❖ MUSLIM WORLD ❖

MODERN MUSLIM
SOCIETIES

 Marshall Cavendish
Reference
New York

Website: www.marshallcavendish.us

This publication represents the opinions and views of the
authors based on personal experience, knowledge, and
research. The information in this book serves as a general
guide only. The authors and publisher have used their best
efforts in preparing this book and disclaim liability rising
directly and indirectly from the use and application of this
book.

Other Marshall Cavendish Offices:
Marshall Cavendish International (Asia) Private Limited, 1
New Industrial Road, Singapore 536196 • Marshall
Cavendish International (Thailand) Co Ltd. 253 Asoke, 12th
Flr, Sukhumvit 21 Road, Klongtoey Nua, Wattana, Bangkok
10110, Thailand • Marshall Cavendish (Malaysia) Sdn Bhd,
Times Subang, Lot 46, Subang Hi-Tech Industrial Park,
Batu Tiga, 40000 Shah Alam, Selangor Darul Ehsan,
Malaysia

Marshall Cavendish is a trademark of Times Publishing
Limited

All websites were available and accurate when this book was
sent to press.

Library of Congress Cataloging-in-Publication Data

Modern Muslim societies.
    p. cm.
  Includes index.
  ISBN 978-0-7614-7927-7
  1. Islamic sociology. 2. Islam--Customs and practices. 3.
Muslims--Social life and customs. 4. Islamic law. 5.
Economics--Religious
aspects--Islam. I. Marshall Cavendish Reference.
  BP173.25.M62 2010
  306.6'9709051--dc22
                                                    2010008612

Printed in Malaysia
14 13 12 11 10 1 2 3 4 5 6

Marshall Cavendish
Publisher: Paul Bernabeo
Production Manager: Michael Esposito

The Brown Reference Group Ltd.
Editors: Felicity Crowe, Jolyon Goddard, Ben Hollingum,
Sally MacEachern, Henry Russell
Development Editor: Tom Jackson
Designer: Joan Curtis
Picture Researchers: Sophie Mortimer, Andrew Webb
Indexer: Christine Michaud
Senior Managing Editor: Tim Cooke
Editorial Director: Lindsey Lowe

CONTENTS

REGIONAL AND NATIONAL SURVEYS

CONTRIBUTORS
AND CONSULTANTS

Sulafa Abou-Samra, Visiting Associate Professor, School of Architecture, Prairie View A&M University, Texas

Jacqueline Armijo-Hussein, Assistant Professor, Department of Social and Behavioral Sciences, Zayed University, United Arab Emirates

Clinton Bennett, Adjunct Professor, Department of Philosophy, State University of New York at New Paltz

Tamsin Bradley, Research Fellow, London Metropolitan University

Jeffrey Burke and Salima Christie Burke, Georgetown University, Washington, DC

Pamela Chrabieh Badine, Teaching Fellow, Department of Theology, Université Saint-Esprit de Kaslik, Lebanon

Dawoud el-Alami, Lecturer, Islamic Studies, University of Wales, Lampeter

Ebru Erdem, Assistant Professor, Department of Political Science, University of California, Riverside

Naznin Hirji, London, UK

Kimberly Jansen, Department of Religious Studies, University of Amsterdam

Shainool Jiwa, Institute of Ismaili Studies, London

Nahid Kabir, Research Fellow, School of Social Marketing, Edith Cowan University, Western Australia

Akel Ismail Kahera, University of Texas at Austin

Mohammad Hassan Kalil, Assistant Professor, Department of Religion, University of Illinois at Urbana-Champaign

Mark Lindley-Highfield, Associate Lecturer and Research Affiliate, The Open University

Ron Lukens-Bull, Associate Professor, Department of Sociology and Anthropology, University of Central Florida, Orlando

Baqie Badawi Muhammad, African Studies Program, Indiana University, Bloomington

Mentor Mustafa, Department of Anthropology, Boston University

Shakir Mustafa, Assistant Professor, Modern Languages and Comparative Literature, Boston University

Florian Pohl, Assistant Professor, Department of Religion, Oxford College of Emory University, Oxford, Georgia

Riham Rizk, Lecturer in Accounting, Duham Business School, University of Duham

Patricia K. Spurles, Associate Professor, Anthropolgy Department, Mount Allison University, New Brunswick, Canada

Dona J. Stewart, Associate Professor, Department of Anthropology and Geography, Georgia State University, Atlanta

Seval Yildirim, Assistant Professor, Whittier Law School, California

Kornel Zathureczky, Assistant Professor, Religious Studies Department, Saint Francis Xavier University, Nova Scotia

Lawrence Ziring, Professor Emeritus, Department of Political Science, Western Michigan University

FOREWORD

The Islamic call to prayer, repeated five times a day around the globe, may be the most tangible tie among the world's Muslims, but a love of soccer is almost as universal in Muslim-majority countries. When Zamalek and Al Ahly, Cairo's top teams, play, the streets of the Egyptian capital are quiet while fans crowd around TV sets. The fortunes of national teams from Bahrain to Tunisia are followed by Muslims around the world.

In 2010 nearly a quarter of the world's population was Muslim. Most Muslim majority countries are in western Asia and North Africa. This is the Muslim cultural hearth, home of the prophet Muhammad, Islam's holy places, and Arabic, the language of the Koran.

More than 60 percent of the world's Muslims live in Asia. Indonesia, with a population of over 240 million, has the largest Muslim population in the world. China, where only 1 or 2 percent of the population is Muslim, has more Muslims than many countries in western Asia. Muslims in Asia have been profoundly influenced by interactions with Hinduism, Confucianism, Buddhism, and, more recently, Christianity.

About 20 percent of the world's Muslims live in countries where Islam is a minority religion, including in Europe and North America. In such countries Muslims, or at least those who wear "traditional" dress, tend to be easily distinguishable from the majority. Mere appearance helped attract suspicion and scrutiny to Muslims after the terrorist attacks of 9/11 in 2001.

European immigration patterns often reflect the continent's imperial past. Muslims from North Africa are heavily concentrated in France, while many Muslim immigrants from South Asia live in Britain. The presence of Muslims, especially those who are religiously conservative, has sparked intense debate. How can Islam be accommodated in a largely secular society?

CHANGE IN MUSLIM SOCIETY

Muslim lives reflect a great variety of traditions, practices, values, and beliefs. The differences between a Muslim U.S. attorney and a Bangladeshi laborer living in Dubai are vast. Even within Muslim countries the lives led by educated elites differ greatly from those of rural farmers. There is no single view in Islam on the details of what it means to be Muslim and lead a "Muslim" life.

Change is characteristic of Muslim societies around the globe. In recent decades, often as a result of globalization and technology, Muslim societies have experienced rapid change, challenging traditional values and beliefs. Today much of the Muslim world wrestles with defining Islam and its role in society. Key questions include: What acts, beliefs, and institutions are Islamic? What role should Islam have in government and education? Which interpretation of Islam is most suitable?

These questions are reflected at the national level, where conformity to Sharia is debated or the content of educational curricula discussed. Within families, where some younger women have adopted clothing standards that are more restrictive than their mothers' while others have resisted parental pressure to wear the veil, the debate over Islam reaches a deeply personal level.

Family has traditionally been important in Muslim societies. Children often live at home until marriage and after marriage remain closely tied to their extended family. The decision over whom to marry is often not made by the individual but by the family. Interaction between unrelated males and females may require a chaperone; young people often socialize in groups or in public places.

As in the West, mobility has changed the traditional family structure. In lower income Muslim majority countries, such as Egypt, Pakistan, and Bangladesh, males may migrate to the cities or to wealthier countries, such as the Gulf States, for work, leaving their families behind. Economic necessity and educational opportunities have led to greater female participation in the workplace, further changing traditional gender roles.

STATUS OF WOMEN

The status of women in the Muslim world is a complex issue. The veil, or *hijab*, is the most visible and most contentious symbol of Islam. Only two countries, Iran and Saudi Arabia, and the Taliban-controlled areas of Afghanistan require women to conceal their bodies and hair. Elsewhere, women may choose to wear the veil for a variety of reasons. Although the obligation to veil is much debated, many Muslims believe that it is a religious requirement (the Koran calls for modesty in dress by both men and women) or are more comfortable wearing a veil because it is common in their society. Some women may be pressured to wear the veil by relatives concerned with family honor and reputation. Wearing the veil is also a way to publicly claim an Islamic identity: this was a way to challenge the Western imperial powers before independence and today to challenge unprecedented levels of Western intervention in the region.

The presence of the veil is a poor indicator of women's status in Islam or in any particular country. More important is the legal status enjoyed by women, such as the right to education, participation in political life, and economic opportunity. Women in Turkey received the right to vote in 1926, for example. Although women in the United Arab Emirates live in a socially conservative society, they tend to be more educated than males, taking advantage of free university education. Yet overall female literacy in western Asia lags significantly behind that of men. As elsewhere, a women's socioeconomic status is the strongest determinant of her educational and employment opportunities and ability to exercise free will.

YOUNG PEOPLE

Throughout the Muslim world there is enormous pressure for change, driven especially by the large youth population (up to 25 percent in some countries). Many young people lack jobs or educational opportunities, leading to frustration with their governments. New technologies are giving the most affluent and tech-savvy of these youth new ways to challenge authority. In Iran, Twitter was used to organize election protests, and Facebook was used by Egyptian youth to organize a demonstration supporting Egyptian labor unions. The Internet has also been used to recruit young people into militant Islamic organizations. Bluetooth technology allows youth in conservative societies, where unsupervised contact is not allowed, to discreetly exchange contact information and skirt parental control, much like teenagers around the world.

Dona J. Stewart
Center for Middle East Peace, Culture, and Development; and Department of Anthropology and Geography; Georgia State University

FAMILY LIFE

*Individuals in any community are tied together by bonds.
One of the strongest bonds is that of the family. Islam represents a
faith-based order that Muslims see as crucial to creating healthy
families and communities and correcting the damage done by modern
society. However, many Muslims, especially second-generation
immigrants, find it difficult to balance their religious commitments
with a Western lifestyle.*

The family is the most important part of the Muslim community. It is so highly regarded that it is protected by the Islamic scripture, the Koran. The family is considered to be the first school in which children learn the basic morals and ethics that will guide them through their lives. While the well-being of the individual is extremely important, Islamic Sharia—the system of law interpreted by learned scholars and based on the Koran—focuses on the duties and rights of every individual through the eyes of the community as a whole. All punishable actions are prohibited because of the destructive outcome those actions would inflict, not only upon the person responsible but also upon his or her family and the community as a whole.

THE MUSLIM COMMUNITY

This idea of thinking about "others" rather than just the "self" is so deeply rooted in Islam that it is often commented upon by those outside the religion. The British humanitarian and civil rights lawyer Clive Stafford-Smith (b. 1959), a non-Muslim, once stated: "What I like about Islam is its

focus on the group, which is opposite to the West's focus on individuality."

Many countries in the modern world follow constitutions based on Islamic Sharia. Different people interpret these laws in different ways, however, so there is often much diversity between Muslims from different countries. Regardless of the social,

What I like about Islam is its focus on the group, which is opposite to the West's focus on individuality.

linguistic, and political background, there is an immediate bond between Muslims from different parts of the world. They abide by the same jurisdiction and follow the same basic rules. Muslims worship together, as they are ordained to do so, to strengthen their faith and their ties, which is based on *ukhuwah al-Iman* ("brotherhood of faith"). Muslims have an obligation to ignore their differences and personal disagreements and focus on improving relationships for the good of the community as a whole.

A Muslim family prays to God in thanks for the food they are about to eat.

A father tends to his newborn son. Muslim parents share the responsibility for raising their children and look to each other for guidance and support.

THE CONCEPT OF MOTHERHOOD

Islam has long recognized that women are equal to men—the two sexes complement each other, although they are not identical. Similarly, men and women share the same responsibilities as fathers and mothers. In any Muslim family, the mother's role as the primary caregiver is no less important than the father's role as protector and family provider. Both the mother and father are there to complement each other. Children are raised equally by both parents, who consult each other on important family-related matters.

In many respects, however, Islam places more emphasis on the importance of the woman's role in the family and society as a whole. According to the Koran, being a mother is one of the greatest gifts God has given to women. In one story, a man asked the Prophet which one of his parents he should honor more. The Prophet answered: "Your mother." The man then asked: "And then?" The Prophet gave the same answer three times, and only on the fourth occasion did he say "Your father." Finally the Prophet said "Paradise lies at the feet of mothers."

In fact, the woman's role in the family is so important in Islam that women are often called "the school of the nation." This reflects the fact that it is usually the mother who plants the first seeds of knowledge about life and God at home.

THE EXTENDED FAMILY

The family unit has a wider connotation than husband, wife, and their immediate children. The traditional Muslim family often spans three or more generations, and many homes include one or more grandparents, as well as unmarried aunts and uncles. In the modern world, however, these extended family ties have become increasingly broken. People are moving away from their hometowns, and in many cases the extended family may include only one grandparent. This is especially true in big metropolitan areas—cities such as Cairo, Dubai, Istanbul, Jakarta, Islamabad, and Tehran—which have been more accepting of Western influences.

The rapid pace of modern life and the need to relocate to gain employment are two factors that have contributed to this breakdown in the extended family. In the towns and cities, however, where Westernization has had less of an impact on traditional Muslim ways of life, family relations continue to be enforced. Even if family members do not live in the same house, relatives continue to uphold strong family bonds. An extended family structure offers many advantages, including stability, coherence, and physical and psychological support, particularly in times of need.

MUSLIM VIEWS ON ABORTION AND CONTRACEPTION

Islam considers the human body to be a trust, which every mother has to preserve and maintain. It also confirms that the fetus is God's bounty. No one has the right to abort the fetus unless its presence threatens the life of the mother. In that particular case, Islamic law does allow for abortion. However, there is one condition. Islamic law will only permit an abortion if saving the life of the mother is the "lesser of two evils." Different schools of Muslim law hold different views on whether any other reasons for abortion are permitted.

The Koran makes no direct references to abortion, so Muslim jurists instead refer to verses that relate to infanticide, such as: "Kill not your offspring for fear of poverty; it is We who provide for them and for you. Surely, killing them is a great sin" (17:32). This verse, as well as several Hadith that discuss miscarriages caused by physical violence, have led most Muslim jurists to conclude that neither parent has the right to terminate their child's life because they were not the ones who granted it to the child in the first place.

Abortion is only allowed to be performed during the early stages of the pregnancy—before the end of the first trimester. However, different schools of Muslim law hold different views about the exact timing of the abortion. Some permit abortion in the first sixteen weeks of pregnancy, while others permit it only in the first seven weeks. Even those scholars who consent to early abortion in very specific cases still consider abortion to be wrong. The more advanced the pregnancy is, the stronger the prohibition.

Birth control is allowed as long as it is not permanent. For example, a woman cannot have a hysterectomy (removal of the uterus) or be sterilized, since both methods lead to a permanent inability to conceive. Likewise, an Islamic text forbids castration in men.

Elders in the Family

In Muslim families, as with many other traditional cultures, respect and esteem increase with age. Elderly family members are respected for their life experiences and their senior position within the family unit. The opportunity to serve and care for parents and grandparents as they grow older is viewed as a gift from God. In fact, this provision of care is not an optional task but a duty.

Your Lord has decreed that you would worship none other than Him and that you show kindness to your parents. If one or both of them reach old age, do not grumble and do not rebuke them, but be kind to them, befriend them and lower for them the wing of humility and mercy; and say "My God, have mercy upon them, as they raised me up when I was an infant." (17:23–24)

Muslim families maintain close contact at all times. If they do not share the same house, family members often live close to each other, which means it is easier to care for elderly relatives. A typical Muslim family is large, with an average of five or six children, so there will always be someone around to look after elderly relatives. If special care is needed, for example, if a grandparent is disabled, family members usually pool together and hire nursing care. Nursing homes exist in Muslim countries, especially in the large metropolitan areas, and they are either

Brothers, sisters, uncles, aunts, parents, and grandparents share lunch as a traditional extended Muslim family.

luxurious private nursing homes or state-owned facilities with basic services. However, many older people refuse to be placed in these establishments, as they feel they are being abandoned by their families. In the same way, relatives often reject the idea of nursing homes because they feel they are responsible for their parents before God. There are exceptions, for example, when all the children have migrated abroad and the elderly parent prefers to remain in his or her country of origin. The children may then pay for their parent to stay at a nursing home.

HEALTHY RELATIONSHIPS

The Koran offers explicit guidelines to govern an individual's relationships with other people.

Show kindness to your parents and your kindred, to the orphans and to the needy, to your near and distant neighbors, to your fellow travelers, to the wayfarers, and your servants. Allah does not love arrogant and boastful people. (4:36)

Family members try to connect with one another to maintain healthy relationships with relatives. Grandchildren and grandparents socialize to reinforce the bond between young and old. Parents are to be treated with love, utmost respect, and attention until their death.

It is not only parents and grandparents toward whom mercy and love are to be shown, but also all dependents, including permanently sick or handicapped aunts and uncles. Otherwise, a Muslim person would bring social embarrassment upon himself or herself.

In some Muslim countries, such as Libya, Sudan, and Yemen, it is a social obligation to offer assistance and extend hospitality to neighbors, even if they are not relatives. Tunisians are relatively egalitarian in their relations with others. However, a strong sense of etiquette prevails. In traditional Muslim families, a man should not show too much curiosity toward female relatives outside his own immediate family. In some cases, for example, brothers would not visit each other because female relatives would be present. Men and women are also supposed to show respect for each other. Sons and

In some Muslim countries, such as Libya, Sudan, and Yemen, it is a social obligation to offer assistance and extend hospitality to neighbors, even if they are not relatives.

daughters are not supposed to smoke in the presence of their father or mother. Brothers and their wives might frequent different cafes so that the presence of a brother would not hinder relaxation by their sisters-in-law. However, these rules are relaxed in the urbanized upper classes.

WOMEN IN MARRIAGE

Much has been said and written about Muslim attitudes toward and treatment of women. While some of the most extreme statements are exaggerated, excessively generalized, or based on ignorance, there are indeed major differences between the status of women in Islam and that of their counterparts in the Western world. However, it would be wrong to suggest that Christianity is necessarily more liberal and inclusive than Islam. For example, the Koran does not subscribe to the theory of "original sin." According to the Christian Bible, original sin occurred when Adam and Eve ate the forbidden fruit in the Garden of Eden. Since Eve was tempted into eating the apple (by Satan, in the form of a snake), the Biblical story suggests that women were the cause of the fall of humanity. The Koran blames both Adam and Eve for eating the apple, and both are punished, suggesting the equality of women and men. Marriage is encouraged and approved as the only lawful relation between a man and a woman. Procreation is a natural instinct and is permitted within the framework of marriage, as a vital element for the continuation of life.

THE MARRIAGE CONTRACT

According to the Sunna of the Prophet Muhammed—his sayings, actions, and traditions—marriage is a noble activity. In one story, the Prophet meets a man who vows that he will not have anything do with women. The man believed that marrying a woman would prevent him from becoming spiritually closer to God. The Prophet responded very firmly, "I swear I am the most God-fearing amongst you! Yet. . . I marry."

In Islam, marriage is a legal contract between man and woman. The marriage must be announced to the public, and the contract must be signed by at least two adult witnesses. There may be certain conditions written into the marriage contract, which must be agreed upon by both husband and wife.

A marriage contract must include two very important points. It must demonstrate that both spouses give their consent to be married, and it must include details of the dowry owed to the bride by the groom. The dowry is a sum of money that acts as an insurance policy for the wife, which she can collect if her husband decides to terminate the marriage. The bride can take the dowry in full at the time of marriage

CAREGIVING AND SUPPORT AMONG MUSLIMS IN THE UNITED STATES

Despite the fact that the Koran does not specify how or where elderly relatives should be cared for, most Muslims invest all available means to support them by themselves. However, the families of Muslim immigrants who live in the United States or any other Western country in which the situation may be more complex may have to consider all possibilities when they make decisions regarding disabled and elderly parents.

Since families living in the West travel in search of work, it is much rarer for the families of Muslim immigrants to live as "extended families." Brothers and sisters rarely live in the same town, so it may be impossible to share the responsibility of caring for a relative. A third problem occurs when the husband and wife are both working long hours and may have to leave an older relative at home. In these cases, it may be sensible to look for help when caring for an elderly relative, even though the onus traditionally falls on the immediate family.

According to a Gallup poll (2008), 18 percent of Muslim Americans are helping to care for an elderly or disabled relative or friend. In the same poll, a majority of Muslim Americans (76 percent) say they have people, either relatives or friends, who form a support network to help them in times of need.

or defer it. The dowry then converts into a loan that the groom must honor whenever the payment is requested.

Islamic law allows a man to marry many wives—this practice is known as polygamy. However, a bride who may not agree with this practice can insist on adding a clause to annul the marriage if the husband chooses to marry another woman. Polygamy also carries financial obligations. A man must provide for all of his wives, as well as any of their unmarried female relatives, for example, sisters and widowed mothers, regardless of their financial status.

The Significance of Marriage

No greater example of the perfect Islamic marriage exists than that of the Prophet Muhammad, who told his followers: "The best of you are those who best treat their women. And I am the best of people to my women."

Marriage is a way to uphold Islamic morals and values. It is the only permissible arena in which men and women can fulfill their sexual desires. It is seen as a form of worship through which Muslims protect themselves from destructive and illegitimate sexual relationships. In most traditional Islamic states, adultery is punishable by laws based on traditional Sharia.

Just as Muslim men and women are warned about the dangers of adultery, they are also introduced to the benefits of marriage. In the eyes of Muslims, marriage is an integral part of a couple's religious devotion and promotes moral virtues such as compassion, forgiveness, love, and mercy. Through marriage, couples can educate their children to appreciate these values and contribute to the welfare of their family and the whole community. In this way, marriage promotes social cohesion.

Whom Can a Muslim Person Marry?

In Sharia law, the term *mahram* means a relative with whom sexual intercourse is considered to be incestuous. *Mahram*s for a woman include any blood relatives— brothers; father, grandfathers, and great-grandfathers; sons, grandsons, and great-grandsons; uncles, great-uncles and grandparents' uncles; and nephews, grandnephews, and great-grandnephews. *Mahram*s for a man can be derived in a similar manner.

Relatives with whom a Muslim becomes *mahram* through marriage include: father-in-law; son-in-law; and if the marriage is consummated, stepfather (mother's husband) and stepson (husband's son). These relatives continue to be *mahram*s even if the marriage is dissolved.

One important exception to the blood relative rule is the marriage of cousins, which includes cousins from either paternal or maternal sides. The marriage of first cousins is a relatively common event in Islamic nations such as Pakistan, Saudi Arabia, and other Gulf states. In the broader Muslim world, however, the practice is very rare.

In Islam, a man can legally marry any woman who follows one of the religions associated with Abraham, which usually refers to Judaism, Christianity, Islam, and the Baha'i faith. However, a Muslim woman can only marry another Muslim man. As a result, any non-Muslim man interested in marrying a Muslim woman would have to convert to Islam.

The Role of the Family in Islam

The aim of any married Muslim couple is to build a balanced, happy family. Islam supports many different ethical codes and moral practices that the married couple must adopt so they can be good role models for their children. The family is supposed to be the social foundation from which younger generations attain their religious and moral values. Through the instruction and guidance of both parents, a child can formulate his or her interactions with other relatives and society at large.

Within the traditional Muslim family, the father is the shepherd over his wife, children, and extended relatives. As head of the house, the father's role is to protect and provide for his family and to be a good role model for his children. The mother is the shepherd over the house. Her role is to guard her family and bring about a supportive and loving atmosphere that is necessary to build healthy relationships between family members. Both parents are responsible for the guidance and education of their children, but a mother who chooses to stay at home and raise her children remains in charge of their needs while the father is at work.

CHILD CUSTODY

While Muslims strive to build a happy environment within the family, many marriages still fail for a wide variety of reasons. Following a separation, questions about the custody of children are addressed through traditional laws. In most cases, these laws provide for the best interests of the children involved and allocate custody to the most reliable and compatible parent. In situations where the breakdown is less amicable, disagreements may be resolved by extended family members. The main aim is to protect the family unit from the consequences of a painful separation. In the worst cases, divorce may be granted.

SHARIA AND CUSTODY

The Koran does not offer any particular advice on the breakdown of marriage; rather, it deals with the child's right to be nurtured. The Koran does not state which parent should assume custody. If a divorce is granted for whatever reason, it is usually the mother who assumes child care, although she can choose to relinquish her responsibility. While the Sunna of the Prophet did not leave any guidelines, the Prophet used to grant the child the option to choose the parent he or she wanted to be with. In cases in which the mother dies, the Prophet would usually give the child to her or his maternal aunt. There is the general consensus that the mother,

Within the traditional Muslim family, the father is the shepherd over his wife, children, and extended relatives. As head of the house, the father's role is to protect and provide for his family and to be a good role model for his children.

aunts, and any female relatives have a greater capacity for child care than any male relatives.

However, there is a distinction to be made between the provision of child care, or guardianship, and financial protection. In all cases, a father must sponsor his child financially. When this is not possible, the burden falls on the male relatives of the father, for example, the child's grandfather or his uncle. This applies even when the mother is the main care provider. However, this division of

A bride and groom make their way to the mosque during a wedding ceremony in Khiva, Uzbekistan.

responsibility rarely reflects reality in a modern Muslim family. In the past, women usually had limited education and little experience in managing daily affairs, so a male relative was assigned to the mother and the child to take care of practical matters.

THE COURT AND CUSTODY

In Islamic law, the courts must look at a wide range of factors when the outcome of a custody case is to be decided. These include the age, gender, and religion of all the children involved, as well as the moral characteristics and capabilities of the

A young couple ask the local imam for advice to help them resolve a family dispute.

parents or guardians. The courts will also consider the wishes of the children if they are old enough to form an intelligent opinion of their own. If the children are very young, the courts will usually award custody to the mother.

In most Islamic countries, modern family law is based on an interpretation of traditional Sharia law. However, family law does not always conform to the essential nature of Sharia, as intended by its founding jurists, and the regulations are constantly changing. Since religious leaders in different countries interpret Sharia in different ways, family law also varies widely among Islamic states.

In 2004, the authorities in Morocco reformed their family laws. Child custody is almost always first granted to the mother, then the father, and then the grandmother on the mother's side. If these options prove

unfeasible, the judge will entrust custody to the most competent relative in the child's family. In all cases, the well-being of the children is the most important deciding factor. If the courts award custody to the mother, who subsequently remarries, she no longer relinquishes her custody right, as she would have done before the modern era. The mother can also appeal if custody is awarded to the father.

In Tunisia, both parents have equal rights in child custody and guardianship. Even if the parents remarry, they both enjoy similar rights and responsibilities concerning their children. Following a divorce, the judge will award custody based on the best interests of the children. If this turns out to be the mother, she will assume responsibility for the child's travel, education, and financial affairs.

Many other Islamic countries, such as

Egypt, Lebanon, and Jordan, apply a similar type of model. Child custody in Pakistan continues to be governed by the Guardians Act of 1890, which places the welfare of the child above all other considerations and favors neither fathers nor mothers.

MUSLIM BIRTH CUSTOMS

The birth of a new child is time for much celebration in the Muslim community. The new parents must respect their religious duties and may follow local customs and traditions to mark the important event. According to the Sunna of the Prophet Muhammed, the father whispers the Islamic call to prayer, the *adhan*, in the right ear of his newborn child. The baby's first taste should be something sweet, and the parents usually chew a piece of date and gently rub it against the baby's gums. On the seventh day, the baby's head will be shaved to show that he or she is a servant of Allah.

The *Aqiqah* Ceremony

The *aqiqah* ceremony follows in the tradition of Millat-e-Ibrahim—the religion of the Prophet Abraham. Essentially, the ceremony consists of two steps: shaving the hair from the head of the newborn baby and sacrificing an animal as a mark of celebration. The hair on the newborn's head is weighed, and the equivalent of its weight in silver is given to charity. A sheep or ram is then sacrificed and shared with family, friends, and the poor. Some of the meat is kept for the parents to eat.

Egyptian Birth Celebrations

In Egypt, the birth of a new child is accompanied with pride and joy. Birth is seen as a divine blessing of both parents, who have sealed the sacred union of their marriage and ensured the continuation of their family line. The *sebou* ceremony is one of Egypt's oldest and most cherished festivities. The family gathers seven days after the birth of a new child (the word *sebou* means "seventh"). All social classes—rural and urban, Christian Coptic and Muslim—in Egypt celebrate this important family occasion.

Traditionally, the birth rituals start during the mother's pregnancy period. If the mother looks healthy, full of life, and happy, it is assumed that she is expecting a boy. If the mother's face and body are covered with rashes, or there is discoloring or redness, then the baby is expected to be a girl. The preparation for *sebou* ceremony

> The baby's first taste should be something sweet, and the parents usually chew a piece of date and gently rub it against the baby's gums.

begins when the parents know if they have a boy or girl. Bracelets, earrings, and necklaces are bought for girls. Lucky charms and written prayer rolls, which may be kept in a gold or silver case that is decorated with precious stones, protect the baby from diseases and the "evil eye." The family also ensures that essentials such as soap, cleansing powder, herbal medicine, and powdered, crystallized sugar are available. These items are kept in small white bags, which should be made from silk if the family can afford it.

Following the birth, the baby is washed in warm water and dressed in a long white cotton dress. On the day of the ceremony, the baby has a bath and is dressed in a new

The role of the Muslim father is to protect his children and act as a good role model.

will be offered a local sherbet and hot food called *kachee*. The umbilical cord is cut and tied with two blue and white threads. The midwife then dresses the baby in a special outfit called the dress of resurrection. The dress is a long piece of white cotton with a hole for the head in the middle. The newborn is then dressed with a white shirt or dress on top. If the newborn baby is a boy, his head is covered with a small hat. If she is a girl, her head is covered with a scarf. Once the baby is dressed, one of his or her fingers is dabbed in blessed clay from the city of Karbala in Iraq. The same finger is then placed in the baby's mouth while prayers are recited. This is believed to protect the newborn child.

For the first three days after the birth, the mother feeds her baby tiny pieces of butter and a few spoonfuls of crystallized sugar dissolved in warm water. Wealthy families hire wet nurses, who are usually new mothers themselves, to breast-feed their babies. The midwife has a duty to check on the mother and her newborn child several times until the sixth day. On this day, which is significant in the Zoroastrian system (an ancient philosophy based on the teachings of the Prophet Zoroaster), the girl's ears are pierced. Boys are circumcised on an odd day, but the decision to complete the procedure is based on the baby's health and well-being and the availability of the person who performs the procedure. Circumcision is an Islamic ritual. Popular entertainments might be held for the circumcision, including a puppet show depicting stories about heroes, ancient legends, love stories, or popular children's tales.

Another custom linked to the Zoroastrian philosophy connects the sixth day to a sizable danger that might fall

outfit. All the women, including the mother, prepare a feast and cook the slaughtered sheep or lamb. The ceremony starts by scattering salt on the mother and around the house, which offers protection against the evil eye. The baby is then put in a decorated basket and taken on a tour around the house. Children and other family members follow the baby in a procession, carrying candles. During this ceremony, the mother steps over her baby seven times without touching it, and the older women make loud noises to make the baby aware of sounds. After the feast, bags full of candies, sweets, and gold and silver coins are distributed to all attendees.

IRANIAN BIRTH CUSTOMS

In Iran, the mother and her baby are given baths immediately after the birth. The mother then retires to her bed and upon the mother and her baby—dark spirits are thought to be the source of a possible attack. In fact, a newborn child will never be left alone in the first forty days after his or her birth due to the fear of bad spirits. To protect the house against danger, the midwife burns camphor until it turns into ashes, while reciting the verse called *ayat ul korsi* from the Koran. Traditionally, women in the family use the ash from the burned camphor to make beauty marks on the mother. They paint the marks between her eyebrows and on her palms and feet. The baby's eyes are also darkened with the ash. Two pieces of thread, white and blue, are twisted around each other to form a bracelet, which is placed around the mother's right wrist.

Further measures are taken to protect the house from danger on the sixth day. First, the mother spreads raw grains and rice in all corners of the bedroom and around the bed. The mother also walks around carrying a sword or large kitchen knife, lightly touching the walls of the room while repeating loudly that she is creating a fort. When she has finished, the mother leaves the knife by the bed. Two elderly women, either family members or friends, repeat these steps using a meat skewer to touch the walls. The two skewers are placed in fire until they are burning hot and then immersed in water to cool. The mother must drink this water, which is assumed to be fortified.

On the sixth night, the baby is named by the local imam. Before dinner, the baby is brought before the imam, who asks about names the parents have in mind for their child. The imam writes down the names on paper and randomly places them inside a copy of the Koran. Then the imam recites prayers in the right and left ears of

the baby and pulls out one name, which will be given to the baby. The imam repeats the name into the baby's ears along with some prayers. The imam is usually given money or gifts to perform the naming ceremony. If the family cannot afford an imam, one of the baby's grandfathers is chosen to select the name of his grandchild. After the naming ceremony, the baby receives gifts, which may include titles to properties in the most wealthy families. The celebration lasts until the first sign of daylight on the seventh day. As the threat has now passed, it is safe to relax and sleep. Traditionally, on the seventh day a sheep is slaughtered in the baby's name. One of the legs is sent to the midwife—this practice is called *aghigeh*—and the rest of the meat is shared by everyone except the parents.

The imam is usually given money or gifts to perform the naming ceremony. If the family cannot afford an imam, one of the baby's grandfathers is chosen to select the name of his grandchild.

Another major event in the first few days after childbirth occurs when the mother and baby take their first bath together. This event takes place on the seventh day for a girl and the tenth day for a boy. In Iran, most families use public bathhouses. The mother's female relatives and friends may accompany her on the first bath, and the midwives also participate in the occasion. Preparations begin the night before. The mother's waist and belly are massaged with honey, covered with herbal powder, and wrapped with fabric. In the

Family members bless a baby with holy water during the *aqiqah* ceremony in the village of Lui in Malaysia. *Aqiqah* is a traditional Muslim ceremony for newborn babies and is normally performed after the seventh day of birth.

morning, all the women gather and accompany the new mother and her baby to the bathhouse. A copy of the Koran is held over the heads of the mother and baby as they leave the house. The mother wears a talisman and other lucky charms around her neck. One of the charms is a small cup made from copper or brass with forty small pieces engraved with *bismallah,* which means "in the name of God."

On the way to the bathhouse, the mother and her group sing happy songs. When they arrive, the group is greeted with incense, songs, and drums. The mother then washes and puts oil on her skin. She may be given a massage, and other body treatments, such as henna, may be applied.

Food, fruits, sherbets, and sweets brought in by the group are served. At the end, the mother eats two lightly boiled eggs and some sweets, which have been treated with more incense. Blessed clay, called *torbat bebe,* is rubbed on the mother's forehead. (*Bebe* is the name of an ancient Iranian goddess.) The celebrations continue when the group returns home. Dinner is served to the family and friends, and street entertainers might show up unexpectedly if they were not already invited.

Many of these Iranian birthing customs follow ancient pre-Islamic traditions, and Muslims in other countries in the Middle East do not observe them. They are still popular in Iran, although some of the customs are changing with the times.

RAISING CHILDREN

The Koran makes it clear that it is the responsibility of the parents to educate and guide their children in matters relating to morality and acceptable behavior. The parents must constantly remind their children, especially the daughters, to be cautious and to adhere to Islamic traditions. From a very early age, Muslim parents lay out guidelines concerning relationships with members of the opposite sex. Children are cautioned not to ignore their social position and to avoid any form of unsupervised interaction with both sexes. Islam recognizes the natural urges young people have and never denies it. So, just as Islam strictly forbids sex outside the institution of marriage—and all means leading to it—it also prohibits celibacy.

To observe these moral guidelines, young men and women continue to live with their parents until they get married. A young man who is physically and financially capable of marrying should be encouraged to do so as soon as possible. Similarly, a woman who is ready should get married as soon as she approves of a suitor who proposes to her. Even when a young man and woman are engaged to be married, they are not allowed to date unaccompanied by a sibling.

MAKING MARRIAGE WORK

A Muslim marriage can be successful if the couple are compatible in their religious views and share their commitment to Islamic values. Marriages work if husband and wife are willing to struggle to fulfill their objectives and to support each other when dealing with the challenges the world has to offer. Compatibility is the key to guarantee the success of a marriage, but compatibility can be different from one Muslim community to the next. It can relate to economic and social class, how educated someone is, and what type of job they do.

MARRIAGE MATCHMAKING

Many people assume the role of matchmaker—not only the parents but extended family, friends, and work colleagues. In fact, the whole community feels a responsibility to help young men and women find suitable partners so that the young adults do not make unwise choices. Muslims consider marriage as an act of union between two families, so it is the responsibility of the parents to arrange the marriage. In countries such as India

> The Koran makes it clear that it is the responsibility of the parents to educate and guide their children in matters relating to morality and acceptable behavior.

and Pakistan, families start planning their children's futures and looking for potential partners from an early age, based on their relationships with other families. While the approval and consent of both the bride and groom are essential, the parents' decision is usually respected. The practice of choosing marriage partners from within the family's community is considered to be important by young and old. However, some parents are evidently beginning to understand the marital concerns of their children.

In Cairo, as in many other large metropolitan areas in the Muslim world, all areas of life are becoming increasingly Westernized. It is becoming exceedingly difficult to make suitable marriage choices, and young Muslim men and women are facing an undeniable dilemma. On the one hand, they have unlimited opportunities to meet with each other at universities and in the workplace. On the other hand, they must conform to traditional Islamic values and respect the rules of their parents. In spite of all of these difficulties, Muslim families have continued to maintain their strong family bonds.

BONDING BETWEEN PARENTS AND THEIR CHILDREN

The strong bonds that exist between children and their parents continue as young boys and girls grow into men and women. These strong family bonds are associated with traditional Islamic values such as belonging, connectedness, contentment, and forgiveness. They contrast with Western values such as personal perseverance and individual performance. Young Muslims are confronted with conflicting expectations at different stages of their life, and they may struggle with ideals of individual autonomy. Peer pressure and cultural norms play a major role in building people's sense of identity.

MUSLIM FAMILIES IN THE UNITED STATES AND THE MUSLIM WORLD

Muslims in different parts of the world are facing different problems. Factors such

An imam delivers gifts to newborn babies at Ibn Batouta hospital in Basra, Iraq, on the eve of the Muslim Eid al-Fitr festival.

as birth order, parents' education, gender, and urbanization and their impact on the emotional and financial connectedness of young Muslims are perhaps felt much stronger in America than the Muslim world. Despite regional variations, young Arab Muslims, both men and women, seem to be more attached to their families than young American Muslims. While there has been an increase in urbanization and industrialization in the Muslim world, Muslims have managed to preserve family bonds and foster connectedness.

MUSLIM FAMILY TIES IN THE UNITED STATES

In the modern globalized world, bringing up Muslim children in a predominantly Muslim country is an increasingly complex task. However, it is made much more challenging when Muslim couples are raising their children in the United States or another Westernized country. The Muslim family faces a dilemma: How do they balance a deeply structured lifestyle in which they have to perform ritual prayers and conform to a different physical, moral, and dietary structure than that of Western culture.

Muslim parents who live in the West must guide their children through their non-Islamic environment and teach them to avoid the temptations of alcohol, drugs, sex, and crime. A young person's respect for his or her parents and the elderly is a highly valued trait, which ranks second only after obedience to God in Islam. The Muslim family structure does not leave much room for individuality, which is at the core of Western social values. Many young Muslims are finding it difficult to express themselves as individuals without raising confrontation with their families.

Many young Muslims are finding it hard to fit in with their non-Muslim peers. Some feel under pressure to drink alcohol or have a girlfriend or boyfriend to become accepted by their peers.

In addition, many young Muslims are finding it hard to fit in with their non-Muslim peers. Some feel under pressure to drink alcohol or have a girlfriend or boyfriend to become accepted by their peers. For Muslims, these activities are contrary to everything they have been taught about right and wrong behavior and will have serious consequences for family relations.

THE ROLE OF FAITH

Religion looms large in the lives of people across the Islamic world. In the traditional Islamic state of Egypt, virtually all of the population believes that their religion plays an important part in their daily lives. The story is much the same in Bangladesh (99 percent), Indonesia (99 percent), and Morocco (98 percent). In the United States around 80 percent of Muslims believe that religion has a big effect on their daily lives, which is higher than the American population as a whole but about the same as that reported by some Christian groups. The role of the mosque is central to the faith and the Muslim community, and most Muslim Americans attend at least once a week. In Europe, Muslims living in Germany are far more likely to say that their religion is an important part of their daily lives

(82 percent) than Muslims in France (69 percent) or Britain (70 percent).

Muslim Families in Bosnia

Many Muslims had to adapt quickly following the atrocities of the Bosnian War (1992–1995), which often led to the displacement of families from their homes. Bosnian Muslims are a resilient people who refuse to allow the negative influences of the war to compromise their cultural identity. They continue to uphold their traditional rituals and retain a strong cultural identity to support children and family as a whole. The strong custom of

Bosnian Muslim women must observe strict codes of privacy to protect the family, for example, by not talking about issues such as a family argument, since it would bring shame on the family.

respect for the elders and the unconditional support for younger Muslims made the transition from war to peace much easier. Muslims devote a lot of time helping their children achieve their academic and professional goals. Over time, the children of Muslim families repaid this investment by using their skills to help rebuild their country. Another advantage for Muslims trying to resettle after the war is their acceptance of other cultures, which is one of the key teachings outlined in the Koran.

Family is the main social structure across Bosnia, in both urban and rural areas. Until the 1970s, adult children commonly lived with their parents, and many generations shared the same house.

Today, however, it is usually only the immediate family—father, mother, and children—who live in the same house. Extended family members often live nearby. Drinking coffee and sharing food, accompanied by the essential element of lively conversation, are very essential aspects of social life. Traditional music and folk dances are an important part of cultural celebrations.

Bosnian Muslim women must observe strict codes of privacy to protect the family, for example, by not talking about issues such as a family argument, since it would bring shame on the family. However, many women are finding it difficult to balance their traditional roles in modern society, especially as Bosnia strives to become more accepted in the Western world.

Growing Up as a Muslim in the United States

As a minority within a population who do not hold the same religious beliefs, Muslims in the Western world in general, and in the United States in particular, struggle to establish their religious identity. Muslim parents must raise their children as Muslims regardless of where in the world the family lives. Parents start to teach their children some of the basic principles of Islam from a very early age, including how to pray and perform the ritualistic wash. They also learn about the fasting month and the religious holidays and celebrations. The next step is for young Muslims to go to the local mosque and Islamic school. Some wealthy parents may pay for their children to attend full-time Islamic private school, where they memorize the short Koranic chapters and some Prophetic traditions. Most young Muslims living in the United States receive

this type of religious instruction until their mid-teenage years. By this time, many feel they have learned as much as they can or become too busy with schoolwork. Muslim American parents are often reluctant to interrupt their children's religious education, but they may not want to burden them with more structured Islamic scholarship at this stage.

THE JOURNEY OF DISCOVERY

During their teenage years, many young Muslims begin to discover their religious identity. Some think that being born into Islam is not enough to understand the principles of the religion. Many teenagers attend discussion groups to find out how to overcome any doubts about their religion and discover their faith in Islam. During

these discussions, teenagers will begin to ask questions about the instruction they have received from their parents and develop their own understanding of Islamic beliefs and practices. Gradually, they will start to reconcile conflicts between what they have been taught and what they experience. This is especially important when young Muslims grow up in a predominantly Western society, when Islamic principles and practices are often in conflict with what they see in the world around them. One example is the use of alcohol in social celebrations in the West— Muslims are forbidden to consume alcohol. Similar problems can arise when a teenager forms a relationship with someone of the opposite sex. For example, how deep can a Muslim teenage boy become involved in a

The hands of a Muslim bride in India are covered with henna decoration, called *mehndi*. *Mehndi* is a cultural rather than religious tradition and is common to both Muslim and Hindu weddings.

FAMILY ISSUES IN THE MIDDLE EAST

In 2006, researchers published a study summarizing the conclusions of various reports from Arabic-speaking Muslim communities in the Middle East. The researchers made the following observations.

1. Cultural and religious factors play an important part in the formation of bonds between an individual and his or her family members. However, the report found that bonds between close relatives, such as parents or grandparents, are just as strong as those between the extended family, for example, aunts, uncles, and cousins.

2. Despite the various degrees of religious conservatism in the Muslim world, the bonds between family members are equally strong when you compare two different countries. Most young Muslims in Lebanon said that they followed their parents' directions in important life matters, such as marriage and employment. Most embraced this close relationship rather than reject it.

3. In 2003, the Arab Woman Developmental Report suggested that 87 percent of the young Muslim women in Lebanon and Bahrain thought that their relationship with their parents was good.

4. A study carried out among college students in Saudi Arabia suggested that the vast majority of students looked to their parents to help them make decisions on important life matters. For example, 100 percent of the students interviewed consulted their parents before making a decision about getting married and 70 percent discussed travel plans with their parents. Furthermore, 12 percent consulted their parents before choosing their majors in the university. Most of the students reported that their parents and relatives had a great impact on their motivation to study.

5. Among college students in Egypt, 64.4 percent of women and 33.1 percent of men favored "absolute submission" to parents (which echoes the way in which all Muslims submit to God). The same study suggested that 57.7 percent of female students and 25.7 percent of male students would prefer their children to have similar characters and morals as their parents.

6. Parents with higher educational attainment were just as connected with their children as parents who were less well-educated. Most young Muslims enjoy a collective type of personality rather than an individualistic type.

relationship with a girl? At what point does it become too dangerous for the couple to continue their relationship?

Many young Muslims do not share the same ideas about how to practice the basic tenets of Islam. While their parents find it difficult to separate religion from everyday life, many second-generation Muslims living in the West experience an identity crisis as they try to balance their religion with Western influences. Eventually, this can pull them away from following the structured Islamic guidelines. As a result, many second-generation Muslim parents reassess their faith to meet their obligations toward their own children.

FACTORS CONTRIBUTING TO RELIGIOUS IDENTITY

Many young Muslims struggle to find their Islamic identity. Some find it hard to discuss matters of faith with their parents, while others face pressure to conform to the social and cultural environment in which they live. In the United States—and elsewhere in the West—young Muslims may find it difficult to juggle their strict religious commitments and practices with American ideals such as freedom of expression and individuality. Young Muslims will also be exposed to alternative belief systems, which may conflict with their own religious beliefs.

Parent and Child

Muslim parents who were born and raised in an Islamic country but then immigrated to the United States—either to pursue higher education or for any other purpose—may feel uncomfortable discussing certain issues with their children. Since the parents did not have to deal with the added pressures of living in a Western society as they grew up, there may be a cultural gap and some unfamiliarity with their children's situation. As second-generation Muslim children grow into adults, it may become increasingly difficult to seek guidance from their parents about issues that may be deemed important. Communication between family members

In the United States—and elsewhere in the West—young Muslims may find it difficult to juggle their strict religious commitments and practices with American ideals such as freedom of expression and individuality.

is the most important factor that helps young Muslims form their own religious identity and build faith. As with many Eastern cultures, those built around Islam are profoundly family oriented. Muslims do not see themselves as individuals, rather they are part of their family. The support network includes the immediate family—parents, grandparents, brothers, and sisters—as well as the extended family, such as uncles, aunts, and cousins. By discussing their concerns and sharing their discoveries with so many family members, who may

have a vast range of life experiences, young Muslims can develop their personal beliefs and continue on their spiritual path.

Alternative Belief Systems

Second-generation Muslims living in the West do not always imitate the religious and cultural convictions of their parents. Crossing these boundaries may lead to family discord or resentment. Furthermore, young Muslims meet people from different religious backgrounds—sometimes through discussions with friends at school or from a personal desire to learn about other religions and cultures. Exposure to other philosophies and belief systems naturally encourages young Muslims to examine their personal convictions on faith, God, and religion and serves to strengthen their maturing religious identity.

Family Guidelines

As Muslim children grow and develop into young adults, it is only natural that they start to ask questions about their place in the world. Many young Muslim Americans turn away from their parents' beliefs and values and follow the appealing secular American lifestyle. Some Muslim American children commit to their religious principles under the guidance of their parents, only to step away from it as they grow into young adults. Following open communication with family and friends, they may readopt a more observant religious path later in life.

The Importance of Discussion

It is extremely important for Muslim Americans to feel they can explore their concerns and question what they have been taught through open discussions with their families. Many young Muslims feel that this is an essential part of discovering their spiritual path and developing their faith. In particular, the mother is considered to be a pivotal part of this journey of spiritual discovery. Islam emphasizes the importance of the mother within the family, as the Prophet said: "Your Heaven lies under the feet of your mother."

Islam is a universal religion that welcomes people from different ethnic, professional, and racial backgrounds.

Culture and Religious Identity

Islam is a universal religion that welcomes people from different ethnic, professional, and racial backgrounds. It even welcomes people of different faiths, who may want to form a new religious identity. Islam may be practiced anywhere, and it is not held back by the necessity to follow a clergy or any specified structures.

Many African Americans, for example, have experienced problems relating to ethnicity or have witnessed a breakdown in community relations. Islam offers a way to channel these negative experiences into avenues for life improvement. Through Islamic rituals such as prayers, people from different backgrounds can start to feel part of a large family as they are accepted into the wider Muslim community.

CONVERTING TO ISLAM

The Muslim world has come under a lot of criticism in recent decades due to the activities of extremists, who commit acts of terrorism in the name of religion. These people hide behind Islam but show no real understanding of Muslim morals and values. The actions of these criminals alienate the majority of Muslims from the

Muslims gather to pray at a mosque of the Islamic Society of Orange County, California, in the United States.

rest of society, many of whom view all Muslims with suspicion. As a result, it has been difficult to bridge the perceived cultural gap between Muslim Americans and the population as a whole. However, the gap between the two groups may be narrower than many people think since both share similar values. This is reflected by the increased number of Americans who are converting to Islam.

The importance of family in Islam is one of the main reasons that many non-Muslims decide to convert to the religion. Islam appeals to women in particular since it emphasizes the role of the mother as a teacher and loving guide to the children and grandchildren. Living as an extended family is rare in the United States. In many cases, even the immediate family does not live together. Many families break apart as fathers travel to work and siblings move to college. There are also many families in which one parent, usually the mother, acts both as the breadwinner and caregiver. Islam promotes traditional family values, where the mother is not burdened with the responsibilities of both parents.

BRIDGING THE GAP

Western converts to Islam act as cultural and political mediators and bridge the gap between the Muslim community and the American population as a whole. Converts can also act as guides for second-generation Muslims who may be struggling between inherited cultural customs and traditional Islamic values. Converts also establish their own religious identity by directing their everyday life toward God, for example, through the structured daily rituals such as washing and prayer. By embracing these new practices, the convert's non-Muslim friends and family members learn about

the Islamic traditions and rituals, too.

Carol Anway shares her experiences of her daughter's conversion to Islam in her book *Daughters of Another Path* (1995). The book charts the journey of reconciliation and gradual acceptance of her daughter's change in tradition. Anway also interviews 53 American-born women who converted and asks how and why they came to Islam and what their lives are like as a result of the decision. The interviews and her own experiences suggest ways in which non-Muslims can relate to Muslim relatives, friends, and coworkers. The interviews suggest that children of these converts rarely absorbed and retained a Muslim identity. Anway suggests that the presence of a community of Muslims and a Muslim peer group, as well as a committed Muslim father, is most influential in the converts' successful transmission of Muslim identities to the next generation.

A woman in a shop at the KL City Center in Kuala Lumpur in Malaysia. Western influences have had a major impact on the lives of Muslims throughout the world.

Polygamy

Polygamy is permitted in the Muslim world, but it is not encouraged. In the Koran it is asserted that polygamy is only acceptable in certain circumstances.

The term *polygamy* describes the practice of marriage to more than one partner at the same time. The most common form of polygamy, and the only one practiced in the Muslim world, is called *polygyny*, in which one man takes multiple wives. Polygamy was an established custom in many parts of the Middle East prior to the rise of Islam, and since that time it has been tolerated in a limited, modified form within Muslim societies. The customary practice of polygamy in pre-Islamic Arabia allowed men to take as many wives as they wished, without any obligation to treat them equally or fairly. In addition, it was the custom that, after a man's death, his wife, or wives, would be obliged to marry either his father, uncle, or any of his brothers—even if these men already had several wives.

DEFINITIONS OF ISLAMIC POLYGAMY

The source of the majority of the rules and customs of marriage and polygamy in the Muslim world is the fourth sura of the Koran, *An-Nisaa* (The women), which discusses issues of marriage, inheritance, and family. In Islamic societies, polygamous marriages are permitted, but only in certain circumstances—primarily in situations where a man's death has left his widows with no means of support. The basis of these rules can be found in verse 4:3, which states: "And if ye fear that ye will not deal fairly by the orphans, marry of the women, who seem good to you, two or three or four; and if ye fear that ye cannot do justice (to so many) then one (only)." In addition, verse 4:3 states that it is better for a man to marry a captive slave woman, who does not have a bride-price, than for him to marry a free woman and, in paying the bride-price, deprive his children and his other wives of an acceptable standard of living.

The practice of polygamy as dictated by the Koran is more strictly regulated by ethical codes than it was in the societies of pre-Islamic Arabia. Polygamy is neither mandatory nor encouraged, but merely permitted. The Koran's conditional endorsement of polygamy stresses that self-interest or sexual desire should not be the reason for entering into a polygamous marriage. It is a practice associated with the social duty Islamic men have to protect the social and financial standing of the

The Koran's conditional endorsement of polygamy stresses that self-interest or sexual desire should not be the reason for entering into a polygamous marriage.

widows and orphans in their community. The permission to marry up to four wives is discouraged unless the children of a widow are in danger of being disinherited or forced into unsuitable marriages.

In addition to the charitable motivations described in the Koran, Islamic scholars have suggested other circumstances in which polygamy is acceptable. Some of these are backed by statements in the Hadith and Koran, while others are based more on social expedience. The most commonly proposed of these arguments is that it is better for a husband to take an additional wife than for him to engage in forbidden extramarital activity or to divorce his current wife. In common with the instructions

A Muslim man pictured with his three wives in Zouar, Chad. In many parts of Africa the practice of polygamy existed long before the arrival of Islam.

given in verse 4:3, these interpretations do not encourage polygamy but view it as preferable to the alternatives.

POLYGAMY AND FAIRNESS

Of the conditions that Islam places on the practice of polygamy, it is the husband's duty to treat his wives and children equitably and fairly that is emphasized above other considerations. The concept of a social or sexual hierarchy within a polygamous marriage is rejected; it is not permitted to make social distinctions between wives based on their age, how long they have been married, or whether or not they have had any children by their husband. Those men who choose to take multiple wives are under an obligation to treat them equally. The husband is fully responsible for the equal distribution of housing, food, material goods, kind treatment, and must must not engage in sexual intercourse more often with some wives than others. If a man is not sure if he will be able to deal justly with his wives, the Koran urges him to take only one. If a wife feels that she is not receiving an equal share of her husband's time, affection, or resources, she is generally allowed to request a divorce.

The importance given to equal and fair treatment serves to emphasize the undesirability of polygamous marriage in Islamic society. This is demonstrated in verse 4:129, which acknowledges that "You will not be able to deal equally between (your) wives, however much you wish (to do so)." This means that the actual practice of polygamy will inevitably fall short of acceptable standards of personal conduct. The same verse does, however, establish the limits of acceptable behavior, urging Muslim men to, at the very least, "turn not altogether away (from one [wife]), leaving her as in suspense."

A Muslim man poses with his two wives and six children in Xinjiang Province, People's Republic of China.

Verse 4:129 has been viewed by some as an implicit prohibition of polygamy. For example, in 1958 the Tunisian government cited this verse to support their decision to ban polygamy. They claimed that its assertion that no man could ever actually treat his wives fairly or equally meant that any real-world example of polygamy was a violation of Islamic law.

POLYGAMY AND TEMPORARY MARRIAGE

Both Shia and Sunni interpretations of the Koran allow the practice of polygamy. Followers of Shia Islam (and a minority of Sunni Muslims), however, allow another form of marriage, called *nikah mut'ah*, which creates a marriage bond that lasts for a fixed period of time before being dissolved. These temporary marriages have long been a source of controversy in Islamic scholarship, both because of their possible social consequences and their debated Koranic origin. In addition, there is a similar practice in Sunni Islam, called *nikah misyar*, in which a wife waives certain aspects of the conventional Islamic marriage contract, such as complete financial support, cohabitation rights, and equal treatment to the man's other wives.

When a man and a woman agree upon a temporary marriage, they make an irreversible agreement stating the period they will be married and the compensation the man owes to the woman for it. The period may be any length of time from one day to weeks, months, or even several years. The wife's financial compensation can be any amount of money, estate, jewelry, or some other type of guarantee that the wife stipulates. Once the agreed-upon period expires, the man is under no obligation to provide for the wife's needs or any of her expenses. The *mut'ah* marriage does not need to be witnessed, nor does it have to be legally recorded. If by the end of this temporary marriage both parties agree to extend the marriage, they can enter into either another temporary marriage or a permanent one.

In the context of Islamic polygamy, the practice of *mut'ah* marriage presents a number of issues. As such marriages place the man under no permanent obligation, it has been argued that such temporary marriages can be entered into even if the husband already has four wives.

Similarly, the lack of financial or social obligations in the Sunni *nikah misyar* make it possible for married men to avoid the responsibilities of formal polygamy.

CONTEMPORARY VIEWPOINTS

In the majority of present-day Muslim nations, the practice of polygamy is legally and socially permitted, although, as in the Koran, no nation encourages the practice under normal circumstances. In the secular states of the Muslim world, such as Turkey and Tunisia, polygamy is illegal in any form, although polygamy is still practiced secretly in many parts of Turkey. Even in the nations where it is permitted, however, polygamy is only practiced by a small minority. For example, polygamous marriages represent only around two percent of marriages in Lebanon, eight percent in Jordan, and two percent in Algeria.

Before a man can take an additional wife, he is required to obtain the consent of his existing wife or wives.

In the Islamic world today, where most nations' laws are based on principles laid down in Sharia law, laws governing polygamy have a number of shared features. These features come primarily from the restrictions of polygamy specified in the Koran, but they are also inspired by social circumstances and the application of Islamic ethical principles. Before a man can take an additional wife, he is required to obtain the consent of his existing wife or wives. He must also prove that he has the means to support an additional wife without harming the well-being of his existing wives or children. In some cases, men are also required to provide reasons for taking an additional wife that are justifiable under Sharia law, such as an existing wife's infertility or unwillingness to engage in sexual activity. In some countries, acquiring this legal permission is a formality, while in others, such as Malaysia and Morocco, entering a polygamous marriage requires the husband to prove his financial means and justify his motivations at a court hearing.

Chapter 2

MARRIAGE

Marriage has tremendous religious and social importance in the Muslim world, and it forms an important part of community and family life. Marriages in the Muslim world can be monogamous or polygamous, lifelong or temporary.

In the Muslim world there is a commonly quoted Hadith in which Muhammad states: "when a man marries, he has fulfilled half his religion." This Hadith sums up the importance of marriage within Muslim society. Muslims believe that marrying and having children pleases Allah more than any number of extra acts of worship. As a result of these beliefs, there is no ascetic or monastic tradition in mainstream Islam; all Muslims, even those who wish to devote their lives to the study of scripture and service of Allah, are expected to marry and procreate. The Koran asserts that the existence of the two sexes and the potential for love between them are evidence of Allah's generosity. This is stated most clearly in Sura 30, verse 21, which says:

> And among His Signs is this, that He created for you mates from among yourselves, that you may dwell in tranquillity with them, and he has put love and mercy between you.

In the Muslim world it is only through marriage that relationships between men and women can be considered socially and morally valid. Many, but not all, Muslim countries have rigid laws or social conventions limiting the degree to which unmarried men and women can interact, in many cases prohibiting it entirely. In this context, marriage is not only a religious dutybut also a necessity for any couple who wish to cohabit, begin a sexual relationship, or just spend significant amounts of time together.

There is no ascetic or monastic tradition in mainstream Islam; all Muslims. . . are expected to marry and procreate.

The rules that govern the practice and form of marriage in the Muslim world are primarily based on religious rather than secular principles. Islamic marriages are expected to be permanent, although divorce is permitted and considered preferable to an unhappy or abusive relationship. Adultery and premarital sex are strictly forbidden; however, polygamous marriage is allowed by Islamic law under certain circumstances. Both Sunni and Shia Islam allow forms of marriage that permit a couple to have a sexual relationship without the full range of rights and responsibilities that go with a conventional marriage.

An Indian bride wears traditional Muslim dress at her wedding ceremony in the western Indian city of Ahmedabad in 2004.

Guests and family at a *walima*. The *walima*, or wedding banquet, is a requirement for marriage in most parts of the Muslim world.

There are two main terms used to refer to marriage in Islam: *nikah* and *zawaj*. These are Arabic words, and the roots of both are found in the Koran. Both are used to refer to marriage in Arabic-speaking countries. In most non–Arabic-speaking Muslim countries, the word *nikah* is the conventional term used to refer to the contract of marriage (*aqd al-nikah*), as it is the term used by the Muslim jurists. In some countries the term also refers to the wedding ceremony, incorporating the contract. The difference between the two words is linguistic. *Nikah* incorporates the meaning of the act of physical union between spouses as well as the legal and social institution, while the root of the word *zawaj* denotes pairing. There are various terms for the wedding itself in Arabic-speaking countries, most commonly *urs*, but also *farah* (from a root meaning "joy"), and naturally non–Arabic-speaking communities have words in their own languages, for example *shadi* in Urdu. In Iran the word *aghd* is used, which is the Persian equivalent of the word *aqd*, or contract.

MARITAL JURISPRUDENCE

The separation of genders, marriage and divorce law, and even some of the customs related to weddings are dictated by the rules and guidelines established by Islamic law. The preferred source of all Islamic law (Sharia) is the Koran. If the Koran contains comprehensive and unambiguous instructions on a given subject, then Islamic law relating to the issue is based purely on these instructions. However, in cases in which the rules in the Koran are incomplete or their meaning is not clear, scholars refer to the Sunna, or actions and sayings of the Prophet Muhammad. These are recorded in Hadith, which are reports of events and sayings, complete with a short description of who narrated them and how they were connected to the Prophet. In cases in which neither the Koran nor the Sunna provide an answer to a particular question, scholars refer to the *fiqh*, which is the historical consensus opinion of experts on Islamic ethics. Laws based on interpretation of the Koran and Hadith are usually consistent and unchanging, but those based on *fiqh* can vary between regions and often change over time according to social circumstances.

The topic of marriage is a broad and complex one that presents a number of difficulties to scholars of Islamic law. References to marriage and divorce are found in many places in the Koran, but the majority of the verses that Islamic legal scholars draw on as sources are contained in three chapters: 2 (*Al-Baqara*), 4 (*Al-Nisa*), and 65 (*Al-Talaq*). The verses of the Koran that deal with marriage do not specifically cover all aspects of this complex subject, however. In relation to some contentious issues, such as polygamy and temporary marriage, the Koran's instructions are ambiguous or may seem to be internally inconsistent. Additionally, there are few simple clarifications of these instructions to be found in the example of Muhammad's actions and sayings. Muhammad was personally exempted from many aspects of marriage law by a revelation detailed in sura 33:50. This raises the question of whether or not Muslims are encouraged, or even permitted, to follow Muhammad's example in marriage and marital life. As a result of these problems of interpretation, many laws and customs related to marriage are based on *fiqh*, meaning that the details of marriage law or custom often vary from one region to another. In addition to these differences in scriptural interpretation, the influence of Western and secular concepts has brought changes to the laws of some countries.

MARRIAGE TO NON-MUSLIMS

A Muslim man may marry a woman who is of the "People of the Book," the other Abrahamic faiths, that is, a Jewish or Christian woman, but he may not marry outside these limits. In practice, however, such marriages are often controversial, and their acceptability has been questioned in some countries. A Muslim woman may not under any circumstances marry a non-Muslim man, however. Marriage between a Muslim woman and a non-Muslim man will not be legitimate and, if it occurs, will be considered tantamount to adultery. If a Muslim man who is married to a Muslim woman renounces Islam or converts to another religion, his wife will automatically be divorced from him (apart from any other punishment he may receive for apostasy). There have been some unusual cases in which this provision has been used for political purposes, such as a case in Egypt in 1995 when Nasr Abu Zeid, a professor of Arabic language and literature, was accused of apostasy on the basis of his academic writing about the Koran. Although he denied that he had renounced Islam, a group of religious scholars raised a court case against him using a practice called *hisba*, which allows any Muslim to take legal action against an institution or individual who they think has harmed Islam. As apostasy is not a crime in the Egyptian penal code, they sought to punish and humiliate him by petitioning to have his marriage dissolved on the grounds of apostasy in an attempt to force him to retract his academic views. Before the sentence could be enforced, Abu Zeid and his wife, fellow academic Ibtihal Younis, fled to Europe.

FORCED MARRIAGES

Forced marriage is a term used to describe marriages that take place without the consent of one or both parties. The term is usually applied to situations in which an individual capable of giving informed consent is threatened or coerced into marriage against his or her will. However, the term is also applied to marriages in which at least one party is considered too young to give informed consent. A clear distinction must be made between arranged marriages to which the partners give their free consent—albeit perhaps circumscribed by custom and social expectation—and forced marriages.

Forced marriage sometimes involves physical kidnap, but it does not always involve the use or threat of violence. Very often young women living in close communities simply have no realistic way of resisting family pressure to marry. If they object or attempt to escape, they risk estrangement from their families, social exclusion, and sometimes even physical abuse or death. Very often they simply do not have anywhere to go or any access to financial or practical support.

Forced marriage and child marriage are a problem throughout the developing world. The practice is not limited to a particular geographic region and is influenced by local cultural traditions more than religious doctrine. Due to several high-profile cases involving Muslim women living in Western nations, however, the practice is frequently associated with the Muslim world in the Western media.

With the exception of Iran, Somalia, and Sudan, the countries of the Muslim world are all signatories of the United Nations Convention on the Elimination of All Forms of Discrimination Against Women (CEDAW). Among other things, this document commits nations to the principle that all women have "The same right freely to choose a spouse and to enter into marriage only with their free and full consent" (Article 16b). Although Muslim nations were widely criticized within the UN for refusing to apply the principles of this document in cases where they conflicted with Sharia, these objections were mostly informed by the mistaken belief that Sharia endorsed such practices as forced marriage. The opposition of Islam to such practices was reiterated in 2005 when the grand mufti of Saudi Arabia gave a fatwa banning forced marriage in the kingdom, blaming it for the growing divorce rate. He recommended that fathers who forced their daughters to marry should be jailed until they "changed their minds."

SELECTION OF A MARRIAGE PARTNER

The process by which a marriage partner is chosen varies considerably from one country or region to another. In the Muslim world it is common for the parents of a young person to have at least some influence or control over whom their child marries. This control can be absolute; in some more conservative nations, arranged marriages are still common. In other countries, parents may have little more than an advisory role.

Although interactions between unmarried men and women are restricted by law and social custom in many countries, the growing number of women in higher education and the workforce makes it increasingly common for young people in the Muslim world to choose to marry partners they have met on dates or socially through work or school, rather than partners selected or suggested by their families.

Despite the fairly minor role that Muslim parents may play in the selection of marriage partners, however, the Islamic law followed in many parts of the Muslim world contains provisions under which the father or guardian of a woman may veto, or even in extreme circumstances dissolve, the marriage of a daughter to a man who does not meet a social or educational standard that he deems necessary. This provision has been a source of controversy in some parts of the Muslim world, particularly Saudi Arabia, where judges have dissolved seemingly valid marriages because of objections raised by the bride's father.

In other parts of the Muslim world, the traditional systems of arranged marriages are still commonplace. In Arab tradition, for example, the most desirable marriage is one arranged between cousins. Such a marriage is expected to be harmonious due to the common background of the partners and the support and supervision of the extended family. It is intended to cement families and communities and preserve family property. This tradition persists in Arab society and throughout the Arab world but to a lesser extent than in the past. It is most commonly found in relatively close communities, particularly rural and village communities, and in very conservative Arab society.

Marriages may also be arranged between more distantly related or unrelated families within a community or social circle. A man may ask his family to find him a wife, in which case the family will make inquiries among family and acquaintances looking for a suitable bride. Intermediaries will delicately attempt to ascertain whether or not the woman's family might be open to a proposal from the family of the man; if so, the first steps toward betrothal may be a visit by the mother of the suitor to the mother of the potential bride. The visitors will make the proposal of marriage to the woman's family, who, if willing, will normally reply that they must ask their daughter's consent before replying.

A young man introduces his prospective wife to his parents. It is becoming increasingly common for young people to decide whom they wish to marry, rather than relying on their parents to choose for them.

A mixed group in a university class in Tehran, Iran. Higher education institutions have become a common place for men and women to meet socially.

Traditional matchmakers have always existed in Muslim society. They mediate between compatible individuals and families who are unable to find suitable marriage partners through their own range of contacts. In the twentieth century, marriage agencies appeared throughout the Muslim world and among Muslim communities in non–Muslim countries. These have been overtaken to a considerable extent by Internet agencies that carry listings by families and individuals and offer the facility of online communication to allow people to get to know each other before any further steps are taken. These are particularly useful for diaspora communities and are also used by converts to Islam seeking Muslim marriage partners.

IMPEDIMENTS TO MARRIAGE

According to Islamic law, there are various factors that may make marriage between two people forbidden. These may be permanent impediments due to factors that cannot be changed, such as the prohibition of marriage to immediate family, or merely temporary impediments that prevent a marriage until certain requirements have been met, such as marriage to members of the family of a spouse or the former spouse of a closely related family member.

The Koran goes into considerable detail regarding the degrees of familial relationship that prohibit marriage. The instructions in the Koran are addressed to Muslim men, but the rules apply equally to both sexes. Sura 4:23 makes it clear that marriage between certain close blood relations is permanently and absolutely prohibited. This includes all direct ancestors and descendants as well as siblings, half-siblings, nieces, nephews, uncles, and aunts. In addition to blood relations, sura 4:23 also forbids marriage between individuals who were raised in the same family, regardless of whether they are blood relations. There are no explicit prohibitions of marriage between more distant relatives, however, and sura 33:50 specifically permits marriage between cousins.

There are also in-law relationships that prohibit marriage. Most of these are permanent impediments, but there are certain cases in which the prohibition ends when the in-law relationship ceases. The evidence for these prohibitions is found in sura 4:22–23.

Muslim men are not allowed to marry any woman from whom their wife is directly descended. Similarly, men are not allowed to marry any woman descended from their wife, including the offspring of any previous marriage. These prohibitions are permanent and continue to apply in the event that a man's wife dies before him, if they divorce, or if their marriage is never consummated. In addition to these prohibitions, Muslim men are also forbidden from marrying the women divorced or widowed by their wife's descendants or ancestors.

There is a further degree of relationship that prohibits marriage: relationship by suckling. This prohibition is based on a tradition that the Prophet is believed to have said: "That which is prohibited by blood relationship is also prohibited by suckling." As a result, when a child is breast-fed by a woman who is not his or her mother, a relationship is established between the two families that prohibits marriage between certain members of those families in degrees of relationship that resemble the prohibited degrees of blood relationship. Thus a man is forbidden to marry the woman who breast-fed him

or any of her daughters or other women whom she breast-fed as infants. There is some disagreement between legal scholars on the amount of the breast-feeding required to make marriage impossible; some believe that a single suckling is sufficient, while others consider that a certain number of full feeds is required. Although the practice of wet-nursing is not as common as it was historically, it remains in use in some communities, particularly in rural communities, and this issue is therefore still relevant. As an example of the way in which such issues can also affect the modern world, the question has also arisen with regard to the use of milk banks for special care babies.

There are no explicit prohibitions of marriage between more distant relatives, however, and sura 33:50 specifically permits marriage between cousins.

Certain circumstances create only a temporary impediment to marriage. These include marriage to two sisters, or a woman and her aunt, at the same time. There is, however, nothing to prevent a man from marrying the sister, aunt, or niece of his divorced or deceased wife. Marriage to four women concurrently is also considered to be a temporary impediment to any further marriages. A man who divorces one or more of his four wives or who is widowed may marry further wives up to the maximum of four. A man may not remarry a woman whom he has divorced irrevocably

A husband and wife sign their marriage contract. Although a written contract is not a requirement, it is often required for legal reasons.

unless she has subsequently married another man and then has been divorced by the latter or widowed.

BETROTHAL OR ENGAGEMENT

The betrothal, or *khutba*, is a way of expressing the intention to marry. It is not a legally binding agreement, but it expresses a form of commitment within a community, and if the parties are not yet in a position to conclude the marriage it makes the status of the woman clear and serves to deflect the attentions of other suitors. If one party breaks off the engagement, there are no direct legal implications, but if gifts have been exchanged certain conventions apply. If the man has presented gifts such as money, jewelry, or other items of value, he may not reclaim them if it is he who

has broken off the engagement. If it is the woman who has terminated the engagement, then there will be an expectation that she will return any gifts that she has received from the man.

Marriage itself may take place immediately or shortly after the betrothal, or it may be some time later. In some communities, betrothal may take place even during the infancy of future spouses. In general, however, lengthy betrothals or engagements are discouraged in Muslim societies.

THE CONTRACT

In Islamic law, marriage is a contract, and in every formal sense it complies with all the requirements of any other contract. In many Islamic countries, family or personal status laws, including marriage laws, have been codified so that the legal provisions are clearly defined and subject to enforcement by the civil courts. In some countries, however, the law remains uncodified and subject to interpretationby legal scholars and enforcement in local Sharia courts.

The main feature of the contract is the mutually understood expression of intention to marry by the two parties or their representatives. As with any contract, there must be two parts: offer and acceptance. Normally, the offer will be issued by or on behalf of the groom and accepted on behalf of the bride. There is no strict requirement in the Sharia that the contract should be concluded in writing, but this is normally the case.

LEGAL CAPACITY TO MARRY

For the marriage to be valid the two parties must have the legal capacity to marry, that is, they must be of legal marriage age and mentally competent to understand and assent to the contract. Any woman who has not previously been married, even if she is above the age of full legal majority, is required to have a marriage guardian, who will usually be her father, grandfather, brother, or uncle. In practice, in almost all cases a woman will be represented at the signing of the contract by her guardian. In religious and cultural terms, this practice is usually explained as a matter of modesty and etiquette rather than a denial of her freedom of action. The contract takes place in a gathering of men, and in conservative societies it is not considered appropriate for a woman to represent herself.

In the majority of present-day Muslim societies, the minimum age for marriage is enforced by law. The age of consent is usually lower for women than it is for men, and it varies considerably from one country to another. In Algeria, for example, the minimum marriageable age is 21 for men and 18 for women, while in Pakistan it is 18 years for men and 16 for women. However, in many of the Muslim countries with legally established ages of consent, marriages are permitted at ages as young as 13 if the couple's parents give permission for the marriage or if the marriage is approved by a judge. Additionally, in some

MUHAMMAD'S MARRIAGES

Muslims take their model for married life from the life of the Prophet Muhammad. There are well-known Hadiths, related by al-Tirmidhi, that express his attitude toward women. "The best among you are those who are best to their wives."

Muhammad married for the first time at the age of about 25 to a wealthy widow, Khadija, believed to be some 15 years his senior, for whom he worked as a business agent. Their marriage lasted around 25 years, until her death, and is reported to have been a happy and loving one. It was Khadija who first comforted and supported him when he came to her overwhelmed by the first of the Revelations. He took no other wives during her lifetime. Following her death he was persuaded to marry a widow for companionship; shortly after that marriage, he was betrothed and later married to Aisha, who was to become his closest companion for the rest of his life.

Muhammad made other marriages that are considered to have been mostly to establish relationships between tribes that would cement political alliances, or to offer protection and support to women who had lost their husbands in battle. Indeed, it is held by Muslims that, for these reasons, Muhammad was given a special dispensation to marry more than the prescribed maximum of four wives. The Hadiths suggest that Muhammad's household was often difficult to manage harmoniously, although Aisha is quoted as saying that of all his wives, she only ever felt jealous of Khadija, whose memory stayed with Muhammad until his death.

countries the statutory minimum age is routinely ignored. In Afghanistan, for example, it is estimated that nearly 60 percent of marriages involve girls below the minimum marriageable age of 16.

A significant number of Muslim countries, particularly those in the Arabian Peninsula, do not have any fixed minimum age of consent. Islamic law establishes no minimum age for marriage, only a requirement that husbands wait until after their bride has reached puberty before consummating the marriage. Attempts to reform marriage laws in countries such as Saudi Arabia have drawn protest from some conservative Islamic scholars and organizations. The religious traditionalists reject the right of the state to dictate what is in the best interests of their

children and believe that young people, particularly girls, should be given in marriage as early as possible to avoid moral corruption.

WITNESSING AND PUBLIC ACKNOWLEDGMENT OF MARRIAGE

The contract must be witnessed by two adult male witnesses, or occasionally one male and two female witnesses. This practice prevents either the bride or groom from later denying that the marriage had taken place in order to avoid the responsibilities that go with it. The witnesses must actually be present when both the bride and groom give their assent to the terms of the marriage contract; they cannot merely agree to put their names on the contract after the event. Witnessing also serves to

A marriage ceremony in Bandar Seri Begawan, Brunei. Muslim marriage traditions in countries like Brunei or Indonesia are often very different from those of western Asia.

ensure that the marriage is acknowledged as valid by the community as a whole. Traditionally, the most effective way of ensuring that the whole community is aware of the marriage is through the customary wedding banquet, known as a *walima*. Muslims have a social obligation to attend such celebrations if they are invited, and the families of the bride and groom are expected to invite as many people as they can afford to feed. This custom ensures that as many members of the couple's community and extended family are aware of the marriage as possible.

Most Muslim countries now require official registration of marriages. This is a civil procedure for administrative purposes, but it is not a requirement for the religious legitimacy of the marriage. Unregistered

Unregistered marriages are not considered fornication, but the woman's rights in marriage and divorce cannot be protected by the courts.

marriages are not considered fornication, but the woman's rights in marriage and divorce cannot be protected by the courts. It is in this situation that testimony from witnesses and members of the community who knew of the marriage may be used to enforce the terms of the marriage contract.

In some Muslim countries, individuals who are able to prove their unregistered marriage took place can obtain a retroactive marriage certificate. In Egypt, for example, this practice grants women who were married in unofficial ceremonies full inheritance rights and enables them to hold their husband to account if he

neglects his duties as a husband and father. Until 2000, however, women could not have their case heard in the courts unless they had children.

Dowry

An essential element of the marriage contract is the *mahr* or *sadaq*, also known as *ujr* or *fareeda*, which is the dowry payable to the wife as a marriage gift. This sum of money or property becomes the property of the wife to dispose of as she pleases. Her parents are not allowed to take it, and her husband may not reclaim it. It is paid in two parts, known as the prompt and the deferred dowry. The prompt portion is customarily paid when the couple sign the marriage contract, and the wife may legitimately refuse to cohabit with the husband until it is paid.

The deferred portion is payable upon divorce, if instigated by the husband, or upon his death. This practice serves to ensure the wife's financial security in case she is divorced or widowed. It also acts as a deterrent to ill-considered divorce by the husband, as he will automatically become liable to pay the dowry. The dowry is negotiated between the two families; traditionally, families would insist on substantial sums to emphasize the enormous value that they placed on their daughter. In particular, while they might request a fairly modest sum for the prompt portion, they would demand a very large sum for the deferred part in the hope that this would make it extremely difficult for the husband to divorce their daughter. There are typically no upper or lower limits, and there are therefore vast potential differences between rich and poor. The sum asked for is usually dictated by custom and by the sums that have been paid to other women in the bride's family or women of comparable social status in her community.

Among modern urban communities in many countries, only a nominal amount is agreed upon, simply to complete the formal requirements of the contract. Although the dowry is intended to be the absolute property of the wife, in reality and

The husband must provide, furnish, and equip the marital home to an appropriate standard, normally to the standard to which the wife has been accustomed in her family's home.

in particular in poorer communities it is often taken by her family. It is not unheard of for it to be used to supply a dowry for another member of the family, such as the brother of the bride.

MAINTENANCE

In Islamic law it is the husband's responsibility to provide for his wife. He must provide her with food, clothing, accommodation and the necessities for running a household. There are complex arguments between Islamic scholars over what the husband must provide. This includes disputed topics such as whether or not the husband is obliged to provide such things as medical care or anything above basic living expenses. The actual level of maintenance for which the husband is liable is based on the social and financial circumstances of both parties. If the husband fails to provide maintenance, the wife may make a claim to the courts asking a judge to force the husband to pay, but

only in the most extreme and protracted situations can she seek separation. Before matters reach this stage, a judge may authorize deductions from his salary or accounts, sale of items of his property, or the incurring of debt in his name. The husband will only be entitled to withhold maintenance in some circumstances. These include if his wife renounces Islam, or if she is *nashiz* (disobedient)—a label applied to women who leave their husband's home without his agreement or work without his permission.

Sometimes problems arise with regard to maintenance in cases in which the husband deserts the wife but does not divorce her, or when he takes a second wife but does not comply with the requirement of equal treatment. It may also occur when the husband goes away to work and fails to send maintenance for his wife and family.

The husband must provide, furnish, and equip the marital home to an appropriate standard, normally to the standard to which the wife has been accustomed in her family's home. He may not make her share the home with other relatives, not even his parents, without her agreement. The only exception to this is a very young child from a previous marriage. If he has more than one wife, each is entitled to her own separate accommodation.

In reality, circumstances are as varied as they are in other societies. In the modern world, many women work outside the home, and in this case normally both partners will contribute to the running of the household. In some Muslim cultures it is customary for married couples to live in the home of the husband's family, although in urban communities the nuclear family has become the norm.

TEMPORARY MARRIAGE

With conventional Islamic marriages there is an unwritten understanding that although divorce is permissible, the marriage is intended to be a lifelong bond, and those entering into it are expected to view it as such. There are other forms of marriage permitted under Islamic law, however, which differ from conventional marriage in some ways, by waiving the requirement that the marriage is permanent, that the marriage be witnessed, or that the husband must fully provide for the wife. In Shia Islam there is a form of marriage called *nikah mut'ah*, which is a temporary bond in which the duration of the marriage and the material compensation that the man owes the woman are agreed before the signing of the marriage contract. This type of marriage

was originally intended to regulate the actions of men who were forced to spend long periods away from their wives and families fighting in Muhammad's army. *Nikah mut'ah* is mentioned only once in the Koran, in sura 4:24, which states:

> Lawful for you is what is beyond all that, that you may seek, using your wealth, in wedlock and not in license. So those of them whom you enjoy, give them their appointed wages; it is no fault in you in agreeing together, after the due apportionate. God is All-Knowing, All-Wise.

It is the word *enjoy* (*istamta'tum*—from the same root as *mut'ah*) in this verse that is taken to refer to this particular form of marriage. Shia Muslims believe that this

Bulgarian Muslim women display dowry. The dowry does not have to be a sum of money; it can instead be valuable gifts or property.

constitutes approval of the practice, while Sunni scholars maintain that in the context of the verses around it, 4:24 is in fact a prohibition of the practice. Both Sunni and Shia scholars can produce numerous Hadith to support their arguments, so the debate is largely focused on whether or not these Hadith are authentic. Sunni scholars concede that Muhammad did originally allow *mut'ah* marriages during military campaigns in order to preserve morale but assert that he later decided that it was not acceptable under any circumstances.

The *mut'ah* marriage contract may be concluded between a Muslim man and a Muslim, Christian, or Jewish woman. There is no upper or lower limit to the term of the marriage, but the period must be specified in the contract, as must the amount of the dowry or compensation to be paid by the man. The contract may include additional conditions added by the parties, provided these are not unlawful, and it may even specify the number of acts of intercourse that may take place during the term of the contract (although a contract that specifies only this without fixing the duration of the marriage will be void). The contract cannot be terminated by divorce, there is no mutual right of inheritance between the parties, and there is no entitlement to maintenance. Children conceived during a *mut'ah* marriage will, however, be legitimate and entitled to inherit from both of their parents. A *mut'ah* marriage cannot be converted to a regular marriage during its term. If the couple wish to continue the relationship as a regular marriage, they must make a new contract in the normal manner.

This form of marriage is not uncommon in Iran; in recent years, with the resurgence of the previously marginalized Shia population in Iraq, it has become more popular there. At one extreme, it may be considered to constitute a form of thinly disguised prostitution. Sometimes it is used by those working or studying away from home, who are not in a position to set up a permanent home. Among young people it provides an alternative to illicit relationships and can prevent accusations of fornication. It is also used in other ways to facilitate everyday living by removing the need for veiling among people who spend time together, for instance when they share a house, but who do not have an intimate relationship. In this case they may make a *mut'ah* contract but stipulate as a condition that there should be no physical relations between them. There are reports of cases where a *mut'ah* contract is made between a young daughter of a household and a male servant or gardener

There is no upper or lower limit to the term of the marriage, but the period must be specified in the contract, as must the amount of the dowry or compensation to be paid by the man.

so that she may go about the house and garden unveiled.

The Isma'ili Shia are of the same opinion as the Sunna in prohibiting *mut'ah* marriage. Most Sunni jurists and schools of jurisprudence hold that a marriage contract concluded for a fixed period is invalid, but one opinion of the Hanafi school claims that the marriage contract itself is valid but the condition making it temporary is void. They will therefore consider any such

WEDDINGS IN PAKISTAN

Weddings in Pakistan incorporate rituals of both social and religious origin and, due to the history of the country, reflect many varied customs and traditions imported from neighboring cultures.

Rural areas of Pakistan remain socially and religiously conservative. With some exceptions, arranged marriages are the cornerstone of village and community life. It remains the responsibility of senior members within the family to identify and arrange a suitable partner for their younger relatives. Preference is given to finding matches within the same family, tribe, or community. It is quite common to have the marriages arranged and words of commitment exchanged between the two parties when the girls are around 16 to 20 and the boys 18 to 24 (although it is not unusual for an understanding to have already existed between families for many years).

Usually, one well-known male member of a community is chosen to go door to door throughout the village to announce the wedding and to invite people to the wedding feast. Most commonly, the wedding celebrations begin with a prayer gathering at the local mosque or at the house of the wedding party. The Koran is read and the imam concludes the ceremony with a special prayer to bless the forthcoming wedding.

The first main gathering in the sequence of wedding events is the *mayun*. This is a gathering that marks the beginning of the bride's seclusion, usually a week or so prior to the wedding, during which she is relieved of household work and concentrates on beautifying herself for the wedding. Senior relatives give the bride gifts of money, which are later distributed to the poor. A similar gathering is held for the groom by his relatives.

The next main event is an informal ceremony known as *mehndi* (henna), which is held at the bride's house and is attended mostly by the women and girls of the village.

This event usually takes place one or two days before the wedding itself. *Mehndi* is a cultural tradition and does not have any religious significance. Young women adorn their hands and feet with *mehndi* in elaborate traditional patterns and dance to traditional music. Village women will sit outside the house to apply mehndi to the hands of all the guests in exchange for very small amounts of money. At this gathering the wedding gifts received and household items collected over the years by the bride's family in anticipation of her wedding are put on display. This will be a colorful array of clothes, ornaments, crockery, furniture, bedding, and other household items.

This event is followed within a day or two by the official wedding ceremony. It is held at the bride's house. The groom and his family are welcomed with garlands of flowers. The imam is asked to conduct the *nikah*, or marriage contract. The contract is concluded between the groom and the father or marriage guardian of the bride and is attended by male members of the family and male guests, often in the courtyard of the house. The bride and other women remain inside, and only very close male family members are allowed to go to the bride to ask her official consent to the marriage. Once the process is completed, the imam makes the announcement by congratulating the groom. All of the guests will meet and congratulate the groom personally. A meal is then provided by the bride's family. This is not the *walima* required by the Sunna, but a purely social event.

The next event in the sequence of celebrations is a dinner hosted by the groom's family, known as the *valima* (the same word as the Arabic *walima*), or banquet. This event is usually held on the day following the *nikah* or sometimes a day later. This completes the requirement of announcing the marriage and ensuring public acknowledgement to prevent any denial of it at a later time.

MASS WEDDINGS

The rules governing Muslim marriages require that the man should be able to pay an often substantial amount of money as a dowry, and to be able to provide his wife with a marital home. In the modern world, in which both men and women work, it has become difficult for many men to meet their obligation to pay these expenses on their own. When combined with these problems, the expense of a wedding ceremony, with the accompanying banquet, is beyond many young couples. As a result of this, mass weddings in which hundreds of couples marry at the same time have become common in some countries as a way of reducing costs while keeping within the instructions of the Koran. They are most common in comparatively urbanized countries like the United Arab Emirates, which have a large young working population and a high cost of living.

Muslim bridegrooms, in traditional attire, wait for their wedding ritual during a mass marriage ceremony.

marriage as a permanent marriage. The only Sunni jurisdiction in the Arab world that mentions *mut'ah* marriage is Jordan and then only to indicate that a marriage that meets the requirements in all other ways will be treated as a permanent marriage.

OTHER FORMS OF MARRIAGE

In addition to the *nikah* and the *nikah mut'ah*, there are two other types of marriage practiced in the Muslim world. They are similar to the *nikah mut'ah* in that they allow a couple to have a sexual relationship without being judged to have committed the sin of fornication, while allowing them to avoid the financial and social commitments of a normal marriage. The most commonly practiced of these are known as *nikah misyar* and *nikah urfi*.

Nikah misyar is the name given to a marriage in which the wife waives some or all of the rights associated with traditional marriage, including the right to a home, full financial support, and, if her husband is already married, an equal share of his time and resources. In a *misyar* marriage, the husband has the right to visit his wife whenever he wishes, day or night, but is not obligated to do so. It was originally intended as a way of providing companionship for widows and divorcees who were not considered eligible for remarriage.

Misyar marriage is a controversial issue in the Muslim world, as many see it as a practice that encourages marriages for purely sexual purposes, or allege that it is used as a cover for a form of prostitution. For many couples in the Muslim world, however, *misyar* marriages are a way of marrying without having to obtain the substantial amounts of money needed for the dowry, ceremony, and shared home that are considered a requirement for a conventional marriage. In 2006 the Institute of Islamic Religious Law, an influential Saudi Arabian authority on Islamic law, declared that *misyar* marriages, while not encouraged, were morally and legally acceptable as long as the woman's guardian was informed and there were two witnesses and a state official present.

A related form of marriage known as *nikah urfi*, or customary marriage, has become increasingly popular in Egypt and some other parts of the Muslim world. Like the Saudi Arabian *misyar* marriage, the *urfi* marriage is commonly used by couples who do not have enough money to pay for a traditional marriage or establish a household together.

Normally they will make a verbal agreement to marry in the form of offer and acceptance in front of witnesses, sometimes in the presence of a religious scholar. Sometimes this will be recorded in

Misyar marriage is a controversial issue in the Muslim world, as many see it as a practice that encourages marriages for purely sexual purposes.

a document with the signatures of the witnesses. Very often it is done without the knowledge of their families. Other scenarios include cases in which women and young girls who are homeless or have no family are vulnerable to men who offer them marriage and protection. Having no better option, they agree to *urfi* marriages but are often abandoned after the man has taken advantage of them. Very often, these men will already be married and committed to a

family and have no intention of acknowledging a second family. It is also alleged that *urfi* marriages are used in some parts of the Muslim world to facilitate a form of sex tourism in which young girls, sometimes encouraged by their families, are given in *urfi* marriage to visitors from wealthier parts of the Muslim world. These marriages are almost always dissolved at the end of the visitor's stay, either formally or through abandonment.

This practice can have serious consequences, especially if the woman becomes pregnant and the man denies the marriage. Since 2000 the Egyptian law has allowed claims of proof of marriage in unregistered marriages, but evidence is required and if the woman has no document and no witnesses support her, she can find herself in severe difficulty. Besides the social stigma and the need to prove the paternity of her child, she runs the risk of accusation of polyandry if she attempts to marry again and the first husband has not formally divorced her.

WEDDINGS

Wedding customs vary throughout the Muslim countries but tend to focus around the three main stages of the process of marriage: the betrothal or engagement, the conclusion of the marriage contract, and the commencement of married life. These three stages may be very close together, or they may be separated by periods of months or years.

A wedding is a joyous event and a cause for celebration as lavish as the means of the family will allow. Weddings always involve feasting and in most cultures, with the exception of some of the most conservative communities, they include music and dancing.

After the ceremony itself, the next most important part of any Islamic marriage is the *walima*, or wedding banquet. The *walima* is strongly encouraged by Islamic scholars and is considered by some to be essential for a marriage to be considered valid. Inviting friends, neighbors, and relatives to a wedding banquet ensures that the marriage will be acknowledged and recognized by the community. This ensures that the couple's rights are respected and prevents either party from trying to escape from responsibilities. According to most jurists, Muslims have a duty to attend such banquets if invited.

The timing of the *walima* varies between cultural groups; some hold that it should take place immediately after the marriage contract is signed, or between the signing of the marriage contract and the consummation of the marriage. Others maintain that it should take place on the occasion of the wedding procession, when the bride leaves her family home for her husband's house. The most commonly accepted custom, however, is for the *walima* to be held after the marriage has been consummated, a custom believed to originate with the Prophet Muhammad.

A Bulgarian Muslim bride with special make-up stands next to her husband during their wedding ceremony in the village of Ribnovo, in the Rhodope Mountains, Bulgaria.

The *walima* can be a celebration that lasts for up to two days, in order for everyone to be able to attend. The *walima* is not supposed to be a lavish occasion, however, and using one to display wealth—whether by extending the feast to more than two days, or by serving extravagant meals—is strongly discouraged. The emphasis is traditionally on simplicity. Some Hadith quote Muhammad as saying that a *walima* should be held even if the hosts have nothing more than a single sheep to feed their guests.

DISSOLUTION OF MARRIAGE

There is a saying of the Prophet Muhammad, found in many collections of Hadith, which states that "Of all the things that are permitted, divorce is the most hated by God."

Although the partners should enter the marriage with the intention of it being permanent, Islam recognizes that discord may arise, and divorce is permitted when partners cannot find a way to continue their married life together. When marital problems occur, it is considered to be the responsibility of the family and the community to attempt to solve the problems, as indicated by sura 4:35; if a breakdown of the relationship is feared, an arbitrator should be nominated from each of the two families to try to bring about reconciliation.

Islamic law gives the husband the right to pronounce divorce unilaterally, but there are other provisions by which a divorce may be sought by either or both parties.

The term for unilateral divorce is *talaq*, which means releasing or letting go. Sura 65, entitled *Al-Talaq*, gives considerable detail on the legal requirements and the behavior expected in unilateral divorce.

The exercise of unilateral divorce takes three different forms: *talaq hasan* (good divorce), *talaq ahsan* (best divorce), and *talaq al-bid'a* (literally, innovative divorce).

Unilateral divorce should be pronounced during a period of *tuhr*, or purity, while the wife is not menstruating and when no intercourse has taken place since the last menstruation. Following this period, there is a waiting period, or *iddah*, during which it is considered revocable; the husband has the right to take his wife back with or without her consent and without formal procedure, either verbally or simply by resuming marital relations. The wife is not permitted to marry another man during this time. The duration of the waiting period is the completion of three menstrual periods or, for women who do not menstruate, three months of the Islamic calendar. If the wife is pregnant at the time of the divorce, the waiting period is until she gives birth (or miscarries). If the husband does not take the wife back during this time, the divorce will be *talaq ba'in baynuna sughra*, or lesser irrevocable divorce. The partners may remarry, but this will have to be by a new contract, and a new dowry will be required. The husband may only divorce his wife this way twice and still be permitted to marry her again. If this is repeated a third time, it will be considered to be *talaq ba'in baynuna kubra*, or greater irrevocable divorce, and the partners will be prohibited to each other, unless the wife subsequently marries another man in a legitimate marriage and is widowed or divorced. This form of divorce is known as *talaq hasan*.

Talaq ahsan is also completed by three consecutive pronouncements of divorce, but these must be in three consecutive periods of *tuhr*, between menstrual periods, during which time intercourse has not taken place. Upon completion of these three pronouncements and the observation of the *iddah* following the final pronouncement, the marriage is dissolved irrevocably.

Divorce may be pronounced verbally by the husband himself or by a person whom he authorizes to do this (for instance, if he is in another country), or in writing. Most Islamic countries today require it to be conducted formally before a *qadi*, or notary. The completion of the greater irrevocable divorce makes the husband liable to pay the deferred portion of the dowry immediately on completion of the *iddah*. The husband is required to house and maintain the woman during the period of the *iddah*, which, apart from being a form of cooling-off period, ensures that if the woman is pregnant there is no doubt regarding paternity.

If a husband divorces his wife before consummation of the marriage, then if the dowry has been agreed upon he must give her half of it as compensation. If it has not been agreed upon, he must give her a gift of appropriate value.

Talaq al-bida—in which the husband pronounces the divorce formula three times in succession on a single occasion, thereby effecting an immediate irrevocable divorce—is strongly disapproved of and widely regarded as contrary to the intention of the Sharia. Nevertheless, *talaq al-bida* is recognized as legal in many Islamic countries. In many countries where registration of a divorce is required, the court will only record it as a single divorce.

The methods by which a wife may seek divorce are more limited. She may stipulate in the marriage contract that she should have the right to terminate the marriage, although this is obviously subject to the husband's agreement at the time of the contract. She may also stipulate other conditions, for example that she should be entitled to a divorce without prejudice to her marital financial rights if the husband takes another wife or if he asks her to emigrate or move away from her hometown with him.

A wife may seek dissolution of the marriage by a *qadi* on grounds of injury if her husband mistreats or abuses her, whether physically or psychologically. In some jurisdictions the taking of a further wife may be construed as harm and serve as grounds for divorce. Persistent failure to pay maintenance or imprisonment of the husband for an extended period are further possible grounds, as is significant mental or physical defect in the husband that the wife was unaware of at the time of the contract.

A further form of access to divorce for women that is supported by the Koran is *khul*. This is a process by which a wife may free herself from an unhappy marriage without having to give grounds or prove any fault or injury by waiving all of her financial rights, including repaying any dowry that she has received. Reformers in several countries have attempted to develop this into a formal workable system to enable women to free themselves from intolerable marriages when their husbands are unwilling to divorce them. The Egyptian legislature introduced a law permitting and regulating *khul* in 2000 in an attempt to provide relief to the thousands of women whose petitions to the courts for divorce are delayed, sometimes by years, in an overworked judicial system. On the surface it appears to offer the possibility of speeding up the process and avoiding the distress and expense involved in lengthy court proceedings, but in reality it is an option that is available only to the privileged few

Henna tattoos on the feet of a woman taking part in a wedding celebration. These temporary tattoos are commonly used in South Asia and the Middle East to adorn the bride and her attendants.

who are able to afford it. It involves sacrificing financial rights, specifically the deferred dowry, to which a woman otherwise may be legitimately entitled.

WIDOWS AND WIDOWERS

Widows are required to observe an *iddah* period in the same way as divorced women, although the term is fixed at four months and ten days or, if they are pregnant, until they are delivered of the child. A widow is not entitled to maintenance during the *iddah*, but the spouses have mutual rights of inheritance according to Koranic shares that vary depending on the presence of other heirs.

Widowers do not have to observe an *iddah* period after the death of a wife and can remarry immediately afterward. The marriage is dissolved from the moment of the wife's death. This means that many cultures forbid widowers from attending to their wife's body after her death or seeing it without a veil.

See Also
Family Life 8-31 ❖
Polygamy 32-35 ❖
Divorce 58-59 ❖
Men and Women
60-83 ❖ Islamic Law
108-129 ❖

Divorce

Traditional Muslim divorce is heavily weighted in favor of husbands and against wives. While that bias remains, there are signs in the modern Islamic world of improved rights for women.

In Islam, marriage is viewed as a union ordained by God, and its dissolution is discouraged. The Koran is clear in encouraging harmonious relations between husbands and wives and in discouraging discord and separation. It expressly instructs the Muslim community to attempt to intervene where a marriage is perceived to be breaking down. However, marriage is not seen by Muslims as a religious sacrament but as a legal contract between two parties and, as such, there is no theological impediment to its dissolution.

A Muslim husband may end his marriage simply by saying "*talaq*" (I divorce you) three times to his wife. No religious or judicial process is involved. Between the first and the final *talaq*, the man may revoke his pronouncement at any time during the *iddah*, the waiting period during which he must still support his wife. If, in the meantime, the wife discovers that she is pregnant, the *iddah* is extended until the birth of the child.

Although this form of divorce—known in Arabic as *talal* (repudiation)—does occur, the notion that it is the only or indeed the predominant method of terminating a marital union is an extreme oversimplification of the complex divorce laws that vary widely from country to country in the modern Islamic world. For example, in most Muslim countries, wives may seek divorce through the courts on the grounds of their husbands' cruelty, desertion, or failure to pay adequate maintainance.

Nevertheless, traditional Muslim divorce laws remain biased against women. While, according to the practice known as *khul*, marriages may be ended by the mutual agreement of the spouses, the wife must pay the husband to secure her release from the union. The price is normally the return to the husband and his family of the dower she received at the time of the marriage. This is a significant problem because the original dowry, though ostensibly a gift to the bride, is often given to her family soon after the marriage. As a result, many women are unable to divorce their husbands because their family is either unwilling or unable to return the dowry. Similarly, for a man to divorce a woman, he is often required to pay her a sum of money known as a deferred dowry, which is arranged as part of the marriage contract. This sum is frequently set prohibitively high by the bride's family, which further complicates the divorce process for many couples.

MODERN PRACTICES

Since the middle of the 20th century (and, in a few cases, earlier), many Muslim countries have attempted to codify the provisions of Islamic family law and to make them enforceable in civil courts or Sharia (religious) courts. Legislation to reform the laws of marriage and

... [M]arriage is not seen by Muslims as a religious sacrament but as a legal contract between two parties and, as such, there is no theological impediment to its dissolution.

divorce has been made with great delicacy and framed in terms that comply with traditional jurisprudence in order to avoid any accusation of contravening Sharia law.

Many countries have attempted to regulate the use by men of their right to divorce. Governments have set out strict preconditions for the repudiation of any marriage and legislated to ensure the provision of

A mullah (Muslim cleric, left) in Iran examines the case of a young couple wishing to divorce. Most Iranian divorce officials are clergymen who observe Sharia law as well as legal rules.

maintenance payments after the divorce. Tunisia is one of several Muslim-majority nations that have gone so far as to require that any unilateral, "triple *talaq*"-type divorce should be pronounced in a court of law. These nations have also legislated to define as clearly as possible the various grounds on which a woman may seek the dissolution of a marriage and the procedure for doing so, as well as to codify the *khul* to comply with the stipulations of the Koran.

To serve the Muslim communities in Western countries, many mosques currently offer marriage guidance and reconciliation services. When there is no conflict with the national law, the service providers may settle disputes over dowry and maintenance. In cases in which they are unable to bring about a reconciliation, they may register a *talal* or a *khul* and prescribe the period of *iddah*. Normally they will do this in parallel with the process of legal divorce in the national courts. However, problems sometimes arise when women obtain a legal divorce but their husbands refuse to pronounce the *talaq* or to accept the *khul*. In these cases, the husband and wife will still be deemed to be married under Sharia law and will therefore be prohibited from remarrying.

Chapter 3

MEN AND WOMEN

After a century of struggle, women in Western societies have won equal rights with men, in many cases enshrined in law. In comparison, Muslim women are perceived to have few rights and to be dominated by men. However, do Muslim women feel unequal? If so, does this inequality come from Islamic teachings?

As with all aspects of their lives, the roles and responsibilities of Muslim men and women are based on two sources: the content of the Koran and the laws established in the centuries after the death of the Prophet Muhammad. These laws were formulated by scholars who used evidence of the Prophet's life as a guide.

On occasion, the rulings set out by the different schools appear to contradict each other, which results in conservative or liberal interpretations of gender roles in different regions.

This form of jurisprudence (lawmaking) is founded on five schools of Islamic thought. Four schools—Hanbali, Shafi'i, Maliki, and Hanafi—follow Sunni traditions, while the Ja'afary school is associated with the Shia branch. On occasion the rulings set out by the different schools appear to contradict each other, which results in somewhat conservative or liberal interpretations of gender roles in different regions.

The relationship between a Muslim man and woman is formalized by Islamic rules and conservative traditions, but the couple are essentially a partnership that works together to raise a family.

MALE DOMINANCE

The mismatches between scholarly rulings are further complicated by the fact that some Muslim-dominated countries have strict gender roles and inequalities that are a product of a society that remains controlled by men. The dominance of men has been gradually reduced in Western societies over the centuries, but chauvinistic cultures have persisted in other parts of the world—including in the Muslim world. Many sexist traditions predate the foundation of Islam, and if anything, the rulings of the religion have improved the status of women in many parts of the world.

WESTERN VIEW

Local traditions apart, Islam does dictate that women have a different role to play in society from men. The rights of men and women in the secular West, however, are now practically identical. As a result, Westerners often regard Muslim women as being persecuted and at a disadvantage. The Western view of Muslim women is partly informed by European stereotypes that stem from centuries of conflict with Muslim states. One well-known myth is that of the harem, a collection of women held prisoner in a house purely for the pleasure of their husband. Such institutions may have existed in the palaces of emperors and sultans centuries ago, but they have no basis in Islam and have no bearing on modern life. Other perceptions of the plight of Muslim women comes from the variations in gender roles reported from around the world. For example, in Saudi Arabia, women are banned from driving cars. Elsewhere, women cannot show their faces in public. The most extreme examples

Muslim women that rebel against inequality in their cultures are often branded as un-Islamic, just as Western feminist pioneers during the 1800s were frequently described as being anti-Christian.

come from Afghanistan during the rule of the Taliban in the late 1990s. In those days, females had no right to an education and could not leave their house without being accompanied by a male relative. A woman convicted of adultery was executed.

Such harsh customs are often reported in the West as being rooted in Islam to the dismay of Muslims living elsewhere. From the perspective of the West, few people understand that Islam infers equal rights on men and women. This theory does not conform with what Westerners perceive as common practice. Muslim commentators point out that injustices are un-Islamic and misguided.

The way of life of Muslim women in countries with more emancipated cultures is seldom reported. For example, in Bosnia, Malaysia, or Kenya, Muslim women are educated to a high level and are not inhibited from playing a full role in society alongside men.

ENCOUNTERING CHANGE

There is much disagreement over whether certain traditions are allowable according to Islamic teachings, with scholars around the world offering different rulings. Muslim women who rebel against inequality in their cultures are often branded as un-Islamic, just as feminist pioneers in North America during the 1800s were frequently described as being anti-Christian.

It is often argued that the restrictions on Muslim women's clothing and movements are meant to protect them from the unwanted advances of men. Two people of the opposite sex are not allowed to be alone together unless they are married or belong to the same family. In Saudi Arabia, among other countries, this act is a crime punishable by lashing and imprisonment. As a result, parents wield a degree of control over their children that would be unusual for a Western family.

When Muslim families migrate to Western countries, they often retain the male-dominated ways of life of their home cultures. Interaction with local people who are used to a more permissive way of life regularly creates tensions within the family, as younger generations question their position in society. However, there is little indication that Muslim women necessarily find Western gender roles more liberating. Quite the opposite, many thousands of women from Europe and North America choose to convert to Islam each year. One of the attractions of Islam is that the Koranic rules offer a life that is liberated from the pressures of Western womanhood.

FOLLOWING ADAM AND EVE

Like Jews and Christians, Muslims believe that humanity is descended from a first couple, Adam and Eve, who were created by God to live in paradise. The relationship between Adam and Eve as reported in the Koran and commented upon by the Prophet Muhammad is the first example of how a man and woman lived together; as such, it forms the foundation of Islamic gender roles.

The Koran describes how God created Adam and Eve from one soul: "Oh humankind! Be pious and conscious of your Lord who created you out of one living soul, and out of it created its mate, and out of the twain God spread abroad countless men and women." The Koran regards males and females to be equally capable of accomplishing God's commands that guarantee their path to heaven.

A Hadith (reported saying and action of the Prophet) relates to Adam and Eve: "Men and women are two parts to one pair." In Arabic, the word *zawj*, meaning "pair," is also translated into "mate" or "spouse"; thus the female spouse was created from the soul of the male spouse in order for them to dwell together.

As in the Jewish and Christian tradition, Adam and Eve were tempted by the devil in the Islamic story. As a result they were thrown out of paradise and ordered to dwell on Earth. Adam and Eve repented, and God forgave them. They were not returned to paradise but were given the ability to conceive children. In other words, procreation was essential in the lives of Adam and Eve. God wanted them to have a family, and it was Adam's job to teach his children God's message—to worship none but the Almighty and strive to live a pious life. Muslims believe that the 24 prophets mentioned in the Koran—ending in the Prophet Muhammad—are all descended from Adam and Eve.

The children of Adam and Eve did not inherit the first sin committed by their parents. (Muslims believe that no person inherits original sin, nor is anyone held accountable for the sins of others.) Therefore God does not penalize all the world's males based on Adam's first sin, nor all the females for Eve's first sin.

Muslims believe that God will evaluate their lives based upon their piety and the depth of their consideration of God's presence in their lives. In other words, whenever someone takes a certain action, he or she would be conscious of whether that action would bring them closer to God or would bring God's wrath. The Koran states in sura 16:97: "Whosoever doeth right,

MARYAM, A DISTINGUISHED MOTHER

An entire chapter of the Koran is devoted to Maryam, the Islamic name for Mary. To Christians she is better known as the Virgin Mary, but to Muslims she is the mother of the Prophet Jesus and is distinguished as an ideal role model for mothers.

Maryam was born in the al-Imran household, a very pious family, and accordingly was selected by God as the purest woman in the world. The Prophet Jesus was created in Maryam's womb by a divine decree rather than conventional conception. In so doing, Maryam's chastity and good virtue were maintained. Jesus is referred to as the son of Mary. Here, the Koran is breaking with the tradition in which individuals are normally identified by their father's name. Named as Maryam's son, Islam teaches that the Prophet Jesus, therefore, was not the son of God. However, the story of Maryam is not just about being a woman. She was chosen for her virtue, nobility, and devotion, as well as her ability to carry children hence she is not confined by her sex and she serves as an example for all humankind.

Islam does not prevent Muslim girls from being taught by men, but the rules that control contact between unmarried people often result in teenage Muslims being taught in single-sex classes.

whether male or female, and is a believer, him verily We shall quicken with good life, and We shall grant them a recompense in proportion to the best of what they used to do." This verse corroborates the fact that men and women are equal.

RELIGIOUS AND SOCIAL ROLES

Sura 33:35 of the Koran makes it clear that faithful Muslim men and women are equal in the sight of Allah:

"Verily, for men and women who surrender themselves unto God, believing men and women, devout men and devout women, honest men and women, patient men and women, men and women who humble themselves [before God], all men and women who give in charity, and self-denying (fasting) men and women, and all men and women who guard their private parts:

and men and women who remember God unceasingly: for them has God readied forgiveness of sins and a mighty reward. It is not fitting for a believer, man or woman, when a matter has been decided by Allah and His Messenger, to have any option about their decision: if anyone disobeys Allah and His Messenger he or she is on a stray Path." Thus the followers of this faith regard their religion as a thorough value system in which the religious and social tasks of men and women are intertwined.

THE EDUCATION OF MEN AND WOMEN

The roles of Muslim men and women in society are influenced by the thoughts and deeds of members of the early Muslim community. Much of the scholarly research into this period reflects on how men and women passed on the teachings of the

Prophet. In turn, this has affected the way Muslim children are educated today.

The very first verse of the Koran revealed to the Prophet was the command: "Read, in the name of your Lord who has created" (sura 1:1). Muslims must seek knowledge and learn to read so they can memorize and recite the Koran and become familiar with their religion. Therefore the education of men and women is an obligation of all Muslims. However, there is debate about what the different sexes should be taught. Conservative Muslim scholars argue that the purpose of a woman's education is to enhance her "natural" roles as the mother and educator of children.

Again, scholars turn to the early Muslim community for guidance. In the early days of the Muslim faith, converts to the religion were taught in schools called *kuttab*. As the years passed, children born into the community were also sent to the *kuttab*. Soon a custom was established in which young children of both sexes attended the *kuttab*s, but teenage girls were withdrawn from school and taught at home by female tutors, while the older boys continued to attend the *kuttab*.

ROLE MODELS

Despite this segregation, adult women can be educated by men, as evidenced by the fact that the Prophet appointed Omar Ibn al-Khattab to teach the newly converted women. Furthermore, the knowledgeable female companions of the Prophet could teach men. Following the Prophet's death, his wives (sometimes known as the Mothers of the Believers) became the role models for future Muslims. Since they were the closest to him at all occasions—especially whenever he used to receive a divine revelation—the wives of the Prophet were the ones who witnessed and got first-hand knowledge from their husband.

The Prophet's wife, Aisha, became a renowned scholar who was an expert of Islamic jurisdiction. She related over 2,210 of the Prophet's traditions; she also used to correct the companions whenever they

The Prophet's wife, Aisha, became a renowned scholar who was an expert of Islamic jurisdiction. He recommended that the Muslims should obtain most of their religious knowledge from her.

would transmit any of the Prophet's sayings, or Hadiths, inaccurately. She was trained by the Prophet to question, discuss, argue, and correct, to the extent that he recommended that the Muslims should obtain most of their religious knowledge from her. Her familiarity with Islamic law entitled her to be ranked as a scholar and issue independent rulings or fatwas.

The early caliphs that ruled in the first 40 years after the Prophet's death used to consult Aisha and his other wives, seeking their advice whenever they faced an issue that had not been considered before or lacked sufficient precedent.

Um Salama, another Mother of the Believers, narrated about 387 of the Prophet's Hadiths. Similarly, during the ninth century, Nafissa, the Prophet's great granddaughter, taught Imam Shafi'i, the founder of one of the Sunni schools of thought. Much later, Ibn al-Arabi, the famous Sufi thinker, was also instructed and greatly influenced by a female mentor.

PUBLIC LIFE

All sources of Islamic jurisdiction make it an obligation upon all Muslims to be literate and to eradicate ignorance. Women of the first Muslim community attended the mosque, took part in religious services on feast days, and listened to the Prophet's discourses. They participated in discussions and questioned, argued, and challenged. A female companion called Um Atiyyah narrated many of the Prophet's Hadiths and taught several scholars among the second generation of the companions about various aspects of Islamic jurisprudence.

Another influential woman was Aisha bint Said ibn Abi Waqqas, who was an expert in Islamic thought. She taught Imam Malik, the founder of the Maliki school of thought, and other famous jurists and scholars of Hadiths.

Just like male companions of the Prophet, several female companions accomplished great deeds and achieved fame, and throughout Islamic history there have been famous and influential women scholars and jurists. However, from the 10th century, women became more secluded from public life, and female social life became restricted to small circles of female friends and relations, who had minimal contact with people outside their homes. It became much harder for women to receive an education, and within a few generations, political and religious life was solely in the hands of men. Women were eventually also excluded from public worship in the mosque.

THE ROLE OF RELIGIOUS LEADERSHIP

Performing the ritual prayers, or *salat*, five times a day is one of the main pillars through which a Muslim submits to God. Prayers can be carried out at home or in the mosque. The latter is preferred so Muslims can interact with the rest of their community and worship God in congregation. Congregational prayers must be led by an imam who, in addition to having memorized the Koran, is also able to pronounce God's words accurately. Congregational *salat* is led by a male imam following in the Prophet's footsteps. The Prophet used to lead congregational prayers for men and women, but all-female groups were led by one of his wives.

Based on an authentic reported account of the female companion Um Waraqa, it was recorded that the Prophet Muhammad used to visit her at her house and ordered her to lead the members of her household in prayer (including the men) because she was best at reciting the Koran. Some jurists who have permitted women to be the

From the 10th century, women became more secluded from public life, and female social life became restricted to small circles of female friends and relations, who had minimal contact with people outside their homes.

imam for a mixed prayer have based their arguments on Um Waraqa's account.

Averroës, or Ibn Rushd, an Andulusian (Islamic Spain) Muslim jurist and scientist from the 12th century, argued that the original rule is that a woman has identical religious duties as a man, unless there is evidence from the Koran or the Sunna (compilation of Hadiths) that proves to disqualify this argument. Averroës agrees with all jurists that women should stand behind men in prayer—with the implication that they would not be leading men in prayer; he also agrees that a woman can lead all-women *salat*. It is permissible for a woman to lead congregational prayers in her household as long as she is the most knowledgeable and the best at reciting the Koran. When it comes to the community as a whole, there will usually be a man who is well versed in the Koran who can be appointed to serve as the imam in the community mosque.

FRIDAY PRAYERS

The Friday congregational prayer—the main religious ceremony of the week—is not an obligatory ritual for women, as it is demanded of all Muslim men. (The Friday sermon is always presented by a man.) Many jurists advocate that it would be preferable for women to perform the Friday *salat* at home, especially in

communities with small mosques with a prayer hall that has hardly enough space for the men. However, husbands cannot prevent their wives from performing their prayers in the mosque or attending the Friday *salat* if they wish to. This is based on a Hadith in which the Prophet says: "Do not hinder women to go to the mosques."

In present-day American Muslim communities, men and women attend mosques jointly, as mosques are designed to be large enough to include many worshippers. Muslim women in the historically Muslim countries have become more involved in religious activities during the last two or three decades of Islamic revivalism.

ECONOMIC OBLIGATIONS

Islamic teachings dictate that men are responsible for the financial needs of their wives, mothers, unmarried sisters, and children. Even if his wife is wealthy, a

Women and girls worship in the same prayer hall as the men in this U.S. mosque, where there is enough room to seat the whole community. However, the females are located behind the males.

husband is still responsible for his wife's and their household's expenses, and he cannot force his wife to share the work of keeping track of the money. Prior to a wedding, the groom pays a dower to the bride. This is financial insurance, which ensures that the woman can access her own money once the marriage has commenced.

Financial responsibilities give most men guardianship of women because men are charged with earning money and supporting the family. In other respects, this amounts to a position of power in the family. While men have responsibility for money, women have the role of procreation and caring for their children—without the pressures of financial concerns.

Nevertheless, neither the Koran nor Sunna contains anything to prevent women from assuming other roles if they choose. In spite of this, some conservative Muslim scholars say that motherhood is the only career available to women.

Such guidance is at odds with the life of the Prophet: Khadija, the Prophet's first wife and the first Muslim convert, had a flourishing business and hired the Prophet to manage her financial affairs before their marriage. Other women achieved positions of responsibility, as was the case with al-Shifa bint Abdullah, who was appointed by the second caliph, Omar, as a market inspector in Medina. Asma bint Abu Bakr, the daughter of the first caliph, also shared the responsibility of supporting her family with her husband by working away from her home and family.

It must be noted that in the Muslim world, the concept of empowerment is not always perceived as a woman's ability to leave her home to participate in the labor force. Just like non-Muslim women, Muslim women around the world make a choice to stay home or get a job depending upon their own social and economic circumstances. If anything, the prevalent view of many Muslim women is that their empowerment can be achieved through success within their household, where they can be key decision makers and respected members of the community regardless of their earning capacity. This viewpoint has perhaps gained some sympathy among Westernized women who may feel unsatisfied with combining the needs of an employer with those of their families.

Although Muslim woman have the right to choose most careers, Muslim scholars direct them that their most important work is raising children.

RIGHTS OF PROPERTY

One of the differences between the rights of men and women in Islam is their ability to inherit from their relatives. Female family members inherit half the amounts awarded to male members. The reasoning behind this is that a man is obliged to provide financial support to the family—and pay a dowry to his wife. A woman does not have to share any of her wealth if she chooses not to. If a marriage ends in divorce, the man is obliged to continue giving money to his ex-wife for the support of their children. A divorced woman is not required to do the same, even if her fortune is greater than that of her ex-husband.

There is sometimes a misconception among non-Muslims that a woman's value is half that of a man. This is a conflation of two separate ideas—the rules on inheritance and the Koranic advice on making business contracts between a man and a woman. In pre-Islamic Arabia, it was common for a man to cheat a woman in business. As a result, sura 2:197 in the Koran explains that when a contract is arranged between a man and a woman, it should be witnessed by a second woman. If the man defaults on the contract, the female witness can testify on behalf of the first woman. However, it does not take two women to sue a single man. The testimony of either woman carries the same legal weight as that of the man.

ENDOWMENTS

Islam's inheritance rules do result in a family's wealth gradually moving from the female members to the men. When a wealthy woman dies, most of her wealth goes to her male relatives, unless there are many more female beneficiaries.

DOMESTIC VIOLENCE

Violent abuse within the home takes place the world over. This crime was hidden for many years as abused wives (and sometimes husbands) chose not to tell the authorities. Today, there are better facilities to help people abused by their spouses, but the problem still remains. Abuse occurs in Muslim families, as it does in households of other faiths. However, it has been alleged that Islam allows a husband to beat his wife. This accusation is based on the Koran, sura 4:34: "As to those women from whom you fear ill conduct, first admonish them, then refuse to share your bed with them, and then, if necessary, beat them. Then if they obey you, take no further actions against them and do not make excuses to punish them." Scholarly rulings say that the sins that qualify for this treatment include drinking alcohol and abusing children. The first two steps need not lead to the third. In other words, the husband may sleep separately from his sinful wife indefinitely if he chooses. The Prophet Muhammad said, "Those men who beat their wives are not the best among you." When asked what a man should use to beat his wife, the Prophet suggested using a toothbrush—he was cleaning his teeth at the time. Scholars have taken this statement to mean that any physical punishments should be symbolic and painless. Some suggest using a handkerchief.

The Islamic endowment, or *waqf* (plural, *awqaf*), is an important financial instrument that allows Muslim people to ensure that their money is put to a good purpose after death. Using a *waqf*, a wealthy person can devote property and its future revenue for specific purposes in perpetuity. (The benefactor's family have no rights over the *waqf*'s funds.)

Although the Koran does not state what type of charity Muslims are supposed to choose, most endowments are used to fund mosques or another religious institution. The Koran forbids people from making a profit by lending money. The funds of a *waqf* are legally a loan, but instead of any revenue going to the benefactor (or to his or her heirs), all profits belong to the establishment itself.

As males and females have the same rights to dispose of property and earnings and participate in business investments and contracts, wealthy Muslim women have historically used endowments to play an active role in improving society. For example, Banafshaa ar-Rumiyah founded a school in Baghdad in the 10th century.

The Gönenli women are trying to live like the pioneers of Islam and offer an alternative to the secular view of women's liberation.

In the ninth century, Fatimah al-Fihriyah used her inherited wealth to build the al-Qarawiyin Mosque in Fez, Morocco. For over 1,100 years, the al-Qarawiyin *waqf* has become famous as a university and religious college that still functions today, as well as for its religious function. Its founder was later given the title "Saint of Fez." At the same time, Fatimah's younger sister, Maryam al-Fihriya, was using another endowment to build the al-Andalusiyin Mosque in Fez.

Centuries later, a third influential mosque was founded by another woman in Morocco. Massouda al-Wazkitia was the mother of the Saadi caliph Ahmed Al Mansour in the 16th century. She built Bab Doukkala Mosque in Marrakesh, equipped it with a library, and set aside funds for future scholars.

Women using endowments to influence Muslim society is not only a past practice. It continues. In 1995, a collection of Sufi

women established the Gönenli endowment in Istanbul, Turkey. The money pays for a Sufi lodge, a place of education and worship, which were once common across the Ottoman Empire until about 90 years ago. Today, the Gönenli women teach, run a pastry shop and a library, and hold their *zikr* circle—the main Sufi ritual—at the lodge. They prefer to stay separate from men in the mosque in order to be able to perform their spiritual activities in private.

The Gönenli endowment earns its members respect and influence as Muslims as well as women. Followers want to be seen as the keepers of traditional values and are trying to live like the pioneers of Islam and offer an alternative to the secular view of women's liberation. Their success reflects a larger picture of how Muslim women are reinvigorating their position in society as the result of religious education, rejecting the secular lifestyle.

THE ROLE OF MEN AND WOMEN IN AN ISLAMIC STATE

After an Islamic state was established in the Arabian city of Medina during the 7th century under the leadership of the Prophet Muhammad, women left Mecca by the thousands, preferring the new Muslim community to living under the control of tribal aristocrats. Islam promised equality and dignity for all people, black or white, man or woman, master or servant.

Every woman who came to Medina when the Prophet was the political leader of the Muslims could gain access to full citizenship and was recognized as a companion of the Prophet—the feminine form of the Arabic word is *sahabyya*. Anyone with that status had the right to enter the councils of the Muslim nation, or *ummah*, to speak freely to their Prophet-leader, to argue with men, to fight for their happiness, and to be involved in the management of military and political affairs on a equal footing with males. The evidence is there in the primary sources of Islamic history, in the biographical accounts of the hundreds of female companions who founded the early Muslim society jointly with their male counterparts.

Their involvement in politics, furthermore, manifested itself by the fact that they openly corrected their rulers, whom they believed were incorrectly implementing Islamic principles. There is a well-known example in which a female companion publicly opposed Caliph Omar, who ruled from 634 to 644 CE. The caliph wanted to pass a law limiting the size of dowries due to women at the time of marriage. After disclosing his ruling, a woman told Omar that he was mistaken, and she quoted the following Koranic verse: "Even if you had given one of them

[the wives] a whole treasure for dower, take not the least bit back. Would you take it by false claim and manifest sin?" (sura 4:20). Upon listening to her argument, Omar said: "The woman is right, and the man Omar is wrong."

POLITICAL CONSULTATION

Shura, the Islamic term for "mutual consultation" is one of the foundations of the Islamic political system. It is a tool by which an Islamic state can achieve the objectives of the Sharia—the God-given law. Every Muslim must commit to Shura, its general principle being that individual members of the community must seek the advice of others most expert in tackling their query. For example, legal problems concerning the Sharia require the assistance of specialized jurists. Technical issues demand consultation with experts in those fields. However, general issues concerning the whole community or nation ideally require some form of consultation with

WOMEN'S MOSQUE MOVEMENT

The Egyptian women's mosque movement began in the late 20th century in response to a perception among women from all walks of life that Islamic education was becoming inadequate under the governance of a secular regime. Members believed that the plight of women in the country was getting worse as a result. The women's mosque movement does not have a feminist agenda in the Western sense of the word. Its role is to promote the four schools of Sunni Islamic thought. Although most Egyptian women traditionally have some measure of training in piety—how to live a good life—the women's mosque movement is unique in making a religious discourse that had previously been the preserve of male-dominated institutions popular among women from a variety of socioeconomic backgrounds. The need for women to be involved in interpreting the Koran and Sunna is important because the requirements of modern life are quite distinct from those previously encountered by Egyptian women. Whether it is working in mixed-sex offices, riding on public transportation, attending coeducational schools, or consuming contemporary forms of mass entertainment, women in Egypt have to deal with a variety of situations that their mothers' and grandmothers' generations did not encounter. As many of the mosque participants argue, their movement is precisely a response to the problem of living piously under social conditions that have become increasingly ruled by a secular way of life.

MYTHS ABOUT ISLAMIC FAMILIES

One of the most enduring images of Muslim family life in Western popular culture is that of a powerful ruler surrounded by a "harem" of attractive young women. This false impression arose when the mighty Ottoman Empire threatened the eastern border of Europe between the 16th and 19th centuries. Malevolent rumors of the un-Christian excesses of the all-powerful Ottoman sultans spread across Europe. Painters imagined what a sultan's harem would look like, and their images have become a fixture of Western culture. Undoubtedly, many Ottoman sultans had more wives than the maximum of four allowed in Islam, but the Western word *harem* is based on a misunderstanding of the Arabic term *harim*, which refers to the "off-limits," or simply private, areas of a Muslim home. Male visitors are not allowed into the *harim*, and so women family members can dispense with their head scarfs and relax in seclusion and comfort.

Another myth about Islam's attitude toward women is female circumcision. It is standard practice for Muslim boys to be circumsized in their early years, but not for girls. A female circumcision removes the parts of the genitals that give pleasure during sex. It is not required by Islam. Female circumcision is performed in traditional societies—some of which are Islamic—in Africa and Asia.

A third myth attributed to Islam is honor killing. Girls who bring dishonor to their family by having premarital sex or perhaps refusing to be married have been killed by their relatives. It is estimated that hundreds of such killings take place each year, but it is hard to know for sure because they occur in secret and victims are not reported missing. There is nothing in Islam that allows families to kill their members. In addition, while Islamic teaching places great store in the virtues of young people, honor killings are not restricted to Muslim families.

every member of the community. This could be in the form of a referendum or general election, or through an assembly.

Women can take part in consultations depending on the subject matter and on their individual skills and expertise. There is no specific bar from them being consulted as jurist or technical experts, providing they have the necessary knowledge. They are also able to take part in general public-level consultations on an equal basis with men.

The Prophet used to consult his male as well as female companions; he also used to seek advice from his wives Aisha, Um Salama, and Hafsa. It was reported that the Prophet had to rely upon the guidance of one of his wives, Um Salama, to solve a problem that threatened the Muslims at a very critical period of their history. In 628 CE, Muhammad and his companions were in conflict with the people of Mecca. However, the Muslims wanted to visit that city for their annual pilgrimage. The Meccans did not trust the Muslims to come to their city peacefully. It looked like a bloody battle was about to begin before Um Salama helped the Prophet to solve the problem. The Prophet made the Treaty of Hudaibiyya, in which the Meccans agreed to allow the companions to perform their pilgrimage, but not until the following year. The Prophet entrusted Um Salama with the task of convincing the community to forgo the performance of the pilgrimage ritual for that year. Thus a woman's opinion helped to avoid a very dangerous situation.

The Prophet regularly received delegations of women. Among them was Asma bint Yazid al-Ansari, who used to discuss and argue on behalf of her fellow Muslim women, and the Prophet used to encourage her, expressing his admiration for her intelligence and strong personality.

POLITICAL ENGAGEMENT

Muslim jurists believe that two roles best suit a woman's emotional nature—being a wife and a mother. They argue that most women are feeble and fragile, and such characteristics would hinder them if they ever assumed leadership positions.

A much mentioned Hadith is, "People who entrust power to a woman will never prosper." However, this has been proven to be an unreliable report on several counts. It has only one source and is regarded as being uncorroborated and non-binding in Islamic law. In addition, there is reason to believe the Hadith may have been forged in reference to the leadership of Aisha, the Prophet's widow during the Battle of the Camel. This conflict occurred in 656 CE in Basra (present-day Iraq) when forces led by Aisha opposed the supporters of Imam Ali, who had become caliph following the murder of the previous ruler, Uthman.

In view of the examples set by the few women rulers in history, the restriction on female leaders is clearly untenable. Nevertheless, rules are not formed on the basis of rare occurrences but on the frequency of them. Thus the scholars established that generally "the rare does not constitute a rule." Therefore, for the woman to be a manager, director, parliamentary deputy, or government minister is acceptable so long as she is appointed after considering the interests of the community.

WOMEN'S PARTICIPATION IN WAR

Women in the early days of Islam participated in battle either by organizing food and water or taking care of the wounded. Some also played a crucial part in the actual fighting.

Among the many examples of women who took active part in battle was Safiyya, an aunt of the Prophet, who defended a fortress in Medina at the time of the Battle of the Trench (627 CE) in which the Muslims faced a much stronger enemy. Safiyya noticed an intruder who

Religious scholars—all men—attend a government meeting in Pakistan. Although Islam does not exclude women from being religious experts, centuries of cultural exclusion have made female scholars few and far between.

had penetrated the defenses of the fortress. She managed to maneuver and kill him before he was able to do any harm.

Um Umara was known for her effectiveness with sword fighting. The Prophet commented that she was better than many men. Um Umara fought in many battles and lost her hand. The companion Um Hakim single-handedly killed seven Byzantine soldiers in the Battle of Marj al-Saffar.

In one expedition against a Persian seaport near the Shatt-al-Arab waterway, the women feared that the men would not be able to defeat the enemy alone. Led by Azdah bint al-Harith, the women turned their veils into flags and marched in formation toward the battlefield. They were mistaken for fresh reinforcements and contributed to the victory of the Muslims.

ALGERIAN RESISTANCE

For more than 130 years, the French colonized Algeria between the 19th and the 20th centuries. In order to preserve their cultural identity from the French impact on their language and traditions, the Algerians had clung even more closely to Islam and Islam-based traditions. They rebelled against the occupation several times until the French forces eventually left in 1962. Algerian women played a heroic role in the fight. They took advantage of two elements of their femininity during the resistance. They used to hide weapons under their Islamic garments, knowing that the French soldiers would not search them because the French abided by the Muslim tradition and did not touch Muslim women. The second element they used was their good command of the French language. Algerian women dressed to look like French women (nearly a million French people lived in the country) and they would seduce the soldiers at the checkpoints, allowing their counterparts to get around security and kill French residents.

CHINESE MUSLIM WOMEN

"Although it is not unusual in Islam for women to lead other women in prayer, China's female imams are part of a trend of greater leadership roles for Muslim women in many nations." So said Omid Safi, professor of Islamic Studies at the University of North Carolina. Nevertheless, the unusual phenomenon of an exclusively women-only mosque is unique to China.

China's Muslim community—known

A maid cannot work in the house of a bachelor, or a male manager cannot have a female private secretary who is required to be alone with him. Muslim women cannot be dancers who excite lustful thoughts or work in a restaurant serving alcohol.

as the Hui—comprises 20 million people. The Chinese Muslim community is a small minority population and has suffered double isolation under secular communist governments and the forced segregation from the rest of the Muslim world community. Since the early 1980s, Chinese Muslims have been able to establish their own mosques. Usually, women's prayer halls are adjacent to a main mosque, as in the provinces of Gansu and Ningxia. In many of the mosques in Gansu, women pray in a curtained section or in an annexed room of the main prayer hall.

Because they run shops that sell Islamic goods, participate in public markets, and serve in religious and educational roles, Hui women have carved out for themselves a

sustainable and active presence in China's public sphere. These women consider their lifestyle to be pure and true, equivalent to the Arabic term *halal*. It is expressed by maintaining Muslim schools, homes, and families, and by marrying within the community and raising their children together as Muslims. In fact, this is one of the ways Islam has spread in China over the past 1,400 years, from its roots in the Silk Road trade among Arab, Persian, Turkish and Mongolian traders.

Hui women have developed extensive social and marriage networks allowing them to reach out to the other Hui communities in the different locations in the country. Trade centers and local market communities are therefore vital venues for the Hui women to connect with other Hui men and women. It is through these social and educational networks that Muslim Hui women have maintained contact with each other and preserved their religious and cultural traditions in a nation in which they form less than 1.5 percent of the total population.

WOMEN IN EMPLOYMENT

Women working outside the home is not forbidden by Islamic law. According to the jurists, however, there are a number of conditions that legitimate employment for both males and females. The type of employment should be a legitimate one under Sharia law. For instance, a maid cannot work in the house of a bachelor, or a male manager cannot have a female private secretary who is required to be

Muslim women reading the Koran in the mosque for women in Guyuan, a mountainous area in northwest China's Ningxia Hui Autonomous Region. The mosque's all-female facilities include a changing room and a bathhouse, as well as a special room for evening dining during Ramadan.

Muslim women are not allowed to be alone with unrelated men, which poses problems for them in the modern workplace.

alone with him. Muslim women cannot be dancers who excite lustful thoughts in their audiences or work in a restaurant serving alcohol. She is not supposed to accept employment wherever there is a potential to commit a prohibited act that is forbidden for both men and women.

The majority of present-day scholars are convinced that a woman's first and greatest work is to rear the next generation, as God has prepared her both physically and psychologically, and she should not be distracted by major functions that could lead to exposing her children to any type of risks. They say that nobody can replace her in that great work on which the future of any nation and its wealth depends. At the same time, no one has the right to forbid women's employment. It may

even become essential if she has no other form of income and wishes to avoid the humiliation of asking for charity. It could be the family who needs her work, such as to help her husband, or to provide for her children, or young brothers and sisters, or her elderly parents.

Within the traditional Muslim household, a woman lives within the financial protection of her father and then of her husband. Egyptian Muslim scholar Aisha Abdel Rahman argues that the right path is the one that combines modesty, responsibility, and the integration of women into public life. In spite of the fact the many contemporary jurists approve of her opinion, they attach much more value to the work that men do. Domestic work is no less of a good deed than going out of the house to work, according to Sharia law. Many believe that there is a way within Islam to attach monetary value to domestic work done by wives and mothers. Indeed, some classical scholars have stated that women should be paid even for nursing their own children. If the criteria for valuing any function is a monetary one, then Muslims should insist that all these functions have financial values attached to them.

Jurists limit legitimate employment for women to certain categories of jobs for which society itself might benefit from having females in those roles. For example, women are best suited at giving medical treatment to other women and looking after them, teaching girls, and providing other types of services for women. They believe that it is more proper for a woman to deal with another woman instead of with a man. The acceptance of a man in such roles may be necessary and should be considered accordingly and should not be opposed as a matter of course.

TWO DEVELOPMENT PROJECTS

Two very different communities of Muslim women took part in projects that affected their gender roles. Female participants were given the freedom to make decisions about the financial and social development aspects of their lives. The first research targeted a Bedouin community near Aswan, Egypt, between April 2000 and March 2001. It was hoped that the project could increase the women's confidence in their own abilities as well as respect from others for their contributions to the household. The second development project is a micro-lending mission in the rural areas of Bangladesh. The project has been in operation since 1983. It was not initiated

to empower its female participants but was intended to bring the entire community out of poverty.

Bedouin Women

The Bedouin women in the study no longer migrate with the men but have settled next to Lake Nasser, moving only to follow the shore as the water line in the huge reservoir moves up and down. Men take the household herds to distant parts of the desert in search of grazing and to trade in markets at Aswan. Women are not mobile and must be accompanied by a male relative on their rare visits to town, normally due to illness or an important family occasion. The Bedouin women and their children are responsible for the management of sheep and goats, even during the periods when men are present, such as the dry summer months. The absence of men from the area for varying periods of time has placed a greater burden on women to take over tasks and make them in charge of

Bedouin woman spend long periods away from their nomadic husbands and are responsible for raising the children and looking after the family's livestock.

managing resources. Sheep are not simply economic resources, as many women link sheep ownership with social status and security. They also believe that their presence is a blessing, and sheep are given to women at weddings as a financial safety net. When offered alternative opportunities, such as education, Bedouin women did not see the point of them, saying "the sheep are our lives."

It is only those women who do not have male relatives who undertake tasks originally designated for males, or those women whose entire family is limited by poverty, who show an interest in these activities. Such women who are active in agricultural activities are the poorer and most marginal members of the community. Research shows that most of them regard the rearing of livestock as demeaning, not least because it is traditionally men's work. To those who suggest that their access to such work is a form of women's liberation, they answer that they would prefer either to produce food crops for direct consumption by their own families or to raise feed crops for livestock.

Micro-Lending in Bangladesh

Muhammad Yunus's mother struggled to raise him and his eight brothers and sisters in the city of Chittagong, Bangladesh, but she always managed to look after anyone who knocked on the door needing help. Yunus went on to become a professor of economics and, inspired by his mother's charity, he set up the Grameen Bank in 1983. The bank lent small amounts of money, just a few cents worth at a time, to the poorest members of the community, generally the women. Nevertheless, the loans had an enormous economic and social impact, for which Yunus was awarded the Nobel Peace Prize in 2006. Many of the loans were used to start small businesses, micro-enterprises that offered women new power in their male-dominated society.

At present the bank has over 6 million borrowers of which 96 percent are females. While empowering Muslim women, Yunus's work also empowered their families. Husbands are more likely to respect their wives and show them admiration and love, instead of shirking their responsibilities.

Instead of forcing women to seek factory jobs away from their families, the bank allowed women to become self-employed. According to Yunus, the women are very cautious with money, and his bank has transformed families under the poverty level into a new class of empowered businesswomen and men. Furthermore, it does not violate Islam's ban on charging interest because its clients own the bank, as in essence they are reinvesting the interest they had to pay.

Studies of the Grameen system have shown that having joined the bank, women are more likely to seek an education, less likely to get divorced, and exercise greater control over their fertility—and reduce their birth rate.

IMMIGRATION TO THE WEST AND RELIGIOUS PRACTICE

In the West, the conduct of gender relations between first-generation immigrant Muslim men and women often differs from the practices in the central Islamic world. Western Muslims of both sexes use Islam as a flexible resource to support their own views and practical requirements within a largely non-Muslim social context. Their adaptations of Islam confirm that the religion is not an inflexible monolith but, like Christianity and Judaism, a tool kit that can be used to support a range of views and practices among its adherents.

For many Muslim immigrants to the West, religion is the most important aspect of their identity.

Analysis shows that the views of first-generation Muslim immigrants on gender roles and their actual practices are complex and sometimes contradictory. Meanwhile, the rhetoric of religious leaders calls for a straightforward complementary ideal. Studies of men and women in Muslim countries have confirmed variations in how people live and think. Such variations,

however, have only recently become the focus for research in immigrant communities in western Europe and North America.

Academic studies suggest that immigrant Muslims in many Western countries actively use Islam to support their own gender views and practices, both in the private household and in relation to the labor market. For many Muslim immigrants to the West, religion is the most important aspect of their identity. Because social norms influence religious culture, it is necessary to undertake studies of religious believers and communities in local settings. The social conditions of immigrants affect the status of both women and men. Women can become marginalized in some aspects of their lives, yet they may gain ability and power to act in other areas.

Women members of the Grameen Bank in Bangladesh salute the future as they wait to repay the loans that have freed them from poverty.

Muslim men and women in the West have been able to pursue higher education on an almost equal footing and have begun to contribute to the acquisition of knowledge. There is a significant number of highly educated, professional Muslim women all over the world who are working as architects, psychologists, physicians, scientists, lawyers, engineers, and in business enterprises; others occupy high political offices as ministers and hold important decision-making positions.

Research does not support the popular notion that first-generation male Muslim immigrants to the West are opposed to equality of opportunity for women. A 2001 survey conducted by the Department of Psychiatry at the University of Toronto, Canada, showed that Muslim men who abuse Muslim women are motivated not by religion but by the same psychological problems that lead to such behavior by non-Muslims.

AMERICAN MUSLIM WOMEN

In addition to the political and social roles played by nationwide Muslim organizations in the United States and Canada, North American Muslim men and women are working jointly to make a place for Muslims in the West. The Islamic Society of North America (ISNA) is an association of institutions and individuals who represent as wide a range of American Muslims as possible. Through offering social, educational, and religious support, ISNA is providing a common platform for Muslim communities. In addition to its social and outreach programs, ISNA is developing stronger ties with the other American religious communities, as well as civic and service organizations. Moreover, in 2006, ISNA elected Ingrid Mattson, a Canadian

Muslim, as its first female president. She had previously held the position of a vice president of ISNA. In 1987 and 1988 Mattson lived in Pakistan where she worked with female Afghan refugees. In 1995 she served as advisor to the Afghan delegation to the United Nations Commission on the Status of Women. During her graduate studies in Chicago, Mattson was involved with the local Muslim community, serving on the board of directors of the Universal School in Bridgeview and as a member of the Interfaith Committee of the Council of

Professional Muslim women all over the world are working as architects, psychologists, physicians, scientists, lawyers, engineers, and in business enterprises; others occupy high political offices as ministers and hold important decision-making positions.

Islamic Organizations of Greater Chicago. Mattson earned her Ph.D. in Islamic Studies from the University of Chicago in 1999. Her research remains focused on Islamic law and society and she encourages Canadian Muslims to become active participants in society at large. In 2003, she became Director of Islamic Chaplaincy and Professor at the Macdonald Center for Islamic Studies and Christian-Muslim Relations at Hartford Seminary in Hartford, Connecticut, the earliest Islamic chaplaincy program in the United States. She has also lectured at such institutions as the U.S. Naval Academy.

LITTLE MOSQUE ON THE PRAIRIE

It is difficult for non-Muslim people to understand the family life of Muslims. Without spending time with Muslim men and women, people have little more than crude stereotypes and incomplete reports on which to form their opinions. Mass media helps to bridge the gap, although news media seldom focus on ordinary, uneventful lives. Movies tend to present a dramatic view of Muslim people for the sake of entertainment. However, comedy is a powerful tool for reflecting the similarities and differences between otherwise disconnected people. A good example of this is the Canadian TV comedy *Little Mosque on the Prairie*.

It is a funny look at a Muslim community living in a little prairie town in Canada. It shows that Muslims have family spats, romantic problems, generational issues, and must balance their secular and religious lives. The creator of the series is a Muslim woman named Zarqa Nawaz. She said she wanted to show "that Muslims can be funny and are just like everyone else." Muslims have reacted very favorably to the show because they love to be portrayed as real people. *Little Mosque on the Prairie* is not meant to be a political show, but such entertainment presents a friendly image of Muslim men and women and helps defuse cultural conflict.

FEMALE CHAPLAINS

The participation of women in Western armed forces is one area that has challenged the roles of Muslim women. Shareda Hosein is a Muslim who has been in the U.S. Army Reserves for the last 28 years. The attacks of September 11th, 2001, motivated her to become academically qualified as an army chaplain. She enrolled at the Hartford Seminary, yet the U.S. Army rejected her application for the chaplaincy position, based on the Islamic law stipulation that a woman should not lead men in the congregational daily and Friday prayers. Hosein attained an acknowledgment from Muslim scholars that even though women cannot lead men in prayers, they are not excluded from chaplaincy positions. She was also endorsed by the American Muslim Armed Forces and Veterans Affairs Council and became a chaplain at Tufts University in Medford, Massachusetts. Nevertheless, the armed forces have continued to turn down her application.

Mumina Kowalski fulfills perhaps the most challenging Muslim chaplaincy in America as a religious leader in a Pennsylvania female correctional facility. Under the very harsh and dangerous circumstances of women's prisons, Kowalski works to transform the lives of the female inmates into an Islamic lifestyle.

COMMUNITY SERVICES

It should be noted that although the following account concerns an exceptional Muslim American woman, such phenomena take place daily in many Muslim states. The last 30 years have seen a resurgence in observant Muslim females making regular trips to nursing homes, where they volunteer to care for the elderly. This work is mostly driven by the incentive of assisting their societies to win divine rewards.

Mary Lahaj's parents established the first mosque in New England. She is the first female Muslim chaplain in a hospital's acute-trauma unit. Muslim patients take great comfort that there is a Muslim staff member around them as they recover. Lahaj's responsibilities in the hospital include daily visits to all patients, Muslims and non-Muslims; she participates in their prayers and invokes supplications for them. Her role also involves engaging with bereaved relatives in the remembrance of God—the Sufi ritual of *zikr*. Lahaj has broken new ground because there are almost no other Muslim female chaplains working in American hospitals.

A Congressional Bill Recognizes the Fasting Month of Ramadan

A Muslim sociologist from Texas, Ilham Jaafer, won an internship on Capitol Hill in Washington, D.C., to work in the office of Congresswoman Eddie Bernice Johnson and was soon offered a permanent position in her office. As a foreign-policy legislative assistant, Jaafer introduces and tracks legislation related to her field. She also organizes conferences and dialogues dealing with diversity and tolerance as well as

women's leadership roles in the world. One of these diversity dialogues resulted in a discussion about why and how Muslims fast during Ramadan. Following this discussion, Congresswoman Johnson introduced a resolution that the Muslim holy month should be recognized by Congress. The resolution was passed unopposed in 2007. This is an example of how the mobility and opportunities of American society can be embraced by Muslim women without the need to contravene Islamic laws.

Veiling and Empowerment

The most obvious sign that a woman is a practicing Muslim is her dress. Muslim women are not allowed to wear revealing clothes that might induce lustful thoughts in a man. She is also commanded to cover her hair when in public.

The common idea that Muslim men and women always study and worship separately has little foundation in fact.

In the Islamic world, the wearing of the veil need not imply a woman's separateness or detachment from men. It can be viewed as similar to wedding rings worn by Western married couples. Veils also provide privacy, which many people regard as desirable, making this form of dress liberating rather than oppressive.

Some Muslim women also choose to hide their faces behind a veil. In the Western context, masks are culturally associated with threats. Many people find it disconcerting that they cannot see the face of a stranger they are talking to or who is nearby. Also some Western men feel insulted that the veiled woman assumes that the man would behave inappropriately if she showed her face.

Objections to veiling are numerous and widespread. Nonetheless, even though many people of both sexes—religious and secular Muslims and non-Muslims, Westerners and natives of the Islamic world alike—regard this form of dress as repressive, significant numbers see the veil as liberating, as an opportunity for privacy and an expression of difference.

In the middle of the 20th century, women in Egypt, Morocco, Syria, Jordan, and many other Muslim nations chose to wear Western dress. By the 1980s, a movement of Islamic revivalism was sweeping the Muslim world, and many younger women were choosing to adopt hair covering and traditional clothing. Some of these religious women were able to attain positions of dominance over others as enforcers of codes of dress intertwining with behavior. Adopting a full veil also offered better social acceptance to attend mixed-sex colleges, as well as allowing women to get involved in other public pursuits while avoiding undesirable sexual attention from men.

Even in the West, middle-class and educated Muslim women living in Texas gave several reasons for choosing to veil in a recent study. The main reasons were to display their religious identity and to be part of a community.

Thus veiling is not always a symbolic denial of modernization. It can be a way of combining traditional family values with urbanization, education, and women's careers, as it is helping married, employed women to gain more respect among their male coworkers. Hence, the veil is empowering and in some respects a symbol of opposition to secular values.

Wearing the Veil

The practice of covering the hair and, in some cases, the face,
with a veil or head scarf is common in many Muslim societies.
The custom's origins lie in both religious law and tradition.

The veil today is often portrayed as the symbol of Islam. Yet donning the veil has never been an exclusively Muslim practice. Centuries before the advent of Islam, women of various societies covered their hair. As a means of distinguishing the elite, ancient Assyrian (around 1200 BCE) law required upper-class women to cover their hair. Jewish and Christian sects would also adopt the concept of covering, albeit for different reasons. In his First Epistle to the Corinthians, Paul of Tarsus instructs righteous Christian women to cover their hair when praying.

With the coming of Islam, the veil was incorporated into the fabric of Muslim societies. Among the various kinds of veils popular among Muslim women today, the most popular is the *hijab*, which covers the hair and usually the neck. Less prominent are *niqabs*, which cover the lower half of the face (leaving eyes exposed), and burqas, which cover the entire face and body. There are also veils and veil styles that reflect particular cultures and social groups.

VEILING AND THE KORAN

There are few direct references to women's clothing in the Koran, and there is some controversy among Muslim thinkers on the correct interpretation of the verses that address the subject. The Koran commands Muslim men and women to lower their gaze and guard their modesty, and instructs women to "display of their adornment only that which is (ordinarily) apparent." It also requires women to draw the head scarf, or *khimar*, over the chest when in the presence of certain men (24:30–31). Elsewhere, the Koran instructs women to "draw their cloaks close round them. . . so that they may be recognized and not molested" (33:59). In addition to these references in the Koran, supporters of the practice of veiling point to a number of Hadith that suggest veiling was practiced and encouraged during the lifetime of Muhammad.

Opponents of the practice of veiling are often critical of this interpretation of scripture. Opponents assert that

The Koran commands Muslim men and women to lower their gaze and guard their modesty, and instructs women to "display of their adornment only that which is (ordinarily) apparent."

verse 24:31, which discusses women's dress, does not make any reference to the covering of the hair or face, and point out that it is not known what the garments described, such as the *khimar*, actually looked like at the time. Further references to veiling and the separation of men and women in the Koran are often interpreted as specific references to the wives of Muhammad, which are not necessarily applicable to all Muslim women. Many of the Hadith used to further support the practice of veiling are seen as being of weak authenticity.

There is a consensus among most Muslim thinkers that both women and men should adopt modest dress. It is in determining what constitutes modesty that reveals differences of opinion. Following precedents of the past and certain contested sayings ascribed to the Prophet,

A Muslim woman in a burqa holds a young girl. It is not considered necessary for parents in the Muslim world to make young children conform to adult standards of modesty.

the overwhelming majority of traditional scholars adopt the view that, simply for the sake of modesty, women in public spaces should cover the entire body except for the face, hands, and possibly feet. Some argue that the face should also be covered, while others find the practice to be unwarranted and even disliked. Many nontraditional Muslim thinkers argue that what is required is simply modesty and that the veil is at best optional—a cultural rather than religious symbol.

HISTORY OF VEILING

Historically, most Muslim women, like many non-Muslim women, covered their hair, with some choosing to cover their faces as well. During the early part of the 20th century, more and more women began to stop wearing the veil, in large part due to European colonization and influence. One famous example of this occurred in 1923 when Egyptian feminist Huda Sha'rawi, having just arrived from a feminist conference in Rome, removed her

veil publicly in the streets of Cairo. As the Muslim world became increasingly secularized, and with nationalist movements gaining momentum, the veil came to represent backwardness in the eyes of many. By the mid-20th century, the overwhelming majority of Muslim women went about their business in public with their hair uncovered. Throughout much of the Muslim world, it became extremely rare to find upper- or middle-class women who were veiled. In countries such as Turkey and Iran, veiling had even become prohibited in various public arenas. Nevertheless, beginning in the late 1960s, customs began to change, and numerous Muslim countries witnessed a re-veiling movement that continues to this day. During the 1970s the veil became a political symbol. Supporters of groups such as the Muslim

In Singapore, women wearing head scarves and traditional Islamic dress take part in a procession to mark the day customarily associated with the birth of Muhammad.

Brotherhood in Egypt wore the veil and conservative clothing to make a political statement. Today, the *hijab* is worn by the overwhelming majority of women in many Muslim countries.

One possible explanation for this development is a disillusionment with the values of secular nationalist movements, a sentiment that was widespread among Middle Eastern Muslims following Israel's triumphant victory over Egypt, Syria, and Jordan during the Six-Day War in 1967. It was during this period that the Muslim world began to witness a religious revival with the veil being the most noticeable symbol of this movement. Also significant was the increasing influence of pro-veiling scholars, who now reached many, using new technology, and a growing foreign labor force in Saudi Arabia, which included individuals who eventually returned to their homeland with a new religious outlook.

VEILING AND THE LAW

The practice of wearing the veil and the degree to which it covers the face and head have been subject to a many different legal regulations and rules in different regions.

In Turkey, for example, the practice of wearing the veil was restricted by the social reforms of Mustafa Kemal Ataturk's nationalist government. Although these restrictions have been partially lifted over the years, the strictly secular constitution of modern Turkey does not allow women to wear the veil in government buildings because of its religious and political significance. In 2008 a reform to the constitution that allowed women to wear the head scarf at universities was passed, but it was subsequently struck down by the Turkish supreme court. A similar situation exists in France, where all religious symbols, including the veil, are prohibited in government buildings and schools.

At the opposite end of the scale, there are many countries in the Muslim world that strictly enforce the practice of veiling. Not long after the 1979 Islamic revolution in Iran, for example, veiling became mandatory, and women were expected to wear a long, loose black outer garment called the chador. Women who did not comply with this rule were often subject to abuse and could be arrested and detained for inappropriate clothing.

A more recent and more extreme example of mandatory veiling can be seen in the Sharia law enforced by the Taliban regime in Afghanistan in the 1990s and early 2000s. Under the Taliban, women were required to wear burqas—a garment that covers the entire body, including the hands and face—at all times. Women who did not, or whose actions were deemed immodest, were subject to beatings or imprisonment. This ruling caused widespread outrage throughout the Muslim and non-Muslim world.

In the United States and most other Western countries, there are no laws prohibiting or encouraging the practice of veiling. While discrimination on the basis of the decision to wear the veil is generally prohibited, exceptions are made for practical or social reasons. In the United Kingdom, for example, it has been ruled that schools can dismiss teachers who cover their faces on the grounds that it distances them from their students. Similarly, a federal court in the United States recently established that Muslim police officers do not have the right to wear the veil while on duty, because it constitutes a social and political statement.

In the United States and other Western nations, Muslim women who cover have experienced increasing difficulty due to prejudice, which intensified following developments that include the fear of terrorism by Muslims, Taliban rule, and the wars in Afghanistan and Iraq. While anti-*hijab* sentiments have become more apparent in recent years, the *hijab* has simultaneously become more widely accepted among certain groups. This was demonstrated just after the September 11, 2001, attacks, when non-Muslim organizations initiated *hijab* campaigns on college campuses to encourage non-Muslims to stand by and support their veiled Muslim peers. In some nations there is a growing number of independent, professional Muslim women who choose to wear the veil. Some have begun donning the veil for the first time, wishing to make their religious views known as a means of challenging certain stereotypes. On the other hand, given the current climate, many others have chosen to remove their *hijab*s. Given how dramatically both Muslim and Western views of the veil have changed in recent decades, one can only anticipate more remarkable developments in the near future.

Chapter 4

EDUCATION AND EMPLOYMENT

There has sometimes been a tension in the Islamic world between religious and secular education—should the two forms be separate or complementary? Such uncertainty has damaged employment prospects and remains both a socioreligious problem and an economic challenge.

Islam is founded on education and recognition of the importance of acquiring wisdom in all areas, practical as well as intellectual and spiritual. According to the Koran (sura 96), the first revelation made by Allah (God) to the Prophet Muhammad began with the command "*Iqra!*" ("Read!"). This has been widely interpreted to mean that Islam places the importance of reading above even prayer and worship.

❖

Islam is founded on education and recognition of the importance of acquiring wisdom in all areas, practical as well as intellectual and spiritual.

Boys and girls read passages from the Koran at a class in Nigeria. The verses are written on a *lawh*, a wooden tablet used for learning the Koran.

The Koran also contains more than 800 occurrences of the word *ilm* (knowledge), notably in instructions to the faithful— "God will exalt those of you who believe and those who have knowledge to high degrees" (58:11)—and in prayers, such as "O my Lord! Increase me in knowledge" (20:114). Also highly significant is the Muslim tradition of honoring monotheists, especially other "People of the Book" (Arabic: *Ahl al-Kitab*), whose faith, like Islam, is founded on divinely inspired works of literature. The main Peoples of the Book are Jews, Christians, and Zoroastrians, whose beliefs are based on, respectively, the Torah, the Gospel, and the Avesta.

ORAL TRANSMISSION

The Koran became the principal Muslim teaching and learning text long before printing made possible the large-scale reproduction of books and during a period when the overwhelming majority of the world's people were illiterate. The earliest printed versions of the Koran date from the 10th century, by the start of which Islam had been established for almost 300 years and had spread from its base in Arabia to become firmly rooted throughout northern Africa.

The earliest copies of the Koran were handmade by calligraphers. Later copies were pressed onto paper from carved wooden blocks, one block per page. The work was next printed by lithography, a method that transfers text onto paper from a master sheet made originally of stone and

Al-Azhar University in Cairo, Egypt, was founded in the 10th century. Its imam is regarded as the foremost scholar in Sunni Islam, and his rulings are studied around the world.

subsequently of metal. Not until the mid-16th century was the Koran first reproduced by movable type.

The rapid spread of the Koran's influence during the first three centuries of Islam is therefore attributable not to reading but to oral tradition. The practice of learning a story by heart and then reciting it to new audiences was well established in the pre-Muslim era; the early tales thus transmitted were mainly historical narratives and myths. Rote learning had practical applications, too, as it enabled recipes, chemical formulae, multiplication tables, and other such data to be passed from parent to child and from teacher to pupil. During and after the lifetime of

Muhammad (570–632 CE), the oral tradition also adopted the text of the Koran, which, having been revealed to the Prophet by Allah (God), could not be embellished or changed in any way.

The limitation of this method of instruction—committing the sacred text to memory and then reciting it in order—was that it provided no opportunity for commentary or criticism. As Islam extended its influence, and especially as writing became widespread, it was only natural that believers should wish to discuss the significance of the Koran. However, because the holy text was sacrosanct, commentaries on the work had to be partitioned off and clearly shown always to be separate from the divine revelations. Thus Islamic education developed two strands. One strand, *kalam* (theology), explained and justified the Muslim faith. The other strand, *falsafah* (philosophy), dealt with the whole range of scientific matters.

THE ROLE OF THE MOSQUE

Central to the rapid spread of Islam were mosques, which, though primarily places of communal worship, soon became at least equally important as educational centers. Some of them began to attract more students than worshippers, and thus their main function changed from prayer hall to schoolroom. Children of both sexes as young as four or five were enrolled in *kuttabs* (elementary schools attached to or within mosques), where they learned by heart extensive passages of the Koran. Traditionally, their first task was to memorize the 99 names of Allah.

The first school of this type was opened in 653 CE in the Masjid an Nabawi (the Prophet's Mosque) in Medina, Saudi Arabia. Another *kuttab* opened at the mosque in Damascus (the

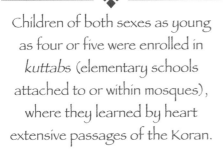

Children of both sexes as young as four or five were enrolled in kuttabs (elementary schools attached to or within mosques), where they learned by heart extensive passages of the Koran.

capital of modern Syria) in 744 CE. At the start of the 10th century, nearly every mosque had its own *kuttab*. There were 300 *kuttabs* in Baghdad alone. By the middle of the 13th century, there were

HALAQAS—MUSLIM LEARNING CIRCLES

The literal English translation of the Arabic noun *halaqa* is "ring," but the term may be more generally applied to any gathering of students in a circle around a teacher. The word is often used by extension to mean "lesson" or "class."

The original *halaqa*s were conducted in mosques, where pupils sat on the floor around an imam, who heard them recite passages from the Koran and corrected them when they went wrong.

This basic format soon developed into discussion and dialogue. On a visit to Baghdad, al-Bahluli (d. 930 CE) observed a *halaqa* at which a scholar, whom he described as "aflame with intelligence," fielded his students' questions, not just on religious matters but on a whole range of diverse subjects. During the Islamic renaissance, this format became standard throughout the Muslim world. The teachers were the final authority, but the range of topics was unrestricted, and the disputes often became animated and sometimes heated.

In the largest mosques, *halaqa*s attracted large audiences and several might be conducted simultaneously. In his celebrated book *Rihlah* (Travels), Ibn Battuta (1304–1369) describes a class of 500 in the Ummayad mosque in Damascus. Another Arab travel writer, Al-Maqdisi (946–1000), recounts a visit to Al-Azhar mosque in Cairo where he saw 110 *halaqa*s in progress at the same time.

establishments of this kind all the way from the Atlantic Ocean to the Himalayas. Outside Arabia, the main centers of education were Seville, Córdoba, and Toledo (Spain); Fez (Morocco); Cairo (Egypt); Jerusalem; Bukhara and Samarkand (Uzbekistan); Balkh, Ghazni, and Herat (Afghanistan); Esfahan, Hamadan, Neyshabur, Rey, and Shiraz (Iran); and Mary (Turkmenistan).

In many *kuttabs*, the elementary curriculum expanded beyond rote learning and recitation of the Koran to include reading, writing, and arithmetic. Some of the biggest mosques in the main population centers then began to offer advanced courses in a wide range of subjects, including algebra, Arabic grammar

In contrast to the early Western universities, to which Christianity was for many years a condition of entry, there was little religious discrimination in Islamic higher education.

and poetry, biology, history, law, logic, and theology. This important development laid the foundations of the first universities, many of which are still in operation today. The earliest university in the Islamic world is generally agreed to be Al-Karaouine in Fez, Morocco, which was founded in 859 CE. It was followed in 972 CE by Al-Azhar University in Cairo, Egypt, which became the largest and most influential higher learning establishment in the Arab world. One of the most significant common features of all these seats of learning was libraries, which quickly became comprehensive, with thousands of volumes in dozens of languages.

Among the greatest early products of mosque-based universities were the polymaths Ibn Bajja (Avempace, 1095–1138) and Ibn Rushd (Averroës, 1126–1198), who both studied in Spain (Zaragoza and Córdoba, respectively). Ibn Bajja was an astronomer, logician, musician, philosopher, physician, physicist, psychologist, and poet. Ibn Rushd was a philosopher and physician who wrote more than 60 original works and extensive commentaries on Aristotle and Plato.

Universities not only educated young people of both sexes but also attracted established experts from far away. Among the many distinguished resident lecturers at Al-Azhar university were the Basra-born Ibn Al-Haytham (965–1039), a leading scientist, and the Tunisian Ibn Khaldoun (1332–1406), who taught medicine.

In contrast to the early Western universities, for which adherence to Christianity was for many years a condition of entry, there was little religious discrimination in Islamic higher education; non-Muslims were accepted without being required to "revert" (the

STUDYING MEDICINE

As often in the West, Muslim physicians generally learned the theory and practice of medicine in hospitals rather than in universities. The first public teaching hospital in the Islamic world opened in Baghdad under Harun al-Rashid (r. 786–809 CE), the third Abbasid caliph. By the time of the seventh Abbasid caliph, al-Mamun (r. 813–833 CE), this foundation was issuing its own diplomas to graduates in general medicine and surgery.

The first public teaching hospital in Cairo was opened in 872 CE, more than a century before the city's Al-Azhar university. During the 11th century, similar establishments emerged throughout the Islamic world, from the Iberian Peninsula to Persia.

MAKING THE MODERN WORLD

From its earliest days, the Muslim world has been home to many centers of learning. A thousand years ago, Islamic universities and academies stretched from Spain to India and from Zanzibar to Uzbekistan. Today's students can still draw inspiration from the learned traditions and scientific breakthroughs that come from that time.

One of the earliest and greatest Islamic research centers was the Bayt-al-Hikmah (House of Wisdom), which

The tomb of Ibn Sina in Hamedan, Iran.

was established in Baghdad in 830 CE. Scholars at the Bayt-al-Hikmah worked with philosophy and science garnered from the Greek and Roman world and the knowledge passed down from Persian and Indian civilizations, building on them to make many new discoveries. A few years after Bayt-al-Hikmah, the al-Qarawiyin school was set up in Fez (now in Morocco). This institute of learning was followed by Zaytouna in Tunisia and the renowned school at Córdoba in Spain, which was founded in the 10th century. Every Islamic city in medieval times had a library, with Córdoba and Baghdad claiming to have had more than 400,000 books each. Islamic scientists remembered from these times include al-Khwarizmi, an astronomer working at the Bayt-al-Hikmah in the 9th century. He is known as the father of algebra, the name of which is derived from the Arabic word for "completion." A century later, Ibn Sina (also known as Avicenna) from Central Asia produced the *Canon of Medicine*, which was used to teach doctors for 700 years. Around the same time in Cairo, al-Haytham (Alhazen) laid out the basic concepts of the science of optics.

Muslim term for "convert to Islam"). Among the foreigners who studied at Al-Karaouine was Gerbert of Aurillac (c. 945–1003), who subsequently became Pope Sylvester II (r. 999–1003). He is widely credited with introducing Arabic numerals (1, 2, 3, 4, 5, etc.) to the West, where they replaced the old Roman numerals (I, II, III, IV, V, etc.).

FROM RENAISSANCE TO SUBJECTION

The importance of *kalam* increased as Islam spread and the Koran became adopted across northern Africa and the Iberian Peninsula (modern Portugal and Spain) by people who spoke no Arabic, the language

in which the book is written. Meanwhile, the development of *falsafah* was both a cause and an effect of the great flowering of intellectual life that occurred in the expanding Muslim world between the 10th century and the 13th century. During this period, Islamic scholars adopted *ijtihad* (rational principles) making possible immense contributions to science and almost every known form of art. Without being constrained by *kalam*, the Islamic world advanced its knowledge of astronomy, biology, chemistry, geology, mathematics, and physics far beyond anything achieved contemporaneously in Europe. One of the reasons for this disparity was that the Muslims studied and learned from ancient Greek works, many of which were disapproved and banned by the Christian church of the time because their authors were pagans.

The Islamic renaissance was brought to a conclusion in the 14th century by a resurgence of religious orthodoxy, which first advocated and then insisted on *taqlid* (blind obedience). As ultraconservative ulama (Muslim legal scholars) gained ascendancy over scientists, independent thought was discouraged. Primary education was again restricted to memorizing the Koran, and academic study became closely confined to scholarly commentaries on existing works. Inquiry and research were discouraged when they were not expressly forbidden. Even during the halcyon intervals between armed conflicts, originality was commonly regarded as subversive.

There then followed an extended period of foreign attacks on Muslim territory by Christians, Mongols, and other invaders, during which intellectual pursuits were generally subordinated to the struggle for survival. In the 18th century, Islamic educational methods were overtaken by those of Europe, which had made great advances during the Enlightenment, a period and an intellectual movement that valued human reason above divine revelation and inspired the separation of church and state as well as the distinction between religion and science. Although almost 500 years had passed since the golden age of Islam, Muslim educators were still shackled by *taqlid* and by the widely held belief that all aspects of existence are inseparably interrelated, and that there could be no scientific research without constant reference to the Koran and the Hadiths (the sayings of Muhammad).

The following era of European colonialism further inhibited the development of education in the Islamic world, as foreign rulers tried to impose secular teaching systems on Muslim societies that wanted to preserve their own traditional religious values. Thus there emerged two, apparently parallel but often conflicting, types of schools—the European, which taught mainly the administrative skills needed by the government, and the madrassas, to which Muslim children were still sent to keep in touch with their faith.

MODERN EDUCATION

By the start of the 21st century, the philosophy of education in some parts of the Muslim world exhibited significant progress toward the reconciliation of the previously conflicting aims of acquiring knowledge or learning to live life as Muhammad had done. In Bangladesh, Egypt, Indonesia, Malaysia, Morocco, and Nigeria, madrassas no longer confine their syllabi to Koranic studies but follow the same curricula as the nations' nonreligious schools. However, the madrassas of six other countries—Guinea, Mali, Pakistan, Senegal, Uzbekistan, and Yemen—teach only religious subjects. In between these two extremes is Morocco, whose madrassas use elementary instruction in the Koran as the foundation for literacy in Arabic.

Clearly, therefore, there is no great homogeneity in Muslim education. This is only to be expected, given the diversity of Islam itself and its geographical spread. The Organization of the Islamic Conference (OIC; founded 1969) has 57 member countries widely distributed across Africa, Asia, Australasia, and South America.

Although it is impossible to generalize

about Muslim education, there are certain challenges that are faced throughout the world of Islam. The most widely publicized of these is exclusion. Education is theoretically intended to be available to everyone but, in practice, girls, older children of both sexes, and rural dwellers commonly derive less benefit from it than boys, younger children of both sexes, and urban residents. Even in Bahrain, one of the richest Arab nations, where state education is now free, compulsory, and universally available to all residents aged 5 to 17, the level of participation is still only just over 50 percent. Throughout the Islamic world there are thought to be 10 million children between 6 and 15 years of age who are not in school; this number is increasing annually. Among other badly affected nations are Guinea and Mali, where, respectively, only 59 percent and 53

percent of those eligible for primary education are in fact receiving it. There is also a significant dropout rate, not through disaffection but because of inadequate provisions. In Senegal, for example, more than 10,000 children who completed their primary education in 2001 in the public system were unable to proceed to secondary schools because there was no room for them in the classrooms. Almost 10 years later, only 25 percent of all Senegal's elementary school graduates were provided for at the next stage. The students thus excluded either drop out or continue their studies in the madrassas.

According to a 2009 report by the United Nations Educational, Scientific, and Cultural Organisation (UNESCO), the Muslim nations have the world's highest percentages of primary-age girls not enrolled in school. The worst affected country is

Male and female students sit separately during assembly at a high school in Malaysia.

A student in Timbuktu, Mali, practices writing in Arabic. The Koran is taught in its original Arabic, so all Islamic schools teach the language.

their rural counterparts. This is a symptom of a malaise that afflicts many parts of the Muslim world, but Pakistan has further problems of its own that affect pupils, regardless of their sex. The nation has a three-tiered educational system—public schools, private schools, and religious schools (madrassas). Public schools offer a predominantly secular education in Urdu which, though the nation's official language, is spoken as a mother tongue by only eight percent of the population. The largest group—48 percent of the population—are Punjabi speakers. In the private schools, the medium of instruction is English, and many graduates of these establishments go on to further study in

Of course, education is not restricted to formal instruction in classrooms and lecture theaters. Knowledge is also disseminated by communications media, and modern technological innovations have enabled Islamic preachers to be heard and read all over the world.

Egypt, where 96 percent of the 232,000 children of elementary school age who were not attending school that year were female. For boys and girls alike, absence from school at this age is a setback from which many of them are unable to recover in later life because governments throughout the region lack the finances, the infrastructure, and the political will to accommodate those who missed out earlier.

In Baluchistan, a province of Pakistan, 85 percent of girls in urban areas attend school, in contrast to only 40 percent of

anglophone nations, principally Britain and the United States. The madrassas concentrate on Koranic studies and the commitment of the text to memory; they may also provide boarding and lodging facilities for students from the most deprived backgrounds.

One of the numerous shortcomings of the Pakistani education system is that it cultivates and perpetuates the division of society along socioeconomic lines: the richest speak English and are the best educated; the poorest have little more than a religious education.

Throughout the Islamic world, another problem for those Muslims who do attend school regularly is that the quality of education is often poor. This is due mainly to underqualified, undertrained teachers and inadequate learning materials. Because of these shortcomings, 4.6 percent of boys and 3.3 percent of girls have to repeat a grade of elementary school, a situation that exacerbates the other main problem—overcrowded classes.

Of course, education is not restricted to formal instruction in classrooms and lecture theaters. Knowledge is also disseminated by communications media, and modern technological innovations have enabled Islamic preachers to be heard and read all over the world. The great leap forward in this area began in the late 1970s when the speeches of Ayatollah Ruhollah Khomeini (leader of the Iranian revolution, ruled 1979–1989) and the posthumously published sermons of Sheikh Abdul-Hamid Kishk (Egyptian dissident, 1933–1966) reached a global audience through audiocassettes. The speed of change increased with the advent of satellite television and, above all, of the Internet. The latter increased the fame of Egyptian Muslim televangelist Amr Khaled (b. 1967) to such an extent that in 2009 *Time* magazine

Boys read the Koran at a madrassa in Islamabad, Pakistan, where the sacred text is being taught by rote—learning by repeating verses over and over.

EMPLOYMENT LEVELS (2008)

The figures in this table refer to the countries of the Organization of the Islamic Conference (OIC) for which full and reliable statistics are available. The OIC members omitted are Benin, Chad, Gambia, Guinea, Guinea-Bissau, Niger, Palestine, Sierra Leone, Somalia, Togo, Turkmenistan, and Uganda. The number of guest workers in Qatar makes the total workforce larger than the population. For the purposes of comparison, the U.S. population in 2008 was 307.2 million and its workforce was 154.3 million, with 5.8 percent unemployed.

Country	Population (millions)	Labor Force (millions)	Unemployment (percentage)
Afghanistan	28.4	15.0	40.0
Albania	3.6	1.1	12.5
Algeria	34.1	9.4	12.8
Azerbaijan	8.2	5.7	0.9
Bahrain	0.7	0.5	15.0
Bangladesh	156.0	70.8	2.5
Brunei	0.4	0.2	3.7
Burkina Faso	15.7	6.6	77.0
Cameroon	18.8	6.7	30.0
Comoros	0.75	0.3	20.0
Djibouti	0.5	0.3	59.0
Egypt	83.0	24.6	8.7
Gabon	1.5	0.6	21.0
Guyana	0.8	0.3	11.0
Indonesia	240.0	112.0	8.4
Iran	66.4	24.4	12.5
Iraq	28.9	7.7	18.2
Ivory Coast (Côte d'Ivoire)	20.6	7.3	50.0
Jordan	6.3	1.6	12.6
Kazakhstan	15.4	8.4	6.6
Kuwait	2.7	2.0	2.2
Kyrgyzstan	5.4	2.3	18.0
Lebanon	4.0	1.5	9.2
Libya	6.3	1.6	30.0
Malaysia	25.7	11.0	3.3
Maldives	0.4	0.1	14.4
Mali	12.6	3.2	30.0
Mauritania	3.1	1.3	30.0
Morocco	34.8	11.3	9.5
Mozambique	21.7	9.7	21.0
Nigeria	149.0	51.0	4.9
Oman	3.4	1.0	15.0
Pakistan	176.2	50.6	13.6
Qatar	0.8	1.1	0.4
Saudi Arabia	28.7	6.7	11.8
Senegal	13.7	5.0	48.0
Sudan	41.0	11.9	18.7
Suriname	0.5	0.2	9.5
Syria	20.2	5.6	8.6
Tajikistan	7.3	2.1	2.3
Tunisia	10.5	3.7	14.1
Turkey	76.8	24.1	11.0
United Arab Emirates	4.8	3.3	2.4
Uzbekistan	27.6	15.4	1.0
Yemen	23.8	6.5	35.0

placed him 13th in its list of the world's one hundred most influential people.

Without access to new media people cannot benefit from its content. At the end of the first decade of the 21st century, the OIC member countries had almost 300 million illiterate people aged 15 and over. This figure—which is higher than that for any group of comparable size in the world—has a severe negative impact on the prospects of individuals and on Muslim society as a whole.

EMPLOYMENT

The problems of education in the modern Islamic world are strongly linked with the region's demography and economics. The most significant single datum is recent population growth in the Arab countries of western Asia and northern Africa. At the outbreak of World War I (1914–1918), the region was home to around 68 million people; by 2000, that total had increased to 407 million. This growth rate—a factor of almost six in less than a century—was the second highest in the world. It was exceeded only by the Sahel—the semidesert on the southern rim of the Sahara that extends from Mauritania to Chad—which is also predominantly Muslim. It is estimated that, by 2020, the population of western Asia and northern Africa will have grown to around 550 million and that the median age will then be 30 years. The consensus among analysts and commentators is that this population bulge will require the creation of some 80 million new jobs in the region in the 15 years following 2010. However, at the start of this period there was little sign of the economic activity required to create such opportunities—the Arab countries of the region supplied only 2 percent of world exports and received only 2 percent of foreign investment.

That is not to say that there has been no growth. On the contrary, according to statistics compiled by the World Bank, between 2000 and 2006 the economies of western Asia and northern Africa grew on average by 5.2 percent. That they have continued to suffer from high unemployment rates is attibutable to four factors. The first factor is that the growth has been mainly capital intensive (banking, for example), while the only form of growth that creates large numbers of new jobs is labor intensive (construction industry, for example).

> It is not that the job market contracts and then finds new areas into which it can once again expand, but rather that there simply are no jobs and no discernible prospects of their creation.

The second factor is that, in contrast to the developed nations of Western Europe and North America, where unemployment is cyclical, in the Arab countries it is typically structural. It is not that the job market contracts and then finds new areas into which it can once again expand, but rather that there simply are no jobs and no discernible prospects of their creation.

The third factor is that too many of the individual national economies are either exclusively dependent or overly reliant on a single commodity or a very small number of products. Saudi Arabia is the prime

example of a country that has relied mainly on oil production, although it has, since the last decade of the 20th century, made efforts to diversify into other areas, notably power generation, telecommunications, natural gas exploration, and petrochemicals. Other countries of the region depend excessively on industries that generate insufficient revenue in the modern world. Egypt, for example, relies on agriculture, in which 32 percent of the national workforce is engaged, and on textile manufacture. The overdevelopment of the latter industry is a legacy of the colonial period, during which the British made Egyptians concentrate on the production of cotton products to compensate for the inability of English mills to satisfy their own domestic demand. Even the late-20th-century boom in the Cairo stock market and the increasing exploitation of Egypt's extensive natural gas and hydrocarbon deposits have failed to revitalize antiquated practices and kickstart the economy.

The fourth factor, known as frictional unemployment, is a condition that occurs in economies where there are available jobs but the work force lacks the qualifications required to perform them. All four factors are matters of concern to world economists, but it is frictional unemployment that most worries politicians because of the fear that it will propel the people affected into a downward spiral of frustration, disillusionment, and—in the worst case scenario—political extremism, which, in some parts of the Muslim world, is taken to be virtually synonymous with Islamic fundamentalism.

At the start of 2010, the unemployment situation was exacerbated by failures in education. Nonetheless, for all the shortcomings of the school system

A Muslim woman works in a medical research laboratory. To a Muslim, science reveals the mechanisms by which God's creations work.

The adverse consequences of this situation can be seen throughout the Muslim world but nowhere more clearly than in Egypt, where, in 2009, 42 percent of the working population had completed secondary school education but 80 percent of the people thus qualified remained unemployed.

The competition for jobs in Muslim countries has intensified as a result of the vast increase in the number of educated, employable women. An extreme example of a widespread trend is Saudi Arabia, where, in 2009, 55 percent of university graduates were women. However, in the same year, only 3 percent of those women were working. In the Arab countries bordering the Mediterranean Sea—Morocco, Algeria, Tunisia, Egypt, Syria, and Lebanon—there are currently 50 million women aged 15 to 64 who represent half the population of working age but comprise only one-quarter of the workforce.

The adverse consequences of this situation can be seen throughout the Muslim world but nowhere more clearly than in Egypt, where, in 2009, 42 percent of the working population had completed secondary school education but 80 percent of the people thus qualified remained unemployed.

outlined above, the formal credentials that it supplies to graduates are still highly sought after by Muslim youth. However, too many of the courses studied have few or no practical applications in the modern world. Muslim schools still place greater emphasis on religious subjects and—in a hangover from the colonial era— administrative and clerical qualifications. These are of limited use in a commercial age that seeks, above all, highly skilled electronic and mechanical engineers and entrepreneurs who can start new businesses or develop existing ones.

In the view of some commentators, the fact that there are more workers available than there are jobs for them to do is a convincing case in favor of barring women from the employment market. That, after all, has been official policy at various times in several Muslim societies, most recently in Afghanistan under the rule of the Taliban. However, this proposal appears counter to statistics supplied by the World Bank, where analysts have noted that, throughout northern Africa and western Asia, the number of women in the work force bears an inverse relationship to the total number of people unemployed—in other words, the more women who work, the greater the number of men and women in employment. Thus, the active participation of women in the labor market appears to correlate with a healthy, flexible economy. Whether there is a causal link between the two phenomena remains a matter of debate, but it seems clear that women's jobs are often different in kind from men's jobs, and that in the modern globalized economy the former are often more productive than the latter. World

UNEMPLOYED YOUTH

At the start of the 21st century, of all the people in the Muslim world as a whole—an estimated 1.5 billion—more than half (836 million) were under 24 years of age. In northern Africa and western Asia, 25 percent of youths were unemployed.

Teenage girls travel to school in burqas in Afghanistan. Under Taliban authority, Afghan girls are not allowed to go to school at all.

FOR RICHER. . .

In the United Arab Emirates (UAE), the richest Muslim nation, schooling is free to every resident but compulsory only at elementary level (ages 6 to 12). There are more than 300,000 children in public schools throughout the country. Boys and girls have equal access to education but are taught in separate schools. Each village has a primary school, and the cities have secondary schools with boarding facilities. Most teachers are foreigners from other Arab countries. A measure of the success of the UAE's education policy is the rapid rise in literacy, from 20 percent in 1980 to 80 percent in 2010. Statistically, the main beneficiaries have been female: 81.7 percent of Emirati women can read and write but only 76.1 percent of Emirati men are literate.

There is also a large private education sector, which accommodates nearly 40 percent of Emirati students. In many of the private schools, the language of instruction is one of those spoken by the largest expatriate communities, mainly English, French, German, and Urdu.

In 1977, the UAE government opened the Emirates National University in Al-Ayn, the second largest city in Abu Dhabi. Modeled on U.S. practice, the university has nine faculties—arts, science, education, administrative and political sciences, law and Sharia (Islamic law), agriculture, engineering, medicine and health sciences, and postgraduate studies—and offers instruction in Arabic or in English.

The federal government of the UAE provides financial support in the form of grants and scholarships not only for undergraduates at Al-Ayn but also for graduates of the university who wish to study for further degrees abroad.

In 2009, the Emirates National University had around 12,000 students, three-quarters of whom were women. Many female students at Al-Ayn have come from more conservative Arab countries to take advantage of educational opportunities that are not available to them at home.

Bank statistics also show that the total household income of a family in which the woman works increases on average by 25 percent, a rise that would be sufficient to lift millions of Arab families out of poverty.

Nevertheless, such views are not unchallenged, and old prejudices remain strong in many parts of the Muslim world. At the start of the 21st century, of the 65 million adult Arabs who were illiterate, two-thirds were women. The nations with the highest female illiteracy were Morocco (62 percent) and Egypt (56 percent). Female participation in the job market— 30 percent of all women of working age— is lower than anywhere else in the world.

Even among this narrowly defined group, unemployment is 60 percent higher than among men aged 15 to 65.

CURRENT VACANCIES

The richest Muslim nation, the United Arab Emirates (UAE), has a relatively small population (4.8 million) and high employment, mainly in the oil and gas industries. The economy needs to diversify, in order to reduce its dependence both on these products and on the large numbers of expatriate workers.

The most populous Muslim nations are Bangladesh, Indonesia, Iran, Morocco, Nigeria, Pakistan, Sudan, and Turkey. In all eight countries, the majority of the workforce is engaged in occupations that are labor intensive but produce only low commercial yields. For example, nearly two-thirds of Bangladeshis work in agriculture, mainly in rice cultivation; most of the remainder are employed in service industries. Neither area is very productive or profitable, and, as a result, many Bangladeshis work overseas—principally in the UAE and other oil-producing nations of western Asia, or in Indonesia and Malaysia. The economy of Bangladesh is currently over reliant on remittances sent home by nationals working abroad.

. . . FOR POORER

In Guinea-Bissau, the world's poorest Muslim country, education is compulsory between the ages of 7 and 13, but in 1999 only about 54 percent of eligible children attended grades one to four, and only 26 percent stayed on to complete grades five and six. Only 32 percent of girls went to school, compared with 58 percent of boys, and only 58 percent of girls finished the fourth grade. At the start of the 21st century, the average size of a class in Guinea-Bissau elementary schools was 44 pupils. In the United States, the pupil to teacher ratio was 16:1 in public schools and 14.5:1 in private schools.

Female students look for their exam results at the campus of An-Najah University in the West Bank. In some Muslim countries, high unemployment rates leave many successful graduates struggling to find appropriate work.

In 2007, Keith Ellison (pictured here with his wife, Kim) became the first Muslim to win election to the U.S. Congress. He is a representative from Minnesota.

The economy of Guinea-Bissau—the poorest Muslim nation and one of the five poorest countries in the world—depends on farming, particularly rice, cashew nuts, and peanuts, and on fishing. There are significant deposits of petroleum, both on land and offshore in the Atlantic Ocean, but these remain unexploited because of domestic unrest and a lack of foreign investment. As a result, most of the working population lives at subsistence level—the people farm mainly for their own sustenance, and make little or no profit from any surplus. Guinea-Bissau survives only through frequent cash injections from the World Bank, the International Monetary Fund (IMF), and the United Nations Development Programme (UNDP).

EUROPE

The employment experiences of Muslims who have come to live and work in the West can be broadly divided into two categories, along continental lines, European and North American.

Into Europe, there have been three main immigration routes: from Bangladesh, India, and Pakistan to Britain; from Algeria and Morocco to France; and from Turkey to Germany. The first two trends are consequences of British and French colonial rule in South Asia and northern Africa, respectively.

In Germany, Muslim immigration began after World War II (1939–1945), when Turks left their impoverished homeland to earn relatively high wages in the construction industry as what was then West Germany underwent a rapid economic recovery.

The incomers to Europe had mixed experiences in the job market but, in general, Muslims started out in working-class jobs and rose no higher. There was no main single reason for this phenomenon, but among the contributing factors were the prejudice of the indigenous peoples and the Muslims' own uncertainties and disagreements about whether and where to draw the line between integration and maintaining their traditional identities. Also influential were the vagaries of the

The experience in the workplace for Muslim immigrants to the United States and Canada has been markedly different from that of their coreligionists in Europe.

European job market. In Britain and France, the industrial sectors of the economy shrank drastically in the last quarter of the 20th century, reducing the number of blue-collar jobs. In Germany the reunification in 1990 of the capitalist West and the formerly communist East brought economic hardship for many. The economy of the former East Germany had collapsed following the fall of the Soviet Union, and many unemployed East Germans traveled to the West in search of work. This economic upheaval increased unemployment, and many of those who lost their jobs were low-paid Muslims of Turkish heritage.

Before the reunification of Germany, most of the nation's Turkish workers made little effort to integrate and were not encouraged to do so. Under the German

law of the time, children born to foreigners in Germany were not entitled to German citizenship. However, since 2000, the naturalization process has been made easier, and German citizenship may now be granted to the German-born children of foreigners. Turks are now Germany's largest ethnic minority, totaling around 2 percent of the population of 82.3 million.

NORTH AMERICA

The experience in the workplace for Muslim immigrants to the United States and Canada has been markedly different from that of their coreligionists in Europe. On the whole, it has been happier and more rewarding.

Again, the reasons for this are not straightforward, but they include the socioeconomic background of the incomers, most of whom are academics, engineers, or physicians—middle-class professionals who have entered nations that can use, and have often sought to attract, their expertise.

Another reason is that, unlike their European counterparts—many of whom were economic migrants motivated mainly by the need to leave their native lands, rather than by a positive desire to settle in Britain, France, or Germany—most North American Muslims have made a positive decision to relocate to the United States or Canada. Also important is distance; American Muslims have relocated farther from their roots and, indeed, farther from each other, all over the continent, thus increasing their incentive to adapt to their new surroundings.

The biggest factor, however, remains each individual immigrant's level of educational attainment, because, in all but the most distressed economies, the skills and expertise acquired at school and in college are of crucial importance to employment prospects.

Pesantren

Comparable to madrassas elsewhere in the Muslim world, pesantren *are Islamic boarding schools in Indonesia run by* kyai—*respected leaders of the Islamic community.*

The most common term used to describe a *pesantren* is an "Islamic boarding school." A *pesantren* does have certain features of a boarding school, but it also has aspects of a seminary (an institute for training priests) and a monastery or a convent (establishments for people who have taken religious vows).

At a minimum, *pesantren* teach religious subjects, including memorization and interpretation of the Koran, Hadith (traditions of the Prophet), and *fiqh* (Islamic jurisprudence—the science and philosophy of Islamic law). Institutions similar to *pesantren* are found throughout the other countries of South Asia, where they are also called *pondok* or *pondok pesantren*.

Today, the teaching at **pesantren** *covers four basic areas: religious education, character development, government-approved "secular" subjects, and vocational training.*

Pesantren are the focal points of classicalist—also called traditionalist—Muslim communities in Indonesia. These communities maintain the practices and traditions of *Wali Songo*, the nine saints who brought Islam to Indonesia. From the 11th to the 17th centuries, to be a Muslim was to be a Sufi (mystic) and to be a member of a Sufic brotherhood, known as a *tarekat*. The *Wali Songo* legends are clear reminders of this heritage and are filled with tales of mystical prowess. The legends also incorporate aspects of ancient Indonesian culture, including gamelan (music) and *wayang* (puppet theater), based on Hindu epics. This accommodation of pre-Islamic traditions helped Islam spread throughout Indonesia.

The leaders of a classicalist Muslim community are not the men in charge of places of worship; instead, they are the men and women who run *pesantren*. By creating networks of students who will always owe respect and allegiance to the *kyai* (the headmaster of a *pesantren*), as well as to other fellow students, *pesantren* are at the core of the community. The status of a *kyai* is measured, in part, by his ability to attract students. Indeed, any visitor to a *pesantren* will soon be told the number of students in attendance and the places in Indonesia from where they have come.

No Compulsion

To this day, the *kyai*, who are considered to be the intellectual inheritors of the *Wali Songo*, emphasize the mysticism of Islam (but not to the exclusion of its everyday aspects). Rather than preaching against popular practices, the *kyai* accept that people want to do these things and strive to teach them a more conventional, or orthodox, way of conducting and understanding these practices. The Koranic injunction that there should "be no compulsion in religion" is frequently used by *kyai*, and most Indonesian Muslims reject the establishment of Sharia as a national law.

Before the 20th century, all formal education in Java—an island of Indonesia that contains the national capital, Jakarta—was *pesantren* education. Anyone who needed to be literate, including teachers, religious leaders, princes, and court poets, attended *pesantren*. The 20th century brought with it new forms of education, sponsored and influenced by the Dutch colonial administration, which ran Indonesia (Dutch East Indies) from 1800 to 1942, then by nationalist movements, and later by the Republic of Indonesia (declared in 1945 and recognized internationally in 1949). The new forms of education, which focused on math, sciences, and other secular subjects, were viewed as giving students a better preparation for work. As enrollment in *pesantren* gave way to secular schools, *kyai* were faced with having to embrace the new forms of education or else lose their legitimacy and standing.

FOUR BASIC AREAS

Today, the teaching in *pesantren* covers four basic areas: religious education, character development, government-approved secular subjects, and vocational training. The curriculum at particular *pesantren* always includes the first two areas and may take on one, both, or neither of the other two. In addition, character development is the core area in many *pesantren*, because there can be wide variation in the other three areas. Pursuing both religious and government-approved curricula often means that the religious training in *pesantren* is not as strong as it once was. The graduates of *pesantren* are not as accomplished in the skills needed by religious teachers, preachers, and leaders as they once were. However, this is generally not met with too much concern, as long as some graduates are able to move into these leadership roles. It is agreed that not all students can become *kyai*, nor does the country need them all to become *kyai*, but that the nation needs them all to have the morality and character of *kyai*, regardless of their future careers.

In addition to meals, students are provided with low-cost housing or dormitories at their *pesantren*. Some students spend up to 20 years—from ages 4 to 24—in a *pesantren*.

Chapter 5

ISLAMIC LAW

At its most basic, Islamic law—the definition of what is permissible for a Muslim and what is not—is derived from the Koran and the Sunna. However, different interpretations by various scholars resulted in several schools of Islamic law. In present-day Muslim-majority countries, the extent to which Islamic law applies varies from almost entirely to not at all.

People throughout the world, for the most part, are citizens of countries, with defined borders, ruled by central governments. Consequently, each individual has multiple allegiances, among them allegiance to his or her country and religion. With the exception of only a few countries, present-day states have crafted their own sets of laws with which to govern their citizens.

Some of these laws are based on religious doctrine, but all apply to all

Although religious law is often discussed in strict and dogmatic terms, it is not much different from any other set of laws that govern societies.

citizens governed by the state. In this respect, Muslims are like any other citizen in a given country. At times, their understanding of their obligations under Islam may come in conflict with the demands of the state law. This article explores the various implications of law in

Muslims' everyday life in different parts of the world.

After a discussion of the main concepts of Islamic law, this article surveys a few countries, some of which follow a strict separation of state and religion, and others where the laws and the legal processes are based on religion.

INTRODUCTION TO ISLAMIC LAW

Although religious law is often discussed in strict and dogmatic terms, it is not much different from any other set of laws that govern societies. All law starts from one or more primary sources and is then interpreted by qualified experts in law called jurists. For example, positive law—laws made by human beings—starts from a source, such as the U.S. Constitution, and is then explained and interpreted by judges and legal scholars. Islamic law—the law that governs Muslims in their daily lives—should be thought of in this sense. The term *Islamic law* is often used ambiguously, referring to a variety of different meanings. However, it is rarely discussed in terms that explain what Islamic law is or what its sources are. To understand what Islamic law refers to in the modern world, it is

An Iranian police officer, photographed in 2005. Law enforcement in Iran is strongly based on upholding Shiite Islamic law.

important to understand its sources, the methods by which it is constructed, and the various stages of change it has gone through over time.

The phrase most often used to refer to Islamic law is *Sharia*. However, there is disagreement over the precise terminology used to refer to Islamic law. Some scholars argue that Sharia is Islamic law generally, and *fiqh* is the principles developed from the primary sources of Islamic law (the Koran and the Sunna).

Other scholars argue that Sharia refers to the experiences of Muslims at large, legal and otherwise, whereas *fiqh* is the correct terminology for Islamic law. They believe that without the interpretation of scholars, primary sources alone do not constitute law. Many scholars, however, use Sharia and *fiqh* interchangeably and do not recognize a significant difference between the two terms.

There is no single Islamic law—rather, there are several different schools of Islamic law. The main division is between the Sunni and Shiite branches of Islam, which have further divisions among themselves.

These divisions are discussed in detail later, but at this point it is important to note that different schools of law—even within the same branch—may accept or reject different Islamic legal rules as well as different legal methods used to reach such rules. These numerous differences make it difficult to speak in terms of one Islamic law.

In other words, although all schools of Islamic law base their understanding on the same primary sources, their interpretations have differed, which at times has led to different and even contradicting rules. These principles are further diluted as different Muslim communities may practice them differently, based on different interpretations of the primary sources.

SOURCES AND CONSTRUCTION OF ISLAMIC LAW

As stated earlier, the two primary sources of Islamic law are the Koran, Islam's holy book, and the Sunna, the acts and sayings of the Prophet Muhammad (c. 570–632 CE) during his lifetime, as reported and recorded by those who witnessed them.

Muslims believe that the Koran embodies God's exact words as revealed to Muhammad over a period of 23 years. Muhammad shared these revelations with his followers throughout his life, and upon his death, the revelations were written down as the Koran.

The Koran was revealed to Muhammad in the two cities where he lived—Mecca and Medina—both in present-day Saudi Arabia. When Muhammad started to receive divine revelation, he lived in Mecca as a merchant. The revelations, or Koranic verses, received in this period (610–622 CE) mainly concern the newly revealed faith and its moral principles. These were predominantly about the salvation of the individual and his or her relationship with God, reflecting the needs of the small Muslim community in Mecca at that time. After Muhammad moved to Medina in 622 CE, he and his followers confronted broader community needs. The verses revealed during that period (622–632 CE) deal more with the administration of a state and everyday affairs among members of a community. About 500 of the Koran's 6,000 verses deal with legal matters, which provides a source for Islamic legal principles. Islamic scholars disagree on whether some of these verses are legal verses at all, and some argue that no more than about 50 verses are truly legal verses.

Regardless of the dispute over the number of Koranic verses with legal content, the substance of the verses deals with numerous areas of daily life in a settled community. Some of the main areas covered are criminal conduct, inheritance rights, and marital relations.

The Sunna is the second primary source of Islamic law. It consists of Muhammad's deeds, sayings (Hadith), advice, and interpretation of Koranic verses throughout his lifetime. The Sunna as a primary source of law is prescribed by the Koran itself. It was written after Muhammad's death.

Muhammad received revelations until the end of his lifetime. Many of the verses were not clear to the believers, so he commented on them, explaining their meaning and application. In addition, at times, Muhammad either through his actions or his words would guide his followers as to how to conduct themselves properly. Many of the sayings of Muhammad were written after his death. An entire science developed to ensure which sayings can be viewed as authentic. Of the number of collections of Hadith written, only two have found widespread acceptance. These are collections written by Muhammad ibn Ismail al-Bukhari (810-870) and Muslim ibn al-Hajjaj (c. 821-875).

When thinking of the Sunna as a primary source of Islamic law, it is important to remember that different schools of Islamic law accept different Hadith collections as more or less authentic, leading to different conclusions of law on the same issue.

THE ROLE OF JURISTS

During Muhammad's lifetime, if an issue arose on which there was no relevant Koranic verse, Muhammad could comment on the issue based on revelations he had already received. At times, he would even receive further revelations to help him respond to his followers' queries. After Muhammad's death, however, this process of clarification based on divine guidance and original sources was no longer possible. With new or novel legal issues came the need for further clarification and

AUTHENTICATING HADITH

To authenticate a Hadith (a saying attributed to Muhammad), scholars need two main requirements. First, they look to see whether the substance of the Hadith is logical and not in contradiction with the Koran or a previously authenticated Hadith. Second, they look to see whether the individuals in the chain of transmission from the time of Muhammad's life to the time of the Hadith's recording met certain standards. For instance, all the people who passed on the Hadith must have been trustworthy individuals. Furthermore, each transmitter of the Hadith must be the contemporary of the transmitter immediately preceding him. Shiites further require that the original transmitter came from Muhammad's family. If the transmitters meet these requirements, then the scholars analyze the frequency with which a Hadith is reported throughout the chain of transmission. A Hadith that is frequently reported, leaving no doubt as to its accuracy and honesty, is deemed authentic, whereas a Hadith reported with less frequency or with variations along the chain is more vigorously scrutinized. Over time, Hadith collections have been given values of authenticity: authentic (*sahih*), good (*hasan*), or weak (*daif*).

interpretation of the primary sources. In this way, *itjihad*—making legal decisions by independent, individual reasoning—evolved. Muslim jurists—called *fuqaha* (singular, *faqih*)—began developing the body of what is today referred to as Islamic law. The following is a list of secondary sources that jurists have used to find answers to new legal issues. It must be noted that not all jurists accept all these sources as valid and not all schools of Islamic law agree on the way in which they may be used.

Consensus (*ijma*). Consensus refers to agreement on a given issue. Initially, different jurists formulated different interpretations of primary sources. Over time, some of these opinions gained greater acceptance by other jurists. This culminated in a consensus over a given opinion by a jurist. In other words, an opinion that is just the product of a single jurist's practice of *itjihad*—individual reasoning—may become a legal principle if it gains the consensus of the community of legal scholars over time. Consensus building may take as long as a few generations. Consensus has been a significant source in the construction of the body of Islamic law.

Analogy (*qiyas*). Analogy is a method that uses deduction to formulate a legal ruling based on primary sources. When a legal case arises, the facts of which are not explicitly covered by the Koran or the Sunna, the jurists look at these primary sources for a ruling on a pattern of facts similar to the novel one before them. In order to formulate the new rule, the jurists first identify the rationale (*illa*) of the rule stated in the primary sources. They then apply that rationale to the new facts. For

example, the Koran prohibits alcohol consumption. The rationale of the prohibition is that alcohol is intoxicating and impairs the mental faculties. To figure out whether a narcotic substance would be allowed or prohibited, an analogy to alcohol may be made. Because narcotics are intoxicating and impair mental faculties, the narcotic substance would also be prohibited by analogy.

Custom (*urf*). All schools of Islamic law recognize that reference to community custom is permissible as a secondary source of law. These pre-Islamic customs may not contradict Islamic principles.

Common Good (*maslaha*). When no legal resolution is possible from the primary or secondary sources, it is permissible for the jurists to consider the common or public good to determine a legal ruling. Public good (*istislah*) is important in Islamic law. By asking what best serves the members of a community, jurists can reach fair and reasonable rulings that are in harmony with people's everyday lives. Moreover, when a strict adherence to analogy could lead to undue hardship to Muslims, jurists may exercise a preference for a less harsh outcome for the benefit of the public. This ruling is referred to as *istihsan*. Another related concept is *darurah*, or necessity, in which the jurist makes an exception from strict adherence to analogy because of considerations of public good.

Using these sources, jurists have compiled a vast body of Islamic law. The two main areas could generally be summed up as *ibadat*, the area of law that deals with the individual Muslim's relationship with God, including forms of worship; and *muamalat*, the area of law that deals with

Muslims' relationships with one another and the state, including civil relations such as commerce and commercial dealings.

Moreover, unlike in some other legal systems, such as the U.S. legal system, where the law either prohibits or allows certain conduct, Islamic law has five general categories of conduct: obligatory (*fard*), recommended, permissible, reprehensible, and prohibited or forbidden (*haram*). In other words, some acts are explicitly forbidden or required, whereas Islamic law is silent on others, making them permissible. Yet some other acts are either recommended—therefore encouraged—and others are reprehensible, and Muslims are advised to refrain from them.

FORMATION OF DIFFERENT SCHOOLS OF LAW

Although the law that emerged from the Koran and the Sunna is referred to as Islamic law, there are multiple schools of law that have emerged since the death of Muhammad in 632 CE.

Before his death, Muhammad had not given clear instructions as to the identity of his successor. The main division in Islam, between Sunni and Shiite factions, is a result of disagreement over the identity of Muhammad's successor. The division was a result of political differences among the followers of different leaders after Muhammad's death.

Immediately after Muhammad's death, some of his companions who had been with him throughout his leadership argued that the Muslim community should be united under a single ruler and that initially this ruler should be one of his companions. Abu Bakr (c. 573–634) was elected as the first caliph, or leader, of Muslims. Sunnis believe that the first four caliphs were the rightly guided leaders of the Muslim community. However, Shiites believe that the rightful successors to Muhammad should be based on familial descent. Those who held this view after Muhammad's death supported the leadership of Ali ibn Abi Talib (c. 598–661),

The primary sources of Islamic law are the Koran and Hadith collections, seen here for sale in a bookstore in Turkey.

Muhammad's cousin and son-in-law. As a result of this disagreement, the first major split within the Muslim community occurred. Different spheres of influence developed within the Sunni and the Shiite branches, leading to multiple schools of Islamic law.

Over time, certain jurists emerged as more influential than others, and they acquired a following among later jurists. Some of these jurists significantly helped construct Islamic law into what it is today. For example, an early jurist, Abu Abd Allah Muhammad ibn Idris ash Shafi'i (767–820 CE) was the first to write a volume on sources and methods of Islamic law. The period between the 7th and 13th centuries is known as the Golden Age of Islamic law because of the many significant legal collections written during this time.

The development of more varieties of opinions during the early stages of Islam subsided as an increasing number of jurists began to follow the collected opinions of certain earlier jurists. This allegiance to certain jurists led to the formation of schools of law, or *madhahib* (singular, *madhab*). Four main schools developed in the Sunni branch of Islam.

Maliki School. This school follows the teachings of Abu Abd Allah Malik ibn Anas (711–795 CE). It is predominant in North Africa.

Hanafi School. Most popular of the Sunni schools, this follows the teachings of Abu Hanifa al-Nu'man ibn Thabit al-Taymi (699–767 CE).

Shafi'i School. This school follows the teachings of al-Shafi'i (767–820 CE) and is common in Egypt, Palestine, and Jordan.

Hanbali School. Following the teachings of Ahmad ibn Hanbal al-Shaybani (780–855 CE), this is the official school of law in Saudi Arabia and Qatar.

These schools of law all agree on certain legal issues but differ significantly from one another on other matters. For example, some argue that the Hanafi School is the more liberal of the Sunni schools on issues of individual freedom and women's rights. The Maliki School puts a great emphasis on Hadith; whereas the Shafi'i school rejects *maslaha* as a valid source of law. In fact, in the early stages of school formation, even jurists within the same school of law would differ on certain issues. However, the major trend has been toward rigidification of schools as uniform bodies of law. Increasingly, jurists practiced *taqlid*—imitation of the founders of schools of law. *Taqlid* as a method in law does not leave much room for change and does not give much leeway for the jurist to use some of the methods discussed earlier. A jurist practicing *taqlid* looks to the rules in the teachings of his school of law. For instance, a Hanafi jurist would look to the teachings of Abu Hanif to come to a judgment on an issue of law, or to the rulings of earlier Hanafi jurists rather than apply methods such as analogy or use his own judgment on the issue, based on his interpretation of the primary sources.

Many scholars have argued that by the 13th century CE this "setting in stone," or rigidification, of the schools of law had reached such a degree that only the collected rulings of the four main scholars were being used as Sunni Islamic law. Individual jurists were no longer using their own reasoning to come to legal conclusions—in other words, *taqlid* was being used as the only valid legal method.

It is said that by this time "the door of *itjihad* was closed." Contemporary Islamic legal scholar George Makdisi (1920–2002) wrote that it is unclear who first coined this phrase or where its origins come from. However, a significant number of scholars have argued that the door of *itjihad* could

---

❖

The period between the 7th and 13th centuries is known as the Golden Age of Islamic law because of the many significant legal collections written during this time.

---

never close. They have argued that because each jurist must make a decision as to how the rulings of the founder of his school applies to the facts before him, every jurist necessarily exercises *itjihad*. The concept of *itjihad*, whether the door to it has been closed or not, has emerged as a necessary tool in the current debates of those seeking to reform Islam and Islamic law.

Differences also emerged within the Shiite branch of Islam. Four main schools of law developed in the Shiite sect of Islam: Ismaili, Ja'fari, Zaydi, and Ithna Ashari (the Twelver Shiism School). Iran, discussed in further detail later, is one of the few countries with a Shiite majority. The city of Qom in Iran is the center of Twelver Shiism, which is the largest sect of Shiites. The Shiite schools have never accepted that the door to *itjihad* had been closed. This is in part because the Shiite schools have always accepted *itjihad* as a necessary part of Islamic law formation and have rejected certain other methods, such as *ijma*, as valid. Moreover, unlike the Sunni schools, the Shiite schools, specifically

Twelver Shiism, have looked to individual jurists as leaders and have given them more authority to formulate legal opinions. These jurists are referred to as *marja* in Farsi (the official language of Iran).

LEGAL DEVELOPMENTS IN EXPANDING MUSLIM STATES

The expansion of Islam added to the changes that Islamic law experienced. Not only were there schools of law that jurists belonged to, but certain Muslim states were growing in power and territory. Such growth also created the need for centralization of state power to ensure that the Muslim world could be effectively controlled and governed. The Ottoman Empire emerged at the end of the 13th century CE as a central power that successfully invaded other lands, spreading into Asia Minor, the Arabian Peninsula, North Africa, and eastern Europe.

Unlike contemporary legal systems where the judge interprets the legal sources and also decides cases before him or her, the Islamic legal system divided the tasks. Jurists interpreted the law and formulated legal rules and principles, but they never actually heard cases. Muslims who wanted the courts to resolve their disputes went before a judge, or *qadi*, who heard the particular facts of each case, and by applying the rules formulated by the jurists, decided what the outcome of the case should be. A judge typically had the discretion to turn to more than one jurist. Even after the claimed closure of the door of *itjihad*, the judges would look at jurists from more than one school of law if the facts of the case before them demanded so. In a way, jurists were the theoreticians and the judges were the implementers of law. Generally, this system had no oversight. The decisions of the judges were not scrutinized by another authority.

Although this flexibility helped resolve Muslims' daily problems in a fair manner, with the rise of large empires, this lack of uniformity was seen as increasingly undesirable. The Ottoman Empire, the largest Muslim state in history, provides a good example of how the law had to adapt to the demands of changing circumstances. The Ottoman rulers believed that the need to control vast lands also meant that legal uniformity was necessary. In the Ottoman Empire, the basis for identity was religion —for legal purposes, a citizen belonged to a religious group, rather than to a racial or ethnic group. Following Islamic legal principles, religious minorities were ruled by their own religious laws. Muslims made up the majority of the Ottoman Empire, and they were ruled by Islamic law.

To achieve legal uniformity, the Ottoman state declared the Hanafi School of law as the official law of the Ottoman Empire. Many Muslim scholars have therefore argued that Hanafi law was applied in Ottoman courts. However, increasingly, scholars studying case law from different locations and time periods in the Ottoman Empire have found that there was never absolute legal uniformity in the Ottoman courts. For example, in his study of Ottoman cases, historian Haim Gerber concludes that judges decided cases by trying to achieve justice more than by trying to abide by the legal rules of any one school or any one jurist.

Although Islamic law was the legal system of the Ottoman Empire, with new developments in everyday life, the rulers found that certain issues were not covered by Islamic legal principles. They therefore formulated another set of laws, referred to

as *qanun*. These were positive laws formulated by the Ottoman state and not based on Islamic legal sources. *Qanun* focused on agricultural and criminal regulations—issues on which Islamic law was silent. Despite existing as a complementary legal system to Islamic law, *qanun* could not contradict Islamic legal rules. The significance of *qanun* came from its nonreligious nature; it later provided a background for legal reforms.

The Ottomans changed the legal system with codification—the process of putting laws into codes. Codification is widespread today throughout the world.

Another Ottoman legal structure that was a break from traditional Islamic law was the office of Sheikh-al-Islam, the lead Islamic scholar in the Ottoman Empire. The official's job was to ensure that the *qanun* and the decisions of the state and all its branches throughout the empire were in compliance with Islamic law. As a result, not only did the Sheikh-al-Islam have tremendous power in state affairs, but he was a religious legal scholar who was a part of the state-appointed political structure.

The Ottomans changed the legal system with codification—the process of putting laws into codes. Codification is widespread today throughout the world. For example, the United States has the Uniform Commercial Code, which outlines what the legal principles of commerce are. Similarly, beginning in the 19th century, Muslim populations saw widespread codification of their laws. The Ottomans were already familiar with the concept of a code, because *qanun* was in the form of codes. When writing a code, the state decides which laws should be in the new code and which laws should be omitted. The trend of codification that began in the 19th century is significant for this reason— it meant that states (for political reasons), and not jurists (for purely legal reasons) were selecting which Islamic laws would be included in the new codes.

The first civil code in the Muslim world based on Islamic law was the Mecelle-i Ahkam-i Adliye, or the Ottoman Mejelle of 1877. As the Ottoman Empire began to lose territory, its rulers increasingly believed that there was a need to modernize. Legal reform and codification was a significant focus of these reforms.

The Mejelle was a part of the Ottoman state's effort to modernize to keep up with the European states, which had surpassed the Ottoman Empire in military capability and power. The Ottomans had already set up codes of commerce with other states, but those codes were not based on religious law. The Mejelle codified which rules would govern relations between the subjects of the Ottoman Empire. It is significant because its laws were based on Islamic law. Consistent with the Ottoman state's allegiance to the Hanafi School, most of the rules were based on Hanafi jurisprudence (the science and philosophy of law). In this way, the Ottoman state's affiliation with the Hanafi School was also codified.

Although the Mejelle was the first act of codifying Islamic law, it was only the beginning. Implementation of Islamic law in present-day states has almost exclusively taken the form of codification. Although the act of codification gives the state

significant power over choosing which parts of traditional Islamic law are enforced, various legal methods used in the process of codification have proven highly useful in advancing certain individual rights, as will be discussed later.

TAKHAYYUR AND TALFIQ

The two legal methods that were widely used in constructing new Islamic law codes were *takhayyur* and *talfiq*. *Takhayyur* is the method of selecting principles from different schools of law on a particular topic. *Talfiq* refers to the process of combining or piecing together these various principles into a legal code governing that particular topic.

Women's access to divorce provides a good example of how *takhayyur* and *talfiq* have been used. In some cases, women's rights in marriage and divorce have improved as a result of using these two methods. Traditionally, different Sunni schools of law differed as to whether a woman could initiate divorce. Under Hanafi law, a woman could only obtain a divorce through annulment if her husband was unable to consummate the marriage or if her husband was missing for a long period. Clearly, with only these options, women's access to divorce was severely limited in countries such as those that were part of the Ottoman Empire, where the state applied Hanafi law. Women who wanted to get out of their marriages had severely limited options.

Other schools of Sunni law offered additional grounds of divorce for women. For example, under Maliki law, a woman could petition the court for a divorce if her husband treated her with cruelty, if he deserted her, if he had an ailment making marital life dangerous, or if he failed to provide for her as agreed to in the marriage contract. Hanbali law had similar provisions.

The Ottoman Family Law of 1917 adopted these grounds from the Maliki and Hanbali schools. The Ottoman lawmakers used *takhayyur* to choose these principles from Maliki and Hanbali law, and then combined them, using *talfiq*, into one single code, the Ottoman Family Law of 1917.

ISLAMIC LAW IN THE CONTEMPORARY WORLD

Modernization and legal reform is ongoing in most countries of the world, including Muslim states. Since the 19th century, Muslims have experienced various colonial powers taking over their lands, followed by stages of decolonization and the formation of new states. Codification has remained a main method of new law formation in Muslim-majority countries.

Muslims live under two main types of states: where they constitute the majority of the population (Muslim-majority states) and where they constitute a minority of the population (Muslim-minority states).

LAW IN MUSLIM-MAJORITY COUNTRIES

Muslim-majority countries are scattered throughout Africa, Asia (including the Middle East), and in eastern Europe. These Muslim-majority countries have different political structures—such as democracies, military dictatorships, or monarchies—as well as different legal systems, each of which gives differing degrees of importance to Islamic law.

The legal systems of these countries may be divided into three main categories:
• Countries that identify themselves as Islamic countries or whose laws are based mostly or entirely on Islamic law.
• Countries whose legal system is based on Islamic law only in some areas of law.
• Countries with entirely secular (nonreligious) legal systems, where Islamic law is only relevant in individual citizens' private lives.

Saudi Arabia

This state is perhaps one of the better known countries in the category of self-identified Muslim states. Governed by the Hanbali School of Islamic law, Saudi Arabia is an absolute monarchy, where the governing dynasty rules the country according to its interpretation of Islamic law. The Koran is the basis of all law, and religious courts interpret and apply Islamic law in all matters, with the exception of certain administrative legal matters.

Saudi Arabia—along with the few other absolute monarchies such as Brunei and Qatar that apply a conservative interpretation of Islamic law—is often criticized for its violations of international human rights. These violations of human

Saudi Arabia is an absolute monarchy ruled by a king. Saudi law is based on the Hanbali School of Islamic law. Pictured here is Saudi king Abdullah (born 1925), who came to the throne in 2005.

rights include amputation of limbs as a punishment for noncapital crimes and prohibition of women being allowed to drive cars on public highways. However, it is important to note that Saudi Arabia is at the same time a signatory to various international human rights treaties, such as the Convention on the Elimination of All Forms of Discrimination Against Women (CEDAW), although with significant reservations. The reservations allow Saudi Arabia to maintain its participation in the international treaty while resisting certain changes to its laws, which are arguably in violation of treaties such as CEDAW.

Iran

Another country with an Islam-based legal structure is Iran. Unlike Saudi Arabia, which has always been a monarchy, Iran has gone through various stages of political governance, which in turn brought about various reforms and changes in the country's legal system.

The current political regime of the Islamic Republic of Iran began in 1979 with what has come to be known as the Islamic Revolution. Before the current regime, Iran was a constitutional monarchy ruled by the Pahlavi Dynasty, specifically Reza Shah Pahlavi (1878–1944) and later his son, Mohammad Reza Shah (1919–1980). The Pahlavis undertook a number of legal and social reforms similar to those of Mustafa Kemal Atatürk in Turkey. A part of these reforms was a codified law, the Family Protection Law (FPL) of 1967, governing marriage, divorce, and other aspects of interpersonal relations. Through this amended codification of Shiite family law, the Pahlavi shahs brought about reform toward gender equality in marriage and divorce. Unlike traditional

Shiite law, the codified family law required that all marriages and divorces be registered and gave expanded and numerous grounds on which women could initiate divorce.

Although the Pahlavi dynasty is remembered for its progressive reforms, it also used harsh methods to ensure the effective implementation of its policies. Due to the dynasty's close ties with the United States, increasing foreign control— mainly by the United States—of Iran's oil reserves, and the increasing income disparity between the common people and those close to the Shah's regime, discontent with the dynasty grew until it culminated in the 1979 Islamic Revolution.

After the revolution, spiritual leader Ayatollah Khomeini (1902–1989) returned to Iran from Europe, where he had been living in exile. Khomeini and his supporters established a new regime: the Islamic Republic of Iran. The laws and the legal system were entirely reformed to be in compliance with the Shiite law–based principles of the new regime.

Under the new government, legal reforms consisted of dismantling the justice system and replacing it with new Islamic courts. For example, in the area of family law, the FPL was annulled and replaced by Shiite family law. After the abolition of the FPL, the new government formed family law courts staffed by Shiite law–trained judges. These courts have been applying a new code, the Iranian Civil Code of 1979, which incorporates the principles of the Ithna Ashari School of Shiite Islamic Law.

Although Iran is now a country where the law is generally based on religious law, it is important to note that the codified laws of the state are not always identical to the traditional principles they claim to uphold. For example, the Iranian Civil

Ayatollah Khomeini, shown here on Iranian currency, became Iran's Supreme Leader in 1979. His government reformed the legal system to follow Shiite Islamic law.

that marriage and divorce be registered with the courts.

In her extensive field studies in post-revolutionary Iranian family courts, legal anthropologist Ziba Mir-Hosseini has found that women often negotiate various provisions in marriage contracts. Under Islamic marriage law, a contract is drafted in which the groom must promise the bride a specific amount of money, referred to as *mahr*. In addition, under Islamic law, the husband has an unconditional right to divorce for which he need not give any reason. Under the best of circumstances, the wife may only divorce her husband if certain conditions are met and the court agrees with her claims.

Mir-Hosseini's field research has found that women often use their *mahr* as a negotiating tool to control their husbands' unconditional right to divorce. Instead of receiving payment of their *mahr* at the beginning of the marriage, many women defer receipt of either part or all of their *mahr*, claiming it only if they divorce. Consequently, a man has to consider whether he is able to pay the *mahr* amount owed to his current wife under their marriage contract. In other cases, women might forgo their claims to the *mahr* amount in return for the husband's consent to a divorce initiated by the wife. In short, even though the law places various restrictions on the woman's right to divorce, at least some women are able to utilize their Islamic legal right to circumvent the restrictions placed on them.

Although the Islamic Revolution of 1979 was a popular revolution—in that it enjoyed the support of most Iranians—the strict and rigid application of religious laws have led to widespread unrest, especially among young Iranians. Reformist groups

Code of 1979 retained some of the reforms achieved under the FPL. One of these reforms was the registration requirement for marriage and divorce. Unlike traditional Islamic law (of all branches), in which marriage and divorce are treated as contractual relationships between two individuals, the Iranian Civil Code (as did the FPL) requires have been working through Iran's parliamentary system to bring about progressive change in the country's laws. Their path is paved with obstacles, but they have succeeded in certain instances. For example, in 2002, the reformist members of the parliament succeeded in changing the law regarding the minimum age of marriage. The minimum age for females was changed from 9 to 13 years and for boys from 14 to 15 years.

Nigeria

In 1999, twelve regions, or states, with Muslim-majority populations in northern Nigeria declared that Islamic law would govern their legal systems. Accordingly, they each set up a new judicial system, with new courts applying their understanding of Islamic law. There has been widespread criticism of these courts and the ways in which they have applied Islamic law. The courts have been accused of incorrectly applying Islamic law and at times not enforcing certain procedural safeguards that Islamic law provides. For example, one area in which the inadequacies of the courts have been most frequently discussed is enforced death by stoning as a punishment for adultery.

Under traditional Islamic law, adultery (extramarital sexual intercourse) is a crime. If the man or woman accused of the crime is single at the time, the punishment is a certain number of lashings. If the accused is married and has engaged in unlawful

In 2007, Iranian policemen launched a crackdown on women flouting Islamic law by not adequately covering themselves in public.

relations with someone other than his or her spouse, then the punishment is death by stoning. Although the punishment is clearly very severe, traditional Islamic law also places significant procedural safeguards, which are very difficult to satisfy. Specifically, to prove that adultery has occurred, there must be at least two adult witnesses who have personally observed the accused engaging in the act. Moreover, in order to combat false witness testimony or false accusations, the punishment for falsely accusing another of adultery is a specific number of lashings. Even though the punishment for adultery is severe, the law makes it difficult to adequately meet the requirements for proof.

After the implementation of Islamic law in northern Nigeria, the courts have been reported to either forgo or loosely apply these procedural requirements for proof in adultery cases. These flaws came to light in the international news in 2002 when a Nigerian woman, Amina Lawal, was

sentenced to death by stoning after giving birth to a baby more than nine months after divorcing her husband. She was brought before an Islamic court for the crime of adultery. The court, applying a strict interpretation of Islamic law, held that pregnancy itself was proof of adultery and did not require testimony from witnesses. Lawal's lawyers took her case to the Sharia Court of Appeal. The Court of Appeal accepted Lawal's argument that the procedural safeguards had not been applied and Lawal's right to a fair trial under Islamic law had been violated.

The legal issues involved in the application of Islamic law in northern Nigerian states are especially interesting in that they involve not only issues of religious law but also raise concerns about how the differences between state-level and federal-level laws may be resolved in a contemporary constitutional federal system. For example, had Lawal's death sentence not been overturned by the

Nigerian Amina Lawal waits in an Islamic courtroom in northern Nigeria after being sentenced to death by stoning for having a child out of wedlock. Her sentence was overturned by the Islamic Court of Appeal.

appeals court and then proceeded to the Nigerian Supreme Court—a nonreligious court—what would have been the outcome? Presumably, applying the Nigerian Constitution, as it is bound to do, the Nigerian Supreme Court would have found that Lawal's rights had been violated under the Nigerian Constitution. This would in turn raise issues about the boundaries of religious law applied locally in a secular federal system.

COUNTRIES THAT APPLY ISLAMIC LAW IN CERTAIN LEGAL AREAS

A significant number of present-day Muslim-majority countries apply Islamic law only in certain areas. Many of these countries retain Islamic law in the area of personal laws or, more specifically, family law. Family law governs issues about marriage, divorce, and custody. In many of the countries in this category, Islamic family law is codified. As discussed earlier, codification is a process in which certain legal principles are preferred over others. Various Muslim-majority countries have a document called the Family Code, in which different schools of Islamic law have been combined. The code differs among countries because each country selected the principles and schools of law it favored to draw up the code. As a result, it is generally difficult to make broad statements about what Islamic family law is unless referring to a specific country.

Some of the interesting examples of countries that apply Islamic laws to certain areas of their legal systems are Southeast Asian countries. Generally, after gaining independence from colonial powers, Southeast Asian Muslim-majority countries, such as Indonesia, Malaysia, and Singapore, have retained many of the characteristics of the laws implemented by their colonialist governments. These include codified laws and laws covering matters for different religious groups. In fact, this legal characteristic is common in most countries that were colonized by western European states. However, a unique characteristic of Southeast Asian states is an additional source of law referred to as *adat*, or customs. Although customs are often supplementary legal sources in other contexts (for example, the Swiss Civil Code), in countries such as Malaysia and Indonesia, *adat* is recognized as a primary source of law. This practice is very significant because these countries use Islamic law only as one source of law— even in areas where Islamic law applies. Although this legal use of *adat* is common in Southeast Asian countries, there are significant differences between the countries. For example, in Malaysia, women are not generally accepted as judges, whereas in Indonesia, women constitute a significant percentage of judges.

There is no consensus among legal or political scholars whether countries that apply religious law in certain areas only can be considered secular. Perhaps, the issue is not as significant as the ways in which individuals are affected by the laws, and whether the laws provide sufficient protection for individual citizens, especially given each country's obligations under international human rights treaties and agreements. Despite the general negative portrayal of Muslim-majority countries in mainstream Western media, almost all of the Muslim-majority countries are signatories to international human rights treaties and are thereby bound by the mandates of those treaties. However, because these international treaties allow for reservations, not all of their provisions are followed by all the signatories. An example of this problem was the case of Lina Joy.

Lina Joy, a Malaysian woman born as Azalina Jailani, wanted to officially convert from Islam to Christianity. Her application to the Malay Islamic law court to change her religion was rejected. The Malay governmental office accepted her name change but not her conversion. Arguing that the freedom of religion provision in Article 11 of the Malay Constitution mandated the Malay State to recognize her conversion, Joy appealed her case to all levels of courts in Malaysia. Court after court, including Malaysia's federal court—the court of last resort in Malaysia—rejected her appeal. The federal court, in its 2007 decision, ruled that only the Islamic law court had the authority to accept or reject Joy's petition regarding her conversion from Islam to Christianity. To date, Joy's conversion remains unrecognized by the Malay state.

COUNTRIES WHERE ISLAMIC LAW IS NOT A SOURCE OF LAW

Only a small number of Muslim-majority countries do not derive any part of their present-day laws from Islamic law. These countries are Turkey, Albania, the ex-Yugoslav state of Kosovo, and the ex-Soviet states of Azerbaijan, Kazakhstan, Uzbekistan, Tajikistan, and Turkmenistan.

With the exception of Turkey, all these countries have retained the secular legal systems they had while under communist or socialist rule. As a result, the laws in these countries do not refer to Islamic law or any other religious law. They are secular states where religious belief and practices are left to individual citizens. That the state law does not incorporate religious law does

not necessarily mean that people will abandon religious customs. In the absence of state-mandated religious law, some citizens continue to follow their beliefs, guided by the religious leaders in their communities. However, at times, religious law as practiced by private citizens may clash with the state's secular law. This is also an issue in secular countries where Muslims constitute a religious minority, as discussed later in this chapter.

The Turkish Republic, the successor of the Ottoman Empire, was the first Muslim-majority country to change its laws entirely after the demise of the empire. Formed in 1923, the new Turkish Republic formulated all its laws following the ideology of its leader in its independence struggle, Mustafa Kemal Atatürk. Atatürk and his followers believed that in order to modernize, their new country had to be secular and had to leave Islamic law behind. They adopted western European codes as the basis of their new laws. For example, they took on modified versions of the Italian Criminal Code and the Swiss Civil Code. As they gained their independence, other countries such as Egypt and Lebanon followed this trend of adopting European codes.

These legal reforms, complemented with social and political reforms, were mainly top-down reforms. In other words, these reforms were decided upon, formulated, and implemented by governments, often without any meaningful input from the population they would govern. Arguments over whether they were ever desirable or whether their continued influence is desirable is an ongoing debate in almost all Muslim-majority countries. The idea of secularism and secularization (the process of taking religious law out of the laws of a country) is the main focus of current debates. Although secular laws have existed in the Muslim world for a long time (since the Ottoman *qanun*), secularism as a dominant political and legal system is not always welcome. This is true not only in Muslim-majority countries but is a reality for all peoples of the world. The debate on secularism is really about the place of religion in the social, political, and legal structures of a country. It is unlikely that these debates will be resolved in the foreseeable future.

According to official records, 99 percent of Turkey's population are Muslim. Under the Turkish Constitution, Turkey is a secular republic, which means its laws are based on positive law and are not derived from religious law. Accordingly, Turkey is a secular country and it resembles other secular countries such as the United States and France. However, different countries have interpreted secularism differently, and as a result, they have different legal systems, even though all are referred to as secular.

Some countries, such as France and Turkey, have legal systems that limit religious expression in public spaces such as schools or governmental offices. Some countries, such as Sweden and the United Kingdom, have official state churches. Others, like the United States, interpret secularism as a strict separation of the state and its law from religion, and the state may not interfere in religious affairs.

In Turkey, Islamic law is a choice for private individuals to practice according to their understanding in their daily lives. However, while none of the country's laws is based on religion, the Turkish state regulates religious institutions, including mosques. Although Turkish lawmakers

initially adopted western European (especially French) legal systems as the model of their laws, Turkish secularism has evolved into a distinct type of secularism.

The Turkish Constitution grants all citizens freedom of religion in belief and practice. However, the Turkish state maintains the authority to regulate certain parts of religious practice. For instance, Muslim clerics, or imams, who preach in the mosques are employees of the Turkish state. Within the centralized Turkish educational system, the government prescribes a course on religion and ethics to all schoolchildren. The textbook on religion is written and distributed by the government, and it explains how Muslims should understand Islam. Moreover, certain laws prohibit religious separatism—which contradicts certain aspects of Islamic law—and inciting religious hatred.

Another area in which the Turkish state regulates religious activity is in clothing. Religious garb worn by clergy outside of religious institutions and houses of worship is prohibited. The debates surrounding female head coverings, commonly referred to as *hijab*, are also prevalent in Turkey. Through various regulations issued since the mid-1980s, Turkish law prohibits covering one's hair in educational institutions and governmental offices. Therefore female teachers, professors, administrators, and students who wish to cover their hair for religious reasons may not do so while at work or school. Although primarily a political and social issue, the courts, especially the Constitutional Court of Turkey, have been the arbiters of the issue. The Constitutional Court of Turkey is the court of last resort on legal issues that are based on constitutional claims. Since the mid-1980s the Constitutional Court of Turkey has thrown out two legislative attempts to allow head coverings for religious purposes in educational institutions. The court has found that allowing religious garb, even for solely private purposes of religious expression or worship, in public institutions would violate the principles of secularism as outlined in the Turkish Constitution.

Having found no help in the Turkish legal system, Leyla Sahin, a Turkish medical student, took her complaint to the European Court of Human Rights (ECHR). The ECHR is a regional court that enforces an international treaty, the European Convention of Human Rights, among signatory countries. Turkey is a signatory to the convention and is therefore bound by its terms, including guarantees of religious freedom. Sahin, a devout Muslim who believed she must cover her hair, was not allowed to take her examinations wearing her head scarf. In her appeal to the ECHR, Sahin argued that Turkey's refusal to allow her to complete her education wearing her head scarf was in violation of her right to religious freedom, as well as her right to an education without undue restraints from the state. The court found that Turkey was in violation but that the violation was justified because the state sought to maintain its secular structure, and head coverings in public institutions such as schools could be used as political symbols of fundamentalist Islam. The court further reasoned that such symbols could jeopardize Turkey's protection of secularism.

Although similar issues, especially those regarding head coverings, are also common in countries with Muslim minorities, Sahin's case is unique because it occurred in a Muslim-majority country. As such,

it reflects that even in a Muslim-majority country there are disagreements over the extent to which religious freedom implies religious practice and to what degree secular laws restrict religious practices.

MUSLIMS LIVING IN COUNTRIES AS RELIGIOUS MINORITIES

Today, many Muslims live in countries where they are a religious minority within the overall population. Depending on the legal structure of their adopted homeland, some Muslims live in countries where secular laws apply equally to all citizens regardless of their religion, while other Muslims live in countries where only in certain areas of law, such as family law, are they governed by Islamic law. Being a minority comes with various issues regarding laws. Discussions about reform in Islamic law are alive and flourishing in Muslim-minority countries, as they are in Muslim-majority countries. For example, in Canada and the United States, Muslim women have led prayers for men and women in certain mosques— traditionally an uncommon and mostly unaccepted practice.

Muslim groups in these countries are forming organizations both as a way to identify themselves to the rest of the Muslim communities and as a way to foster solidarity of different voices within Muslim communities. For instance, Muslim sexual minorities have formed the international organization Al Fatiha, with member groups in England and the United States. Al Fatiha challenges traditional interpretations of Islamic law, which views homosexuality as sinful.

Clashes between secular law and traditional Islamic law are a part of life for Muslim minorities. These issues are

numerous, ranging from the need to find accommodation and dietary restrictions to recognition of their very existence as part of society. In these respects, Muslim minorities face multiple challenges. India and the United States, two countries where these challenges have been disputed in the courts, provide interesting examples.

India

Muslims constitute the largest religious minority in India. Under India's laws, applicable religious law governs each religious community in personal matters (such as marriage, divorce, and inheritance). Accordingly, Islamic personal law as implemented by Islamic law courts governs India's Muslim minority. Decisions of

Islamic law courts are subject to appeal to secular courts, including the Supreme Court of India, the country's court of last resort. Although this might be desirable for the purposes of recognition of religious differences, it also leads to problems, many of which remain unresolved to this day.

One of these problems is the question of who speaks for India's Muslim community and who decides whether India's Muslim laws should be reformed. The debates often involve women's position in marriage and divorce. These issues were fiercely debated during the case of the Muslim woman Shah Bano Begum in the mid-1980s. Shah Bano's husband divorced her after many years of marriage. Under traditional Islamic divorce law, he

Many Turkish girls and women observe *hijab*, but they have not been permitted by Turkish law, which is entirely secular, to wear head scarves in schools, colleges, and government offices.

only had to provide her with three months of financial support. Shah Bano sought help from the courts, and the Indian Supreme Court eventually heard her case.

In 1986, the Indian Supreme Court found that Section 125 of the Indian Criminal Code—a secular code applicable to all Indian citizens—prescribed payment of alimony, and therefore even a Muslim man was bound by its mandate, regardless of Islamic law. The court's decision drew

There is a growing Islamic population in the United States. Many American Muslims follow Islamic personal laws, including this woman in a burqa.

adverse reactions and criticism from many in India's Muslim community, although Muslim women's rights groups applauded the decision.

Fearful of a political backlash from the main groups of the Muslim community, India's government at the time passed an act called the Muslim Women's (Protection of Rights on Divorce) Act of 1986, exempting Muslim men from Article 125 of the Criminal Code. This act also amended Section 125 of the Criminal Code, explicitly annulling its protection for Muslim women to receive financial support after divorce beyond the three-month period provided under Islamic law.

The Shah Bano case illustrates the continuing tensions between Muslim-minority communities' desire to maintain their identity in the face of a dominant culture that may differ from theirs in various ways. It also highlights the need to reform certain laws to provide equality to men and women. This debate remains unresolved in law and society.

The United States

There is a significant and growing Muslim population in the United States. Unlike India, the United States only has secular laws that are binding for all its citizens. However, at times, lower courts have heard cases in which mainly immigrant Muslims have sought to have their Islamic marriage contracts enforced. Often it is the wife who seeks to have her *mahr* paid upon divorce. There is no consistent practice by the courts as to whether Islamic marriage contracts entered into in a foreign country are binding in the United States. Because of the multitiered nature of the U.S. legal system, there is no clear result as to the enforceability of Islamic marriage contracts until the U.S. Supreme Court decides on the issue. However, Muslim couples who get married in the United States may circumvent these potential problems by simply placing the terms of the marriage contract in the form of a prenuptial agreement, which is common practice among many U.S. citizens, Muslim and non-Muslim alike.

In addition to seeking help in secular courts, Muslims in the United States (and in Canada and various countries of western Europe) have formed unofficial religious councils or tribunals, sometimes referred to as Sharia councils. These act as arbitration boards. Whether these unofficial community councils could one day issue binding legal decisions remains to be seen. In Canada, attempts to make decisions by these councils legally binding have been defeated various times in the last few years. In late 2008, some Sharia councils have been given the power to make decisions that are legally binding under U.K. law. To what extent this trend will flourish in other countries with Muslim minorities, including the United States, remains to be seen.

Another issue that remains unresolved is whether and to what extent secular law accommodates Muslim religious practices, specifically the Muslim women's head covering (*hijab*). In the United States, the Supreme Court has not yet heard a case on this issue, and the lower courts have found that governmental concerns over security trump individual religious liberties. Police officer Kimberlie Webb's case illustrates the ongoing tensions surrounding *hijab*.

Officer Webb is a 14-year veteran of the Philadelphia Police Department. She converted to Islam soon after she joined the force. Like many Muslim women, she did not always believe that she had to cover her hair at all times. For a number of years she did not mind removing her head covering while in uniform. However, her belief changed, and she now believes, as do many Muslim women, that she must never reveal her hair to men who are strangers, and, accordingly, she must cover her hair in or out of uniform. Webb's repeated requests for religious accommodation were denied by the Philadelphia Police Department on the basis that religious headgear was not allowed under the uniform hat. Another reason the department gave was the need for uniformity in the police department, which would be compromised if Webb were allowed to cover her hair. Webb's initial case at the trial court was dismissed. Receiving significant support from the Muslim community, as well as other religious communities, Webb appealed the lower court's dismissal to the U.S. Court of Appeals for the Third Circuit. The appeals court did not accept Webb's argument that her religious freedom outweighs the Police Department's need for uniformity.

Although the Court of Appeals for the Third Circuit was the highest U.S. Court to hear a case on a Muslim woman's head covering, its denial of Webb's claim does not represent a uniform practice on the issue in the United States or in western European countries with Muslim minorities. For example, in the United States, various police departments and correctional officer corps allow officers to cover their hair for religious purposes while in uniform. Likewise, in the United Kingdom, police departments and other military and paramilitary organizations allow for religious headgear, including Muslim head coverings and Sikh turbans.

See Also

Banking and Finance 130-131 ◆ Institutions and Organizations 132-141 ◆ States, Politics, and Political Groups 144-163 ◆ Civil and Human Rights 168-187 ◆

Banking and Finance

Islamic banking and finance are among the fastest-growing areas
in world finance. They follow the principles of Sharia law,
including the prohibition of all forms of interest.

With its origins in Egypt and Dubai as recently as the 1970s, Islamic banking and finance have since grown into a big industry, with increasing interest from Western governments and global financial services institutions. Estimates of the size of the industry vary. Most experts place the worth of global Islamic finance assets at close to U.S.$1 trillion, with annual growth rates predicted to be between 15 and 20 percent—more than twice the rate of growth of other financial sectors. Although Muslims account for about 20 to 25 percent of the world's population, Islamic banking is estimated to represent only 1 to 2 percent of global financial services. It is therefore seen as a potentially strong and untapped market.

Although the industry is mainly concentrated in Bahrain, Dubai, and Kuala Lumpur (the capital of

Malaysia), it has recently taken off in the Western world, especially in the United Kingdom. In 2004, the Organisation for Economic Co-operation and Development (OECD) established the Islamic Bank of Britain, which is the first wholly Islamic retail bank. In 2006, another bank opened—the European Islamic Investment Bank. In 2007, Islamic mortgages accounted for U.S.$ 1 billion in London alone—a 50 percent increase over the 2006 figure.

WHAT IS ISLAMIC FINANCE?

The set of principles and guidance that govern the financial affairs of Muslims is generally referred to as Islamic, or Sharia, finance. The best-known and dominant principle is the prohibition of all forms of interest. Islamic banking works on the basis of profit sharing for any risk undertaken. The customer and the bank (or lender) share the risk of any investment on agreed terms and divide the profits between them. For example, this could include an investment in which the customer risks losing money if it is unsuccessful, but the bank would not charge a handling fee unless the investment makes a profit. The prohibition on fixed interest stems from Islam's concern for social justice. Interest, it is argued, reinforces a tendency for wealth to accumulate in a few hands, to guarantee gain without the risk of loss, and to hamper investment and employment.

In addition to the prohibition on interest, there is also a strict ban on investments in any forbidden, or

The Islamic Bank of Britain, established in 2004, has six branches in the United Kingdom. It offers Muslims (and non-Muslims) financial services in line with Sharia law.

haram, activities, such as those involving alcohol, gambling, pornography, and pork-related products. This is very similar to the notion of ethical investing in secular societies, although the Islamic definition of ethical is wider than its secular equivalent.

Islamic financial products include current accounts, mortgages, insurance, personal loans, bonds (without interest), and trust funds. It is worth noting that the products available at present are not religious products. They are merely a means to allow Muslims to raise and invest in finance in a way that does not compromise their religious beliefs.

To ensure compliance with religious beliefs, Islamic banks and other financial services providers must hire Sharia scholars to review and approve each product and practice as lawful, or halal. These scholars—educated in

❖

Islamic financial products include current accounts, mortgages, insurance, personal loans, bonds (without interest), and trust funds.

Islamic jurisprudence (the science and philosophy of law) in addition to modern finance—are not involved in the design of the products but merely give an opinion on whether or not they are Islamic.

Despite a growing presence in world finance, Islamic finance and banking are still very much in their infancy. Issues, such as the need for standards, governance structures, tax implications, and a lack of qualified practitioners, have yet to be fully addressed. These obstacles, however, are not insurmountable, as evidenced by the many conventional financial institutions that have successfully developed Islamic offerings, such as the U.K. bank HSBC (whose name is derived from the Hongkong and Shanghai Banking Corporation) and the U.S. financial services company Citigroup. Islamic banking and finances are here to stay and may offer a bright future for investors who are prepared to address the hurdles and grasp the opportunities—both within the Muslim world and beyond.

ISLAMIC FINANCIAL TERMS

Western Islamic finance experts use a number of terms taken from Arabic:

Amanah *is not a contract as such, but a feature or requirement in some contracts that requires disclosure of cost price as well as negotiated sales price.* **Amanah** *relates to the part of the buyer/seller relationship based on trust.*

Ijara *is a leasing agreement whereby the bank (or lender) buys an item for a customer and then leases it back over a specific period.*

Ijara-wa-Iqtina *is a leasing arrangement in which the customer can buy the item at the end of the contract (e.g., a lease with option to own).*

Mudaraba *offers specialized investment by a financial expert in which the bank and the customer share any profits.*

Murabaha *is a form of credit that enables customers to make a purchase without having to take out an interest-bearing loan. The bank buys the item and then sells it to the customer.*

Musharaka *is an investment partnership in which profit-sharing terms are agreed in advance, and losses are pegged to the amount invested.*

Sukkuk *(singular,* **sakk***) are financial certificates that can be regarded as the equivalent of bonds.* **Sukkuk** *securities must comply with Islamic Sharia and its investment principles.*

Takaful *is Islamic "cooperative" insurance in which resources are pooled. It is in line with the principles of compensation and shared responsibilities among the community.*

Chapter 6

INSTITUTIONS AND ORGANIZATIONS

Muslim communities have formed regional, national, and international institutions and organizations to provide a wide range of support services, emergency relief programs, long-term development assistance, advocacy, and guidance to its people. International networks connect Muslims around the world, enabling them to access expertise and resources.

M any charities, institutions, and organizations help Muslims who are living in an environment of poverty, violence, or political instability. These organizations are extremely important in countries where Muslims form a minority group within the larger population. They help Muslims live alongside—and build strong relationships with—people who live their lives according to different values and belief systems, or who have no religion at all. Most Muslim organizations provide practical and educational support, for example, legal, advocacy, and financial advice. Some hold overtly political goals that aim to change public perception of Islam. Representatives of these groups lobby politicians to change policy and raise awareness of Islam to ensure that the Muslim voice is heard within the larger national and international decision-making institutions. Many Muslim organizations act as umbrella groups for a network of smaller enterprises, all of which seek to foster and promote the harmonious existence of Muslims in the modern world.

A volunteer for the Red Crescent helps an elderly man receive relief goods following floods in Bangladesh in 2004. One of the main aims of the Red Crescent is to provide humanitarian relief following natural disasters.

There are two main types of Muslim organizations and institutions. In the first category are groups that offer guidance and support to Muslims in their country of residence. Although they may demand legislative and policy changes, these groups are primarily social and advocacy organizations and do not lobby political

Many Muslim organizations act as umbrella groups for a network of smaller enterprises, all of which seek to foster and promote the harmonious existence of Muslims in the modern world.

parties. This type of organization is common in countries where Muslims form a minority group within the larger population. The second type of organization includes groups that focus mainly on charitable or development work. Charities, aid organizations, and nongovernmental development agencies support Muslims who are living in poverty, for example, families who may have been displaced from their homes following a war or a natural disaster such as a drought or an earthquake. The concept of charity is one of the central tenets of Islam and explains why there are so many Islamic charities and nongovernmental development agencies.

On September 11, 2001, Islamic extremists committed horrendous acts of terrorism. Al-Qaeda terrorists intentionally

The ethos behind most Muslim charities and development agencies is a desire to build equality between all people regardless of religion, race, or nationality and foster harmony around the world.

crashed four commercial airliners into the Pentagon, World Trade Center, and a field near Shanksville in Pennsylvania. Since then, Islamic groups—both charitable and political—have come under the close scrutiny of Western governments. Many Islamic organizations have been subject to intense official and media investigation to clear suspicion of links with Islamic fundamentalists and global terrorist networks. Fearful of the increased threat of Islamic extremism, governments in the United States, Britain, and other Western countries have expressed concerns that some organizations are acting as fund-raising bodies for terrorists. Despite investigations into the affairs of Islamic organizations, few have ever been proved to act in this way. Only a very small minority of Muslims support extremist views. The

ethos behind most Muslim charities and development agencies is a desire to build equality between all people, regardless of religion, race, or nationality, and to foster harmony around the world. Most Islamic institutions and organizations work across faith and secular boundaries and do not limit their support, financial and welfare based, solely to other Muslims. Despite this valuable work, many Islamic organizations feel vulnerable and under greater scrutiny than other faith-based support groups.

LOCAL AND NATIONAL SOCIAL INSTITUTIONS AND ORGANIZATIONS

One of the largest Muslim organizations in the United States is called the Islamic Supreme Council of America (ISCA; www.islamicsupremecouncil.org), which was founded by Shaykh Muhammad Hisham Kabbani in 1997. The ISCA aims to provide practical solutions for Muslim Americans based on traditional Islamic Sharia—the system of law based on the Koran and interpreted by a board of highly respected scholars. Members of the minority Muslim population in the Western world are finding it hard to act out their faith within a country in which the majority may not appreciate and respect Islamic principles. As a result, Muslims may need the support of organizations such as the ISCA to help them voice their beliefs and practices in an environment that may be apathetic or even hostile to Islam.

Councils exist in most countries in which Muslims are living in a minority. The Muslim Council of Britain (MCB; www.mcb.org.uk) was founded in 1997 and carries out similar work to the Islamic Supreme Council of America. The MCB is one of the largest bodies representing

Muslims living in Britain. The council comprises 500 affiliated national, regional, and local organizations, mosques, charities, and schools. The MCB works closely with local and national government departments to ensure that polices are sensitive to the views of the Muslim population. The MCB supports and guides Muslims living in Britain and helps them play a full role in public life. Many British Muslims live in areas of economic deprivation or in communities where their neighbors do not understand or respect Islam. As a result, the council funds projects that work with young Muslims to help them combat experiences of social exclusion. Much of the work of the MCB identifies and funds initiatives that aim to empower Muslim groups. The MCB also enables Muslims to

develop the skills needed to make a meaningful contribution to Britain.

More than one Muslim organization exists in many countries. In the United States, different Islamic movements and organizations have slightly different objectives. Some organizations represent a specific group of Muslims or focus on a particular issue. Islam is a diverse religion, which makes it difficult for any one organization to represent the full range of views in the Muslim population as a whole. The American Society of Muslims is one of the largest Muslim organizations in the United States, with an estimated membership of around 2.5 million. This group emerged in 2002 from another organization called the Nation of Islam. The American Society

Suleiman Ghali (right), president of the Islamic Society of San Francisco, voices his condemnation following the terrorist attacks in London on July 7, 2005. Many Muslims feel that non–Muslims blame them for the terrorist activities of a few Islamic extremists.

135

of Muslims represents a specific group of Muslims—African American Muslims who identify with Warith Deen Mohammed (1933–2008), the former leader of the Nation of Islam. Members of the Nation of Islam did not recognize Muhammad as God's final Prophet—a view that differs sharply from traditional Islam. Today, the American Society of Muslims aims to establish Islamic community life and portray an accurate representation of Islam in all areas of life. Other popular Muslim organizations in the United States and Canada include the Islamic Society of North America, the Islamic Circle of North America, the Islamic Assembly of North America, and the Muslim Student Association.

Some Muslim institutions in the United States have political aims. The Council on American-Islamic Relations (CAIR; www.cair.com) was established in 1994 by Nihad Awad, Omar Ahmad, and Rafeeq Jaber. CAIR claims to be the biggest Islamic civil rights and advocacy group in the United States and aims to be a leading advocate for justice and mutual understanding. The council's mission is to enhance understanding of Islam, encourage dialogue between different groups, protect civil liberties, empower Muslim Americans, and build coalitions that promote justice and mutual understanding. CAIR has been accused by its political opponents of having links to extremist groups, but no credible evidence of these links has ever been produced.

A charity supports destitute Pakistani Muslim women by offering them their first meal to break the fast during Ramadan—the holiest month in the Islamic calendar.

CHARITABLE ORGANIZATIONS

Zakat is the third of the Five Pillars of Islam. The word *zakat* means "alms-giving," and it is the responsibility of every Muslim to make compulsory donations to charity. Donations come in many different forms, which have evolved over time. Today, all Muslim adults must give 2.5 percent of their income or savings every year. This forms a kind of tax that Muslims pay to fulfill their social responsibilities to others. *Zakat* must be paid on precious metals such as gold, merchandise used in trade, and crops and livestock from agricultural land, but it is not payable on personal possessions such as cars, clothing, houses, and jewelry. In countries with a ruling Muslim government, *zakat* was once collected and distributed according to pre-established patterns. Today, it is usually left to the conscience of the believer. Many Muslims therefore make monthly donations to one of the many Islamic charitable organizations. Muslims are allowed to earn a minimum amount, called *nisab*, before they have to pay *zakat*. *Nisab* is an amount equal to the essential needs of a person or family for one year. Measured in terms of livestock, *nisab* is equivalent to five camels, thirty cows, or forty sheep or goats.

Charity is such an important part of Islam that Muslims will often donate voluntarily in addition to the compulsory *zakat*. *Sadaqah* is a voluntary donation for the cause of Allah. It is a sign of gratitude for the material provision that Allah has provided. *Sadaqah* may be given as a blessing on special occasions such as anniversaries and weddings or as a mark of respect for bereavement. *Zakat al-Fitr* (also called Fitrana) is a one-time payment Muslims make between the first day of the month of Ramadan and the first day of

Shawal. Adult Muslims are obliged to pay *zakat al-Fitr* regardless of their age, status, or wealth. The amount to give should be approximately 6½ pounds (3 kilograms) of stable food or the cash equivalent. Another charity is *sadaqah-e-jariya*, which can take many forms—from the ongoing provision of clean water to a specific community to the building of hospitals. Many Islamic charitable organizations have a *waqf* fund, which is an endowment used to fund projects such as mosques, hospitals, and schools. *Sadaqah-e-jariya* donations are paid into the fund to ensure that the money brings ongoing benefit. *Qurbani* is another charitable donation given on Eid al-Adha.

Today, all Muslim adults must give 2.5 percent of their income or savings every year. This forms a kind of tax that Muslims pay to fulfill their social responsibilities to others.

This important celebration commemorates the command given by Allah to Abraham to sacrifice his first-born son as a sign of his faith. Muslims celebrate Eid al-Adha with a feast. Muslims who can afford to do so sacrifice an animal, usually a sheep, as a symbol of Abraham's sacrifice. Some of the meat is given to the poor— this is the *qurbani*.

There are around 1,000 Islamic charitable organizations in the United States and a similar number operating in Britain. In wealthy countries such as these, a network of funding offices collect the donations and channel the money into field offices located in Muslim countries

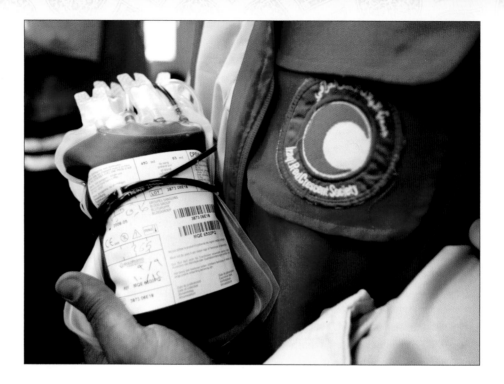

An official of the Red Crescent in Iraq holds up a bag of blood during a blood donation campaign to help the victims of violence during the Iraq War.

that are most in need. The cash is used to fund local development initiatives, ranging from emergency relief efforts to longer-term social and economic development projects that are aimed at improving lives and creating a more self-sustaining environment. One of the best-known organizations is the Aga Khan Foundation.

RED CRESCENT

The Red Crescent is the Islamic equivalent of the Red Cross; the two organizations combine to form an International Federation that operates in almost every country in the world. The International Federation of Red Cross and Red Crescent Societies (IFRC) is the world's largest humanitarian organization, providing assistance without discriminating on grounds of class, race, religious beliefs, or political opinions. The founding charter of the IFRC was drawn up in 1863 and now

comprises 186 member Red Crescent and Red Cross societies with a secretariat in Geneva, Switzerland, and more than 60 delegations strategically located to support local activities around the world. Swiss businessman Henry Dunant (1828–1910) inspired the IFRC. In 1859, Dunant witnessed the aftermath of the Battle of Solferino. He was appalled at the suffering of thousands of men and watched with horror as they died without any efforts being made to save them. On his return to Switzerland, Dunant proposed the creation of national relief societies made up of volunteers who could provide neutral and impartial help to relieve suffering at times of war. As a result, a committee was set up in Geneva, which later became the international committee of the IFRC.

More than 97 million volunteers work for the IFRC, which operates through its national societies. These are supported by other strands of the organization and are headed by the secretariat. The vision of the IFRC is as follows:

> We strive, through voluntary action, for a world of empowered communities, better able to address human suffering and crises with hope, respect for dignity and a concern for equality.

The IFRC carries out relief operations to assist victims of disasters and combines this with development work to strengthen the capabilities of local people. The four core areas of the IFRC are: prompting humanitarian values, disaster response, disaster preparedness, and health and community care. More information about the history and activities of each of the national societies can be found on the IFRC Web site (www.ifrc.org).

The IFRC represents a federation in the truest sense of the word. Each national society is autonomous and controls its activities and approach to humanitarianism. Unification comes in the form of shared values—all the representatives and volunteers share the commitment and belief in the importance of the work they do. The IFRC holds an international conference every four years. In 1965, at the conference in Vienna, Austria, the IFRC adopted seven basic principles. They are:

Humanity. There is a desire to bring assistance without discrimination to the wounded on the battlefield and to prevent and alleviate human suffering wherever it may be found. The IFRC seeks to protect life and health and to ensure respect for the human being. It promotes mutual understanding, friendship, cooperation, and lasting peace among all peoples.

Impartiality. The IFRC makes no discrimination as to class, nationality, race, religious beliefs, or political opinions. It endeavors to relieve the suffering of individuals, being guided solely by their needs, and to give priority to the most urgent cases of distress.

Neutrality. The IFRC may not take sides in hostilities or engage at any time in controversies of a political, racial, religious, or ideological nature.

Independence. The IFRC is an independent movement. While the national societies are auxiliaries in the humanitarian services of their governments and are subject to the laws of their respective countries, they must always maintain their

> "[The IFRC] strive[s], through voluntary action, for a world of empowered communities, better able to address human suffering and crises with hope, respect for dignity and a concern for equality."

autonomy so they can act in accordance with the principles of the IFRC.

Voluntary service. The IFRC is a voluntary relief movement and is not motivated by desire for personal gain.

Unity. There can be only one national society in any one country. It must be open to everyone and carry on its humanitarian efforts throughout its territory.

Universality. The IFRC is an international federation. Every society has equal status and shares an equal responsibility and duty to help each other.

These seven principles were added to the official statutes of the IFRC in 1986

THE AGA KHAN FOUNDATION

The Aga Khan Foundation is a "nondenominational" international development agency established in 1967. It emerged out of, and is still connected to, the Ismaili Muslim community and was designed to realize the social conscience of Islam. The foundation is the main grant-making agency for social development within the Shia Ismaili imamate. The Shia Ismaili Muslims are a community of ethnically and culturally diverse people living in more than 25 countries around the world. The foundation is named in honor of Prince Karim Aga Khan, the 49th hereditary imam of the Nizari Shia Ismaili Muslims. (The Ismaili community of Muslims consist of various groups—the Nizari is the largest one.) Prince Karim al-Hussayni became the present Aga Khan IV on July 11, 1957, at the age of 20, succeeding his grandfather. Nizari Muslims believe the Aga Khan lineage can be traced directly to the Prophet Muhammad. The Aga Khan provides funds for administration and new program initiatives as well as contributions to its endowment. The Ismaili Muslim community contributes volunteer time, professional services, and substantial financial resources. Other funding sources include income from investments and grants from government, institutional, and private sector partners, as well as donations from individuals around the world.

The Aga Khan family has vast wealth and believes it must put it to good use by helping others. Through the foundation, the family aims to develop and promote solutions to social challenges, primarily in Asia and East Africa. The foundation currently works in Afghanistan, Bangladesh, Britain, Canada, India, Kenya, Kyrgyzstan, Mozambique, Pakistan, Portugal, Switzerland, Syria, Tajikistan, Tanzania, Uganda, and the United States. The Foundation chooses which countries and regions to work in based on an assessment of need. Priority goes to the poorest communities. Additional support is given to initiatives that are already in place. The foundation likes to intervene where it has a strong volunteer base. Local volunteers are best-placed to achieve positive results through the design and implementation of long-term development programs.

With a small staff, a host of cooperating agencies, and thousands of volunteers, the foundation claims to reach out to vulnerable populations on four continents, irrespective of their gender, race, religion, or political persuasion. In 2004, it funded more than 130 projects in 16 countries with a budget of U.S.$149 million. To make the most of its resources, the Aga Khan Foundation concentrates on selected issues in health, education, rural development, and strengthening civil society. The foundation funds programs through the Aga Khan Development Network (AKDN). The AKDN consists of a group of development agencies, each possessing different mandates. They are the Aga Khan Health Service, Aga Khan Agency for Microfinance, Aga Khan Fund for Economic Development, Aga Khan Planning and Building Services, Focus on Humanitarian Assistance, Aga Khan Education Services, Aga Khan Trust for Culture, the University of Central Asia, and the Aga Khan University.

All aspects of the foundation are united by core goals:
• To enable poor people to act in ways that will lead to long-term improvements in their income and health, in the environment, and in the education of their children.
• To provide communities with a greater range of choices and the understanding necessary to take informed action.
• To enable beneficiaries to gain the confidence and competence necessary to participate in the design, implementation, and continuing operation of activities that affect the quality of their lives.
• To put institutional, management, and financial structures in place to ensure that program activities are sustainable without foundation assistance within a reasonable time frame.
• To maintain long-term commitment to achieve the goals.

and were adopted by every national society. The principles are extremely important because they link the various societies and branches of the federation together.

ISLAMIC RELIEF

Islamic Relief is an international relief and development charity that aims to alleviate the suffering of the poorest people in the world. Egyptian physician Hany el-Banna founded Islamic Relief in 1984 following the widespread famine in Africa at the time. The organization responds to emergencies and disasters and aims to promote sustainable economic and social development by working with local communities regardless of gender, race, or religious beliefs. The organization divided its activities into four main categories: emergency relief, development, orphans, and a *waqf* fund.

Islamic Relief operates in more than 20 countries. The central headquarters are in Birmingham, Britain. Islamic Relief USA is based in Buena Park, California. Fund-raising offices in Belgium, Britain, France, Germany, Mauritius, Netherlands, South Africa, Sweden, Switzerland, and the United States support field offices in Bangladesh, Bosnia, Chechnya, China, Egypt, Kosovo, Indonesia, Mali, Pakistan, Palestine, and Sudan. The organization also works in Ethiopia, Jordan, Kenya, India, Somalia, and Yemen. Islamic Relief funds projects ranging from emergency relief to long-term development initiatives. Key areas include water, sanitation, health and nutrition, orphan sponsorship, and income generation.

MUSLIM AID

Muslim Aid is an international relief and development agency that was founded in 1985 as a response to the famine in Africa. Muslim Aid began as an emergency relief organization. Between 1992 and 1994, the organization developed its mandate to include long-term development projects aimed at providing a sustainable living for survivors of disasters. The organization seeks to empower and build the capacity of local people to take control over their own future; its programs focus on giving individuals the resources and skills necessary to tackle the problems themselves within their own communities. Muslim Aid also runs an orphan sponsorship program designed to help children left destitute in war-torn countries. The headquarters of Muslim Aid are in London, England, and there are 14 field offices in Bosnia, Lebanon, Iraq, Pakistan, Somalia, Sudan, Kenya, Jordan, Bangladesh, India, Cambodia, Sri Lanka, Indonesia, and Gambia.

OTHER ORGANIZATIONS

Like many other relief organizations, Muslim Hands was founded to respond to natural disasters, conflict, and poverty around the world. Fund-raising offices in Britain, France, and South Africa support field offices in more than 40 countries in Africa, Asia, Central America, Europe, and the Middle East.

Other Islamic charities and aid organizations include the Alavi Foundation, al-Haramain Foundation, the Association of Islamic Charitable Projects, Benevolence International Foundation, Help the Needy, Hidaya Foundation, Human Appeal International, Global Relief Foundation, Inner-City Muslim Action Network, Islamic Aid, Islamic American Relief Agency, Kind Hearts, Ummah Welfare Trust, and the Zakat Foundation.

See Also

Education and Employment 88-105 ❖ Islamic Law 108-129 ❖ Banking and Finance 130-131 ❖ Grameen Bank 142-143 ❖ States Politics, and Political Groups 144-163 ❖

Grameen Bank

*Established to help poor people in rural Bangladesh, the Grameen
Bank gives out small loans, known as "microcredit," so borrowers
can set up businesses and improve their quality of life.*

The Grameen Bank, with its headquarters in Bangladesh, is an innovative banking system designed to help the poor borrow money. Poor people find it hard to get loans from established banks because they do not have sufficient resources to repay the amount. In times of acute hardship, many poor people in Bangladesh turn to loan sharks and other unscrupulous organizations to raise money for essentials, such as food and shelter. Loan sharks charge high rates of interest, forcing poor people deeper into debt. The Grameen Bank is unique because it does not require borrowers to put down collateral—an asset pledged for the repayment of a loan if it cannot be repaid as money—to secure loans. Instead, it relies on trust and a concept of partnership. Combined, these principles help foster a sense of responsibility among its borrowers that makes them feel obligated to repay their loans.

The Grameen Bank (GB) was founded in 1976 by Bangladeshi economist Muhammad Yunus, then a professor at the University of Chittagong, Bangladesh. He put together a research project to devise a credit delivery system for the poor. The word *Grameen* means "rural" or "village." During 1976 to 1979, a pilot program was initiated in a village near the university. The first project was supported by the Bangladesh Bank and other commercial banks. By 1979, the project's success enabled it to expand into other districts. By October 1983, GB became an independent bank. Today, it is owned by the rural poor. Borrowers own 90 percent of its shares and the government owns 10 percent. In 2006, Yunus and the GB organization received the Nobel Peace Prize in recognition of the significant impact the bank has had on alleviating poverty in Bangladesh. The bank has inspired many similar programs across the globe.

The founder of the Grameen Bank (GB), Muhammad Yunus, visits a group of Bangladeshi women who have benefited from a GB loan. The women used the money to set up a successful business in which they buy and rent mobile phones.

Today GB has 7.5 million borrowers, 97 percent of whom are women. GB lends money to people who are part of a five-person group. Loans are given to individuals within the group, and the other members motivate and support one another to make repayments. Interest—which may be permitted by Sharia as long as it is not usurious—is paid at a lower rate than to other banks.

Loans are used for many purposes, including the establishment of "microcredit" plans to set up small-scale businesses, such as making clothing, buying and operating a rickshaw, or establishing a food stall. Loans are also given out for housing and education. GB funds—from its profits—scholarships for poor children to attend school and gain an education.

Interest-free loans are available for destitute people to pay for essentials, such as shelter, food, and clothing. These loans are repaid over a much longer timescale than the other loans GB offers.

HOW THE BANK WORKS

GB works as follows: A branch is set up with a manager, who then works alongside a number of center managers, covering 15 to 22 villages. The managers visit local people to introduce them to the bank and assess their needs. During a visit, a manager tries to identify five people who would benefit from a loan and encourages them to form a group. Two members of the group will each be given a loan. The group is then closely observed over one month to see if they abide by GB rules: Have the loans been used to secure better shelter, replace machinery or tools, or to set up a small business? If the money is used wisely and the borrowers repay money over six weeks, other members of the group then become eligible for a loan.

Overall, the GB believes that its loans contribute toward a wider social-development agenda that raises the social and political consciousness of the people it works with. The focus on women is deliberate, as GB believes women prioritize the well-being of their families and are more likely than men to use their loans wisely. GB monitors the physical and social infrastructure of the areas it covers to ensure that improvements can be seen in peoples' lives.

FOUNDING OBJECTIVES

The founding objectives of the Grameen Bank, as listed on its Web site, are:

Extend banking facilities to poor men and women.

Eliminate the exploitation of the poor by money lenders.

Create opportunities for self-employment for the vast numbers of unemployed people in rural Bangladesh.

Bring the disadvantaged, mostly women, from the poorest households into an organization that they understand and can manage themselves.

Reverse the age-old vicious circle of "low income, low saving, and low investment," into a virtuous circle of "low income, injection of credit, investment, more income, more savings, more investment, and more income."

GB has been widely praised for its work, and its operational model is being used across the world to encourage local people to use microcredit to create their own businesses or to improve their lives. However, research examining the effectiveness of the bank has sounded caution over its direct replication. Each country and region carries its own set of social, political, cultural, and economic conditions, so the model must be adapted if it is to work. In addition, concerns have been expressed that although GB gives loans mainly to women, the money is often spent by their husbands. In these instances, a woman is not empowered to take control over her and her children's future. The success of GB is significant, but the road to eradicating poverty and inequality is fraught with difficulties. There are no quick-fix solutions. The bank must continue to adapt its model to overcome the problems and barriers it encounters.

Chapter 7

STATES, POLITICS, AND POLITICAL GROUPS

Fifty-seven states belong to the Organization of the Islamic Conference (OIC), the intergovernmental body that promotes cooperation and unity among Muslim-majority nations. Another five states are observers, making a total of 62, which is almost one-third of the total membership of the United Nations (UN).

T he member states of the OIC have a variety of forms of government, from dictatorships to democracies. Many of these forms of government are associated to varying degrees with Islamic tradition and do not fit easily into Western political definitions. Moreover, many Muslim states have complex histories; some are ancient, while others have existed in their current form only since the end of Western colonialism.

The range of political systems in the OIC extends from Turkey, which is a constitutionally secular state (religion and government are formally separated), to states that are officially Islamic, such as Afghanistan, Iran, Pakistan, and Saudi Arabia. Nine OIC members are monarchies; they include Morocco, Saudi Arabia, and the United Arab Emirates (UAE). Other OIC states are republics, three of which—Bangladesh, Indonesia, and Iran—have elected governments. While some Muslim monarchies are commonly—but not very accurately—described as "absolute," others, including those of Jordan, Malaysia, and Morocco, are often referred to as

"constitutional monarchies." Libya and Syria are commonly described as dictatorships, and other Muslim countries have had autocratic leaders during their recent history; examples include Iraq,

Several Muslim countries, including Bangladesh, Pakistan, and Turkey, have had democratically elected governments interspersed with periods of military rule.

which was ruled by the dictator Saddam Hussein between 1979 and 2003. The presidents of states such as Egypt have usually held office for very long periods but have rarely been referred to as dictators. Several Muslim countries, including Bangladesh, Pakistan, and Turkey, have had democratically elected governments interspersed with periods of military rule.

The influence of Islam in politics varies from state to state. In some of the OIC

An Iranian woman passes election posters in Tehran in 2004 beneath a mural of the founder of the Islamic Republic, Ayatollah Ruhollah Khomeini. Iranian president Mohammad Khatami questioned the fairness of the 2004 elections after reformist candidates were excluded from the ballot. Similar doubts were expressed about the election of Mahmoud Ahmadinejad for a second term as president of Iran in 2009.

ORGANIZATION OF THE ISLAMIC CONFERENCE

The Organization of the Islamic Conference (OIC), formed in 1969, is now the world's second-largest intergovernmental conference after the United Nations (UN). Currently, the OIC has 57 members, five observer states, and one associate member. The UN and agencies such as the African Union, the League of Arab States, and the Nonaligned Movement have observer status at the OIC. The OIC has observer status at the UN.

The OIC aims to strengthen Islamic solidarity worldwide and to promote political, economic, and cultural cooperation between members. It also aims to eliminate colonialism and to foster good relations with the non-Muslim world. It is committed to using peaceful means to settle disputes between member states. While political cooperation and solidarity are among its goals, a single political system is not. At any particular time, member states include stable democracies, dictatorships, various forms of monarchies, and other types of government.

During the rule of Saddam Hussein in Iraq (1979–2003) and that of Idi Amin in Uganda (1971–1979), both states

Led by King Abdullah of Saudi Arabia, the leaders of the OIC visit the Kaaba in Mecca after a meeting in 2005.

belonged to the OIC. Military coups, too, have taken place in several OIC member countries, including Pakistan, a founding member, where General Pervez Musharraf ousted Prime Minister Nawaz Sharif in 1999. In Turkey (also a founding member), military coups took place in 1971 and 1980.

countries, only marriage, divorce, and some civil matters, such as inheritance, follow Islamic law, while criminal law and commercial law are based on Western legal codes. In other states, much if not all of the legal system is based on Islamic law. The term *political Islam* is applied to efforts to Islamize the state. Islamization often revolves around how Sharia law is understood and applied. Not all Muslims favor political Islam; many regard it as an ideological manipulation of the faith for the purposes of power and control.

DIFFICULTIES OF COMPARISON

In spite of the variety of forms of government in the Muslim world, it is possible to identify four major categories: secular states, democracies, monarchies, and Islamic socialist states.

While the four categories are reasonably easy to characterize in general terms, the labels commonly used in Western political discussion are not easy to apply to the countries of the Muslim world. For example, Saudi Arabia is often described as an "absolute monarchy" but, while the king is undeniably powerful, there are limits to his authority. Yet neither can Saudi Arabia properly be described as a constitutional monarchy because the king can issue decrees. Jordan and Morocco are closer to the Western concept of constitutional monarchies, but their rulers still have significantly greater authority than those of Denmark, Netherlands, or Sweden, for example. Their powers are more easily comparable with those of the president of the United States.

Iran is a republic with an elected president, but there are few effective comparisons between the Iranian constitution and any polity in the Western world. The Supreme Leader, rather than the elected president, is the highest authority in Iran, and he exercises religious and political power. The president is elected by public vote; the Supreme Leader is elected by the Assembly of Experts, which is also elected by the public but from a list of approved candidates.

Terms such as *liberal, modernist, progressive, traditionalist, neotraditionalist,* *revisionist,* and *radical* have been used to describe the various forms of government and the politicians in the Muslim world. The rulers of the Saudi state are usually classed as traditionalists. Abdurrahman Wahid, the president of Indonesia from 1999 to 2001, was categorized as a progressive, while the Taliban, the ultrareligious political faction in Afghanistan, could be classed as radical. Libya's leader since 1969, Colonel Muammar al-Qaddafi, is widely regarded as a revisionist because he rejects many of the traditions of the Prophet Muhammad and the legitimacy of the four main Islamic schools of law. Also under Qaddafi's rule, Libya has dated the Islamic calendar from Muhammad's death in 632, rather than, as is traditional, from the time of the

CHARACTERISTICS OF ISLAMIC GOVERNMENT

Secular States	Islamic Democracies	Monarchies	Islamic Socialism
• The constitution requires that government should be strictly nonreligious. • Islam, as the majority faith, informs ethical conduct and the law. • It is taken as axiomatic that the coalition of religion and the state on the death of Muhammad came about through force of circumstances; the solution that was appropriate in 632 should not be regarded as prescriptive for modern Muslim-dominated polities.	• Such polities have an elected president, a constitutional monarch, or another head of government and advisors to interpret Islamic law. There are variations in who may elect and who may stand for election, but the basic principle is that the whole community guards Islam. • Most Islamic democracies have a common global objective of strengthening the OIC to their mutual benefit.	• The king or (in Iran) the Supreme Leader is the guardian of the law on behalf of Allah and a servant of the whole community. He is advised by religious scholars and a consultative body composed of appointees, elected representatives, or a combination of both. • The ultimate aim of Islam should be the establishment of a single polity of this type for Muslims throughout the world.	• The central tenet is that Muslims need to be liberated from the colonial and neocolonial legacies of the West. Islam is the authentic way forward. • One-party rule is essential to such states because any revolution needs ideological direction by those who understand its aims and priorities. • The ultimate objective is an end to oppression in every state on earth, regardless of whether it is Islamic.

hijra (the Prophet's flight from Mecca to Medina) in 622.

ISLAM AND DEMOCRACY

Countries that are often referred to as democracies, such as Indonesia, Malaysia, and Pakistan, may more properly be called *Islamic democracies*. In each of these cases, *democracy* is defined with reference to Islamic ideals and principles, rather than to any political philosophy from outside Islam.

Some Muslims reject the term *democracy* altogether. They see it as merely a tool of neoimperialism and regard Western rhetoric about spreading democracy as a strategy to resubjugate the Muslim world. They condemn the West as duplicitous in its identification of democracy solely with secular democracy. When the military seized power in Algeria following the electoral victory in 1991 of a religious party, the Islamic Salvation Front (ISF), the West stood by with apparent approval. Although the ISF appeared to espouse democracy, many people—especially non-Algerians—feared that, having gained power, the party would then rule

Some Muslims reject the term *democracy* . . . and regard Western rhetoric about spreading democracy as a strategy to resubjugate the Muslim world.

autocratically in the name of Islamization.

The influential Egyptian political theorist Sayyid Qutb (1906–1966) taught that Islam and democracy are fundamentally incompatible. The Pakistani Sayyid Abul A'la Mawdudi (1903–1979),

another traditionalist, adopted the term *theodemocracy*—a portmanteau word formed by combining *theocracy* (rule by religious leaders) with *democracy* (government of the people, by the people, and for the people)—to stress that sovereignty in an Islamic polity is vested primarily in God. Mawdudi did not object to Islamic government having democratic features but shared with many other Muslims a desire to avoid the use of terms such as *legislature* or *legislators* because they were inapplicable to Muslim polities in which consultative assemblies (*majlis-i-shura* or *shura*) formulate regulations, which are subsequently passed into law by caliphs and classified as *qanum* (administrative decrees) rather than as laws.

Some Islamic democracies veer toward monarchy, while others veer toward democracy, depending on how power is distributed and on the amount of authority that is vested in an elected body or in a nonelected or an elected leader. The main point at issue is that of how the process of interpreting Islamic law is understood. Is the authority shared by all, or are some more qualified to exercise it than others?

In the view of some commentators, what is eternal is the principle behind a traditional penalty, not the penalty itself, even if that penalty is explicitly stated in the Koran. Other people regard traditional penalties as fixed forever. The different interpretations are influenced by local customs, which may themselves change over time. The areas in which legislation is practically changeable are very limited in some polities, such as that of Saudi Arabia, but quite wide-ranging in others, such as that of Jordan.

The extent of the franchise (the number of people who are entitled to vote) varies from country to country in the Muslim world. Non-Muslims sometimes vote in separate constituencies for their own representatives, whose role is restricted to matters that directly concern their constituents. For instance, the parliaments of Egypt, Iran, Jordan, and Pakistan have seats reserved for non-Muslims, to which members are appointed rather than elected.

ISLAMIC MONARCHIES

Muslim monarchies do not practice automatic succession in the Western manner, with power passing from the reigning parent to a child or the nearest relative as a matter of course. Succession in Muslim monarchies is by designation and with the consent of senior advisors. Supporters of this system argue that it follows the example of the Prophet, who appointed his own successors. The succession in Muslim monarchies is often kept within the same family, partly through their self-interest but also for pragmatic reasons of convenience, stability, and the avoidance of civil strife.

Although not strictly speaking a monarch, the role of Iran's Supreme Leader is similar to that of a king inasmuch as he is a guardian of the law. However, the Supreme

SOME DIFFERENCES BETWEEN WESTERN DEMOCRACY AND ISLAMIC DEMOCRACY	
WESTERN DEMOCRACY	ISLAMIC DEMOCRACY
The people are sovereign.	God is sovereign; people are God's vice-regents (normally in the person of caliphs).
People make and can change the law.	God has already revealed his law, which does not change.
Any citizen can stand for public office (with certain restrictions, such as insanity or criminal convictions).	Those considered pious Muslims can be nominated for office (self-nomination is considered suspect vis-à-vis motive and personal integrity).
Those elected are legislators, or lawmakers.	Those elected interpret and administer God's law, but laws are not made by people.
Only the secular ruler (but no religious figure) can veto legislation (which can be overruled by a predetermined majority of legislators).	All regulations are subject to scrutiny (and possibly veto) by religious experts with whom the final authority invariably rests.
Human rights, as defined by the United Nations Declaration of Human Rights, are sacrosanct.	God's rights and human duty toward God take priority. The right to change religion and the realization of human rights are defined, restricted, or denied by religion.
Separation of church and state (the church may be "established" but it has no political role).	Men and women are equal but different, thus their "rights" are also different, taking account of their various responsibilities.

Mohammad Siad Barre, president of Somalia from 1969 to 1991, described himself as a socialist and modeled his government on that of the Soviet Union.

Leader's method of appointment is different from that of a monarch: the succession is decided by a council of religious leaders, rather than passed down automatically within a family.

The Al-Qaeda leader Osama bin Laden and others contend that monarchy is un-Islamic. However, their concept of a global caliphate, headed by a single individual, resembles a monarchy.

Other Muslims regard the whole concept of the state as un-Islamic. In their view, the entire Muslim world should be a single political entity. Some accept the pragmatic necessity of the nation-state but would like to see greater cooperation between Muslim-majority states.

Many Muslim states have not existed for long in their present form; indeed, some of them did not exist at all before they were created by the European colonial powers in the late 19th century and the early 20th century. For example, although ancient entities bore the names of Iraq, Jordan, and Syria, the modern states of those names were formed when the Ottoman Empire was divided between Britain and France after World War I (1914–1918). None of these modern nations corresponds exactly to the territories to which those names were previously applied. The same is true of modern Turkey and Saudi Arabia—both are countries with ancient names but 20th-century frontiers.

Monarchies and democracies in the Muslim world evolved from particular Islamic understandings of governance. Their development was disrupted by European colonialism. Even after the colonial powers had departed, they left behind independent governments that owed more to non-Muslim ideas, precedents, and political philosophies than they did to Islam.

RESPONSES TO THE COLD WAR

In some Muslim countries, the politics of the Cold War and the rivalry between the Eastern and Western blocs catalyzed the emergence of a third category of government—the Islamic socialist state. Countries that fall into this category adapted many of the principles of communism, including its tendency toward an autocratic polity.

Islamic socialism is a term used by Libya's leader, Colonel Qaddafi, and others. Syria, Iraq under Saddam Hussein (r. 1979–2003), Egypt under Gamal Abdel Nasser (r. 1954–1970), and Somalia under Siad Barre (r. 1969–1991) all described themselves as "socialist" states while retaining some degree of Islamic identity. In Syria, Bashar al-Assad succeeded his

father, Hafez al-Assad (1930–2000), but with the title of president, not king.

SECULAR STATES

Secular states are countries in which the government is constitutionally separated from religion. Turkey is a secular state. Pakistan began as a secular state, as did Bangladesh. After declaring independence from the disintegrating Yugoslavia in the 1990s, the Muslim-majority country of Bosnia and Herzegovina took a secular political path to demonstrate a historical commitment to religious and cultural pluralism and harmonious coexistence.

Some secularists find it difficult to gain acceptance for their ideas in the Muslim world. Many secularists have received Western educations, and their critics have been able to undermine their credentials and dismiss them as agents of the West.

POLITICAL PARTIES

Islamic political parties and political organizations play significant roles in many Muslim majority states. In Bangladesh and Pakistan, Jamaat-e-Islami, an Islamist party, has participated in government. In Lebanon, Hezbollah, an Islamist militia, has a political wing that forms part of the ruling coalition. In Palestine, the majority party in the National Authority's Assembly is Hamas, a radical, religious, nationalist group. In Egypt, although members of the Muslim Brotherhood—an organization that advocates a return to earlier and, in their view, purer, interpretations of the Koran—are officially banned from standing for election, they have run successfully as independents.

Some Islamic political groups operate entirely within the prevailing political system, sponsoring candidates for election

POLITICAL ISLAM

Politics and theology—traditionally closely related but kept separate in Islam—come together in the concept of political Islam, or Islamism. The term is usually reserved for those who support a traditional concept of Islamic law (such as amputation for theft and subordinate political status for non-Muslims and women). *Taqlid* (imitating past practice) is stressed, along with a return to Islam's earliest (salafist) practices. This approach is motivated by what is perceived as the economic and political dominance of the West, by opposition to Israel, by criticism of U.S. foreign policy, and by support for Palestinian statehood.

The degree to which manifestations of political Islam have widespread support is unclear. Islamization has often been championed by unelected leaders, while salafist parties have enjoyed little electoral success, with some local exceptions in the poorest parts of Europe (especially in France) and western Asia. On the other hand, many Muslims want reform of state institutions to reflect Muslim values and desire better education, health care, and welfare. Results of a Gallup poll published in 2007 suggest that very few Muslims support terrorism. The majority want greater democracy with little direct role for religious leaders but with laws based on Islamic principles. Most Muslim women want equality with men. Many Muslims see the West as morally bankrupt. Few Muslims want the state to define Islam, but neither do they want religion marginalized, as they think has happened in the West. Many Muslims detest the activities of Al-Qaeda but share its animosity toward the West, so they take some pleasure in Osama bin Laden's ability to avoid capture. Similarly, many Muslims detested Saddam Hussein's treatment of his own people and were aware that he used Islam simply to attract Muslim support, yet they admired him for standing up to the West.

to parliament or to other bodies. Other groups use extraconstitutional means to achieve their aims, including violence and acts of terror. They have also been labeled *jihadist* since they describe their cause as a struggle to defend, extend, or establish true Islam. Al-Qaeda falls into this category. Some of these groups operate among Muslim minority populations to gain moral and financial support or to recruit volunteers to fight.

Some groups aim to reestablish a single, worldwide Islamic polity (often referred to as a "caliphate"). Their interim goal is usually to set up genuine Islamic states, possibly by overthrowing governments that they regard as illegitimate, as a platform toward building a global Islamic polity.

Others want to strengthen an existing global body, such as the OIC, but do not aspire to establish a superstate. Some Muslims even reject the use of the term *political parties*, arguing that there can be only one: the party (*hizb*) of Allah.

Progressive and liberal Muslims tend to support either secular states—those in which, in spite of the strict separation of politics and religion, Islam still influences legislation because it is the faith of the majority—or forms of Islamic democracy in which human rights, women's rights, and minority rights are fully respected. Progressives have not, however, organized themselves into movements comparable with those of Islamist Muslims. They say that "political Islam" is undesirable because it turns a personal faith and a way of life into a state ideology.

HISTORICAL SURVEY

The roots of the different systems of government lie in their historic origins. None of the systems exists in isolation from Islamic political thinking or Islamic history. Advocates of each political system anchor their ideas to Islamic practice, principles, or precedent.

Between 610, the traditional date of Muhammad's revelation, and the Prophet's migration from Mecca to Medina in 622, Muhammad was a religious but not a political leader, although his teachings had political implications and his followers looked to him for advice on social and moral issues. After the migration, however, Muhammad became the political and military leader of an extensive territory. For many Muslims, the belief that all of life is subject to God's will and guidance informs the belief that religion and the state are inseparable in Islam.

When Muhammad died in 632, the territory he ruled began to disintegrate. Some chiefs claimed that they had pledged allegiance to him, not to his successors. The majority adopted a Koranic definition of Muslims as people who govern their affairs by *shura* (consultation). They established the

Mohamed Mahdi Akef, leader of the Muslim Brotherhood in Egypt, votes in presidential elections in 2005. Although the Muslim Brotherhood is prevented from sponsoring political candidates, members running as independents have enjoyed some electoral success.

This manuscript
produced by Mongol
artists in the late 15th
century shows scenes
from the life of Ali,
the Fourth Caliph.

caliphate with the caliph, the symbol of Islamic unity, as commander in chief. The extent to which the caliph was intended to be a religious leader and the extent to which he was bound by the same religious rules as the people he governed remain subjects of debate. The standard view of the Sunni majority is that the community and its leader are subject to the same law, the law of Islam, of which the caliph is the guardian. Should the caliph stray from the law, he loses the right to rule.

The first four caliphs (ruled 632–661) were selected or nominated by a variety of methods. Sunni Muslims regard all those who were chosen as the best possible men for the post. Shia Muslims, however, argue that only a direct male descendant of Muhammad should be caliph. Shiites therefore reject the first three caliphs, who had no blood ties to the Prophet, but acknowledge the legitimacy of the fourth, Ali, the Prophet's cousin and son-in-law.

While not all Muslims took part in choosing the caliphs, a consultative process did take place. The first caliph nominated the second, but the nomination was ratified by oath-taking and public acclamation. After the fourth caliph was murdered, members of the first dynastic caliphate, the Umayyads, governed from 661 until 750. Muawiyah, the founder, justified his assumption of the caliphate against the claim of Hasan (Ali's son) on the grounds that he had more extensive administrative experience and a better understanding of politics. He did not claim to be a religious leader. Two other dynastic caliphates followed: the Abbasid dynasty, which ended in 1517, and the Ottoman Empire, which disintegrated in 1924.

The initial unity of the Muslim world did not last for long. Rival caliphates and semi-independent or autonomous sultanates emerged, some of which paid only lip service to the caliph's supremacy. From 1258, for example, the Abbasids lived under the aegis of the Mamluk sultans of Egypt.

Succession to the caliphate, or to a sultanate, was never strictly hereditary. Sons did succeed fathers, but this was not automatic. Other male family members were sometimes designated to succeed. The succession also depended on the approval of a panel of advisors, known as those who could "bind and dissolve." Keeping the succession within the family, however, was a pragmatic mechanism to ensure smooth transitions in every case.

Some people argued that the "best person" should be the caliph but, because there was no mechanism for widespread participation in a consultative process, it was practically impossible to reach consensus on the identity of the outstanding candidate. Most people agreed that the overwhelming priority was to preserve stability, which was preferable to *fitna* (civil strife), even if a caliph was not the best person for the job.

The idea that the caliph's role was to preserve unity, to protect Muslims, and to administer the law—and that his authority was divinely sanctioned—evolved not only as a pragmatic but also as a theological principle. The Arab jurist al-Mawardi (died 1058) described the caliphate as having been placed on earth by God to take over, after Muhammad's death, the Prophet's role as the defender of Islam. Al-Mawardi wrote that it was a duty for all Muslims to pledge allegiance to the caliph.

Because the caliphs had no privileged right to interpret the law, they were always accountable to the community. Their responsibilities were entirely political or administrative. Trained scholars interpreted the law, either as state employees or in religious foundations. Effectively, this separated the functions and provided checks and balances on the actions of all political leaders.

Classical Arabic texts say less about how caliphs should be appointed than about how they should carry out their duties and the qualities they should possess. Some of the Hadiths (sayings of Muhammad) imply that whoever is in authority should be obeyed, regardless of how they came to power.

SECULARISTS

In the 19th and 20th centuries there emerged a number of Muslim advocates of the secular state. Among the most distinguished and successful of these were the Turk Kemal Atatürk (1881–1938), the Indian-born Sayyid Ahmad Khan (1817–1898), the Egyptian Ali Abd al-Raziq (1886–1966), and Pakistan's founder, Mohammed Ali Jinnah (1876–1948).

Secularists argue that the combination of political and religious authority that Muhammad exercised in Medina was the result of circumstance. Muhammad did not set out to establish a political entity but to call people to walk a path of obedience to God. Islam is a *din* (faith), not an ideology. Religion does not need to be enshrined in the political system as long as Muslims remain free to practice their faith.

Secularists believe that Muslims are not necessarily wrong to combine religion and politics but, more often than not, the machinery of the state and of Islam as a religion have been separated. Muslims can live in a secular state as faithful Muslims. Where Muslims constitute a majority in any democratic state, Islam will inevitably influence legislation, morality, and public and private life.

Turkey was founded in 1923 as a secular state. Atatürk closed seminaries and nationalized religious foundations. Later, the ban on Islamic parties was lifted and two such groupings formed governments, although one of them was subsequently outlawed again. The current government of Turkey remains committed to a secular constitution and now aspires to join the Western-dominated European Union (EU).

In 1995, the nation of Bosnia and Herzegovina (which has a Muslim majority) was created as a multicultural, secular state with a presidium of three members, representing the Bosniaks (Muslims), the Serbs (mainly Orthodox Christians), and the Croats (predominantly

Where Muslims constitute a majority in any democratic state, Islam will inevitably influence legislation, morality, and public and private life.

Roman Catholics) in a deliberate effort to restore multireligious harmony after a divisive regional civil war in the 1990s.

RELIGIOUS INFLUENCE ON POLITICS

Although Saudi Arabia is ruled by a king and sometimes erroneously described as an absolute monarchy, royal power in the country is moderated by religious authorities who run the *siyassa* (administration). The most important of these religious figures is the Grand Mufti, whose office is usually occupied by descendants of the scholar Muhammad ibn Abd al-Wahhab (1703–1792). A measure of the Grand Mufti's power is that, in 1964,

Nationalist demonstrators in Turkey carry a portrait of Mustafa Kemal Atatürk, the creator of the modern, secular Turkish state.

he deposed the ruler, King Saud, for incompetent handling of the economy.

Retention of leadership within a family may not be specifically prescribed by the Koran, but neither is it proscribed. The process of selecting the leader was entrusted to the community, which used *shura* (consultation) and *ijmah* (consensus) to establish the caliphate and proved vital for the preservation of unity and for the protection of Muslims.

Caliphs have been removed for misconduct—Ibrahim in 1648, Mehmed IV in 1697, Ahmed III in 1730, and Selim III in 1897, for example—and have not exercised absolute power. In those Muslim countries where kings rule, they also do not exercise absolute power. As guardians of the law, they have a function that could be fulfilled by any suitable person, such as an elected official, but the dynastic system has worked satisfactorily for hundreds of years, and supporters see no compelling reason to change it.

There has never been agreement on how many people are needed to participate in *shura* (consultation) or indeed on whether its decisions are binding. However, advisors and those who bind and dissolve have always had a say in who succeeds as

Hassan Rohani, chief of Iran's Supreme National Security Council, addresses members of the Assembly of Experts in March 2004.

caliph, sultan, or king. Various verses in the Koran appear to question the concept of majoritarianism, while other verses have been taken to suggest that some Muslims rank above others, which could be taken to justify the concept of a royal family. Nowhere does the Koran state that members of a *shura* have to be elected.

In the Islamic Republic of Iran, ultimate authority is vested in the jurist who is considered the most learned and thus the best qualified to lead. He is elected by the Council of Experts, while the president is elected by the people. The Experts are elected from a slate of candidates drawn up by the government. The whole system is dominated by the *mujtahids* (religious leaders).

The creation of modern Saudi Arabia and Jordan stemmed from a reasserted Arab claim to leadership of the Muslim world, over and above the Turkish caliphate. The founders of the Saudi state were inspired by the 18th-century scholar al-Wahhab, who called for a return to "original Islam" and allied himself with Prince Muhammad ibn Saud (died 1765), whose heirs eventually carved out a kingdom for themselves in 1923. Commonly known as Wahhabis, a term that has become a byword for ultratraditionalism, the rulers of modern Saudi Arabia call themselves *Muwahiddun* (unitarians).

The constitution of Saudi Arabia is the Koran. The king is informally elected from the descendants of Prince Saud by members of the royal family in consultation with the descendants of al-Wahhab. A more formal mechanism has been established for future elections of the king, although it will still be conducted by the royal princes. The king, who is also prime minister, is advised by a *shura* council of 150 members, all of whom are appointed. Steps have been taken to elect a proportion of members at some future date, at local council level as well as at national level. The king can be removed for misrule.

Of the four Islamic legal schools, only Hanbali is recognized in Saudi Arabia.

Saudi Arabia regards itself as the leading Muslim nation and stresses its role as protector of the holy cities of Mecca and Medina, and as host of the hajj.

Based mainly on the Hadiths, Hanbali leaves extensive scope for the incorporation of local customs and regulatory measures. Saudi Arabia regards itself as the leading Muslim nation and stresses its role as protector of the holy cities of Mecca and Medina and as host of the hajj. Women must be accompanied by a male relative in public; they must wear the veil and they cannot obtain driver's licenses. (In contrast, women have been prime ministers in Bangladesh, Pakistan, and Turkey, and Indonesia has had a female president.) Traditional penalties, such as the amputation of limbs for theft, are applied, although forgiveness is also built into the system for the repentant, and the severity of the punishment depends on the value of the items stolen, the number of offenses, and various other circumstances.

Jordan was established as a nation by the British after World War I, alongside Iraq and Palestine, which Britain administered directly. In 1921, the British made Abdullah king of Jordan and his brother Faisal king of Iraq. Iraq became independent in 1932 (the monarchy was overthrown in 1958); Jordan became independent in 1946.

The royal family of Jordan, the Hashemites, is descended from the Prophet Muhammad and claims leadership of the Muslim world in competition with the Saudis. The Hashemite interpretation of Islam is generally more progressive than that of the Wahhabis.

Succession in Jordan is by the designation of the king, and the royal preference may change. For many years, the designated successor of King Hussein was his brother but, shortly before the ruler's death in 1999, he appointed his son Abdullah as his heir. The king of Jordan can veto legislation passed by the elected assembly of 110 seats, but the assembly can override the veto by a two-thirds majority. Christians have reserved seats in Parliament and usually occupy two or three cabinet posts; six seats in the Jordanian parliament are reserved for women. The 50-member upper house, however, is appointed by the king. The Hashemites are active in promoting religious tolerance, Islamic solidarity, nonviolent resolution of conflict, and the religion's role as a peacemaker.

THEODEMOCRACY

Muslim modernists, such as Muhammad Iqbal (1877–1938), who first proposed a separate state for India's Muslims, and Muhammad Abduh (1849–1905), were among the pioneers of the idea that Islamic principles are wholly compatible with democracy as a way of choosing leaders of the community. More conservative Muslims, such as Sayyid Abul A'la Mawdudi and Hasan al-Turabi (born 1932) of the Muslim Brotherhood in Sudan, have argued that democracy can be adapted to meet Islamic requirements, although they do not believe that Western-style democracy can simply be transposed into Islamic contexts.

In the proposed form of theodemocracy, various professional bodies would nominate members as candidates for consultative assemblies, which may be elected. Assembly members then interpret and apply Islamic law. A panel of experts might scrutinize regulations before they become effective, which is the function of the Council of Experts in Iran. In Pakistan, Mawdudi's political party, Jamaat-e-Islami, is organized as a type of government in waiting. The Muslim Brotherhood has a similar structure, with a *shura* council to advise the leader. The Constitution for an Islamic State formulated in 1962 by the Hizb-ut-Tahrir (Global Islamic Political Party) provides for an elected assembly and aims to restore the global caliphate.

Although Sayyid Qutb, who was one of the Muslim Brotherhood's most eminent ideologues, opposed democracy, its members have taken part in elections and won office in Egypt and elsewhere. In 2005, standing as independents, members won 20 percent of the seats and formed the largest opposition group in the parliament. The Brotherhood's founder, Hasan al-Banna (1906-1949), did not believe in political parties, but the Hizb-ut-Tahrir permits them, provided that they are "based on the creed of Islam."

Before achieving independence, Pakistan and Egypt were both parts of the British Empire. Pakistan was partitioned from India in 1947 as a homeland for Muslims but retained much of its preexistent colonial infrastructure, including legal codes. It was established as a secular, democratic state under its founder, Mohammed Ali Jinnah. Islam was to be the main religion and the source of morals. Pakistan became a republic in 1956. It was in two parts, West Pakistan and East Pakistan, separated by 1,000 miles (1,600 km) of Indian territory.

In 1958, a military coup saw the first period of nondemocratic rule in Pakistan under Ayub Khan (1958-1969), who was succeeded by Yahya Khan (1969-1971) before democracy was restored in 1972. The People's Party (PP) leader, Zulfikar Ali Bhutto, then became prime minister and continued the secular policies of Jinnah. Meanwhile, in 1971 East Pakistan broke away and became the independent nation of Bangladesh. Originally secular, Bangladesh declared Islam the state religion in 1988.

In Pakistan (formerly West Pakistan), Bhutto was ousted in a 1977 military coup led by Mohammad Zia-ul-Haq (1924-1988) and executed. Zia, who promised but never delivered free elections, described his government as *nizam-i-islami* (an Islamic system) and launched an Islamization program supervised by an Islamic Ideology Council. Introducing Sharia law, Zia justified his coup by claiming that it was inspired by "the doctrine of necessity." Zia appointed a *shura* council, but it had no binding authority.

Mawdudi had been outspokenly critical of Pakistan as an illegitimate Muslim state until, under Zia, members of Jamaat-e-Islami occupied several important posts. Jamaati members later distanced themselves from Zia, calling for the restoration of democracy. That came in 1988 when

Bhutto's daughter, Benazir, was elected prime minister. She served until 1990 and again from 1993 to 1996, alternating power with Nawaz Sharif of the more Islamist Muslim League (ML). In 1999, Pervez Musharaf, the army chief, seized power. Democracy was restored again in 2007.

Many members of the Pakistan judiciary continued to administer what was mainly a British-based legal system with some adjustments for Islamic personal and domestic law. The future role of Islam in Pakistan remains subject to debate. In 2009, power was shared between the secularist PP and the Islamist ML.

Egypt was a monarchy between the departure of the British in 1922 and the military coup led by Nasser in 1952. Nasser was later elected president. A socialist, he nationalized industry and the Suez Canal. He also used Islam to legitimize his regime, nationalizing

A woman votes in Syria's 2007 parliamentary elections. The turnout in the elections was low after opposition parties urged their supporters to boycott the polls to protest lack of real democratic choice.

mosques and Muslim institutions. The Arab and Pan-Arab nationalists who led Egypt's independence movement were secularists who saw Islam as a moral code, not as a political construct.

Nasser banned Islamist organizations and jailed many of their members. The Muslim Brotherhood was accused of attempting to assassinate him. In spite of all this, Nasser's ideology has been called "political Islam." He recruited Muslim scholars to issue opinions sympathetic to his political ideas. Although family law is based on Sharia, most Egyptian law follows the Napoleonic Code introduced by French colonists in the 19th century. Nasser's successor, Anwar Sadat (1970-1981), was assassinated by a breakaway jihadist group, which declared him an apostate for making peace with Israel in 1978.

In contemporary Egypt, elections are held for the People's Assembly (10 out of 454 seats are appointed by the president) and for an Advisory Council (176 seats; another 88 are appointed), but restrictions on who can run raise questions about the degree to which the system can be described as fully democratic. There is no

MUSLIM MOVEMENTS

The Muslim Brotherhood (MB) was founded by Hasan al-Banna in Egypt in 1928. It aims to establish Islamic states across the Muslim world, ruled by experts in Sharia law. It regards the West as decadent, corrupt, and dangerous. Membership in the MB is a capital offense in Syria, where members led an armed uprising against the state between 1976 and 1982. In 2005, standing as independents (the MB is officially barred from sponsoring candidates), the MB won 20 percent of the seats in the Egyptian Assembly. Although it is a relatively obscure organization today, the ideas of the MB have had an enormous influence on today's Islamic political movements.

Hizb-ut-Tahrir (Islamic Liberation Party) has about one million members in 40 countries. It is banned in many Arab countries and several European ones. Founded in Lebanon by Taqiuddin an-Nabhana in 1952, it aims to reestablish the universal caliphate as an elected institution.

Jamaat-e-Islami was founded by Sayyid Abul Ala Mawdudi in 1941. Although it has enjoyed little electoral success, some of its members have taken part in government in Bangladesh and Pakistan. Jamaati promotes an Islamic state but is relatively open to democracy. Its members have signed Osama bin Laden's fatwas (decrees) calling for jihad (armed struggle) against the United States and its allies.

Hamas (Islamic Resistance Movement) was founded in Palestine in 1987 by Ahmed Yasin, a member of the MB. Hamas's charter rejects diplomacy. The group uses violence, including suicide bombings, to achieve its aim of replacing Israel with an Islamic state. In 2006 it won the majority of seats in the Palestinian National Authority's parliament.

Hezbollah (Party of God, or the Organization of the Oppressed on Earth, or the Islamic Jihad for the Liberation of Palestine) is a Shia political and religious movement founded in Lebanon in 1982. Backed by Iran, it has a humanitarian and welfare program as well as its own militia, which has attacked Israeli targets. It aims to destroy Israel and to establish an Islamic state in Palestine (where the majority of Muslims are Sunni). Hezbollah fought a war with Israel in 2006. It has had considerable electoral success in Lebanon.

limit on presidential terms. So far, all Egypt's elected presidents have more or less served for life. Some people see this as a thinly veiled autocracy. Egypt has also taken a leading role in the Muslim world as a champion of anticolonialism and Muslim autonomy. Syria and Egypt united from 1958 to 1961 in the name of pan-Arabism; the combined state they formed was known as the United Arab Republic (UAR).

ISLAMIC SOCIALISM

Islam may be considered a radical social movement that seeks justice and the liberation of people from oppression, ignorance, and poverty. In the modern world, this tradition shapes the principles of Islamic socialism.

Libyan leader Colonel Qaddafi equates socialism with Islam's emphasis on equality and with the redistribution of wealth (*zakat*) that is built into Islamic practice. In Qaddafi's view, the people rule; he is their guide and philosopher, so he does not need any impressive title of state.

Libya has been condemned in the West as a rogue state that sponsors acts of terrorism. In the Libyans' view, however, they have been exporting the revolution, taking up the cause of all the oppressed and exploited people of the world. Critics say that Islamic socialism began as socialism but added "Islam" in order to gain legitimacy among Muslims. Qaddafi has imprisoned many members of Islamist movements.

In Syria, the Baathist Party that has been in power since 1963 was founded by a Christian, Michel Aflaq (1910–1989), whose agenda was secular pan-Arab nationalism. (Baathists in neighboring Iraq claim that Aflaq became a Muslim before he died, but that is disputed.) Syria gained independence from France in 1946. Neither Libya nor Syria permits multiple parties, so while elections take place, all candidates belong to the state-sponsored party.

MUSLIM MINORITIES

Muslims living in states in which they are a minority often participate in political life through existing, mainstream parties. In the United Kingdom, for example, Muslims are city councillors, mayors, and members of parliament, and hold senior posts in the civil service. Such Muslims tend to favor assimilation, regarding Islam as one of many religious denominations. Other British Muslims have formed separate parties that promote specific changes in the law to accommodate Muslim family law, inheritance law, or even an autonomous Muslim community in which men might be permitted up to four wives, for example.

In other countries, Muslims advocate a type of separatism. Some Muslims around the world are more interested in reforming their countries of origin, promoting Islamist agendas and recruiting Muslims for armed conflicts in places such as Bosnia, Chechnya, or Palestine. Umbrella organizations to represent Muslims in the wider community and lobby governments have also emerged. Sharia Councils or Supreme Muslim Councils handle domestic legal issues for Muslims within the scope of local laws.

The leading Muslim organizations in the diaspora include the Islamic Supreme Council of America, the French Council of Muslim Faith, and the Muslim Council of Britain. These and other similar bodies represent Muslim concerns to the wider public and to their respective national governments. Most of their members take the view that Islam is a belief system and a moral code rather than a political creed.

See Also

Islamic Law 108-129 ❖ Institutions and Organizations 132-141 ❖ Al-Qaeda 164-167 ❖ Civil and Human Rights 168-187 ❖ Islamism in the 21st Century 192-215 ❖

Al-Qaeda

Al-Qaeda is an Islamist terrorist organization. It has been notorious since September 11, 2001, when it carried out concerted attacks on targets in New York City, Washington, D.C., and Pennsylvania.

A l-Qaeda ("the base") was founded in 1989 by Saudi-born Osama bin Laden. It is also sometimes known as the International Front for Fighting Jews and Crusaders, the Islamic Army for the Liberation of Holy Sites, and the World Islamic Front for Jihad Against Jews and Crusaders. Al-Qaeda's ultimate aim is to reestablish the universal caliphate and to make Sharia the law for all Muslims. Other goals are the creation of an Islamic state in Palestine to replace Israel and the removal of U.S. bases from all Muslim countries. Bin Laden's denunciation of the West as manipulative and as preventing Muslims from choosing their own governments implies that Muslims will be economically better off under the caliphate. Many Al-Qaeda recruits, including the perpetrators of the attacks on the United States on September 11, 2001—the atrocities now known simply as "9/11"—are university graduates drawn from middle-class or affluent backgrounds.

Al-Qaeda is loosely organized, so it is not easy to establish whether other organizations are affiliated to it. Among its known associates are the Abu Sayyaf group in the Philippines, whose founder, Abdurajik Abubakar Janjali (1959–1998), fought with bin Laden in Afghanistan; the Egyptian Jihad organization led by bin Laden's chief deputy, Al-Zaqahiri; the Chechen Mujahideen, whose former leader, Ibn Al-Khattab (1969–2007), was also a bin Laden protégé; Indonesia's Jemaah Islamiyah (responsible for the 2002 Bali bombings); and Algeria's Groupe Islamique Armé (Armed Islamic Group; GIA). Al-Qaeda also has links with at least one Islamist group in Thailand, where some Muslims want an Islamic state in the southwest, and with various

Islamist groups in Kashmir and western Asia. It is believed to have run several training camps in Yemen. An association with Hezbollah in Lebanon ended in May 2008, following attacks on Sunni Muslims.

Most notoriously, Al-Qaeda was responsible for the September 11, 2001, attacks on the World Trade Center in New York City, on the Pentagon in Washington, D.C., and on a hijacked airplane in Pennsylvania. . . .

Most notoriously, Al-Qaeda was responsible for the September 11, 2001, attacks on the World Trade Center in New York City, on the Pentagon in Washington, D.C., and on a hijacked airplane in Pennsylvania, in which a total of more than 2,750 people died. Bin Laden does not deny many other acts of violence, even if they are wrongly attributed.

OSAMA BIN LADEN

Osama bin Laden was born in 1957 into a very wealthy Saudi family originally from Yemen, the 17th of 57 children. His family runs a construction company worth billions of dollars. Bin Laden himself possesses a personal fortune of $300 million, to which he may or may not have access. Until 1994, he received $1 million annually

Osama bin Laden calls on Muslims to join his struggle against "infidel" Christians and Jews as seen in a videotaped statement released after the attacks of September 11, 2001.

Time Line

1993   February: bomb attack on the World Trade Center, New York; Egyptian Islamic Jihad (EIJ) leader Sheikh Omar Abdel Rahman is later convicted of this crime.

1995   June: EIJ tries to assassinate Egyptian president Hosni Mubarak.
November: truck bomb attack on the Egyptian embassy in Islamabad, Pakistan, kills 17 people.

1996   June: 19 U.S. soldiers killed in Saudi Arabia.

1997   November: gun attack on tourist bus in Luxor, Egypt, kills 60 people.

1998   August: bombings of U.S. embassies in Kenya and Tanzania kill around 224 people.

2000   October: suicide bombing of USS *Cole* in Yemen kills 17 U.S. sailors.

2001   September: suicide attacks by means of hijacked aircraft on the World Trade Center, New York, and the Pentagon, Washington, D.C.

2002   October: bomb attack on a nightclub in Bali, Indonesia, kills 202.

2004   March: in Madrid, Spain, bombs on rush-hour trains kill 191; links to Al-Qaeda suspected.

2005   July: suicide bombers kill 53 people in London, England; links with Al-Qaeda remain unconfirmed.
November: 57 die in terrorist bombings in Amman, Jordan.

2007   April: 33 die in bombings in Algeria.

Firefighters walk through the dust that still fills the air amid the ruins of the World Trade Center in Lower Manhattan after the buildings were destroyed by hijacked airplanes on September 11, 2001.

from his family. He attended King Abdulaziz University in Jeddah, Saudi Arabia, where he read the works of Syed Qutb and became a convinced Islamist. He may have graduated in economics and business administration in 1981; the details are disputed. Later he became interested in aiding the mujahideen freedom fighters following the Soviet occupation of Afghanistan in 1979. For several years, he traveled back and forth between Saudi Arabia and Afghanistan with equipment, supplies, volunteers, and funds. He may have taken part in some fighting; he is an expert at demolition. In 1984, he opened a guesthouse for jihadists in Peshawar. He actively recruited Arabs and others to fight in the jihad.

The mujahideen received assistance from the U.S. Central Intelligence Agency (CIA), although claims that bin Laden was himself trained by U.S. intelligence are disputed. Technically, bin Laden was number two under Abdullah Azzam, who died in a bomb attack in 1989. With the struggle against the Soviets over and the Islamist Taliban ruling Afghanistan, bin Laden, now in full control, turned his attention to struggles elsewhere. Banned from returning to Saudi Arabia, which he denounces as un-Islamic, he moved his operations to Sudan in 1991 at the invitation of Hasan Al-Turabi of the Sudanese Muslim Brothers. Expelled from Sudan in 1996,

AYMAN AL-ZAWAHIRI

Ayman al-Zawahiri (born 1951) is a physician who served for several years as a surgeon in the Egyptian army. He joined the Muslim Brotherhood (MB) at age 14 or 15 and may have been involved in the attempted assassination of Egyptian president Nasser in 1965. By 1980 he was a leading member of the Egyptian Islamic Jihad (EIJ), which had grown out of the MB to pursue more militant forms of jihad. In 1981 the EIJ assassinated Egyptian president Anwar Sadat for making peace with Israel. The EIJ has also been implicated in the attempted assassinations of Egypt's foreign minister, Hassan al-Alfi, in August 1993, and of prime minister Atef Sedky three months later, as well as in the planning of an attack on the U.S. Embassy in Cairo in 1998. In 1981, al-Zawahiri was imprisoned in Egypt for three years. After his release, he spent a year practicing as a physician in Saudi Arabia before moving, first to Pakistan and then to Afghanistan, where he was joined by Showqi al-Islambouli, who later tried to murder Egyptian president Hosni Mubarak during a visit to Sudan. Al-Zawahiri then reconvened the EIJ and joined Osama bin Laden's circle. In Afghanistan, he affiliated the EIJ with Al-Qaeda. Al-Zawahiri has acted as bin Laden's interpreter and is suspected of being responsible for masterminding the entire terrorist program. In 1991 al-Zawahiri was again coordinating attacks in Egypt, now as the undisputed head of the EIJ. He formally merged the EIJ with Al-Qaeda in 1998. In 1991 he was arrested in Russia attempting to enter Chechnya. He was tried and acquitted. Soon after, he masterminded the attack in Luxor, Egypt, in which 60 tourists died. In 2001 the Federal Bureau of Investigation (FBI) named al-Zawahiri as one of the most wanted criminals in the world for his role as chief planner of the 9/11 attacks.

bin Laden returned to Afghanistan as the guest of the Taliban. He recruited fighters for the wars in Bosnia and Chechnya and for resistance in Algeria and Egypt.

In several fatwas (decrees), bin Laden has explicitly called for jihad against the United States in retaliation for attacks on Muslims during the Persian Gulf War (1990–1991) and for aiding the Israeli occupation of Jerusalem. His fatwa of August 1996 encourages Muslims to rise up against the enemies of Islam. The United States and its allies, in league with the "iniquitous" United Nations, prevents Muslims around the world from defending themselves against attack. In bin Laden's account, these forces were collectively responsible for Muslim bloodshed in Assam, Bosnia and Herzegovina, Burma (Myanmar), Chechnya, Eritrea, Kashmir, Ogaden, the Philippines, Somalia, and Tajikistan. Bin Laden particularly denounced the Saudi alliance with the United States and the presence of U.S. troops in the Arabian Peninsula, which defiled the "land of the two holy places." He referred to a Crusader-Zionist alliance that inhibits what he calls "corrective movement" (Islamic resurgence). Bin Laden's fatwa of February 23, 1998, opens with a Koranic verse: "When the forbidden months are passed, then fight and slay the pagans wherever you find them, seize them, beleaguer them, and lie in wait for them in every strategy of war."

Bin Laden fled Afghanistan after the Allied invasion of 2001 and the destruction of most, if not all, of Al-Qaeda's training camps. It is likely that he lives on or near the Pakistan-Afghanistan border. Several video recordings and audio tapes of Osama bin Laden have been broadcast through the Arab news channel, al-Jazeera, some of which have been authenticated by intelligence agencies. On March 20, 2008, bin Laden denounced the European Union for permitting newspapers to publish cartoons of Muhammad. The U.S. Justice Department has offered a reward of $25 million for information leading to bin Laden's capture.

CIVIL AND HUMAN RIGHTS

To modern Westerners, the Muslim concept of civil and human rights may appear different from their own. Although that view is not unfounded, it is often influenced by adverse publicity. In fact, Islam, Judaism, and Christianity have most of the same core values; many of the differences are created by political considerations.

The most widely espoused definition of human rights is enshrined in the United Nations (UN) Universal Declaration of Human Rights of 1948, which aimed to establish what it described as "global standards"—rights to which all people in all cultures are entitled, simply by existing. These include: the right to health, education, shelter, employment, property, food, and a fair trial; freedom of

❖

To Westerners, such values may seem axiomatic—people in most of the industrialized countries regard the desirability of these rights and liberties as self-evident.

Palestinians such as this schoolgirl from a refugee camp in Bethlehem in the West Bank are subject to Israeli law. The West Bank is one of the main areas of the world in which Islam comes into conflict with other faiths, especially in matters relating to civil and human rights.

speech, thought, and movement; and freedom from torture and slavery.

To Westerners, such values may seem axiomatic—people in most of the industrialized countries regard the desirability of these rights and liberties as self-evident. However, in other parts of

the world, they are highly contentious, not least because they are seen as potential weapons of neoimperialism. They give the most powerful nations a pretext for intervention in the affairs of countries that do not come up to prescribed standards of rights. In this view, there is no consensus that liberal democracy is the only acceptable form of government; indeed, a significant body of political theory suggests that it is sometimes impossible to run a country in that way.

RELATIVISM AND UNIVERSALISM

The UN Declaration is, as its full name suggests, universalist by intention—it seeks to apply a moral and legal standard to the whole world. In practice, however, its prescriptions are diluted by a pragmatic acceptance of variant local customs, at least in the developed world. In Europe, numerous national and regional conventions and charters have developed, including the European Convention on Human Rights and Fundamental Freedoms in 1950 and the Social European Charter in 1961. In 1969, the United

States ratified the Inter-American Convention on Human Rights.

While the Western powers are content with such a heterogeneous approach to human rights in their own territories—a broad statement of desiderata coexisting alongside long-established local customs and practices—they do not always make the same allowances for the nations of the Muslim world.

The same kind of duality also exists in Islam, where there are two schools of thought, known as communalism and universalism. Communalism advocates cultural relativism in which *civil rights* are granted to all citizens of the Muslim state, regardless of whether they themselves are Muslims or non-Muslims. This idea was adopted by three of the four main Sunnite schools of law: the Maliki school, founded in the 8th century by Malik ibn Anas; the Shafi'i school, founded by Muhammad ibn Idris ash-Shafi'i (767–820); and the Hanbali school, founded by Ahmad ibn Hanbal (780–855).

The communalist viewpoint was rejected by the Muslim universalist school, which advocates that basic *human rights*—life, property, freedom of expression, freedom of religion, family, and honor—should be available to everyone, regardless of whether they are citizens of a Muslim state. Universalism was originally codified by the Hanafi school of Sunnite religious law, which was founded by Abu Hanifah (around 700–767). The concept was adopted by the great Islamic empires—the Umayyads, the Abbasids, the Mughals, and the Ottomans. By the 19th century, universalism had lost its original sense of purpose, and there had been an alarming increase in discrimination against non-Muslims, so the Ottomans carried out

a radical overhaul of the system that purged such practices in the name of constitutionalism and democracy. That initiative could not prevent the collapse of the Ottoman Empire in the early 20th century, and after its dissolution the idea of universalism was largely forgotten for almost 100 years. However, some Islamic scholars have recently started calling for a revival of this tradition.

Historically, therefore, there was no consensus on human rights, either globally or within Islam. The debate between universalists and relativists continues, and tension remains between exclusive and inclusive attitudes.

MUTUAL SUSPICION

While, in its basic form, the concept of human rights is easy to comprehend—people either have such liberties or else they do not—the notion is greatly complicated by the way civilizations view each other. Western attitudes toward Islamic practices are strongly influenced by anecdotal evidence that does not always accurately reflect the overall picture. One of the most influential opinion-shapers in the late 20th century in the United States was *Not Without My Daughter* (1987), a book by an American, Betty Mahmoody, that became a 1991 movie starring Sally Field. Both works describe what happened when Mahmoody accompanied her U.S.-born daughter and her Iranian husband to his native country and he subsequently announced that he would not be returning to the United States as originally planned. The Iranians claimed that Betty Mahmoody, by her marriage, was an Iranian citizen and refused her permission to leave the country without her husband's consent. She eventually escaped with her daughter to Turkey, where she found refuge in the U.S. Embassy before being repatriated to the United States. *Not Without My Daughter* solidified American prejudices about Iran and reinforced the already common view that Muslims are violent and oppressive to women.

Several other episodes have entrenched hostility on both sides of the Western-Muslim divide. One was the publication in September 2005 in a Danish newspaper of 12 cartoons that depicted the Prophet Muhammad as a man of violence. This led to a worldwide debate regarding criticism of Islam, censorship, civil liberties, and freedom of speech and the press. Another source of controversy was the release on the Internet in 2008 of *Fitna* (Civil strife), a 15-minute film depicting Islam as an intolerant religion and the Koran as a danger to the preservation of freedom in the Western world. Scenes depicted beheadings, violence against women, and anti-Semitic tirades by imams. The director, Geert Wilders, was a member of the Dutch parliament and the leader of an anti-Islam political party.

These works—and a growing number of others like them—show Islam and Muslims in an unfavorable light, defining the religion as incompatible with human rights, facilitating authoritarianism, and contradicting the values of Western societies. The Muslim response to such attacks is often to reject human rights as an alien ideology imposed without authority by Westernized individuals whose "universal truth" is the truth of colonialists and neocolonialists who seek to exploit the Muslim world. Muslims who take this view often feel that Islam and human rights as defined by the West are alternatives that cannot coexist. For the most devout or politicized Muslims, this may culminate in their outright rejection of human rights as the concept is currently defined.

Betty Mahmoody (left) is the author of the book *Not Without My Daughter*, which tells of her and her daughter's escape from Iran after being held as virtual prisoners by her husband. Zana Muhsen (right) is the author of *Sold: Story of Modern-Day Slavery*, which describes how she was abducted from her native Britain and forced into marriage in Yemen.

Distrust and suspicion have intensified on both sides since the terrorist attacks of September 11, 2001, in which the twin towers of the World Trade Center in New York were destroyed and the Pentagon in Washington, D.C., was seriously damaged. Among Westerners, these atrocities have increased Islamophobia: many Muslim organizations are regarded as training centers for terrorists; Muslim women in the West have been pressured not to cover their heads; and racist attacks on Muslims have increased alarmingly.

The way forward is to develop a sense of urgency that Islamophobia ought to be made unacceptable, just as racism and anti-Semitism are in America.

In 2005, the Council on American Islamic Relations (CAIR) processed a total of 1,972 civil rights complaints (anti-Muslim harassment, violence, and discriminatory treatment), compared to 1,522 cases reported in 2004. Such actions inevitably inspire reactions. According to CAIR's 2006 Policy Bulletin:

> Muslim youth in the West have grown up being preached ideas of plurality, equality, and freedom. When such ideas are not applied towards their own empowerment it can lead to disillusionment, social disorder, and, in the worst cases, irrational violence. . . . The way forward is to develop a sense of urgency that Islamophobia ought to be made unacceptable, just as racism and anti-Semitism are in America. Islamophobia is already beginning to

erode America's image and culture. Opinion leaders should view Islam—a faith with diversity, internal differences, having much in common with Christianity and Judaism—as distinctly different but not deficient, and as a partner in America's future.

HUMAN RIGHTS IN ISLAM

The adoption by Muslim countries of their own declarations of human rights as alternatives to the UN Declaration does not deny the value of the latter and, indeed, seeks to incorporate some of its principles into the Islamic value system. Various Islamic organizations have also formulated declarations of human rights. The Organization of the Islamic Conference (OIC)—which comprises 57 Muslim member states and is the world's second largest intergovernmental organization after the United Nations—has adopted many such declarations, including the Dhaka Declaration on Human Rights in Islam (1983) and the Cairo Declaration on Human Rights in Islam (1990). These declarations confirm human rights, emphasize the role of the community of believers *(ummah)* in asserting and protecting these rights, and honor Islamic law (Sharia), which protects the vital interests of humans and ensures a balance between the obligations and the rights of individuals and groups.

According to the Dhaka statement, humanity constitutes one family and "all men share the same dignity and the same responsibilities and rights, without distinction of race, color, language, religion, gender, political opinion, social status or any other consideration." The articles of the Cairo Declaration assert the right to life and the prohibition of servitude, humiliation, and exploitation of humans, who are all born free. The declaration also affirms the right to private life, family, and home, equality before the law, and freedom of expression and information. In the matter of cultural rights, the declaration states that society and the state are required to ensure that education is "a duty"; in the area of labor law, social guarantees for workers should be upheld by the state.

The Cairo Declaration makes several other provisions, including respect for life and the integrity of the human body (the fetus is considered as a human being from the fourth month and must therefore be protected); the principles of international humanitarian law (it is expressly forbidden "to kill people who do not participate in the fighting, such as the elderly, women, and children"); the prohibition of "taking a person hostage in any form and for any purpose whatsoever"; and the right to a healthy environment.

Further declarations were adopted in the Muslim world, particularly by local nongovernmental organizations (NGOs). The most important of these is the Islamic Universal Declaration of Human Rights of 1981, proclaimed by the Islamic Council, a nongovernmental organization based in London. Most of this document's provisions are similar to those of the 1948 UN Declaration. They assert the human rights to life, justice, protection against torture, asylum, participation in and management of public affairs, social security, and education. They also seek to guarantee freedom of belief, thought, speech, association, and movement, and to ban discrimination. In addition to these broad generalities, a few specific rights have been added, including protection against abuse of power, protection of honor and reputation, and the rights of married women.

IMPACT OF KORAN AND SHARIA LAW

Most Muslim states have ratified the UN Declaration. However, the separate Islamic declarations by which these nations also abide differ from the declaration in several respects, notably by giving priority to the Koran and to Sharia law. In Muslim states, Islam is seen as a set of religious duties that regulate the whole life of every citizen and the functioning of society. Human rights can be guaranteed only within the context

THE APPLICATION OF ISLAMIC LAW IN MUSLIM COUNTRIES

The relationship between Islamic law and the laws of the land vary widely from country to country throughout the Muslim world. The governments of some nations attempt or claim to rule strictly according to the precepts of the Koran, although the original text is, of course, often open to interpretation.

The most literal interpretation of the Koran is generally agreed to be the legal system of Mauritania. In other countries, notably Comoros and Somalia, the Koran is held to be no more than an inspiration for the civil code.

In the largest group of Muslim countries, it is difficult to be sure which, if any, of the secular laws are religiously inspired. That is the case in Algeria, Burkina Faso, Cameroon, Chad, Djibouti, Gambia, Guinea Bissau, Mali, Morocco, Niger, Senegal, Tunisia, and Turkey. Islamic references, whether implicit or explicit, have been deliberately omitted from legislation in all these states.

Although the Muslim world does not have universal suffrage, increasing numbers of women are being given the vote. This photograph shows a woman casting her ballot in the 2005 presidential election in Iran.

of the commandments in the Koran and the precepts of Sharia.

Most of the Muslim states that have ratified the UN Declaration justify their divergence from it in matters of human rights with reference to their constitutions, which take precedence domestically. Iran is one of several Muslim countries where, in matters relating to free speech, the national constitution and Sharia law prevail over the UN declaration. This prevents these nations from ratifying other international agreements, such as the 1979 Convention on the Elimination of All Forms of Discrimination against Women and the 1984 Convention against Torture.

One of the major differences between the UN Declaration and the Islamic declarations is the latter's restriction of the rights of non-Muslims. For example, in the Islamic Universal Declaration of Human Rights of 1981, the right to seek refuge and asylum is broadly guaranteed but reserved for Muslims when it comes to seeking refuge in Al-Masjid al-Haram (the sacred house of Allah) in Mecca. In a similar sense, the right to move freely in the world of Islam is reserved for "all Muslims," which effectively means that non-Muslims are allowed to be excluded from the holy cities of Saudi Arabia. Another crucial difference between the UN Declaration and the Muslim declarations is in matters of sexual equality. The Islamic declarations treat sexual equality only in terms of human dignity and do not give Muslim women the right to marry non-Muslim men.

THE APPLICATION OF HUMAN RIGHTS

The retention by Muslim states of the death penalty and corporal punishment has drawn sharp criticism from the West. Supporters defend it by reference to the Koran, which, while promoting respect for life, also sanctions killing under certain circumstances and corporal punishment, especially in cases of theft or adultery. However, except in Saudi Arabia and Sudan, such extreme sanctions are not invariably enforced; most Muslim countries, while retaining the option of these sanctions in extreme cases, have adopted penal codes based on more flexible Western models.

Based on an analysis of the relationship between Islam, democracy, and individual rights in 23 predominantly Muslim countries, Daniel E. Price argued in *Islamic Political Culture, Democracy, and Human Rights: A Comparative Study* (1999) that the political culture does not have a significant

In the seventh century, the earliest Muslims, under the tutelage of Muhammad, promoted the rights of women to a level that they did not reach in the West for several hundred years.

influence on levels of democracy and protection of these rights. The type of regime (democratic or authoritarian; secular or religious) does not necessarily imply the existence or absence of fundamental rights and civil liberties. Some countries—such as Egypt, Libya, and Syria—adopt autocratic and authoritarian policies; others—notably Jordan, Morocco, and Saudi Arabia—are more liberal monarchies. A third group of nations have democratic systems. They may be secular, as in Turkey, multisectarian, as in Lebanon, or religious, as in Iran.

In Syria and Saudi Arabia, opposition to the regimes is severely punished and human rights violations are widespread. However, Syria protects its religious minorities, and Saudi Arabia has allowed the introduction of compounds on its territory for Western and Arab non-Muslim workers to live in full freedom. In 1923, the bourgeoisie and the army joined forces to create modern Turkey, a secular state that has since developed economically but has continued to violate human rights and suppress democracy.

WOMEN'S RIGHTS

In the seventh century, the earliest Muslims, under the tutelage of Muhammad, promoted the rights of women to a level that they did not reach in the West for several hundred years. Until the lifetime of the Prophet, women in the Arabian Peninsula had been the property of men; they had no say in whom they married, and they were not allowed to inherit property. Under Islam, female infanticide was outlawed and the rights of women in marriage, divorce, and matters of inheritance were significantly increased. These changes were carried out in accordance with the strictures of the Koran.

Today, however, the status of women in many parts of the Muslim world is again restricted. For example, family law in Egypt and Morocco is operated according to a code that treats women as legal minors under the guardianship of male members of their families. The governments of those and other Muslim countries routinely join forces with religious figures in order to curtail women's rights, including their sexual autonomy. Consensual sex outside marriage is criminalized in many countries. In Jordan and Morocco, women who are thought to have "dishonored" their family have been beaten, shot, or stabbed to death by male relatives. Such actions do not go unpunished, but the perpetrators can claim mitigating circumstances, and those whose pleas are accepted usually serve reduced jail sentences.

In many countries in the Muslim world, women's rights to vote, to acquire identity cards or passports, to work, and to travel are granted only with the consent of a spouse or another male family member. Most Islamic countries have permitted only fathers to pass citizenship on to their children. The exceptions are Iran, Tunisia, and, to a limited extent, Egypt, where women can now register their children even if the father's identity is unknown. However, Egyptian women married to non-nationals are denied this fundamental right. Also, in many Muslim countries, no specific laws exist to penalize domestic violence, which is generally regarded as a private matter. Few shelters exist to protect battered women. Spousal rape has not been criminalized; husbands have an absolute right to have sex with their wives at any time. Penal codes in several countries also contain provisions that authorize the police and judges to drop charges against a rapist if he agrees to marry his victim.

Violence and discrimination against migrant women and members of minority groups are also problematic. Non-Muslim women in many countries cannot inherit from their Muslim spouses and are routinely denied custody of their children in cases of divorce. National labor codes that protect

migrant labor also specifically exclude domestic workers, who are predominantly female. Migrant workers in Bahrain and Saudi Arabia have very few civil and legal rights, and, in the view of many jurists, their status is tantamount to slavery. Many countries in the region have also failed to protect the rights of women who are trafficked from eastern Europe and Asia to work in the local sex industries. While little is done to stop the traffickers, the victims of the trade risk being penalized for their actions under laws that prohibit prostitution and extramarital sex.

Although many nations in the Muslim world have ratified the 1979 UN Convention on the Elimination of All Forms of Discrimination against Women, some countries have not adopted the charter because of what they argue are its inconsistencies with Sharia law. Nevertheless, women have always played a vital role in Muslim communities, and not only in traditional roles. Early Muslim women worked as scholars, teachers, and nurses. Among the most famous of them were: Aisha bint Abi Bakr (died 678), the second wife of Muhammad, who became a teacher and a narrator of the Hadiths (sayings of Muhammad); Nusaybah bint Ka'ab, a warrior contemporary of the Prophet; and Rabia al-Adawiyya (d. 801), an Iraqi who is regarded as one of the first Sufis (Islamic mystics).

In modern times, despite women's inferior legal status prohibiting their full participation in public and political life, several Muslim women have become members of parliaments, ministers, and heads of state. Tansu Çiller was Turkey's first woman prime minister (1993–1995) and the first female without a family political connection to head a country with a

Muslim majority. Benazir Bhutto (1953–2007) was the first elected female head of a Muslim state, having twice been prime minister of Pakistan (1988–1990; 1993–1996). Today, the only Muslim states in which women remain disfranchised are Saudi Arabia, where only men can vote, and Brunei, where no one can vote. At the other end of the scale, the majority-Muslim state of Azerbaijan in central Asia has had women's suffrage since 1918.

ISLAMIC FEMINISM

Modern Islamic feminism began in the late 19th century and advanced women's rights in Egypt, Iran, Lebanon, Syria, and Turkey. Islamic feminists may be divided into two broad categories: secular activists, who promote women's rights for humanitarian reasons; and religious feminists, who advocate reforms in the Islamic discourse. The latter movement has grown in strength and number since the 1990s, when women were first admitted to the Islamic university of Al-Azhar in Egypt, and has since spread to Iran, where feminist militancy has increased under the leadership of, among others, the human rights lawyer Shirin Ebadi (b. 1947).

Islamic feminism contends that gender equality is consistent with the Koran's demand that all humans are equal. However, that interpretation of the Muslim scripture is disputed by men who fear losing their privileges and by women who are concerned about the loss of male protection. Other opponents claim that feminism is a Western construct that anti-Muslim forces are attempting to impose on the world of Islam.

While hostility remains, the terms "Islamic feminism" and "Islamic feminists" are gaining increasing acceptance. Islamic feminism has become an integral part of the political philosophy of progressive Islam

A Muslim student hangs up posters at a college in Kolkata, India, during the 2005 Stop Violence Against Women and Girls campaign. The month-long awareness-raising initiative was organized by Swayam, a women's rights organization.

Toujan Faisal, a human rights activist and Jordan's first female member of parliament. In 2002 she was given an 18-month jail sentence for criticizing the prime minister. After a month on hunger strike, Toujan Faisal was granted a pardon by King Abdullah II but banned from standing for public office.

that emerged in South Africa in the 1990s and spread to several other countries, including the United States, where it led to the formation of the Progressive Muslim Union. The first international conference on Islamic feminism—held in October 2005 in Barcelona, Spain—brought together participants from several Muslim nations, including Ziba Mir-Hosseini and Qudsiyya Mirza from Iran, Aziza al-Hibri from Lebanon, Asma Barlas and Riffat Hassan from Pakistan, and the African American theologian Amina Wadud from the United States.

WOMEN IMAMS

There is no verse in the Koran that explicitly prohibits women from being imams, and over the centuries several leading clerics—from Al-Tabari (838-923) and Ibn al-Arabi (1165-1241) to the modern mufti of Egypt, Sheikh Ali Gomaa—have given their support to the practice. However, most Islamic clerics have been intractably opposed to it and, as a result, the recent activism in pursuit of women's freedom to lead prayers in mosques—a movement known as "gender jihad"—has aroused great controversy.

In the vanguard of the campaign were the Muslims of South Africa, where, in the mid-1990s, Amina Wadud became the first woman to make the traditional speech before Friday prayers at the Claremont mosque in Cape Town. A decade after Wadud's historic action, gender jihad had spread to the United States and Canada as Muslims of both sexes demanded women's right to become imams and, in another departure from established practice, their freedom to worship in the main body of the mosque rather than in a specially designated area away from the men.

Then, on March 18, 2005, Amina Wadud led the Friday prayers in the Synod House of the Cathedral of Saint John the Divine in New York City, which was transformed into a mosque for the occasion. This and another similar event shortly afterward in which Naïma Gouhaï, an Italian woman of Moroccan heritage, led a prayer in Siena, Italy, sparked controversy throughout the Muslim world. However, not all the reactions were negative. In April 2006 the Moroccan Ministry of Habous (the land registry) and Islamic Affairs awarded imam status to 50 women, although their powers are restricted: they cannot lead prayers, a privilege reserved for men in accordance with a fatwa (decree) issued by the High Council of Ulemas in Morocco.

CHILDREN'S RIGHTS

In 1994 the member states of the Organization of the Islamic Conference (OIC) adopted the Declaration on Rights and Child Protection in the Islamic World. The document asserted the absolute right to life by banning abortion, the rights of the newborn, regardless of sex, the right to social security, health, cultural and psychological protection, including the principle of equal treatment of children and the prohibition of all forms of discrimination against them; the rights to property and education, as well as particular care in "extraordinary circumstances," such as those that affect children who have lost a parent or parents, been abandoned, or suffer from disabilities, or who are refugees or prisoners in times of war or natural disasters. The OIC recommended that all these principles should be enshrined in national and international law.

Eleven years after the declaration, a joint report by the OIC and the UN International Children's Emergency Fund (UNICEF), entitled *Investing for Children in the Islamic World*, addressed in greater detail the problems afflicting many infants and young people in the region.

The OIC countries account for one-quarter of the world's children and have the highest child mortality rates in the world. Around 4.3 million children under age five die each year from preventable diseases and malnutrition in OIC countries, about 60 percent of them before their first birthday. Only 14 of the 57 OIC member states are on track to achieve the objective of the Millennium Development Goals (MDGs) on child mortality. The greatest hardships are endured by children living in the Islamic countries of sub-Saharan Africa, where the infant mortality rate is twice the global average.

In many OIC countries, high fertility rates and inadequate access to medical care contribute to the highest maternal mortality rate in the world. In African OIC states, the average is one death in every 15 pregnancies, while globally the average is one death in 74 pregnancies. More than one-third of all children living

Ni Putes Ni Soumises (Neither Prostitutes Nor Submissives) is an action group set up in 2002 by French Muslim women to resist pressure to wear the hijab and to enter forced marriages.

in the states of the OIC, with the exception of the Arab region, suffer from persistent malnutrition. HIV/AIDS has a devastating effect on African OIC states, in which the prevalence rate of the disease among adults is 5.4 percent (7.9 million cases). Prevalence rates in the Arab and Asian member nations of the OIC are low by comparison—0.3 percent and 0.1 percent, respectively.

In education, school attendance at primary level is less than 60 percent in 17 OIC member states. More than half of the adult population is illiterate in some of these countries, and the proportion can reach 70 percent among women. In the African OIC member states, 4 out of 10 children do not attend school. This is also true of 25 percent of children in Arab member states of the organization. The OIC/UNICEF report urged governments to work in partnership with regional and

international financial institutions, which should provide funding, and with the private sector, which should provide both funding and technical expertise. A significant increase in development assistance is needed, with the richest OIC member states helping the poorest.

Another important initiative was a manual, produced in 2005 by UNICEF and the International Centre for Islamic Studies and Research on Population at Al-Azhar University in Egypt. The manual, entitled *Children in Islam, Child Care, Protection, and Development*, includes articles written by researchers, together with extracts of verses from the Koran and traditional sources, offering advice on children's rights to health, education, and protection. An older publication, entitled *Child Care in Islam* and published in 1984, focused mainly on the survival of children.

Since then, new problems threatening the welfare of children have been most acute, including female genital mutilation, forced labor, child trafficking, and HIV/AIDS. The manual shows that harmful traditional practices, often wrongly associated with Islam, such as female circumcision and discrimination in education, are not mentioned in the Koran and have no basis in Islamic law. The new manual reflects the broader vision of childhood that has emerged since 1984. The 1989 UN Convention on the Rights of the Child has been ratified by all Islamic nations except Somalia.

RELIGIOUS MINORITIES AND FREEDOM

With regard to religious minorities in the Muslim world, Islam has historically shown tolerance not only toward the Peoples of the Book (Christians and Jews) but also to polytheists (believers in many gods), especially the Hindus in southern Asia. True Islam respects all religions and forbids any coercion in religion, and several verses of the Koran explicitly require that freedom of religion should be given to non-Muslims, not only to the Peoples of the Book. While the constitutions of the majority of modern Muslim states make Islam the state religion, non-Muslim minorities have freedom of religion and the same political rights as Muslims. The principal exception to this general rule is with regard to the head of state, who in most cases must be a Muslim.

In spite of the traditional tolerance of Islam toward other faiths, many Muslim nations still found difficulty in agreeing to the 1948 UN Universal Declaration of Human Rights. Their main objection was to the original draft of Article 18, which concerns religious freedom. The UN responded by altering it to make explicit

SHIRIN EBADI: HUMAN RIGHTS ACTIVIST AND NOBEL LAUREATE

Shirin Ebadi (born 1947) is an Iranian lawyer who, in 2003, became the first Muslim woman to be awarded the Nobel Peace Prize. After graduating with a law degree from the University of Tehran, Ebadi became in 1974, at the age of 27, the first female judge in Iran. She was later president of the court of Tehran for four years.

After the 1979 revolution in Iran, which brought the fundamentalist ayatollah Ruhollah Khomeini to power and resulted in the establishment of an Islamic republic, Ebadi was forced to leave her post, the new ruler having decreed that women were too emotional and irrational to preside over a court. For many years she could only work as a secretary in the court she once presided over. In 1992 she was permitted to resume her career as a lawyer and started her own practice specializing in human rights cases. Ebadi also teaches courses on human rights law at Tehran University.

Ebadi's work concentrates on defending the rights of women and children and providing legal aid to victims of persecution in spite of the threats to which she has often been subjected. She is the founder of the Association for Children's Rights in Iran, the author of several books on women's rights, refugees, and children, and the recipient of the French Legion of Honor as well as numerous awards from international human rights groups. According to Ebadi, historical experience has clearly shown that, without human rights, no democracy can emerge, nor can economic development be achieved. She advocates that human rights should be a part of every culture and enshrined in constitutions.

reference to the freedom to change one's religion. This change was made at the specific request of Lebanon, which had for many years followed a policy of accepting people fleeing persecution because of their beliefs, in particular for having changed their religion.

In its revised form, Article 18 now reads as follows: "Everyone has the right to freedom of thought, conscience and religion; this right includes freedom to change his religion or belief, and freedom, either alone or in community with others and in public or private, to manifest his religion or belief in teaching, practice, worship and observance."

Yet although this altered formula placated one Muslim country, it aroused opposition from others that objected to the additional clause. In many Islamic countries, Christians and Jews remain second-class citizens—they have limited rights and are subject to laws that limit their religious freedoms. For example, in Egypt, the Christian Copts are not allowed to build new churches and are discouraged from repairing their existing places of worship. Elsewhere, attempts at evangelism (persuading other people to change their faith) are frowned on. In Morocco, for example, those who attempt to proselytize (convert) Muslims can be punished with

Amina Wadud (center right) leads a group of women at New York City's first public, mixed-gender Muslim prayer service that was held at Synod House, Cathedral of Saint John the Divine, on March 18, 2005.

SLAVERY IN ISLAM

Slavery was well established in Arabia long before the rise of Islam, and Muslims merely maintained a traditional practice, which they quickly spread all the way from northern Africa in the west to Indonesia in the east.

The main Islamic societies in which slavery predominated were the Ottoman Empire, the Crimean khanate, and the Sokoto caliphate in the lands in western Africa that are now part of Nigeria.

One of the distinctive characteristics of slavery in the Muslim world was that servitude did not necessarily prevent people from rising to positions of power. Some slaves even became rulers, as in eastern Iran, India (the Delhi sultanate), and Egypt (the Mamluk dynasty).

In the 19th and 20th centuries, a series of treaties and international agreements largely put an end to slavery, although some Muslim countries were slow to abolish it—Mauritania made the practice illegal only in 1981. Some critics argue that there are still practices of slavery in the contemporary Muslim world, taking the form of human trafficking, labor exploitation, and domestic workers in the Gulf region and especially in Saudi Arabia. However, many commentators emphasize that these practices are not based on Islamic belief but are the consequences of wars in Sudan and Somalia.

prison sentences of between six months and three years. Repudiation of Islam is still considered to be a crime worthy of death, whereas Muslims have the right to proselytize others. Still, most Islamic countries claim to be tolerant and to guarantee freedom of religion (Egypt, Jordan, Syria), which is part of their laws or constitutions. In Syria, there are many Christians in the government, Easter and Christmas holidays are officially recognized, and atheism is permitted.

Elsewhere, there are many other differences between the principles and the practice of religious liberty. In Indonesia, for instance, freedom of religion is a mandate of the 1945 Constitution, but the government continues to discriminate against the adherents of Ahmadiyah, a minority Islamic Sufi sect that the Indonesians do not consider an official religion. In Yemen, members of the Al-Akhdam minority are subjected to social inequality based on ethnic prejudices because they are of African descent in a country with an Arab majority. A similar case can be observed in northern Nigeria, where the institutionalization of Sharia law has implications for the constitutionally guaranteed rights of non-Muslim minorities. Muslim objections to the methodology of human rights discourse stem mainly from the needs to maintain the integrity of the family, to safeguard the interests of the community in addition to those of the individual, and to preserve religious beliefs as manifested in rituals and in daily life. According to some scholars, the core issue in preserving Muslim values without infringing the rights of the minorities lies in finding a synergy for simultaneous application of Sharia and human rights. Therefore, reconciling Islam with the protection of non-Muslim rights in Muslim-majority constitutional democracies should present fewer difficulties and social tensions than currently prevail.

The civil war and famine in Darfur, Sudan, have affected all the population, but women and children have been particularly badly hit. This photograph was taken in 1991.

FUTURE PROSPECTS

In order for freedoms and fundamental rights to be promoted and protected in the Muslim world at all levels, reforms must be contextualized to local requirements. Failing that, the local population may regard them with suspicion as an extension of foreign interests. To prevent that from happening, many commentators advocate a two-phase response, one phase being politico-legal and the other phase being sociocultural. The former calls for reforms within the political regimes and the judicial systems in most Muslim countries, especially those under authoritarian regimes, whether religious or secular. The latter argues that Islam—while not the sole factor in

APOSTASY

Apostasy—a believer's rejection of his or her former faith—is a problem in all religions. It is discussed in several passages of the Koran, in which there is a specific term to define each type of apostate. A Muslim who turns his or her back on Islam is known as *murtadd*; one who converts to another religion is described as *irtidad;* and one who moves from faith to unbelief (*kufr*) is termed *ridda.*

In strict Islamic societies, Muslims may be accused of apostasy if they fail to pray the prescribed number of times every day without good reason or special dispensation. If two male witnesses testify in front of a judge to such negligence, the offender may be declared an apostate. In that case, there is a wide range of possible penalties, including imprisonment, although different schools of Islamic law have different interpretations. The Maliki school, for example, recommends leniency to women who are pregnant or nursing a baby. The Shiites, however, may insist on a procedure by which an apostate woman is imprisoned and beaten every three days, or even daily, until she recants.

Scholars disagree on the difference between the apostasy of a convert to Islam and that of a person born and raised as a Muslim. They also hold different views on the appropriateness of the death penalty for a penitent apostate. According to strict Shiite theology, repentance is not sufficient to revoke the death penalty. This may be the reason that the death sentence pronounced on Salman Rushdie by Ayatollah Khomeini in a fatwa (decree) of 1989 was not revoked when Rushdie publicly renounced his novel, *The Satanic Verses*, and officially apologized for those passages in it that had been condemned as blasphemous.

In some countries, any denial of any principle of Muslim belief is considered apostasy. If one denies the unity of God or expresses a belief in reincarnation, one is guilty of apostasy. Certain acts are also deemed acts of apostasy, for example, treating a copy of the Koran disrespectfully. Many Muslim theologians take the view that, under Islamic law, apostates must be put to death, although some modern scholars have argued that, in the Koran, apostates are threatened with punishment only in the next world.

Only two Islamic countries address the issue of apostasy explicitly in their penal codes—Mauritania and Sudan. However, the absence of any mention of apostasy in other penal codes does not imply that a Muslim in the country concerned is free to leave his religion. In practice, such loopholes in the secular laws are closed by religious laws. For instance, in June 2008, four Algerians who converted to Christianity were fined and imprisoned for apostasy, while two others were set free after renouncing their conversion.

Families sometimes ostracize their apostate members and, in extreme cases, may take justice into their own hands by murdering the offender.

ensuring reforms in human rights in Muslim states—can be constructively employed as a vehicle for improving human rights. For such reforms to have the desired long-term effects, they must be rooted in the culture of the society, because it is through culture (and thereby through religion) that most people give meaning to their daily life and political life.

In that sense, *ijtihad* (personal judgment applied to Sharia or the interpretation of Islamic tradition) is to be encouraged. Many clerics and community leaders currently oppose human rights and civil liberties in the Muslim world. Thus, an evolutionary interpretation and a contextual interpretive approach are needed. Tunisia, for example, has applied *ijtihad* to a progressive response to the question of polygamy. Islamic feminism uses *ijtihad* to advance women's rights. In Iran, the reformist thinker and philosopher Abdolkarim Soroush (born 1945) is one of a new generation of theologians who openly speak out in favor of human rights. The group, which is supported by forces of social reform in the Islamic Republic, is significant not only for Iran but also for the whole Muslim world. In Soroush's view, a political system can be both Islamic and democratic; the Koran is open to interpretation; Islam and human rights are compatible; human rights are the commandments of human reason and cannot be in conflict with religion because nothing unreasonable can be God's will. Therefore, numerous severe punishments currently practiced under

Islamic law—such as the amputation of hands for stealing in Saudi Arabia—need no longer be applied.

Civil societies—especially youth organizations—play a major role in the promotion and implementation of human rights. Youth constitutes the majority of the population in the Muslim world. More than half of the Arab world's population are under the age of 25, and yet young people are underrepresented politically and they are rarely consulted during the formulation of development strategies and reforms; Muslim youth remains a largely untapped resource.

Even before the terrorist atrocities of September 11, 2001, there was agitation in many parts of the Muslim world for increased political participation, both domestically and on the international stage. In Algeria, Egypt, Indonesia, Iran, Libya, Morocco, Pakistan, Syria, Tunisia, Turkey, and Yemen, independent societies have been

Police guard the gate of a mosque of the minority Muslim Ahmadiyah sect in Dhaka, Bangladesh, in 2004. The Ahmadiyahs endure discrimination and are sometimes threatened by traditionalists, who regard their views as un-Islamic.

formed to pursue those objectives. Centers for human rights studies have been founded. These include the Ramallah Center for Human Rights Studies in Palestine, the Cairo Institute for Human Rights Studies in Egypt, and the Damascus Center for Theoretical and Civil Rights Studies in Syria. One result of the work of these organizations is the Alexandria Declaration, adopted by Arab intellectuals in March 2004 in Egypt, which called for political, social, economic, and cultural reforms in the Arab world and demanded the release of political prisoners, freedom of the press, fair elections, and several freedoms based on the 1948 UN Universal Declaration of Human Rights. The Alexandria Declaration also urges all Arab governments to modernize the Arab Charter on Human Rights and to sign international treaties on human rights abuses, including all conventions relating to the rights of women.

The Alexandria Declaration is the most prominent of numerous initiatives that embody hopes for the realization of noble ideals. That none of the signatories to the agreement is a government reduces its short-term effectiveness, but it is nevertheless optimistically regarded as a clear sign of pressure from below, which is historically often an effective catalyst of change.

If human rights—in the sense of the term that is most widely understood in the West—are to be adopted throughout the Muslim world without being open to the charge that they are instruments of neocolonialism, the change can be effected only through the contributions of non-state actors—individuals and small groups of independent activists rather than government bodies. Such people's efforts will take numerous forms, including declarations, militancy, monitoring human rights and denouncing violations, and signaling improvements, thereby complementing the work of international organizations. Alternatively, advances might be made through teaching, the publication and widespread distribution of documents on democracy, human rights, citizenship, and related issues.

The West and the Muslim world are deeply suspicious of each other's rationale and motives. However, these problems are a challenge rather than an insurmountable obstacle.

It must be noted that, even in normal circumstances, such a process is easier to describe than to implement, particularly in states with effective agencies of repression. The circumstances in the aftermath of September 11, 2001, and the consequent War on Terror in Afghanistan and Iraq conducted by the United States and its allies are anything but normal. The West and the Muslim world are deeply suspicious of each other's rationale and motives. However, these problems are a challenge rather than an insurmountable obstacle. Most people agree that the principles of human rights are plainly enshrined in the Koran and, if that is the consensus view, it must be possible for them to be implemented throughout the Muslim world. For that to happen, there must be dialogue and partnership between all social and political forces at international, national, and personal levels.

See Also

Men and Women 60-83 ❖ Wearing the Veil 84-87 ❖ Islamic Law 108-129 ❖ States, Politics, and Political Groups 144-163 ❖ Civil Rights in the United States 188-191 ❖

Civil Rights in the United States

As a relatively recent immigrant community that has often been associated with terrorism, Muslims in the United States face unique challenges to their civil and religious rights.

F ollowing September 11, 2001, Muslims in the United States became the focus of unprecedented levels of government surveillance, public scrutiny, and media attention. Although Islamic organizations, mosque leaders, and Muslim scholars immediately condemned the attacks, Islam and ordinary Muslims became closely associated with terrorism in the minds of many Americans.

Non-Muslim political and religious leaders denounced any suggestion that Muslims in the United States should be blamed for the attacks, but inflammatory and hostile rhetoric from some public figures is believed to have fueled ill feeling toward Muslim-Americans. In some cases, this hostility was expressed in the form of violence or abuse. There were no large-scale violent reprisals against the Muslim community in the United States, but isolated incidents of hate crimes, ranging from verbal abuse to murder, were reported with greatly increasing frequency in the weeks following September 11th. At times this hostility spilled over to individuals who share outward similarities with Muslims, including Christian Arabs, Druze, Sikhs, and Hindus. The frequency of these attacks went into decline after a few weeks, but even after several years, attacks on Muslim Americans were still more common than they had been before 2001.

In addition to these incidents, the reaction of law enforcement, government agencies, and private institutions to the attacks was a cause for concern for many Muslims. Public anxiety about the possibility of further attacks led to instances of discrimination against Muslims following the September 11 terrorist attacks. This can be most clearly seen in the instances of Muslims being removed from domestic flights due to the concerns of passengers or crew. There were also accounts of disproportionately high numbers of Muslims, or people who looked like Muslims, being stopped and questioned by police near sensitive locations such as transport hubs, landmarks, or bridges.

CONTROVERSIAL LAWS

The acts of discrimination described above represent the result of the judgment of individuals, rather than matters of policy or procedure. Although many argued that these events were influenced by public hostility directed at American Muslims, these discriminatory acts were not condoned by mainstream political figures.

The issue of civil rights began to be raised when provisions allowing racial profiling and the surveillance of Muslim communities were approved as part of new law enforcement guidelines established to counter terrorist threats. These new provisions were seen by many as being implicitly targeted at Muslim Americans. A Department of Justice briefing from February 2002, for example, while asserting that "America has a moral obligation to prohibit racial profiling" in the practices of law enforcement agencies, goes on to state that "race and ethnicity may be used in terrorist identification" and that "federal law enforcement officers who are

Students in Berkeley, Calfornia, protest random attacks on Muslims and groups associated with Muslims following September 11, 2001.

On September 12, 2001, police protect a mosque in New York. In the immediate aftermath of the September 11 attacks, law enforcement agencies were deployed across the country to protect Muslim communities and buildngs against possible retaliatory attacks.

protecting national security or preventing catastrophic events (as well as airport security screeners) may consider race, ethnicity, alienage, and other relevant factors." When placed in the context of fears about Islamic extremism, some argue that these guidelines constitute official permission for law enforcement and security officials to discriminate against Muslims.

THE NO-FLY LIST

Before September 11, 2001, the FBI maintained a list of 16 terrorist suspects who were banned from boarding flights to or in the United States. By November, this list had grown to around 400 names and continued to grow as various intelligence agencies added names from their own watch lists. As of spring 2009, the list had exceeded a million names, representing the names and known aliases of around 400,000 individuals. Not all of these names are of people banned from flying; the list also includes individuals whom airlines are advised to extensively search and question before permitting them to board a plane.

One 2006 investigation found that, in addition to terrorist suspects, the no-fly list contained the names of mainstream political figures, dead or incarcerated terrorists, and thousands of others with only tenuous or unsubstantiated links to suspect organizations. This situation was brought to widespead public attention in 2004, when a flight carrying British musician and Muslim convert Yusuf Islam (formerly known as Cat Stevens) was diverted to an alternate destination when it was learned that he was on board. On landing, Yusuf Islam was questioned by the FBI and ultimately was refused entry to the United States on the basis of his work, six years previously, with a charity that was suspected of having links to the Palestinian terrorist group Hamas.

The list provided to airport security teams gives little information other than names, with the result that all passengers who share the name of someone on the list may be subject to interrogation and search and can be refused permission to board their flight. It has been argued that this violates the civil rights of many thousands of Muslim and Arab Americans because Muslim or Arabic names (each with numerous alternate spellings) are believed to form the majority of the names on the list. Between 2007 and 2009 there were around 51,000 complaints by individuals who had been detained because their name appeared on the no-fly list. All but 830 of these complaints were cases of mistaken identity, and 150 of those who were actually on the list were subsequently removed following further investigation.

GOVERNMENT AND NONGOVERNMENTAL EFFORTS TO PROTECT CIVIL RIGHTS

United States government officials have undertaken a number of initiatives to defend Muslim civil rights. At the federal level, the U.S. Equal Employment Opportunity Commission issued guidelines in 2002 to clarify the workplace rights of Muslims, Arabs, South Asians, and Sikhs. Under the auspices of the United States Commission on Civil Rights (USCCR), advisory committees in several states arranged briefings on Muslim Americans' rights and security in the aftermath of September 11, 2001. In addition, USCCR committees in Illinois, New York, and the Washington, D.C., area held in-depth forums to examine topics such as racial and religious profiling; police responsiveness to hate crimes and harassment of Muslims; and reduced public oversight of law enforcement activities.

Several recommendations emerged from these forums, including encouraging positive relations between Muslim communities and law enforcement, refining the no-fly list to better identify genuine threats, and an end to practices associated with racial profiling. Although steps have been taken to incorporate these recommendations into the practices of law enforcement and government agencies, many Muslim organizations still report widespread problems with racial profiling by law enforcement and airport security.

Islamic nongovernmental organizations have also been active in promoting Muslim civil rights. The Council on American-Islamic Relations, headquartered in Washington, D.C., is the largest of these organizations. Other groups include the Muslim Public Affairs Council, the American Muslim Council, the Islamic Society of North America, the Muslim Students Association, the American-Arab Anti-Discrimination Committee, and the Islamic Circle of North America. These groups have provided information and advice to government agencies and the media on topics related to Islam and the U.S.

Muslim population; supported various community programs and education initiatives; and provided Muslims with legal representation in a number of civil rights cases.

SOCIAL INCLUSION AND RELIGIOUS ACCOMMODATIONS

In December 1997, when the Islamic symbol of the star and crescent first appeared in Washington, D.C., alongside the National Christmas Tree and National Hanukkah Menorah, vandals removed the star and painted it with a red swastika. A public outcry ensued and the display was promptly restored. Since 1997 Islamic symbols have become a common part of such multicultural religious displays, reflecting the increasing social and political visibility of Muslims in the United States.

Some Islamic organizations and individuals are seeking accommodations in workplaces, communities, and schools to enable Muslims to more easily practice their faith. Issues include having times and places to perform prayers while at school or work; being excused to attend congregational services on Fridays; celebrating the two major Islamic holidays (Eid al-Adha and Eid al-Fitr); and preserving modes of dress and grooming, such as head scarves for women and beards for men.

Public schools and universities have been on the front lines in dealing with many of these expressed needs. Some schools with Muslim students schedule recess times to coincide with the Islamic noon-time prayer; others excuse students from the classroom to perform prayers. More than a dozen U.S. universities have installed washroom facilities, including footbaths, for Muslim students, faculty, and staff to engage in ritual ablutions prior to praying. In the case of state-funded educational institutions, questions have been raised as to whether the expenditure of public dollars on footbaths constitutes a breach of the separation of church and state.

Muslim parents also have shown interest in the provision of Arabic instruction. Publicly funded "Arabic-themed" schools have opened in Dearborn and Ann Arbor, Michigan; Brooklyn, New York; and Toledo, Ohio. Critics of these schools allege that teachers mix devotional instruction with academic lessons.

Chapter 9

ISLAMISM IN THE 21ST CENTURY

In the 21st century, the term Islamism *covers such concepts as radical Islam, Islamic fundamentalism, and what is often perceived as Islamic terrorism. This chapter examines the origins and agendas of Islamism and explores the reasons for unrest, poverty, and other development issues in many regions of the Muslim world.*

V ery few of the people who are labeled *Islamist* use this term in self-description. The label *Islamist* is almost always imposed on Muslim thinkers, on Islamic organizations and movements, and on some Islamic governments and political parties by outsiders who may include scholars, political commentators, and journalists. The term became popular in the late 1970s, although it had been in use since the 18th century. It has become increasingly popular since the Islamic Revolution of 1979 in Iran and was used with reference to political movements, such as the Islamic Tendency Movement in Tunisia and the Islamic Salvation Front in Algeria, in the 1980s. It has also been used to refer to the increased activity of the Muslim Brotherhood in Egypt, Sudan, and elsewhere. The word *Islamiyah* is sometimes translated as "Islamist."

Islamism has been characterized as the politicization of religion. However, while some Islamic movements operate almost entirely within the political arena, some also engage in religious activities on the basis that without self-renewal society cannot be

reformed. The Muslim Brotherhood and Hezbollah, for example, engage in religious as well as political activities and both also sponsor extensive social welfare programs. These groups represent two of the most widely known Islamist organizations, both of which have had electoral success. Of the two, Hezbollah, which has its own militia,

The label *Islamist* is almost always imposed on Muslim thinkers by outsiders.

openly employs violence. Although the Muslim Brotherhood has been accused of employing violence and of having a secret paramilitary apparatus (it was implicated in the assassination of Egypt's prime minister in 1948, the same year that its members volunteered to fight in Palestine against the nascent Israeli state), it has been breakaway groups that have engaged in what some call direct action.

An account of the origin and beliefs of the Muslim Brotherhood, for example,

A Lebanese woman holds a portrait of Hezbollah leader Hassan Nasrullah at a rally in Beirut in August 2009. The rally celebrated the third anniversary of the "Divine Victory" of Lebanon over Israel after their 34-day conflict in 2006.

serves to identify how almost all features of Islamism developed in relation to relevant background factors, including historical and political circumstances. In this way, Islamism critiques what many other Muslims believe and practice.

DEFINITIONS OF ISLAMISM

The term *Islamist* can also be used to describe the ideology of such thinkers as Sayyid Qutb (1906–1966) and Sayyid Abul A'la Mawdudi (1903–1979), although they are also often described as fundamentalists. The term *fundamentalist* is used by some Muslims in self-description, while other Muslims are suspicious of a term that derives from the self-definition of some Christians. In fact, Muslims hold as fundamental truths beliefs similar to those of Christian fundamentalists, with reference to the divine origin and infallibility of scripture. It has been claimed, therefore, that all good Muslims are fundamentalists.

The term *Islamist* is almost always used to refer to Muslims whose agenda is to establish their particular version of the Islamic state, a version that regards the Muslim community under Muhammad and the first generation of leaders as ideal. In various ways, the aim of Islamism is to replicate this golden age today. This is also how Salafist Muslims judge the authenticity of any Islamic practice or belief, asking if it was practiced or believed by the earliest generation of believers.

There is considerable overlap between Salafists and Islamists, although the two are not identical. For example, the Muwahiddun who control Saudi Arabia and have supporters across the Muslim world are Salafists, yet the Saudi regime is rarely, if ever, called Islamist. One explanation is that while there is no unanimity among Islamists about how an Islamic state would be governed, almost all see monarchy (the Saudi system) as non-Islamic. Another explanation is that the difference between rich and poor in Saudi Arabia is too extreme for a truly Islamist order, which would, in theory, create a more egalitarian and socially just society.

Islamist Islam is also referred to as political Islam. Again, however, the two are not identical. Many Muslims believe that Islam is a comprehensive system and that a society in which Muslims live as a majority should be organized as a Muslim society with laws and governance guided by Islam. However, such Muslims have a very different view of Islam than do Islamists,

Many Muslims believe that a society in which Muslims live as a majority should be organized as a Muslim society with laws and governance guided by Islam.

and subsequently their Islamic order would also be quite different. Many Muslims believe, for example, that women and minority groups should have the same rights as Muslim men and that by applying the principles behind Sharia (Islamic law) rather than traditional penalties, laws considered fully compatible with international standards of human rights can be developed.

There are also those who, although they support the concept of religious and political unity in Islam, cannot be described as Islamist. Leaders such as Mu'ammar Muhammad al-Gadhafi (born 1942) in Libya and Gamal Abdel Nasser

ZIA-UL-HAQ AND THE ISLAMIZATION PROCESS

Mohammad Zia-ul-Haq seized control of Pakistan in a military coup in 1977, promising to establish an Islamic order that he called Nizam Islami. Members of the Islamic group Jamaat-e-Islami were appointed to the cabinet and the already established Ideology Council, which guided the Islamization process.

Zia's Islamic reforms included the appointment of a nonelected Shura in 1982 and the introduction of Sharia (Islamic law), including penalties such as flogging and amputation (although this was never carried out because doctors refused to supervise) and the death penalty for apostasy. In a 1984 ordinance, Zia declared non-Islamic the Ahmadiyah movement that had been founded at the end of the 19th century and passed a law in 1986 that made defamation of Muhammad an offense carrying a maximum penalty of death. Religious schools were nationalized, and in 1988, the year in which he died, Zia declared that the Ideology Council had ruled political parties to be un-Islamic.

General Zia-ul-Haq pictured in the presidential palace in Islamabad in 1980.

(1918–1970) in Egypt use or used Islam as a political tool but share little in common with Islamists. Nasser used Islam to legitimize his policies, while his opponents denounced what he did in the name of Islam. Deciding who is and is not an Islamist is somewhat arbitrary. In Pakistan under Muhammad Zia-ul-Haq (president from 1978 to 1988) many features of an Islamist regime were in place, but Zia himself is rarely described as an Islamist because neither the policies he adopted nor the measures he implemented could be so described. Islamists generally advocate that an authentic Islamic state will emerge only when Sharia is fully implemented.

Islamists may refer to the use of *shura* (consultation) as a decision-making mechanism, but many are critical of Western-style democracy, which, they say, usurps God's sovereignty (*hakimiyya*) and God's law (*hukum Allah*) with those of women and men. Islamists often speak of an authentic Muslim society as one governed by a traditional interpretation of Sharia, for example, the punishment of theft with amputation and apostasy from Islam with execution. People simply apply God's law and pass regulations to effect its implementation.

Islamists are often accused of being vague about how an emir (commander) or

Ruhollah Khomeini emerged as leader of Iran after overthrowing the last Shah, Mohammad Reza Pahlavi, in 1979. Khomeini became Iran's Supreme Leader, the highest-ranking political and religious authority in the country.

authority and leadership based on personal reputations for piety and learning. Khomeini's position as Supreme Leader was enshrined in the 1979 referendum on the constitution, but Omar, the de facto head of state from 1996 to 2001 with the title of *amir al-mu'minin* (commander of the faithful; a title of the former caliphs), was never formally elected to any position. The official name of the Taliban state was the Islamic Emirate of Afghanistan. Osama bin Laden, among whose aims is the restoration of the global caliphate, regarded the Taliban regime as the only legitimate Islamic government, making Omar, in his opinion, the only legitimate Muslim head of government.

Islamism has been defined as the belief that Islam is both a political and a religious system or as belief in the unity of religion and the state (*din wa-dawla*). However, this definition can be problematic since, with the exception of secularist Muslims, almost all Muslims believe in the unity of religion and politics. Islamist Muslims, however, are also interested in issues of authenticity and identity and believe in a particular type of politics, which includes the application of Sharia as it was traditionally interpreted. They believe that the solutions to society's problems are to be derived from Islam, not from elsewhere. Western systems, including those established in many postcolonial contexts, are rejected as alien and foreign.

ISLAMISM AND RADICAL ISLAM

Islamism is also closely identified with the term *radical Islam*, although they have their differences. For example, some Islamists, such as most members of the Muslim Brotherhood and of Jamaat-e-Islami, use constitutional means, propaganda, education, and participation in the electoral system to advance their agendas. While radicals may

caliph (deputy) would be chosen. Jamaat-e-Islami and Hizb-ut-Tahrir, for example, accept some form of election but would restrict candidacy to a carefully vetted list of people considered sufficiently pious and knowledgeable to lead. In Iran and Afghanistan, two regimes that can be considered Islamist, the choice of leader was circumstantial. There is a view that the leader should be the "best person." Ruhollah Khomeini in Iran and Mullah Omar in Afghanistan emerged largely unquestioned and unchallenged as leaders, rather like Zaydi imams, with their encourage or commit acts of terror, moderate Islamists have condemned them. The practice of dividing Islamists into politically acceptable "moderates" and unacceptable "radicals" is often controversial. Many in the Western world consider the aims of Islamism to be fundamentally incompatible with democratic society and reject the concept of moderate Islamism, while many Muslims argue that the label "radical," and the mainstream media exclusion it brings, is often used as an undemocratic means of silencing legitimate opposition groups.

Sayyid Qutb, a leading ideologue of the Muslim Brotherhood, despised democracy, while the Brotherhood has tended to embrace democracy. In Egypt, the Muslim Brotherhood called for greater democracy and in 2005 won 20 percent of electoral votes by standing as independent candidates. Leaders of other Islamist movements have also supported democracy, although they and members of the Brotherhood are criticized by other Muslims for gaining power by democratic means, which they then intend to abolish. Nonetheless, such Islamists can be described as moderate, that is, as "not so radical," in comparison with those who use violence to prosecute their agendas. Members of Hamas, Hezbollah, and groups affiliated with Al-Qaeda who commit acts of terror and use violence, often self-defined as jihad, could be classed as radical. The terms *jihadist* and *Islamist* are also often used interchangeably.

The difference between moderate and radical Islamists lies less in their perception of what an Islamic state looks like than in their mode of operation. Moderates are more likely than radicals to speak of democracy as an acceptable system through which to choose leaders. The agenda of most if not all Islamists is to establish

Islamic government. Most focus on their own nation states, although some movements have regional agendas. Jemaah Islamiyah (which means Islamic Group), the Al-Qaeda affiliate responsible for the Bali bombings of 2002, aims to establish a pan-Islamic state order across southern Asia. Many see an Islamic state as provisional, pending the formation of a global entity based on the conviction that there is only one Muslim nation, the *ummah*. Some allow for a plurality of political parties; others argue that there is but one true party for Muslims, the party of God.

The difference between moderate and radical Islamists lies less in their perception of what an Islamic state looks like than in their mode of operation.

Islamists understand Sharia in a conservative or traditional way; therefore the status that minorities and women would have in their societies is also a contentious issue, at least for those who do not share their views. Critics argue that non-Muslims and women would be treated as second-class citizens and in ways that violate international standards of human rights. While many Muslims recognize Christianity as a type of sister-faith and Christians as "People of the Book," Islamists often argue that this special status has been forfeited by years of rejecting Islam and by Christian hostility toward the Muslim world. Today, this sentiment is represented by the War on Terror perceived as a war on Muslims, and by Western support for Israel.

PRINCIPLES OF ISLAMISM

Principles shared by moderate and radical Islamists:

- Islam does not distinguish between religion and politics.
- Western secularism and deviation from true Islam have resulted in the decline of Muslim civilization.
- Western-style systems must be replaced by authentic Islamic systems to form Nizam Islami (Islamic Order).
- Sharia must replace Western law codes.
- Inner renewal as well as social and political reform are needed as the foundation of the new society.

Principles advocated by radical Islamists:

- Israel as a state is to be dismantled.
- Governments in the Muslim world that do not apply Sharia (as interpreted by the Islamists) are unfaithful to Islam and should be opposed through jihad.
- Armed as well as peaceful jihad is a duty of all Muslims.

- The West, in alliance with Israel and in collusion with corrupt so-called Muslim governments, is waging a crusade against Islam and genuine Muslims around the world.
- Many traditional *ulama* (scholars) are complicit in propping up illegitimate regimes and are to be opposed.
- A stark distinction is drawn between true believers, who are wholeheartedly committed to the jihad, and those who fail in this duty. This is the same as the distinction between the saved and the eternally damned, the friends and enemies of God.
- The "People of the Book" are no longer entitled to the protection they formerly enjoyed under Islam, and they can be dealt with as harshly as possible to bring about their conversion. They have forfeited the special permission they previously had to remain non-Muslim.

MUSLIM TERRORISTS

Since the terrorist attacks of September 11, 2001, the connection between the Islamic faith and terrorism has been extensively examined in academic, political, and public settings. Al-Qaeda and the many similar terrorist groups operating worldwide consider their actions to be directly inspired and condoned by the teachings of the Koran. This supposed connection between Islam and violence is accepted by many Western political figures and media commentators and forms the basis of a great deal of the prejudice directed at ordinary Muslims today.

Most Islamic scholars, however, disagree with the terrorists' interpretations of the Koran and denounce the indiscriminately violent methods that groups such as Al-Qaeda claim the Koran condones. Many Muslims believe that the continual

association of Islam with terrorism, through phrases such as "Islamic militant" or "Muslim terrorist," unfairly demonizes Islamic religion. The mainstream Western media, by comparison, almost never links the Christian faith to violent acts perpetrated by Christians, even in situations where the perpetrators say they were motivated by their faith. For example, despite the prominent role that sectarian Christian identites played in the formation of terrorist groups in Northern Ireland, media discussion of the subject invariably portrayed it as a political and cultural conflict, rather than a religious one.

Many Muslims who commit acts of terror do so in the name of Allah. Yet, given that the weight of Muslim opinion condemns terrorism and acts of violence against civilians, it can be argued that Muslims who commit such acts are not truly Muslim at all. Although the Koran has been, and still is, interpreted by some Muslims to justify terrorism, the great majority argue that this interpretation is wrong. Suicide bombing has been condemned as contrary to the Koran's teaching on taking one's own life, which it proscribes. If this is so, then the term *Muslim terrorist* falsely perpetuates the notion that Islam not only permits but encourages terrorist acts, or at least that Muslims can carry out acts of terrorism with Islam's sanction and even blessing. Muslims who commit acts of terror may regard themselves as good Muslims, but other Muslims may deny them this status.

ORIGINS OF ISLAMISM

Islamism has its roots in the Salafist and Wahhabi movements. In fact, the terms Salafist and Wahhabi are often used synonymously, although Salafism has predecessors in thinkers such as Ibn Taymiyah (1263–1328) and his protégé, Ibn Kathir (1301–1373), while use of the term *Salafi* dates back to Abu Sa'd Abd al-Kareem al-Sama'ni (d. 1166).

Salafi Islam can be summed up as the belief that during the life of Muhammad, Islam was perfect and that this perfection was more or less maintained by the Salafs, the earliest generations of pious and true Muslims. This view has been described as an ahistorical understanding of history because if the earliest version of Islam was perfect, then any change, innovation, or development is a deviation (*bida*); the ideal would be to imitate or to replicate (*taqlid*) the past. However, Salafists do not argue that there is no scope for change; within the parameters of what is considered acceptable, change can occur in aspects of living covered by local custom. These aspects were

sometimes left unchanged by Muhammad because he considered what was already practiced to be consistent with or not contrary to Islam. Provided that any change in practice is also not contrary to Islam, changes can be made in some areas. Salafists also allow for a degree of adaptation to circumstances. However, changes in such matters as the set maximum penalties for crimes can never be changed, nor a man's right to marry four women.

ORIGINS OF THE WAHHABIS

The Wahhabi movement or school, known more properly as the Muwahiddun or Unitarians, began in what is now the Saudi Arabian peninsula in 1740, when Muhammad ibn Abd al-Wahhab (1703–1792), a Muslim teacher, and Muhammad ibn Saud (d. 1765), then a relatively minor local emir or chief in the central part of Arabia, made a pact agreeing that the sheikh would promote al-Wahhab's religious and political ideas, while Ibn Saud would be the movement's temporal leader. The area over which Ibn Saud ruled was at the time politically insignificant except that, unlike most of the peninsula, it lay outside the Ottoman Empire. Al-Wahhab had studied at various cities, including Mecca and Medina, developing broadly Salafist and reformist ideas. He admired Ibn Taymiyah, who had criticized what he saw as foreign influences and practices among Muslims, especially Sufi Muslims. He was highly critical of such doctrines as *hulul* (divine indwelling) and *ittihad* (union) claimed by or for the Sufi sheikhs. He denounced the Mongols as still living in *jahilia* (ignorance) even though they claimed to be Muslims. Al-Wahhab revived the term *jahilia*—used originally to denounce pre-Islamic paganism in Arabia—

Ouahabys ou Ouahabites   Almée   Enfants et femme Fellahs

Philippoteaux del.   Pierre

This mid-19th-century engraving shows a group of Wahhabi Muslims, followers of the 18th-century Muslim teacher Muhammad ibn Abd-al-Wahhab.

to describe Muslims thought to be heterodox, and it would later be popularized by Sayyid Qutb and Mawdudi in the 20th century. When al-Wahhab looked at what passed as Islam in Arabia in his time, he saw veneration of *walis* (Sufi saints), worship of Muhammad, use of omens, and pilgrimages to Sufi shrines that rivaled the hajj in popularity, while the five daily prayers went unsaid. Some Muslims even venerated stones and trees in rituals reminiscent of pre-Islamic paganism. Al-Wahhab condemned the celebration of the Prophet's birthday and of those of the Shia imams and was as critical of Shia beliefs and practices as he was of those of Sufism. Al-Wahhab also saw what he considered to be un-Islamic practices, such as adultery, passing on of property without reference to Islamic law, neglect of the needy, and a love of luxurious clothes and leisure pursuits. He frowned on what he saw as moral decadence and, in contrast, his preaching emphasized observation of the Five Pillars, and the Oneness (unity) of God, who alone is to be worshipped and to whom prayers are to be addressed.

THE FIRST AND SECOND SAUDI STATES

Legally, al-Wahhab adhered to the school of Hanbali and did not recognize the other three main schools. He thought that obedience to Sharia would reform society. Sharia could best be established and enforced by a strong leader to whom Muslims would owe their allegiance. The object of the alliance between ruler and teacher was to establish a legitimate Islamic entity. Waging a jihad to create this polity and to suppress false expressions of Islam was a religious duty. In 1763, Ibn Saud launched the Wahhabi campaign, destroying shrines and tombs and enforcing this

version of Islamic obedience on those he defeated. In 1802, the Saudi army attacked Karbala, the Shia holy city in Iraq, destroying and damaging shrines; Mecca was taken in 1803. In Medina, even the tomb of Muhammad was damaged. When Ibn Saud died, he was succeeded by his son, Abdul Aziz, who led the movement until he was killed in 1893 by a Shia assassin in retaliation for desecrating Karbala. Abdul Aziz's son Saud (d. 1814) then became emir. By 1811, Saud controlled most of Arabia, with the exception of Yemen.

Hostility to Sufism may have had political motives; the Wahhabi movement was also centralizing authority in the person of the emir, as advised by the leading Muslim scholars. Sufi teachers

Al-Wahhab thought that obedience to Sharia would reform society. Sharia could best be established and enforced by a strong leader.

challenged this centralization of authority; pilgrimages to Sufi shrines also competed with the hajj to Mecca, which the emir controlled. Other Wahhabi reforms included a ban on smoking and ostentatious dress; mosques became simple in design and did not have minarets. This polity is known as the First Saudi State with its capital in Riyadh.

The heirs of al-Wahhab, known as Al ash Shaykh, continued to provide legal and religious guidance. Nominally, Arabia was under Ottoman rule, although the small area that the Saudi family had originally ruled remained outside the Ottoman

Third Saudi State: Saudi Arabia

The Third Saudi State began in 1902 when Abdul Aziz ibn Saud retook Riyadh from the Rashid family and continued to regain lost territory. By 1926, the entire peninsula was again under Saudi rule with Abdul Aziz as king. To achieve this, he also defeated Ali bin Hussain of Mecca, whose family had held the post of sharif of Mecca since at least the 10th century. After the fall of the Ottoman Empire at the end of World War I, the British recognized the rule of Abdul Aziz ibn Saud; his sons Faisal and Abdullah were appointed kings of Iraq and Jordan by the British in 1921 (Faisal was briefly king of Syria in 1920). Abdul Aziz held separate titles as king of Nejd and as king of the Hijaz until the two kingdoms were united in 1932 as the Kingdom of Saudi Arabia.

The Kingdom of Saudi Arabia is defined as a "sovereign Arab Islamic state with Islam as its religion" and the Koran, the traditions of Muhammad, and Sharia as the "source of power." The system of government is a monarchy with rule passing to the sons of the founding king, Abdul Aziz. While descendants of al-Wahhab have occupied senior judicial posts, the role of the Al ash Shaykh, unlike that of the Saudi royal family, is not specified. The king has increasingly defined himself as a religious leader rather than as a temporal leader; recent kings have dropped use of the title "majesty" in favor of the more Islamically authentic "guardian of the Two Holy Places." The king has the power to appoint and to dismiss government ministers and is both head of state and head of government. The Saudi kings can be removed if incompetent. It is also incorrect to describe their power as absolute; they are subject, as are all Saudi citizens, to Sharia. At present, the Shura (Consultative) Council is an appointed body.

Saudi state-sponsored Islam continues the traditions and teachings of al-Wahhab; prayer is regarded as a duty that can be enforced by the state through the *mutawwiin* (religious police) whose job it is to ensure that citizens do good and refrain from wrong. This institution dates back to the First Saudi State, when the *mutawwiin* would physically drag men who were caught not praying at the set times to take part in public prayer. The sexes are strictly segregated; women cannot drive cars. Dress codes can be enforced by the *mutawwiin*. Laughing loudly in public or weeping at funerals has sometimes been banned, and music is discouraged.

Kings of Saudi Arabia

King Abdul Aziz (ibn Saud) (1876–1953) reigned September 22, 1932, to November 9, 1953. Founder of the modern state of Saudi Arabia.

King Saud (1902–1969) ruled from November 9, 1953, to November 2, 1964.

King Faisal (1906–1975) ruled from November 2, 1964, to March 25, 1975.

King Khalid (1913–1982) ruled from March 25, 1975, to June 13, 1982.

King Fahd (1923–2005) ruled June 13, 1982, to August 1, 2005.

King Abdullah (born 1924) ruled from August 1, 2005.

In 2006, the Muslim Brotherhood movement celebrated the centenary of the birth of their founder, Hassan al-Banna (pictured above the podium). Al-Banna founded the Brotherhood in 1928.

Empire. Loss of Mecca especially angered the Ottomans, who commissioned their viceroy in Egypt, Muhammad Ali (1769–1849), to quash the Wahhabi movement and to recover Arabia for the Ottomans. Effectively, the Wahhabi movement was a rebellion against the Ottomans, who described the followers of al-Wahhab as Kharijites because they are said to have killed anyone who refused to accept their form of Islam. The Wahhabi movement, like that of the Kharijites— sometimes described as the pioneers of radical Islam—asserted the right to actively claim political power from illegitimate rulers whether by persuasion or by force. Many Arabs did not fully recognize the validity of the Ottoman caliphate—partly because of a tradition that a Quraishi would always be caliph as long as a single member of that clan still lived—so they supported the rebellion.

Ali and his son Ibrahim, however, defeated the Wahhabis and brought an end to the First Saudi State. Abdullah ibn Saud, ruler from 1814 to 1818, was taken to Istanbul and beheaded. In 1824, Abdul

In a genuinely Islamic society, religion and politics are inseparably linked so that no distinction exists between them.

Aziz's nephew, Turki ibn Abdullah, recaptured territory from the Egyptians and established the Second Saudi State. Never as large as the First Saudi State, the Second Saudi State lasted until 1891 under a succession of emirs. It was then defeated by members of the rival house of Rashid, which was allied with the Ottomans. The Saudi family went into exile in Kuwait.

The Muslim Brotherhood

Hassan al-Banna, founder of the Muslim Brotherhood, was born in Egypt in 1906. Britain had governed Egypt since 1882, and in 1919 al-Banna took part in anti-British demonstrations. At this time, nationalist and pan-Arab movements were sweeping through the Arabic-speaking world. To some degree, the British were responsible for this by having built up the expectation that the sharif of Mecca would head an Arab state in

what had been Ottoman territory following their expected defeat in World War I (1914–1918). Instead, Britain, France, and Italy divided most of the region up among themselves as League of Nations mandated territory. Some in the region wanted independent nation-states on the model of western European states, inspired by the French model. This was especially influential in Egypt because of the brief French occupation (1798-1801), which impacted Egypt in several ways: it was to France that many Egyptians went to study; Egypt's modern legal system drew extensively on the Napoleonic Code; and, in 1919, an Egyptian delegation at the Paris Peace Conference demanded independence. Although independence was finally achieved in 1922, Egypt remained a monarchy under the descendants of Muhammad Ali.

In 1923, al-Banna attended Dar al-Ulum college in Cairo. Graduating in 1927, he became a public school teacher in the Suez Canal Zone, which was still under British administration. Both as a student in Cairo and as a school teacher in the Suez zone, al-Banna was appalled at the extent to which secularism and even atheism were rampant, and about the way in which Egyptians were embracing Western dress, habits, and lifestyles, while the religious scholars were doing little to challenge their behavior. Muslims were almost everywhere under colonial domination and, in comparison with Western civilization, Islamic civilization had lost its vitality. Influenced by Salafism, al-Banna was convinced that Muslims had deviated from true Islam and needed to cleanse Islam of corrupt practices, finding the answers to the problems of the Muslim world in Islam, not in the West. In the Suez zone he saw luxurious villas occupied by foreign workers next to the slums of local employees. Al-Banna disagreed with modernist thinkers that Islam could learn from and adapt ideas from the West. For him, solutions would be Islamic. As a youth, al-Banna had been initiated into membership of the Sufi order and technically remained a member, but he began to criticize Sufis for their lack of political radicalism. To promote his ideas, al-Banna founded al-Ikhwan al-Muslimun, the Muslim Brotherhood, in 1928.

The ultimate aim of the Muslim Brotherhood is to establish legitimate Islamic governance, restore the caliphate, and implement Sharia. Distrust of traditional Muslim scholars as being compromised and in collusion with illegitimate regimes has meant that the Brotherhood bypasses them in favor of its own thinkers, such as Sayyid Qutb. This is a general feature of Islamism. Qutb was not trained as a Muslim scholar and ignored classical *tafsir*, the tradition of exegesis, or how previous scholars understood a passage of the Koran. Instead, Qutb created dialogue between a passage, other passages in the Koran, and his own context. This neglect of historical scholarship follows from the Islamist belief that most of what took place in the Islamic world after the death of the earliest generations was corrupt and deviant. According to some commentators, the fact that many Islamist Muslims have backgrounds in science and engineering may also contribute to the way in which the Koran is used as if it were a manual rather than a book around which discussions of meaning and interpretation have traditionally revolved.

Sunni and Shiite Muslims congregate in Beirut, Lebanon. The rally, held in 2005, was organized by the Muslim Brotherhood to protest against the United States' activities in the Middle East and the UN Security Council Resolution 1559 to free Lebanon from Syrian occupation.

The Brotherhood has an anti-Western, antisecular ethos. It takes as a given that in a genuinely Islamic society, religion and politics are inseparably linked so that no distinction exists between them. In their view, Islam is a total system or a comprehensive way of life that embraces what non-Muslims call politics. The West and much of the Muslim world are decadent because God, God's law, and morality have been removed from the public sphere. In this context, human rights substitute for God's rights, and duty toward God plays no role in political or social discourse. However, in order to construct a genuinely Islamic order, personal renewal followed by social renewal is the first step. Training, spiritual discipline, and moral education, followed by engagement in social action, feature prominently in the organization's program.

ORGANIZATION OF THE MUSLIM BROTHERHOOD

The Brotherhood borrowed organizational ideas from the Sufi orders, whose membership has declined as the Brotherhood's membership has increased. Initially a small organization, by 1939 the Muslim Brotherhood was well established throughout Egypt, and by 1940 had a membership of about 500,000. The Brotherhood's success has been attributed to al-Banna's skilled leadership. Small cells meet to study, pray, and plan. Each cell elects one or more deputies to attend the General Organizational Conference. A Shura Council is elected every four years. Meeting three times annually, this Council appoints and directs the executive, the general leader (*masul*), and his staff, and plans the Brotherhood's activities, although its decisions can be overridden by the General Conference. National groups have a *masul* appointed by the executive. Many of the puritan aspects of Wahhabi are shared by the Brotherhood, such as a dislike of ostentatious dress, dancing, and music, as well as the segregation of the sexes and reservation of senior posts for Muslims. Non-Muslims are allowed to join the Brotherhood, but such members must pay *jizya* (a tax levied by Muslim states on non-Muslims). Al-Banna, Qutb, and other Brotherhood thinkers stress that social justice and a more egalitarian society are key aspects of the true Islamic order and condemn corruption and poverty with equal vigor.

In the late 1940s, tension between the Brotherhood and the king of Egypt reached a climax, resulting in the organization's ban in 1948, not long after members volunteered to fight in Palestine. The following year, the Egyptian prime minister, Mahmoud an-Nukrashi, was assassinated amid rumors that Brotherhood members were plotting to kill him; the Brotherhood was subsequently blamed. A year after that, al-Banna was assassinated. Many members fled to Saudi Arabia, where in 1961 they established Medina University as a substitute for Al-Azhar University in Cairo.

In Egypt, President Nasser had nationalized Al-Azhar University and other Muslim organizations so that he could influence scholars to endorse the legitimacy of his regime. Scholars belonging to the Supreme Council of Islamic Affairs gave fatwas (opinions) favorable to government policy. The Council's journal, *The Pulpit of Islam*, argued that birth control and other policies anathema to Islamism were acceptable. Nasser made use of Islamic symbols to legitimize his policies, but these were condemned and rejected by Islamists. In 1965, accused of attempting to assassinate Nasser, many members of the Brotherhood—including Sayyid Qutb— were imprisoned. Qutb was executed in 1966. Such action did little to curb the Brotherhood's activities. Under Nasser's successor, Anwar Sadat, some of the more extreme members of the Brotherhood split, forming the Jihad Organization. Sadat, like Nasser, was in their view an unbeliever, against whose false regime jihad could be waged. Sadat, who unlike Nasser preferred the separation of religion and politics,

recognized the state of Israel in 1979. Following this action, Jihadists, led by Khalid Islambuli, assassinated Sadat, saying that they had killed a tyrant or pharaoh. The Koran depicts pharoah as usurping the worship due to God alone (28:3-4; 28:38).

Under Hosni Mubarak, who succeeded Sadat in 1981, the strained relationship between government and the Brotherhood continues. The government acts quickly to intervene in disturbances between Christians and Muslims, for which Islamist agitation is blamed. However, Mubarak also released 170 of the men accused of Sadat's assassination as soon as the courts found them to be innocent. While officially banned as a political party in Egypt and other Arab countries, the Brothers have been allowed to take part in state-sponsored television debates with other Muslims whose views differ from theirs. Although the Brotherhood is unable under Egyptian law to sponsor its own political candidates, Brotherhood members standing as independent candidates won 20 percent of the vote in Egypt's 2005 elections, forming the largest opposition group.

Anwar Sadat (left, with arms outstretched) acknowledges the crowd during a motorcade. In the right of the photograph is Sadat's deputy and successor as president of Egypt, Hosni Mubarak.

An armed Hamas soldier stands guard on top of a tank. Since its inception in 1986, Hamas has been involved in both violent and political struggles to secure the establishment of a Palestinian state.

Also imprisoned in 1981 was Ayman al-Zawahiri, who went to Saudi Arabia after his release in 1984 and revived the Jihad Organization, later emerging as leader, or emir. Al-Zawahiri merged the Jihad Organization with Al-Qaeda and also formed an alliance with Iran, believing that an Iran-style Islamic revolution ought to be replicated in Egypt. A series of terrorist attacks are attributed to Jihad, including a 1993 attempt to assassinate Egypt's prime minister, which instead injured 21 people and killed a young girl. In 1999, al-Zawahiri was sentenced to death by an Egyptian court in absentia. In the United States he has been indicted for involvement in attacks

on two U.S. Embassies in Africa in 1998, during which hundreds of lives were lost.

ISLAMISM'S GLOBAL AGENDA

The global agenda of Islamism, as defined by Al-Qaeda, is to bring about the unification of the Muslim world and to free it from Western interference. Al-Qaeda also seeks to promote an uncompromising and intolerant interpretation of Islam throughout the Muslim world. Islamic countries that follow mainstream interpretations of Islam, or cooperate with Western governments, are viewed as enemies of Islam. Global Islamist ideology denounces democracy as un-Islamic and requires that its followers attempt to bring about the movement's goals through violent, direct action, such as suicide attacks.

In the West, Islamism is commonly viewed as an organized, international movement led by stateless, multinational groups like Al-Qaeda. Groups such as Hamas and Hezbollah are viewed by many Western governments as regional affiliates of these global organizations, whose actions form part of a larger plan.

Many experts, however, do not agree with this view and argue that Al-Qaeda has little or no influence over the vast majority of Islamist groups operating today. They believe that while Islamist groups exist around the world, their actions do not represent a global movement but rather a series of unconnected political and social movements, loosely associated through a shared religious emphasis. Some experts have even gone so far as to suggest that the global Islamist movement is largely a myth perpetuated by Al-Qaeda to increase the group's perceived importance.

By targeting civilians as well as military targets, Al-Qaeda and its confirmed affiliates have provoked widespread condemnation in the Muslim world. While support for regional Islamist groups has remained the same or increased in the last ten years, support for Al-Qaeda and global Islamism is thought to have dropped dramatically. As a result, some regional Islamist groups do not want to be associated with global Islamism for fear of losing public support or funding from foreign governments.

Although Islamist groups have shared goals and attitudes, they each have their own political and social objectives and often have specific sectarian or nationalist agendas that contradict the aims of global Islamism. For example, although Hamas and Hezbollah share an enemy—Israel—with Al-Qaeda, they are reluctant to form an alliance or even to be associated with global Islamism. Hamas has publically distanced itself from Al-Qaeda and on several occasions has carried out military operations against Al-Qaeda-influenced Islamist groups operating in Gaza. Like many Islamist groups, Hamas is primarily a nationalist organization and does not wish to risk losing support by getting involved in broader conflicts.

Similarly, Hezbollah, which operates out of southern Lebanon, was formed with the goal of protecting and empowering Shiite Muslims in Lebanon, the West Bank, and Gaza. Its affiliation with Shiite Islam makes it an automatic enemy of Al-Qaeda, whose Wahhabi doctrine maintains that Shiite Muslims are heretics. Furthermore, neither Hamas nor Hezbollah is a purely Muslim organization. The political wing of Hamas includes several Palestinian Christians in senior positions, and Hezbollah has a significant support base among Druze and Christian communities in Lebanon.

In addition to having different objectives for global Islamism, many Islamist groups attempt to achieve their goals through different methods. For example, both Hamas and Hezbollah have enjoyed electoral success: in January 2006, Hamas had a majority in the Assembly of the Palestinian Authority (72 out of 132 seats); Hezbollah has control of about 20 percent of municipal councils and occupies 14 out of 128 seats in Lebanon's parliament, enabling it to share in the governing coalition.

Although Islamist groups have shared goals and attitudes, they each have their own political and social objectives.

Osama bin Laden promoted his Islamist program in Afghanistan, cofounding his Service Bureau in 1984 and Al-Qaeda in 1988. Al-Qaeda shared with organizations such as the Muslim Brotherhood and Hizb-ut-Tahrir the aim of reviving a global caliphate, but in the short term its aim was to defeat the Soviets and to establish an Islamic state in Afghanistan. Among the Afghan jihadists, it was the Taliban under their emir, Mullah Omar, whom bin Laden most favored. Many of those who opposed the Soviets wanted to set up an Islamist order or state. Many also received training and finance from the United States, much of which was channeled through Zia-ul-Haq's Pakistan. When the Soviets were forced out of Afghanistan, the Taliban formed the Islamic Emirate, which lasted from 1996 until the U.S.-led invasion of 2001. Only Pakistan recognized the legitimacy of the Taliban regime, which

U.S. soldiers and their commanding officers at a military ceremony in Baghdad, Iraq. Prior to the 2003 invasion of Iraq and the capture of Iraqi president Saddam Hussein, the area pictured was used for elaborate military parades and political events by the Hussein government.

was nonetheless the de facto government. Rule was more or less through Omar's personal edicts and resembled Wahhabi-style Islam: ostentatious dress, music, and smoking were banned; women were confined to the home and forbidden from entering the workplace; girls were denied education after the age of eight; ancient Buddhist statues were destroyed as idols; and a new penalty of collapsing a wall onto anyone accused of homosexuality was innovated, despite the dislike of introducing anything new into Sharia.

Bin Laden left Afghanistan in 1992 to pursue his wider agenda but returned in 1996, having been expelled from Sudan. In 1998, despite having no training as a religious scholar, bin Laden issued his fatwa in which he declared war on the United

States both for its support of Israel and for propping up the Saudi regime, where, he declared, the presence of U.S. army bases defiled the land of the Two Sacred Places. Bin Laden sanctions any act of violence against U.S. citizens, civilian or military, using the justification that the United States is engaged in a crusade against Islam.

9/11 and the Invasions of Afghanistan and Iraq

On September 11, 2001, 19 members of Al-Qaeda flew hijacked planes into the Twin Towers of the World Trade Center in New York City and into the Pentagon in Washington, D.C. A fourth hijacked plane crashed in Pennsylvania during an attempt by passengers to regain control. Almost

3,000 people died in the attacks. The hijackers, under their leader Mohammed Atta, were carrying out bin Laden's commission that it was every Muslim's duty to kill Americans wherever they found them. Fifteen of the 19 young men were Saudi citizens, none were from poor or uneducated backgrounds, and they had all lived in the West. Atta himself had studied in Germany, where much of the planning was carried out. Many Islamists regard residence in the West as unacceptable unless it is in order to promote the Islamist agenda either in their home countries, from where they may have been banned, or against the West itself. Some critics believe that militant Islam is both present within the U.S. Muslim community and a real threat to U.S. security, with Soviet-style sleepers operating within the apparently law-abiding and even assimilated Muslim community waiting to be activated.

Following 9/11, U.S. president George W. Bush declared the War on Terror. Attributing blame for the terrorist attacks to bin Laden, U.S. forces, with a collation of allies, invaded Taliban-controlled Afghanistan on October 7, 2001. Although bin Laden escaped capture, the Taliban were defeated and a new regime established in its place, of which Hamid Karzai became president on December 22, 2001. The Taliban, however, continues not only to resist the new regime but effectively controls large areas, operating almost with impunity across the border of their former ally, now enemy, Pakistan, where Islamist Islam enjoys considerable support.

In March 2003, the U.S.-led coalition invaded Iraq, where Saddam Hussein had ruled since 1979. Between 1980 and 1988, while fighting a war against Iran, Saddam had enjoyed U.S. support, as had the Taliban

during their anti-Soviet campaign. Accused of possessing weapons of mass destruction (WMDs) that were intended for use against the West and also of supporting Al-Qaeda (which was unlikely, given that Islamists denounced Saddam as an infidel), on March 19 an international force was dispatched to find and destroy Iraq's WMDs. This was called a preemptive strike in the War on Terror. No WMDs were actually found, but the invasion resulted in the defeat of Saddam's Revolutionary Guard and army and in his own downfall. He went into hiding and was finally captured on December 14. Declaring that tyranny had ended in Iraq and that a new democratic regime would be installed, an interim Iraqi government was initially established in June 2004, followed by elections for a permanent government in October 2005. Saddam was tried for crimes against humanity committed during his presidency and was executed on December 30, 2006.

YUSUF AL-QARADAWI

The Qatar-based popular Islamist scholar and broadcaster Yusuf al-Qaradawi is a member of the Muslim Brotherhood and president of the international Union for Muslim Scholars. Although al-Qaradawi is often described as a moderate, he endorses the legitimacy of suicide attacks against any Israeli given the extremity of the oppression under which Palestinians live. However, he has also stated that not all Jews are hostile to the Palestinian cause, but that all Israelis are. Al-Qaradawi has also distanced himself from Osama bin Laden's views on indiscriminately attacking U.S. citizens and targets and condemned the terrorist attacks of September 11, 2001. He has stated that while the U.S. government is hostile to Muslims, not every U.S. citizen shares this hostility. In the United States, a civil court cleared al-Qaradawi of complicity in the terrorist attacks of 9/11 in a case brought by the families of victims.

The new government in Iraq has had to try to balance the agendas and interests of different communities, especially the Sunni who had dominated the country under Saddam, the Shia who form a small majority, and the Kurds, some 17 percent of the population, who mainly live in the autonomous region of Kurdistan that borders Syria, Turkey, and Iran. Some Shia want an Iranian-style government, some Sunnis support an Islamist-style regime, while some Iraqis want a secular state. Following the overthrow of Saddam, various paramilitaries have attempted to disrupt the state with the aim of establishing their government of choice. Among the competing groups are the Mujahideen Shura Council, Sunni nationalists, Ansar al-Islam, the Medhi army, and Badr brigade, as well as Al-Qaeda. The Mujahideen Shura Council is an umbrella for several militias and has Islamist sympathies. The Sunni nationalists comprise former Saddam supporters with Baathist sympathies. The Ansar al-Islam is also Islamist and has the support of Kurds who oppose Kurdish autonomy, wishing to be part of an Islamist entity. The Mehdi army is loyal to the Shia religious leader (often called a cleric), Moqdata Sadr. Although he does not have a rank similar to that which Ruhollah Khomeini had before the 1979 Islamic Revolution in Iran, many people think that Moqdata Sadr sees himself as a future Supreme Leader of a Shia Iranian Islamic order. The Badr brigade is linked with Sciri (the Supreme Council for the Islamic Revolution in Iraq), the majority Shia party in Iraq's parliament, and shares goals similar to the Mehdi army. Armed conflict is further fueled by the fact that Iraq's oil reserves are

THE TALIBAN AND DRUGS

In 2001, their last year in power, the Taliban banned the growing of opium poppies, but they have subsequently encouraged this practice in order to finance their anti-NATO campaign. Although the Taliban do not sell the poppies themselves, it has been estimated that they profit by as much as U.S.$100 million annually by imposing a 10 percent tax on the farmers who grow and sell the poppies. Sources have linked both the Taliban and Osama bin Laden with the illicit drug trade in Afghanistan.

Almost all non-Taliban Muslims apply the same prohibition to drugs as they do to alcohol. However, selling drugs to the West to spread more crime on the streets of Western cities can be seen as part of the jihad of attacking the West whenever an opportunity presents itself and by any means possible.

UN estimates suggest that as much as 90 percent of Afghanistan's opium crop feeds the European drug market, much of it becoming the opium derivative heroin.

mainly in the Shia-dominated south, which raises questions about how revenues should be distributed. As of 2010, Allied troops remained in Iraq.

Syria, governed by a Baathist regime that cannot be described as Islamist, also supports Hezbollah in Lebanon and remains officially committed to the destruction of Israel. First designated by the U.S. Department of State as a terror-sponsoring state in 1979, Syria allows Hamas and Palestinian Islamic Jihad to maintain headquarters in Damascus. It is still categorized as a terror-sponsoring state. Libya has supported Islamic and non-Muslim liberation movements across the globe but was withdrawn from the U.S. list of terror-sponsoring states in 2003 when it announced it was abandoning its WMD program.

OTHER JIHADIST MOVEMENTS

Other jihadist movements with Islamist agendas include the Mujahideen Islam Pattani and several other organizations in Thailand, where acts of terror have been committed. The aim is to establish an Islamic state in southwestern Asia. Operating from Thailand and throughout the southern Asian region, the Jemaah Islamiyah, an Al-Qaeda affiliate, were responsible for the bomb attack in a Bali nightclub in 2002, which killed 202 people, mainly tourists. Jemaah's long-term goal is a caliphate for southern Asia's Muslims, but in the short term it supports separatist movements in Thailand and Indonesia.

Indonesia includes the oil-rich Aceh region of Sumatra, where the main paramilitary group reached a peace deal with Indonesia in 2005. The disagreement with Indonesia focused on the desire for a more Islamist state in contrast to what was perceived as a secular Indonesia. Both Libya and Iran had aided the Free Aceh Movement. Also affiliated with Al-Qaeda, the Abu Sayyaf group in the Muslim majority south of the Philippines aims to create an Islamist state. Its leader and founder, Abdurajak Janjalani (1959–1998) fought in Afghanistan, where he reputedly formed a close relationship with Osama bin Laden. After his death, he was succeeded by his brother, Khaddafy, for whose capture the United States promised $5 million. He was found dead in December 2006. Abu Sayyaf has carried out assassinations, kidnappings, and extortion, infamously beheading an American captive in May 2001. Verses 8:12 and 47:3 of the Koran were cited to justify the beheading of an enemy.

MUSLIMS IN THE WEST AND THE ISLAMIST AGENDA

The fact that the perpetrators of 9/11 had lived in the West and even planned their acts of terror while doing so raised, for some, questions about the activities of other Muslims. Concern about the movement of money and the ease with which the perpetrators had acquired valid driver's licenses and other legal documentation prompted the USA PATRIOT Act of 2001 and the assets of many Islamic organizations in the United States to be frozen.

In July 2005, another terrorist attack in the West caused ripples across the world. In London, four British-born Muslims launched suicide bomb attacks that killed 52 people in the underground railway system and on a London bus. Links with Al-Qaeda remain unproven, but the motive behind the attacks was inspired by Islamist ideology. Links with Pakistani religious schools were also alleged to have contributed to the perpetrators' idealism. The bombers saw the United Kingdom as Islam's enemy for helping to invade Iraq in 2003 and saw their own loyalty as being with the global Muslim community.

Some scholars argue that Islamist Islam is incompatible with Western social values and point to a series of incidents in the Muslim diaspora—such as opposition to Salman Rushdie's 1988 novel *The Satanic Verses*, the murder of Dutch filmmaker Theo van Gogh in 2004 after he produced a short documentary film about violence toward women in the Muslim world, and reaction to cartoons of Muhammad first published in a Danish newspaper in September 2005—to claim that political Islam is a threat to Western, liberal society. Some such commentators support stricter controls on Islamic organizations in the West, especially those suspected of Islamist sympathy, and new immigration policies to discourage new arrivals.

HOW POPULAR IS ISLAMISM?

According to some scholars, Islamists represent a minority of Muslims worldwide. However, many Muslims share some, although not all, Islamist concerns. For example, they want social justice, leaders who uphold Islamic values, and to be able to demand integrity and personal morality of their public officials; they do not want a secular society but a society that is shaped by Islamic principles. Although by no means all Muslims want to see Israel destroyed, they are committed to the creation of a Palestinian state. Many share a tainted view of the West, which they regard as manipulative and as duplicitous in its so-called defense and promotion of democracy; yet the majority of Muslims want greater democracy.

HIZB-UT-TAHRIR: A PROPOSED CONSTITUTION

Hizb-ut-Tahrir was founded in 1953 by Taqiuddin al-Nabhani (1909–1977), a former member of the Muslim Brotherhood. Hizb-ut-Tahrir has members in about 40 countries and is banned in several states, including Libya. It is vehemently anti-Western, although it is very active among Muslim students on campuses in the West. The organization's proposed constitution rejects the view that freedom of speech, of the press, and of religion is an absolute right and believes that, under the caliphate, non-Muslims would not be able to vote for or hold political office, although they would be able to voice concerns related to their own community. They can be members of the Assembly (Majlis ul-Ummah) as long as they only comment on the "misapplication of Islam on them." Shura (consultation) is a "right for Muslims only." According to Hizb-ut-Tahrir, the caliph, who must be male, and senior officials would be elected by Muslims from a slate of approved candidates short-listed by the Assembly; democracy as a system predicated on the rule of, by, and for the people is rejected, but use of the ballot to elect representatives is endorsed. Once the people have pledged their allegiance to the caliph, he cannot be removed. There is no set term of office, but a replacement must be appointed within three days of a vacancy. Multiple parties can exist, but only if founded on the principles of Islam. Hizb-ut-Tahrir does not engage in social and religious activities and is more like a Western-style political party. In some European countries the group's views have attracted calls for it to be banned.

INDEPENDENCE AND ISLAMISM IN ALGERIA

After a bloody war of independence from the French (1954–1962), Algeria was governed by broadly nationalist and secularist French-educated leaders in a one-party system until 1988. In 1989, the Islamist Islamic Salvation Front (FIS) was established by a religious teacher, Abbassi Madani, who preached a Salafist message. In the multiparty elections of June 12, 1990, the FIS won a majority with 54 percent of the votes and was set to form a government. Before it could do so, in January 1992, the army intervened and seized power in a coup. The international community did not condemn the coup or the suspension of democracy. France recognized the new government. In 1993, the FIS began a campaign of armed resistance, and in the subsequent civil war some 100,000 people died. By the end of the 1990s, the more radical Armed Resistance Group (GIA) had overtaken the FIS in popularity, claiming to be the true supporter of jihad in Algeria.

Many Muslims accuse Western governments of a two-faced approach, supporting the Taliban and Saddam Hussein when it suited them and turning against them when their interests changed. Many do not like the way in which education has been divided into Islamic and secular, and few tolerate the way in which religion has been banished to the domestic sphere in the West. While many Muslims want their governments to make decisions that pay due regard to Islamic values, they do not want Muslim scholars to play a dominant role in government.

Many Muslims think that after 50 or 60 years of postcolonial governments based more or less on European models, it is time to try Islamic solutions. In the hiatus created by colonialism and by postcolonial governance, however, many Islamic institutions have stagnated or ceased to exist. The challenge is to revive or to reconstruct these in forms suitable for the 21st century. Islamism in the 21st century will probably continue to feed off poverty as long as the governments of Muslim states fail to address issues of social justice, including wealthy states where there is a huge disparity between rich and poor. Many of those who support Islamist movements, however, are from the educated, urban, middle classes rather than the rural poor. This indicates that Islamism does not only feed off poverty but attracts those who have an ideological commitment to creating change and to bringing about reform (*islah*), or the repairing of Muslim society. Many Muslims believe that capitalism values wealth and property too highly, while communism is too utopian. Islam limits the absolute right to property, placing duties on those who have toward those who do not.

Some Muslims regard Islamism as a total distortion of Islam for political purposes and as an innovation—since no one really knows what early Muslim society was like, it cannot be revived. Others condemn modernists for reducing Islam to what they think is compatible with the West and Islamists for reducing Islam to its political dimension at the expense of its spiritual core. Many Islamists, though, emphasize the importance of inner renewal. Islam, they say, is a faith, not an ideology.

See Also

States, Politics, and Political Groups
144–163 ❖ Al-Qaeda
164–167 ❖ Response to Extremism
216–219 ❖

Response to Extremism

In 2001, the United States retaliated to terrorist attacks against it by invading Afghanistan and Iraq. Critics questioned whether these countries were the root of the problem.

O n September 11, 2001, groups of terrorists working separately but in concert hijacked three commercial airliners in midair and flew them deliberately into major U.S. landmarks. The first hit the North Tower of the World Trade Center in New York City; shortly afterward, the second hit the South Tower of the same office complex. Both buildings caught on fire and collapsed. Half an hour later, the third plane was flown into the Pentagon, the headquarters of the U.S. Department of Defense, in Arlington, Virginia. The building was damaged but not destroyed. A fourth hijacked plane crashed in open fields in Pennsylvania after the terrorists were overpowered by the passengers. In total, more than 3,000 people were killed in these incidents, which became known collectively as "9/11."

Investigations soon revealed that the hijackings had been carried out by Al-Qaeda, an Islamist terrorist group headed by Saudi millionaire Osama bin Laden, which had been responsible for the bombings in 1998 of the U.S. embassies in Nairobi, Kenya, and Dar-es-Salaam, Tanzania. Al-Qaeda's precise motives for these attacks were unclear.

WAR ON TERROR

In the wake of 9/11, U.S. president George W. Bush proclaimed a war against terrorism. The United States began air strikes on suspected Al-Qaeda hideouts in Afghanistan on October 7, 2001, and later sent in land forces to search for bin Laden, who was believed to be hiding there. The focus of the War on Terror then shifted to Iraq, which the United States and its allies invaded in 2003, toppling Iraqi leader Saddam Hussein, who was later tried and executed.

Meanwhile, the United States built a detention camp at Guantánamo Bay, its enclave in southeastern Cuba. Commonly known as "Gitmo," the camp was used to house Muslim militants and suspected terrorists captured in Afghanistan, Iraq, and elsewhere. Several hundred people were held there without charge or legal representation; it later emerged that some of them were tortured.

Gitmo deeply divided domestic and international opinion. Many people and organizations, including the International Red Cross, condemned the violations of human rights that occurred there. Others regarded U.S. actions as a justified response to 9/11 in particular and to Muslim terrorists in general. President Bush stated that normal rules of civilized warfare, as prescribed in the Geneva Conventions, applied neither to Gitmo, because it was not a part of the United States, nor to those held there, whom he described as "unlawful enemy combatants."

THE RIGHT THING TO DO?

Regardless of whether the ends justified the means used to prosecute the War on Terror, doubts remained about whether the U.S. response to extremism was effective. Three main questions arose. Had the United States identified the right enemy? Were the enemy's aims what the United States thought they were? What were the likely and possible outcomes of the conflict?

Some people were concerned that the violent reaction of the United States might have been made in undue

A U.S. soldier stands guard in a watchtower on the perimeter wall of Guantánamo Bay.

FBI TEN MOST WANTED FUGITIVE

MURDER OF U.S. NATIONALS OUTSIDE THE UNITED STATES; CONSPIRACY TO MURDER U.S. NATIONALS OUTSIDE THE UNITED STATES; ATTACK ON A FEDERAL FACILITY RESULTING IN DEATH

USAMA BIN LADEN

haste and directed at the wrong targets. Bin Laden and Al-Qaeda have been widely blamed for provoking the War on Terror, but all over the world there are millions of people who, rightly or wrongly, feel aggrieved at U.S. policy toward their native lands. Prominent among the groups that may harbor grudges against the United States are the Palestinians who have been displaced since the foundation of Israel in 1948. The Jewish state is widely perceived in the Arab world as an imperialist creation that has been used by the West to perpetuate colonialism in the postcolonial era. In addition to more than 1.5 million Palestinians who now live in impoverished camps in Israel in Gaza and the West Bank, there has been a worldwide diaspora of more than 3 million Palestinians. Some of the countries in which these displaced people have taken refuge have been destabilized by immigration. Worst affected is Jordan,

This FBI wanted poster shows Osama bin Laden, the Saudi millionaire widely held responsible for the 9/11 attacks on the United States. Regardless of bin Laden's guilt, some people believe that he and his Al-Qaeda terrorist organization are not the root of extremism but merely a symptom of a deeper malaise in the Islamic world.

whose indigenous population of 6.3 million has been increased by 1.8 million refugees from Israel and, more recently, by another 2 million displaced people from Iraq. Egypt, Lebanon, Saudi Arabia, and Syria have also suffered because of their proximity to Israel.

POSSIBLE CAUSES

Every one of these nations has no shortage of citizens who see themselves as exploited by the West in general and by the United States in particular in a range of areas. One of the most contentious issues is oil. The countries of the region that produce oil do not receive the full benefit, selling it at less than the market rate in order to cultivate Western goodwill. In some states, the profits from oil sales are used to enrich the ruling elites, while the ordinary people receive little or no benefit.

Another cause of friction is the boundaries of these states, many of which were contrived by the West and imposed during the colonial period. Another concern, particularly in Egypt and Saudi Arabia, is harsh rulers who clamp down on internal dissent while adopting what some citizens of those countries regard as fawningly conciliatory attitudes toward the West.

While the disaffected people have no single unifying aim, they are linked by a generalized antipathy to the West and by residing in countries that are either constitutionally or de facto Islamic states. They are not all devout or radical Muslims—many secular Arab businesspeople have commercial reasons for mistrusting the West. Thus Islam may not inspire opponents of the United States but may be merely the banner to which they rally. The Islamic hostility to the United States may be based not on "consciousness and culture," as the *New York Times* columnist David Brooks declared on September 28, 2006, but on political and social circumstances.

CRUSADING SPIRIT

A week after 9/11, George W. Bush described the incipient War on Terror as a "crusade." In the context of relations between the West and the Muslim world, this was a loaded and potentially inflammatory term. The original Crusades were a series of expeditions, undertaken by the Christian countries of Europe between the 11th century and the 16th century, to check the spread of Islam and to repossess those areas of western Asia that had fallen to the Muslims, particularly Jerusalem and Palestine.

In an effort to minimize the damage caused by the president's choice of word, his aides immediately issued clarifications that claimed he had used "crusade" merely as a synonym for "struggle." However, some people took the view that this was not one of the "misspeaks" for which Bush was sometimes satirized. They believed that "crusade" was either a deliberate and considered definition of the United States' war aims or a Freudian slip that revealed Bush's entrenched antipathy to the Muslim world.

UNCLENCHING FISTS

What, then, are the likely and possible outcomes of the War on Terror? It seems that the problem will persist until either the enemy is eradicated or a solution is found. It is now generally agreed that the former will never happen because the grievances—whatever they may be—and the level of support for them have metastasized (spread in the manner of cancer cells). Peace cannot be proclaimed until the United States and its allies have identified the enemy with certainty and ascertained its war aims. The U.S. response to extremism has been spectacular, but there are grave doubts that it has been—or can be—effective. President Barack Obama pointed to a possible change of direction at his inauguration on January 20, 2009, when he said: "To the Muslim world, we seek a new way forward, based on mutual interest and mutual respect. To those leaders around the globe who seek to sow conflict, or blame their society's ills on the West—know that your people will judge you on what you can build, not what you destroy. To those who cling to power through corruption and deceit and the silencing of dissent, know that you are on the wrong side of history; but that we will extend a hand if you are willing to unclench your fist."

In one of his first acts after taking office, on January 22, 2009, President Obama fulfilled a campaign pledge by ordering the closure of the detention camp at Guantánamo Bay within one year and a review of ways to transfer the detainees held there to the United States for imprisonment or trial. He also required U.S. interrogators to use only techniques approved under the Geneva Conventions. In foreign policy, the 44th president began his term by beginning the withdrawal of U.S. and allied troops from Iraq. Meanwhile, he ordered a greatly increased American military presence in Afghanistan. At the end of 2009, Obama won the Nobel Peace Prize. While some commentators questioned what the president had done to merit the award, others took it as symbolic of a promise of future reconciliation.

MER NOIRE
CARA-DENISI aux Turcs CZORNO-MORE aux Moscovites
MAURO THALASSA aux Grecs, autrefois PONT EUXIN

CIRCASSES

GEORGIE

MAWARALNAHRA

IRAN

BEGLERBEGLIC D'ANATOLIE

BEGLERBEGLIC DE SIWAS

TURCOMANIE

BEGLERBEGLIC DE CARAMANIE

BEGLERBEGLIC DE WAN

Mer CASPIENNE aujourd'huy GUALENSKOI MORE ou TABRISTAN aux Moscovites KULSUM ou TABRISTAN aux Perses

TABRISTAN

ADIRBEITZAN

KILAN

DE L'ISLE DE CYPRE

BEGLERBEGLIC D'ALEP

BEGLERBEGLIC DE DIARBEKIR

BEGLERBEGLIC DE MOSUL

ERAK ATZEM

MER DE LEVANT

BEGLERBEGLIC DE TRIPOLI

BEGLERBEGLIC de RIKA

BEGLERBEGLIC de BAGDET

Eschelle

BEGLERBEGLIC DE DAMAS

BERIARA ou
ARABIE DESERTE

CHUSISTAN

DU CAIRE

BARAAB ou ARABIE PETREE

FARS

DE MISIR

KIRMAN

EGYPTE

ESTATS DU CHERIFE DE LA

BEDUINS

A
R
A
B
I
A

GOLFE DE BASSORA ou MER D'ELCATIF

OMAN

Mer ROUGE ou MER DE LA MECQUE

HAGIAZ DE

Ben Seber

MECCA

GEMEN ou IAMAN

DU GRAND SEIGNEUR
TURCS,
IE et EN AFRIQUE,
tous ses
GOUVERNEMENTS:
stats qui luy sont Tributaires
uvelles Relations.
RDAM.
ELWE.
XII.

BEGLERBEGLIC DE HAGIAZ

MER DE CALZEM

TEHMA

BEGLERBEGLIC DE IEMEN ou D'ADEN

MER D'ARABIE

OCEA

ORIENTA

ou INDIEN

FRONTIERES

L'EMPIRE DES ABISSINS

Socotora I.

THE EASTERN MEDITERRANEAN AND THE ARABIAN PENINSULA

This region contains the historic heartland of Islam—it was in the Arabian Peninsula that the Islamic faith originally emerged in the seventh century. In the 21st century, the Eastern Mediterranean is central to some of the greatest opportunities and threats confronting the entire world.

The nations of the Eastern Mediterranean—Jordan, Lebanon, Syria, and Iraq—and the Arabian Peninsula—Saudi Arabia, the United Arab Emirates (UAE), Bahrain, Kuwait, Oman, Qatar, and Yemen—all have large Muslim populations.

The Eastern Mediterranean came under formal European political control following the dissolution of the Ottoman Empire after World War I (1914–1918). The postwar borders of the region—determined at the 1919 peace conferences in Paris and imposed by Britain, France, and the United States—had lasting repercussions on the new nations' economic, cultural, and political development. Throughout the Eastern Mediterranean, French and English are still spoken, alongside Arabic, by educated members of every society. There are sizable Christian minorities throughout the region. The longest-established

Christian group is the Maronites, whose presence in Lebanon predates that of Islam. The colonial legacy also includes European institutions, such as parliaments, in some countries' political systems. European colonialism laid the foundation for the Israel-Palestine conflict, which has dominated political and economic life

The Eastern Mediterranean came under formal European political control after World War I (1914–1918) with the dissolution of the Ottoman Empire.

throughout the region since the creation of the state of Israel in 1948.

The countries of the Arabian Peninsula were not part of the post–World War I

This map shows the extent of the Ottoman Empire in the Eastern Mediterranean and the Arabian Peninsula around 1800.

CREATING THE MAP OF MODERN WESTERN ASIA

During World War I (1914–1918), the Ottoman Empire entered the conflict on the side of the Central Powers, the name given to the alliance between Italy, Germany, and Austria-Hungary. Parts of the Anatolian Peninsula (modern Turkey) and the Eastern Mediterranean became a battlefield between the Central Powers and the Triple Entente of Britain, France, and Russia, with support from Japan and the United States.

During the war, the British officer T. E. Lawrence, known as "Lawrence of Arabia," helped to lead the Arab population in a revolt against the Ottomans. The Arab forces were successful in destroying the Ottoman supply lines and in seizing Damascus and other key cities. In exchange for their support of the Entente, the Arabs sought the guarantee of an independent state if they were victorious over the Ottomans. Letters were exchanged between Henry McMahon, the British high commissioner in Egypt, and the Arab representative Husayn ibn Ali, who was emir of Mecca (1908–1916) and then king of Hejaz (a region of modern Saudi Arabia). In the correspondence, McMahon promised to uphold the independence of the Arabs within certain territories.

At the same time, however, Britain and France concluded, with Russian consent, the secret Sykes-Picot Agreement that determined their respective spheres of

T. E. Lawrence (1888–1935) was a British archaeologist and military strategist who helped the Arabs in their struggle for independence from the disintegrating Ottoman Empire.

influence in the region after the war. Britain would control the territory that corresponds to modern Jordan, Israel, and parts of Iraq. The French sphere would include Syria, Lebanon, and the remainder of Iraq.

This agreement influenced the postwar peace process, led by Britain, France, and the United States. Although the Arabs sent representatives to make the case for Arab independence, a system of mandates was created. Under the League of Nations (formed 1919), Britain and France would administer the former Ottoman territories until the areas had developed sufficiently to be granted independence. In reality, the colonial powers did little to prepare these territories for self-rule. Indeed, colonial policies of pitting various ethnic and religious groups against each other helped to create the instability that continues to undermine these countries today.

For his support in the war, Husayn ibn Ali was given a limited degree of autonomy over Transjordan, part of the British Palestine mandate. For the Arabs, the actions of the Western powers amounted to an enormous betrayal and created long-standing suspicion of Western motives in the region. The Palestine mandate also laid the foundation for the creation in 1948 of Israel and the ensuing conflicts between the Jewish state and its Arab neighbors.

colonial system, but some of them were already under European control as British protectorates. At that time, much of the region did not contain Western-style states, with clearly defined territories and institutions. Instead, tribes living in the area gave their allegiance to local rulers, known as emirs (princes), sheikhs, or sultans to form states known as emirates, sheikhdoms, or sultanates. The emirates concluded treaties in the 19th century under which Britain oversaw their foreign relations and defense. Among the most important of these emirates were Abu Dhabi and Dubai. Collectively, the emirates with formal dependence on Britain were known as the Trucial States. Oman and Saudi Arabia also

had treaties with Britain but were never formally made into British protectorates; they were independent nations from, respectively, 1650 and 1932.

JORDAN

At the end of World War I, the newly formed League of Nations granted Britain a mandate to rule Palestine, the name then used to desribe a large region of the former Ottoman Empire in the Eastern Mediterranean. From that vast tract of territory, in 1920, the British separated out a semiautonomous region known at first as Transjordan. This territorial division was deeply disappointing to the local Arab leader, Husayn ibn Ali (1854–1931), who

The al-Dier monastery—part of the complex of ancient buildings at Petra, Jordan—was originally built in the first century BCE.

The Beirut waterfront has been reconstructed since it was devastated during the Lebanese civil war (1975–1990).

had supported Britain and its allies, France and Russia, in their fight against the Ottomans. However, Husayn accepted the political reality and oversaw the coronation of his son, Abdullah, as the first king of the new nation. Britain then gradually reduced its control over Transjordan, which eventually became an independent kingdom in 1946 and changed its name in 1949 to the Hashemite Kingdom of Jordan. (The Hashemite family, of which Husayn ibn Ali and his heirs are members, traces itself directly back to the Prophet Muhammad; this lineage is the source of legitimacy for Hashemite rule.) At the same time, the foundation in 1948 of the state of Israel created the first wave of Arab refugees into Jordan from the neighboring Jewish state.

Under King Hussein (r. 1953– 1999), Jordan remained stable, despite losing its territory on the West Bank of the Jordan River in the 1967 Arab-Israeli War and almost succumbing in 1970 to a rebellion by a new influx of displaced Palestinian refugees. Hussein was notably pragmatic in

his dealings with Britain, the Soviet Union, and the United States—which had all maintained important interests in the region—as well as with Jordan's Arab neighbors. In 1988 Hussein renounced claims to the West Bank and, in the following year, he introduced a program of liberalization that permitted for the first time the formation of political parties within Jordan. In 1994 Jordan became only the second Arab nation (Egypt was the first) to sign a peace treaty with Israel. It was hoped that the treaty would bring significant economic benefits to Jordan, especially through tourism; the greatest of the nation's attractions is Petra, the site of the ruins of an Arab city that was founded around 1200 BCE.

In 1999, Hussein was succeeded by his son, King Abdullah II (b. 1962). Soon after Abdullah's accession to the throne, the new monarch faced challenges from Islamist political parties and others opposed to his pro-Western foreign policy. Jordan nevertheless assisted the United States during its UN-sanctioned 2003 invasion of Iraq. In November 2005, suicide bombers killed 56 people in attacks on three luxury hotels in Jordan's capital, Amman. In the aftermath of these attacks, which were linked to Al-Qaeda, thousands of Jordanians took to the streets to protest acts of terrorism.

By 2010, displaced Palestinians represented around one-half of Jordan's 6.4 million population, 92 percent of which is Sunni Muslim. In contrast to Egypt and Lebanon, Jordan has granted full citizenship to all these refugees. As a result, Jordanian internal politics is very sensitive to Israeli-Palestinian relations.

LEBANON

Lebanon has accommodated Christianity and Islam, often harmoniously, since the seventh century. In 2010, the country's population of just over 4 million was 60 percent Muslim. Most Lebanese Muslims are Sunnis, but there is an almost equal number of Shiites. The third-largest Muslim group is the Druze.

Following the disintegration of the Ottoman Empire at the end of World War I, France acquired a mandate over Syria and, from it, separated the region of Lebanon in 1920. France, which was largely occupied by Nazi Germany during World War II (1939–1945), granted Lebanon independence in 1943 in order to keep the colony out of German control. The following decades were economically prosperous for Lebanon, as its melding of Arab and French influences attracted international businesses and visitors to its Mediterranean beaches. Known as "the Switzerland of the Middle East," Lebanon became the region's financial and banking center. However, behind Beirut's seafront and glittering skyline, tensions were rising between religious groups over the distribution of political power. In the decades after independence, the growth

THE DRUZE

The Druze are a religious sect that was founded in Cairo, Egypt, in the 11th century. They believe in reincarnation and in the divinity of the Fatimid caliph al-Hakim (996–1021). Members class themselves as Muslims but they are not universally acknowledged as such by mainstream followers of Islam. Druze forbid conversions, either to or from their faith, and marriages to non-Druze.

The Druze became well-known during the Lebanese civil war (1975–1990), when their militia was one of the three main combatant factions, along with the Shiites and the Christian Maronites. In spite of their international fame, the Druze are a small group—

estimates of the exact number vary between 300,000 and one million worldwide. Around one-half of that number lives in Syria; Lebanon is home to between 30 percent and 40 percent; the remaining Druze are scattered throughout Israel and Jordan, as well as in various countries of Europe and in the United States.

The uncertainty about the exact number of Druze is largely attributable to the clandestine nature of their faith. Their doctrines are kept secret, even from many members. They are permitted to deny that they are Druze whenever it suits them to do so, probably as a response to the persecution that they have suffered from time to time throughout their history.

HEZBOLLAH

Members of the Hezbollah militia parade through a suburb of Beirut, Lebanon, in 1986.

In the 1970s, Lebanon, embroiled in civil war, became a base for the Palestine Liberation Organization (PLO), a militant nationalist group that carried out attacks on Israeli towns along the border with southern Lebanon. In 1982 Israel invaded Lebanon with the stated goal of creating a 25-mile (40 km) security zone. Major damage was done to Lebanon's infrastructure, including the capital, Beirut, which was bombed for weeks. Large civilian casualties were sustained and there were massacres in the refugee camps at Sabra and Shatila. The PLO then left Lebanon and relocated to Tunisia; Israel maintained the security zone until 1983.

An unintended consequence of the Israeli invasion of Lebanon was the creation of Hezbollah (Party of God), a Shia militant group with links to Iran. With the goal of resisting Israeli occupation and the ability to deliver social services to the impoverished south, Hezbollah gained much support. Hezbollah regularly carried out rocket attacks on Israel's towns along the border, and their activities could not be brought under control by the Lebanese government's weaker forces. In July 2006 Hezbollah carried out an attack inside Israel, kidnapping two Israeli soldiers. In response, Israel launched a massive bombing campaign, causing extensive damage to Lebanon's infrastructure, including Beirut's international airport. The death toll reached almost 1,000, nearly all of whom were Lebanese civilians. The conflict ended after 34 days with a United Nations–sponsored cease-fire.

The disproportionate scale of Israel's response led to increased support for Hezbollah inside Lebanon and a greater role for the organization in the government. In Israel, an official report severely criticized the inability of the strongest military force in the region to overcome a few thousand militants.

of the Muslim population had rapidly outpaced increases in the Christian population. The creation of the state of Israel drove around 110,000 (mainly Muslim) Palestinian refugees into Lebanon, where they were housed in camps in the south of the country. A further influx of displaced people after the Six-Day War of 1967 between Israel its neighbors increased the population of the camps by a factor of as many as five. With its demographic balance catastrophically altered, Lebanon descended into civil war (1975–1990). Syrian troops invaded the country in an effort to restore order. Although this military intervention failed to end the violence, Syria continued to play a major role in Lebanon's domestic and foreign affairs. So, too, did Israel, whose invasion of southern Lebanon in 1982 inspired the rise of Hezbollah (see box).

The civil war was ended by the Taif Agreement, brokered by the Arab League, which reapportioned political power in Lebanon by reducing the influence of the Maronites, the country's most politically powerful Christian sect. After the war, Lebanon began a massive reconstruction effort, rebuilding the capital, Beirut, which had been one of the main battlegrounds throughout the conflict. However, in the summer of 2006, renewed Israeli attacks, which included massive bombing campaigns against Hezbollah in southern Lebanon, caused enormous damage to the newly rebuilt infrastructure.

SYRIA

The modern republic of Syria emerged after World War I from the division of the Eastern Mediterranean lands that had formerly been parts of the Ottoman Empire. Syria was assigned at first to the French mandate. The nation achieved independence in 1946 but lacked political stability and was ruled by a succession of military dictators who typically came to power in coups and fell in countercoups. In 1958 Syria united with Egypt to form the United Arab Republic (UAR). This unification was a political expression of Pan-Arabism, the idea that the Arab countries should work together to resist continuing efforts by the Western powers to control or influence the region. However, the UAR lasted only three years; its brief existence was characterized by internal strife and Syrian accusations of domination by Egypt. It ended when Syria withdrew.

❖

Under the Abbasid dynasty (750–1258 CE), Baghdad, the main city of Mesopotamia, became the capital of a vast Muslim empire.

In 1963, control of Syria passed to the Ba'ath party (also known as the Arab Socialist Renaissance Party), a secular nationalist political grouping, which has ruled the nation ever since. Although the Syrian party shares a common origin with the Ba'ath party of Iraq, the two parties split over ideological differences in 1966.

During the Six-Day War of 1967, Syria lost the Golan Heights, a plateau in the southwest of the country, to Israel. It failed to regain the territory in the next Arab-Israeli military conflict, the Yom Kippur War of 1973. Israel continues to control this strategic border territory, which is now inhabited by approximately 20,000 Jewish settlers.

In 1970, Hafez al-Assad, Syria's minister of defense, seized power in a nonviolent coup and then served as president until his death in 2000. He was succeeded by his son, Bashir al-Assad (born 1965). Both presidents have consistently been reelected by the population in referendums held every seven years. Although Syria has an elected parliament, the president and the military exercise total control in this authoritarian regime.

Of Syria's current population of just over 20 million, around 15 million are Sunni Muslims; a further 3 million belong to other branches of Islam, notably the Alawites (of which the ruling Assads are members) and the Druze.

IRAQ

The territory that comprises modern Iraq was known historically as Mesopotamia, from the Greek meaning "land between the rivers." The rivers referred to—the Tigris and the Euphrates—created an area known as "the Fertile Crescent," in which emerged one of the world's earliest civilizations. It was there, around 5000 BCE, that humankind first developed writing and a code of laws.

Throughout its history, Mesopotamia has been a cultural crossroads influenced by many foreign powers, including the Persian Empire, under the rule of Cyrus the Great in the 6th century BCE, and the Greek Empire created by Alexander the Great (r. 336–323 BCE). With the rise of Islam, the area came under Muslim rule as the caliphate expanded out of the Arabian Peninsula. Under the Abbasid dynasty (750–1258 CE), Baghdad, the main city of Mesopotamia, became the capital of a vast Muslim empire. It was also a focus of learning and intellectual life. The city's famed Bayt al-Hikma (House of Wisdom)

was the leading global center for the study of humanities and sciences. It hosted scholars from throughout the empire who translated and expanded the works of Persian, Greek, and Indian scholars to create a vast body of scientific knowledge in Arabic. After the destruction of Baghdad by the Mongols in the 13th century and the subsequent rise of the Turks, the area that is present-day Iraq became one of the backwater provinces of the Ottoman Empire.

With the defeat of the Ottoman Empire in World War I, the Ottoman provinces of Baghdad, Basra, and Mosul were combined into a single mandate under British control that was named Iraq. The presence of significant oil resources was a major factor in British interest in Iraq. The new state combined a very diverse population of Arabs (80 percent) and Kurds (15 percent), as well as numerous smaller ethnic groups, such as Turkomen and Assyrians. The new state was also religiously complex, composed of Sunnis (32–37 percent), Shiites (60–65 percent), and a small number of Christians (around 3 percent).

During the mandate period in Iraq, Britain installed a king, Faisal, a member of the Sunni Hashemite family that had supported the British during the war. Although Iraq achieved independence in 1932, Britain continued to exercise control and maintain troops in the country. The Iraqis fought the occupying forces and finally ousted the British-backed monarchy in a 1958 revolution led by the army. Instability marked the first decades after the revolution, although Iraq's economy grew as a result of oil sales. In the 1950s and the 1960s, Iraq was one of the wealthiest countries in western Asia. The government provided free education and health care, and economic success created a large and prosperous middle class.

In 1968 the socialist Ba'ath party seized power and established a tight grip on society. Saddam Hussein, then a Ba'ath party member, rose rapidly through the ranks and claimed the title of president in 1979. Saddam ruled with an iron fist. Iraq's ethnic minorities, especially the Kurds, were targeted and oppressed, as were the majority Shiite population located predominantly in the south of the country. Multiple secret police and military organizations enforced Saddam's policies and quelled dissent.

Between 1980 and 1988, Iraq fought a long and costly war with neighboring Iran. The United States, attempting to contain Iran's influence in the region, supported Iraq with funding and military supplies. In 1998 a cease-fire was declared, with no clear winner. The war left Iraq deeply in debt and with a large military force with no mission. These factors motivated Iraq to invade Kuwait in 1990. Saddam attempted to justify military action by claiming that Kuwait had been a part of Iraq during the Ottoman period. An international coalition, led by the United States and with the backing of the United Nations (UN), took military action in 1991 to force Iraq out of Kuwait. Following the war, Iraq was subjected to economic sanctions and could not sell its oil in the world market. The sanctions were criticized by many members of the international community for harming Iraq's civilian population, especially children, while having little effect on Saddam or his policies.

Iraq was then subjected to an inspection of its weapons of mass destruction (WMD) program by a UN special commission. Iraq had used chemical weapons in its war against Iran and in its actions against the Kurds and was known to have a biological weapons program. The (mainly American) inspectors contended that they were being denied access to key sites, while Saddam argued that the U.S. Central Intelligence Agency (CIA) was using the inspections to gather intelligence. The inspections were suspended in 1998 and restarted in 2002 after Saddam invited the inspectors back in, again under UN auspices. Inspections at that time found no indication that Iraq had an active nuclear, chemical, or biological weapons program.

Accusations that Iraq possessed an active WMD program were the primary justification for the U.S.-led invasion of Iraq in March 2003. Baghdad quickly fell, but Saddam escaped and was not captured until December 2003. An intense search by coalition forces failed to find weapons of mass destruction. After the fall of the Ba'ath regime, the invaders put in place a military occupation government, the Coalition Provisional Authority, which ruled until June 2004, when sovereignty was transferred to an interim Iraqi government; this government executed Saddam in December 2006. Following elections in 2005, a permanent Iraqi government was installed, although disagreements between the elected officials remained frequent. Iraq continues to struggle both with sectarian violence between Sunnis, Shias, and Kurds, as well as with attacks by Al-Qaeda groups. These attacks have claimed a great many civilian lives. In November 2008, the Iraqi government signed a security pact with the United States that requires the withdrawal of all U.S. troops from the country by the end of 2011.

Iraq is religiously divided. Its modern population—around 29 million people—

is divided between 60 percent to 65 percent Shia and 32 percent to 37 percent Sunni.

SAUDI ARABIA

Saudi Arabia is the birthplace of Islam and the site of the two holiest shrines of the religion: Mecca and Medina. The modern population of 28.6 million is 100 percent Muslim.

Saudi Arabia was formed by an alliance that began in the 18th century between the al-Saud family and the followers of Muhammad ibn Abd al-Wahhab, an influential Muslim cleric. Through a combination of the al-Sauds' military prowess and al-Wahhab's ability to attract followers, they were able to consolidate control over the Arabian Peninsula's numerous Bedouin tribes. The modern state of Saudi Arabia was formally declared in 1932, and the relationship between the al-Saud family and the Wahhabi clerics continues to define the country. Wahhabism is an ultraconservative interpretation of Sunni Islam characterized by a very strict adherence to Islamic law as well as to the practices of the early Islamic *ummah* (religious community). Its restrictions include the mandatory covering of women in full-length black cloaks and banning females from driving cars. Only males may vote. The government is headed by a king, who must be a descendant of Abd al Aziz al-Saud, the country's first ruler. Saudi Arabia never came under European control and has been an ally of the United States and Britain since World War II.

This image shows Riyadh City from the observation deck at the top of the Kingdom Tower, the tallest building in Saudi Arabia.

The modern Saudi government faces challenges from Islamist militants who believe that the monarchy is in too close an alliance with the Western powers. The use of Saudi air bases by the U.S.-led coalition in the 1991 Gulf War, in part to defend Saudi Arabia from potential attack by Iraq, greatly angered militants, including the Al-Qaeda terrorist leader Osama bin Laden, himself a native Saudi, who offered to raise an army to defend his country. Although Saudi Arabia expelled bin Laden and revoked his citizenship, his ideas still have influence in the kingdom, especially among disaffected youths who see few opportunities for themselves in a country that, despite its oil wealth, has high levels of long-term unemployment—according to some sources, up to 25 percent of the population are without work.

In recent years, Al-Qaeda has sought the overthrow of the al-Saud family. Militants have bombed housing compounds for expatriate (primarily Western) workers who are vital to Saudi Arabia's oil-export-based economy. Saudi Arabia is the world's leading exporter of petroleum and is thought to have 20 percent of all oil reserves. The nation is a key player in the Organization of Petroleum Exporting Countries (OPEC). The Saudi government redistributes significant wealth to the population, and this helps to restrict dissent. With a rapidly growing population, high oil prices are needed to sustain this system. The government has attempted to diversify the economy through the development of tourism, finance, and education, but petroleum remains the nation's most lucrative product.

Shown under construction, this is one of the artificial palm-shaped islands built off the coast of Dubai at the start of the 21st century to attract wealthy residents.

UNITED ARAB EMIRATES

The United Arab Emirates (UAE) formed after the British withdrew from the area in 1971. Formally the UAE is a federation of seven small states: Abu Dhabi, Dubai, Sharjah, Fujairah, Umm al Qawain, Ajman, and Ras al-Khaimah. In practice, it is dominated by the two most powerful emirates—Abu Dhabi, which has vast oil wealth, and Dubai, a major center of commerce and trade. By tradition, the presidency is held by a member of the Abu Dhabi ruling family, al-Nahyan. In 2004 Sheikh Zayad bin Sultan al-Nahyan, the first president of the UAE, died and was succeeded by his, son, Khalifa bin Zayed al-Nahyan (born 1948).

The UAE has a rapidly growing economy and a very high gross national product due to its vast oil resources. Although many countries in the lands surrounding the Persian Gulf have large numbers of expatriate workers, the UAE economy is extraordinarily dependent on foreign labor. The total number of UAE citizens—approximately 4.8 million, 96 percent of whom are Muslims—represents only about 15 percent of the total population. Expatriate workers include—in addition to Westerners who occupy highly technical or managerial positions—vast numbers of menial workers from India and other parts of South Asia. Many males are employed in the booming construction sector, while females work as domestic help or in tourism services. The treatment of these workers—especially the women, who sometimes face physical and sexual abuse by their employers—is a matter of concern to international human rights agencies. Emirati society tends to be conservative, with most women wearing the veil voluntarily. The educational

attainment level is generally high, and the universities of the UAE are unusual in that they have more female students than male students.

Since independence, the UAE has undergone a rapid economic and infrastructural transformation. Once a land of vast deserts and few buildings, with an economy based on pearl diving and fishing, the UAE is best known today for its glittering skyline and high-end malls. Its spectacular and expensive urban projects include the Burj Dubai, which, when completed, will be the world's tallest human-built structure, with a height of 2,684 feet (818 m). The UAE has also built artificial islands in the Persian Gulf for tourist and residential developments. The shapes of these islands—some in the form of palm trees, another with the outline of a map of the world—are visible from the air.

BAHRAIN

The kingdom of Bahrain occupies a group of tiny islands in the Persian Gulf with a total area of only 253 square miles (665 sq. km). It has a population of 728,000, some 81 percent of whom are Muslim. Fertile due to freshwater springs, Bahrain has been inhabited since ancient times and has been subject to many cultural influences, both in ancient times and today. From the 16th century, it was ruled first by the Portuguese and then by the Persians until 1783, when the Arab al-Khalifa family invaded from Qatar and took control of the island. Unable to secure its gains unaided, the al-Khalifa family appealed for help to Britain, and Bahrain became a British protectorate in the 19th century.

Bahrain achieved independence from Britain in 1971 and became a constitutional monarchy with a bicameral parliament and universal suffrage—women are allowed to vote as well as men. Al-Wifaq, the political party that represents the Shiite majority, currently holds the largest number of seats in the elected legislature. Although Bahrain is noted for its religious and ethnic tolerance, discontent among the Shiite population has erupted in street protests and sporadic violence.

By the end of the 20th century, the oil reserves that underlay the economy were severely depleted. The island kingdom diversified into petroleum processing and refining. Bahrain also benefited from the relocation to the island of many banks that fled Beirut during the Lebanese civil war.

KUWAIT

Kuwait was settled in 1612 by tribes from the Arabian Peninsula that came in search of water resources. Pearl diving and the spice trade were the main economic activities. During the Ottoman period, Kuwait was a distinct territory, not included in the provinces that would eventually be combined by the British to form Iraq. After the defeat of the Ottomans, the British, though they had previously signed a treaty recognizing Kuwait as an independent sheikhdom, declared Kuwait to be a British protectorate. Kuwait became fully independent in 1961.

Kuwait is thought to have the fifth-largest oil reserves in the world. Oil was one of the main reasons for the invasion of the country in 1990 by Iraq, which accused its neighbor of "slant drilling" across the frontier to access Iraqi oil. During the Iraqi occupation, more than 600 of Kuwait's oil wells were set ablaze. The fires burned for months, causing extensive pollution. The

The Kuwait National Assembly building stands near the seafront in the capital, Kuwait City.

invaders were expelled by a U.S.-led coalition of UN forces that liberated Kuwait in 1991.

Before and after the Iraqi invasion, Kuwait was ruled by a hereditary constitutional monarchy. The current emir is Sabah al-Ahmed al-Jaber al-Sabah, a descendant of the first emir of Kuwait, who ruled in 1756. The National Assembly of Kuwait holds elections every four years; in 2006 the right to vote was extended to women. In 2008 a number of women ran for office in the parliamentary elections, although none were elected. Nevertheless, a woman was appointed to the cabinet, as minister of planning.

The current 2.7 million population of Kuwait includes 1.3 million non-nationals. Of the 1.4 million native citizens, 85 percent are Muslim—70 percent Sunnis, 30 percent Shiites.

OMAN

The Sultanate of Oman wraps around the southern tip of the Arabian Peninsula, near the entrance to the Persian Gulf and the Strait of Hormuz, a narrow seaway through which much of the world's oil supplies must pass.

Oman's strategic location caused it to be held by many empires during its history. Persian empires, such as the Achaemenids and the Sassanids, controlled the area before the advent of Islam. More recently, the Portuguese, seeking to protect their sea routes to and from Asia, held control from 1500 until they were expelled in 1648. Subsequently ruled by sultans, Oman entered into a close economic and military alliance with Britain in the 19th century, which endured until the early 1970s. It is a hereditary monarchy. The current sultan, Qaboos bin al-Said, who has ruled

since 1970, has done much to open up a previously closed society, creating a commercial infrastructure and an inclusive educational system.

Traditionally, Oman's economy was based on seafaring and trade, especially with India. Although moderate oil resources have allowed Omanis to enjoy a good standard of living, reserves are dwindling and are expected to run out in the 21st century. Oman has been working to diversify its economy by developing industrial sectors and tourism. Oman still has a close relationship with Britain and has entered a free-trade agreement with the United States to stimulate its own economy.

Omanis are predominantly Muslim and socially conservative. Sunni Muslims are the largest religious group, but nearly one-third of the population of 3 million are Ibadi Muslim. The Ibadis differ from Sunnis on various theological matters, including the question of whether believers will actually see God on Judgment Day, and the process of succession after the death of the Prophet Muhammad. There is also a small Shiite population. Hinduism and Christianity are practiced by the country's significant expatriate population.

QATAR

Qatar is a small emirate located on a thumb-shaped protrusion of the Arabian Peninsula near the mouth of the Persian Gulf. The area was dominated by many groups throughout history, including the Persians and the Ottomans. Like the UAE, Qatar had treaty relationships with the British, who used it a stopover en route to India. The country became independent in 1971 and, although it was briefly included in the agreement that created the UAE, it soon withdrew from the federation. Qatar is ruled by hereditary monarchs from the al-Khalifa family. The current emir, Hamad bin Khalifa al-Thani, took control from his father in 1995 in a bloodless coup.

Qatar is conservative but markedly less restrictive than neighboring Saudi Arabia. The Arab satellite television channel, al-Jazeera, based in Qatar, was originally founded with a grant from the emir of Qatar. As most media in the Arab world are censored by national governments, al-Jazeera was considered groundbreaking because it was independent and willing to criticize the Qatari government. Qatar has a close relationship with the West, especially with the United States. The U.S. Armed Forces Unified Combatant Command unit for the Middle East, known as CENTCOM, is headquartered in Doha, the capital of Qatar, and was the base for the U.S.-led invasion of Iraq in 2003.

The 833,000 citizens of Qatar have the highest per capita income in the world. Their wealth is based on oil, the revenue from which has been used to create a "knowledge economy" that has attracted Western universities and science and technology firms to the country. Georgetown University, Carnegie Mellon University, and Texas A&M University are among the U.S. universities that now have campuses in Doha.

YEMEN

Yemen became one of the first nations to adopt Islam when its Persian rulers converted to the religion in the year 628. Although Yemen was briefly united with the rest of the Arabian Peninsula under Abu Bakr (ruled 632–634), for the greater part of its history it has been distinctively different from the other countries of the region. North and South Yemen developed separately in the 19th century after the former became a part of the Ottoman Empire and the latter became a British protectorate. The North gained independence in 1918. In 1967, the British withdrew from the port of Aden, and South Yemen became a Marxist (communist) people's republic. Hundreds of thousands of refugees then fled to North Yemen, and the two states entered a long period of civil war, which ended in 1990 with their unification as the Republic of Yemen. Islam is the state religion, and most of the 23.8 million population are Sunni, although Shiites predominate in the mountainous north and have from time to time tried to create a separate state.

Yemen is one of the poorest countries in the Arab world. Like its neighbors, it possesses oil, which has been extracted commercially since the 1970s, but only in limited quantities. Its richest resource, natural gas, is currently underexploited, although a liquefaction plant was nearing completion in 2009.

The economy is highly dependent on overseas aid, notably from the International Monetary Fund (IMF) and the World Bank. Poverty and the repressive policies of Ali Abdallah Salih—the former president of North Yemen, who assumed control of the unified state at its inception in 1990—have revived numerous separatist movements, some of which have become associated with Al-Qaeda. The bomb that exploded in 2008 outside the gates of the U.S. embassy in the Yemeni capital, Sanaa, killing 16 people, was the most widely publicized of several terrorist incidents that occurred in that year. Following the attack, tension and uncertainty remained at a high level throughout the country.

See Also
Iran 236-245 ❖
Northern Africa
246-249 ❖ Turkey
and Eastern Europe
322-333 ❖

Chapter 11

IRAN

Iran is one of the oldest countries in the world, with borders that have been fairly intact for centuries. It has a unique position in western Asia as it boasts a long pre-Islamic tradition associated with ancient Persia. Iran has never been a formal colony of Western nations. Despite foreign influence in recent history, Iranians proudly held on to their independence and autonomy.

Iran and its people, who are known as Persians, have a long and esteemed history. In the sixth century BCE, the emperor Cyrus unified Persia and expanded the influence of the Persian Empire. The empire's prominence came to an end with the rise of the Greek ruler Alexander the Great in the third century BCE. The next important shift in the history of Iran came with the Arab conquests in the seventh century CE. The conquests resulted in the conversion of the population to Islam, a new religion that had unified Arab tribes and spurred their remarkable military successes. Although Iranians accepted Islam, they distinguished themselves from their conquerors by embracing a new faction of Islam that emerged among their ranks.

These Shias split from the main Islamic tradition (Sunni Islam) by contesting the succession of caliphs after the death of Muhammad. According to the Shias, the rightful successor of Muhammad was his cousin and son-in-law, Ali. As a result, they do not accept the authority of the first three caliphs who succeeded Muhammad as leaders of the Muslim community (*ummah*). With the rise of the Safavids in 1501, a

Shiite dynasty came to power in Iran, and under their rule Persia became a world power once again. Safavid rule came to an abrupt end because of invasions from Afghanistan in 1722. After a short period of unrest, the Safavids were replaced by the much less competent Qajars. The Qajar dynasty, riddled by widespread corruption and incompetence, disintegrated as a result of a movement that culminated in the Constitutional Revolution of 1905 to 1911.

The Arab conquests resulted in the conversion of the population to Islam, a new religion that had unified Arab tribes and spurred their remarkable military successes.

The process of democratization initiated by the Constitutional Revolution was soon replaced by the authoritarian rule of Reza Shah Pahlavi (originally Reza Khan), a military officer who declared himself the new emperor of Persia in 1925. Reza Shah's rule united the country under a strong central government. He established

This late-16th-century map shows the extent of the Persian Empire under the rule of the powerful Safavid dynasty. Persia had converted to Islam during the Arab conquests some 900 years earlier.

a modern army and secularized the educational and judicial systems. After his foreign policy maneuvers in World War II met with the disapproval of the Allied Forces, he abdicated the throne to his son, Mohammad Reza Shah Pahlavi.

The postwar era was characterized by the short-lived democratic rule of the widely revered prime minister Mohammad Mosaddeq (in office 1951–1953). Mosaddeq completed the nationalization of Iran's oil industry, largely controlled by Britain and the United States. He became a central figure in the resurgence of Iranian nationalism. He was quickly removed from his position by the Shah with the aid of the British and the Americans. Mosaddeq's removal from power and the involvement of the U.S. Central Intelligence Agency (CIA) in a clandestine plot became an important point of reference for Iranian nationalists. The CIA plot has been often used to fuel anti-American sentiments. Mosaddeq's overthrow was followed by a return of the autocratic rule of Mohammad Reza Shah Pahlavi. His modernization program, called the White Revolution, created growing resentment among Iranians, especially the clerical class, who rejected the Westernization program as anti-Islamic. The Shah did not tolerate dissent in the country. The gap between the affluence of Westernized elites

MOHAMMAD REZA SHAH PAHLAVI

Mohammad Reza Shah Pahlavi was the shah, or emperor, of Iran from 1941 to 1979, the year he was deposed by the Islamic Revolution. He succeeded his father, Reza Shah Pahlavi, who established the Pahlavi dynasty in 1925. Reza Shah Pahlavi was forced into exile in 1941 by Great Britain and the Soviet Union, who feared that Iran would join World War II on the side of Nazi Germany.

Mohammad Reza Shah was a devoted modernizer and planned to establish Iran as a major world power through a succession of Western-style modernization efforts. His open pro-Western sympathies and the influence of Western oil companies brought him into conflict with Mohammad Mosaddeq, a popular nationalist leader, who was prime minister of Iran between 1951 and 1953. A CIA-engineered coup finally removed Mosaddeq from power and reinstated Mohammad Reza Shah into power. His authoritarian rule ended with the Islamic Revolution in Iran; after fleeing Iran he was given asylum by Egyptian president Anwar el-Sadat in Egypt, where he soon died.

Mohammad Reza Shah Pahlavi is seen here (center right) on arrival in Rome, Italy, after the first, unsuccessful attempt to oust the prime minister Mohammad Mosaddeq.

and the rural and urban poor widened to the breaking point. The anti-Shah and anti-Western sentiments culminated in the Islamic Revolution of 1978 to 1979. The Shah, already sick with cancer, fled the country and died from his illness in 1980 in exile in Egypt.

THE ISLAMIC REVOLUTION

Mohammad Reza Shah's efforts at modernization had mixed results. The country remained heavily dependent on oil revenues. This dependency was revealed as vulnerable after 1973, when an oil crisis led to a sharp drop in Western oil consumption. A growing economy, coupled with the largely credit-based buying power of the population, led to runaway inflation. The increasing prices of everyday items caused growing discontent. In addition, vast land reforms initiated by the Shah did not have the expected results. Huge numbers of people left rural areas seeking better opportunities in Iran's urban centers.

> Mohammad Reza Shah's efforts at modernization had mixed results.

Economic reforms were not followed by political liberalization. The two parties of the political system provided only the appearance of choice, as the Majles (the Parliament) gave unquestioning approval to the policies of the Shah. The Shah used his feared secret service, the SAVAK, to put down, sometimes by the use of torture, all forms of dissent. Indiscriminate repression united diverse groups in their mutual resistance to the perceived tyranny of the

TWELVER SHIISM

Shia Islam has several branches, differentiated by how far the various groups acknowledge the line of imams beginning with Ali, the son-in-law of Muhammad. The main branch, which is the reigning form of Islam in present-day Iran, is Twelver Shiism. Twelvers profess that Muhammad, along with the spiritual and political leadership he represented, was succeeded by 12 imams, starting with Imam Ali. The last imam, al-Mahdi, mysteriously disappeared in 874 and is known as the Hidden Imam. Al-Madhi is believed to be in a state of concealment, or occultation, until his return. Shia Islam is therefore infused with strong messianic expectations. It distinguishes itself from the majority Sunni tradition, which does not share expectations of a future spiritual political leader who will appear and establish his rule on earth.

Shah. More and more people turned to the leadership of the religious establishment, the ulema, especially to Ayatollah Ruhollah Khomeini. The Shia cleric was most vociferous in his criticism of the Shah's secular regime and its close ties to the United States and Israel. Although Khomeini had been in exile since 1963, his sermons and messages were recorded on tape and were disseminated within Iran.

In early 1978, a major newspaper defamed Khomeini. Students of religious institutions and madrassas took to the streets in great numbers to protest. Their protests emboldened others, mostly young urban intellectuals and university students, who were deeply dissatisfied with the Shah's regime. The mass protests took the ailing Shah off guard and he lost control of events. The brutal response to the protests led to their escalation. Khomeini, in exile first in Iraq and then in France, masterminded the spread of a protest movement that was increasingly looking to his political leadership.

Members of the Revolutionary Guard parade at the former U.S. Embassy in Tehran, later used as a military training college. The Revolutionary Guard was established by Ruhollah Khomeini in 1979.

After the Shah fled Iran and appointed a provisional Regency Council led by Shahpuhr Bakhtiar, events came completely under the control of Khomeini. He returned to Iran on February 1, 1979, and was received by more than one million supporters on the streets of Tehran. Following a national referendum, Iran was declared an Islamic Republic on April 1, 1979.

With the declaration of the Islamic Republic, conservative clerics, led by

Khomeini, quickly set out to exclude their former allies—leftists, secular nationalists, and intellectuals—as they sought to impose strict religious norms on public life. The Islamic legal code, Sharia (in its Shia interpretation), was declared the ultimate arbiter of social and political life, and strict religious dress codes were enforced. Women were obligated to wear the veil, and previous advances in women's rights were quickly rescinded. Religious militias began to patrol the streets and reprimand those who did not adhere to the religious norms set by the Revolutionary Council. The Revolutionary Guard established by Khomeini systematically eliminated all opposition to Khomeini's rule, often exceeding the brutality of the SAVAK. The glory of the Revolution that brought together Iranians from all political affiliations slowly deteriorated into a reign of religion-based terror. The new regime launched an offensive to eradicate all traces of Western influence. The Westernized elite fled the country, while the Marxist left, former allies of Khomeini, were also gradually marginalized.

Khomeini presented himself as the most credible force to resist the imperialist threat of the United States and establish national unity. He also initially portrayed the Islamic system as devoted defenders of the poor and the dispossessed. However, his support base among the conservative merchant class, the *bazaaris*, made him less willing to make good on his promises to the poor.

The elimination of leftist voices from politics was followed by the suppression of clerics and political leaders who did not fully fit the conservative mold of the new regime. As a result of their disagreement regarding the handling of the subsequent hostage crisis, both the provisional prime minister, Mehdi Bazargan, and the first president of the Islamic Republic, Abolhsan Bani-Sadr, were pushed out of power. The conservative takeover of the Revolution was thus complete.

IRAN HOSTAGE CRISIS

The Revolution brought about a significant change in Iran's relationship with the United States. The Shah's regime had close ties with the United States, but the perceived U.S. support for the increasingly repressive regime of the Shah created a backlash against the United States in the early days of the Revolution. The American Embassy became the frequent target of public demonstrations. When in October 1979 the deposed Shah was admitted to the United States to obtain medical help, the embassy in Tehran became the target of further hostilities. A mob of 3,000, mostly university students posing as leftist revolutionaries, overran the embassy and took hostage about 70 American staff.

The hostages were caught in a power struggle within the less than unified revolutionary movement. The efforts of the Carter administration to negotiate the release of the hostages became repeatedly frustrated. The United States tried to put pressure on Iran, freezing Iranian assets and suspending the purchase of Iranian oil while lobbying the United Nations to condemn the Iranian government. The situation was made worse by the failure of a secret U.S. military operation to free the hostages in April 1980, when a military aircraft crashed in the desert. The debacle was highly damaging to the presidency of Jimmy Carter, who later lost presidential elections to Ronald Reagan. As a symbolic act of humiliation, the hostages were released virtually minutes after the new president of the United States was inaugurated in 1980.

THE IRAN–IRAQ WAR

On September 22, 1980, Iraqi forces, having mobilized around the Iranian border, invaded western Iran. The invasion had been precipitated by a string of territorial and political disputes. Iraq, led by President Saddam Hussein, had its eye on the oil-rich region of Khuzestan, largely inhabited by Sunni Arabs. Saddam claimed that the

Sunni population expressed its allegiance to his Sunni-led Iraqi regime. Iraq was also looking to take over both banks of the Shatt al-Arab waterway, a natural border between the countries. In addition, Saddam was concerned about the perceived attempts of the new Islamic Republic in Iran to spread revolutionary ideas among the majority Shia population in Iraq.

The surprise invasion was halted by the stronger than expected resistance put up by the Iranian Revolutionary Guard, making it impossible for the Iraqis to capture the target of Abadan, with its major oil refinery. Within a few months, the Iraqi troops could push no farther into Iran. The

Iranians launched a counteroffensive and recaptured most of their territory. By 1982, the Iraqis started to seek a peace agreement with Iran. By then, however, the Iranians were determined that only the overthrow of Saddam Hussein could guarantee an acceptable resolution of the war. Still, Iranian forces could not achieve significant gains against the Iraqis, who were now defending their own territory, and the frontlines were frozen for several years. The war resulted in enormous losses, especially on the Iranian side, which relied on sheer numbers of untrained but devoted infantry. Most Western powers supported Iraq, until it became known that Iraq used chemical

RUHOLLAH KHOMEINI

Ruhollah Khomeini was an influential Shia cleric who became the political and religious leader of Iran after the overthrow of Mohammad Reza Shah Pahlavi in 1979. He was educated in Islamic schools and became a prominent Islamic thinker, publishing various writings on Islamic theology, philosophy, and law. He developed the notion of the *velayat-e faqih* (governance by the religious jurist), a doctrine that he endeavored to personify after the Revolution. He received the title of ayatollah, a designation of a major religious leader in Shia Islam, in the 1950s and was further recognized as a grand ayatollah in the 1960s, becoming one of the most important religious leaders in Iran.

Khomeini was vocal in his opposition to the Shah's regime and to the spread of Western, secular influence in Iran. After he openly criticized the Shah, Khomeini was arrested and forced into exile. During his exile, at first in the Iraqi holy city of Najaf, he continued to call for the end of the rule of the Shah and for the establishment of an Islamic Republic. After Saddam forced Khomeini to leave Iraq in 1978, the grand

ayatollah settled in Paris, from where he coordinated the growing public protests of the early days of the Islamic Revolution.

Khomeini proved a smart manipulator of the conservative religious sentiment prevalent among revolutionary Iranians. He moved quickly to undo all traces of the Westernizing tendencies of the Shah's regime. He made it obligatory for women to wear the veil in public, banned Western music and the consumption of alcohol, and reinstated physical punishments for the transgression of Sharia (Islamic law), which became the foundation of Iran's legal system. Khomeini's militant message of political Islam resulted in his opposition to both the United States and the Soviet Union. His determination to spread the Islamic Revolution to other Muslim majority countries further alienated his regime, hindering Iran in its eight-year war with Iraq. Khomeini refused to accept a peaceful solution to the war, hoping instead to overthrow Saddam. As a result of its international isolation and drawn-out war, Iran experienced a long period of economic stagnation and decline under Khomeini.

and biological weapons against both its Iranian foes and its own minority Kurdish population. Iran had its own regional allies, most notably Syria and Libya, while Iraq was financially supported in the region by Saudi Arabia and Kuwait.

The war depleted the resources of both countries, as oil revenues dropped sharply. Almost every family in Iran was touched by the loss of a male relative, which had significant repercussions on the postwar development of the country. The war ended formally when diplomatic ties were reestablished between Iran and Iraq during Iraq's invasion of Kuwait in 1990.

REFORMS

With Ruhollah Khomeini's death in 1989, the competition between various factions within the Islamic Republic became clearly visible. Facing a serious economic crisis in the aftermath of the war, officials were divided about how to rebuild the economy. Although they all supported a conservative social and religious Islamic state, members of the government had different visions. One faction supported greater government control, while an opposing group wanted a smaller role for government. A movement for reform also began whose interest lay beyond economics. Reformists argued that the Islamic Republic needed liberalization of its social and political structures, and that it needed to come out of its self-imposed international isolation.

Changes began immediately after the Assembly of Elders named the president, Ali Khameini, as supreme leader, or *rahbar*, in 1989. Khameni's rise to higher office left the position of president vacant. Elections were organized in 1989 to choose a replacement. The winner, Ali Akbar Hashemi Rafsanjani, was previously speaker of the Majles.

Rafsanjani immediately began to implement policies for economic liberalization and privatization of state property. He also tried to normalize relationships with Western countries and attract desperately needed Western capital. Rafsanjani's policies were met by stiff opposition from the clerical elite, which tried to suppress dissident movements among students and intellectuals. Despite the conservative reaction, new forms of communication with the outside world created new possibilities to address various social issues, especially women's rights. Signs of democratization were slowly emerging in a society that had experienced decades of oppression, first under the Shah and than under Khomeini.

The liberalization process initiated by Rafsanjani gained further impetus with the election as president of Mohammad Khatami, a moderate. Following Khatami's election, hundreds of new newspapers were set up to support the reformist program. The conservative religious establishment, headed by Ayatollah Khameini, tried to suppress the resurgent reformist movement; members of Khatami's administration were removed, and public intellectuals were jailed or died under suspicious circumstances. Freedom of the press was also stifled with the banning of reformist newspapers. Khatami won new elections in 2001 but was seriously weakened by both the attacks of the conservatives and the concessions he was making to please them.

Khatami's efforts to forge links with the United States were also frustrated. Despite his condemnation of the terrorist attacks in the United States on September 11, 2001, Iran was nonetheless named as part of an "axis of evil" by U.S. president George W. Bush in 2003. The reformist agenda became paralyzed and Khatami resigned, which led to the rise to power of the conservative populism of Mahmoud Ahmadinejad.

Mahmoud Ahmadinejad became president of the Islamic Republic in 2005 after defeating Ali Akbar Hashemi Rafsanjani, the favorite to win, in a run-off election. There were rumors that Ahmadinejad participated in the hostage-taking at the American Embassy in Tehran in 1979, but these claims were later refuted. After Iran's invasion by Iraq in 1980, he became a member of the Revolutionary Guard. Following the war, Ahmadinejad was involved in provincial politics, holding several administrative positions before being elected mayor of Tehran in 2003. As mayor of the capital city, he gained a reputation for being devoted to the Islamic revolutionary principles of Khomeini, calling for a return to the religious rigor advocated by the grand ayatollah.

Ahmadinejad's 2005 presidential election campaign ran on a populist and conservative platform that promised to end the growing corruption in Iranian government and to institute new economic policies to address the plight of the growing number of poor in Iranian society. Although his economic policies did not fulfill people's expectations, Ahmadinejad maintained his public appeal by turning to populist nationalism, emphasizing Iran's nuclear ambitions, and calling for the eradication of the State of Israel. His conservative religious platform also helped him strengthen the role of the president in Iranian politics.

SUNNI-SHIA CONFLICT

The traditional conflict between Sunni and Shia Islam reached a conflagration point with Ayatollah Khomeini's rise to power in 1979. Khomeini saw himself as a leader of the whole Islamic world and expressed his desire to export the Islamic Revolution and help overthrow regimes he considered un-Islamic. He was especially critical of the

IRAN-CONTRA AFFAIR

Iran-Contra refers to a complicated political scandal in the United States that implicated influential members of the National Security Council during the Reagan administration. In an effort to gain favors with Hezbollah, a terrorist group in Lebanon that had kidnapped numerous American citizens during the Lebanon civil war, the United States secretly sold weapons to Iran. In addition, the administration used the revenues it garnered from these arms sales to provide clandestine financial support to the Contras, anti-Communist insurgents in Nicaragua. In 1985, Ronald Reagan gave the green light to selling missiles to Iran, which was then deeply entrenched in a war with Iraq, in exchange for Iran's help with negotiating with Hezbollah, a Shia group with close ties with Iran. This decision contradicted explicit U.S. policy not to negotiate with terrorist organizations, or to get economically involved with countries that supported terrorist groups. By November 1986, the arms-for-hostages transaction became public knowledge, putting Reagan in a highly embarrassing situation. The embarrassment further intensified with revelations about how funds from the arms transaction became diverted to support the Contras, an insurgency group known for its atrocities against the civilian population in Nicaragua. The two main players, Oliver North and John Poindexter, were fired, and a special commission was appointed to investigate the scandal. Although Reagan denied direct involvement and knowledge of the details of the transactions, his role in the Iran-Contra Affair was never sufficiently clarified.

regime in Saudi Arabia, whose rulers were major supporters of Saddam Hussein during the Iran-Iraq War. Khomeini's opposition to Sunni-majority Saudi Arabia, where Wahhabism had become the official form of Islam, reignited the age-old rivalry between Sunnis and Shias. The opposition between Iran and Saudi Arabia is often characterized as the clash of state-funded fundamentalism. Khomeini drew on Shia sacred history and the martyrdom of Imam Ali's son Huseyn at Karbala to mobilize his supporters and wage an unrelenting war against Sunni-minority-led Iraq.

Conflict between the two main branches of Islam again gained significance with the invasion of Iraq by the United States and its allies in 2003, which quickly led to the overthrow of Saddam Hussein's Sunni regime. Following the invasion,

violence erupted frequently between the two religious communities within Iraq, where Iran supported the Shia majority. Post-invasion Iraq saw the rise of Shiism in the country where Shiites had been largely suppressed and kept out of power under Saddam Hussein. The rise of Shiism in Iraq and its increasing presence in the political life of the country resulted in an often violent response from the Sunni community in the region. On the other hand, however, it has helped to strengthen the position of Shia communities in Lebanon and Bahrain, where members have been demanding an increased role in the political life of their respective countries. Many observers believe that the resurgence of Shiism will strengthen Iran and allow it to become the major political player in the region.

Mahmoud Ahmadinejad was the surprise winner in the 2005 Iranian presidential elections, beating favorite and rival Ali Akbar Hashemi Rafsanjani. In 2009 he won a second term in a controversial election marred by accusations of corruption and violent protests.

See Also

The Eastern Mediterranean and the Arabian Peninsula 220-235 ❖ South Asia 274-291 ❖ Central Asia 304-313 ❖

S   10   15   20   25   30   35   40   45   50   55   60   65   70   75

GALLIA

HISPANIA

ITALIA

GRAECIA   ASIA MINOR

MARE · MEDITERRANEVM ·

Sardinia.   Sicilia.   Cyprus.   I

Mauritania.   Africa minor.   Marmarica.

Bagrada fl.   Cyrene.   AEGYPTVS.   Sin' Arabic

Sulfus fl.

Cagapola   Getulia   Vsargala mõs.   Garamates.

Chausarus.   Girgiris.   Chelanida pal?

Nuius fl.   Nigritę   Libyę palus.   Meroe.

Massa fl.   Nigri fl.   Sabath

Nigrisisii pal?   Nuba pal.

Darati   Ryssadius.

Caphas.   LIBYA.   Afia

Stachiris.   Interior.   Garamantica   Aftabora   Gar

Leucaethiopes.   Thala mos.   ualis.

Nia fl.   Nilus fl.

Mellitou.   Deorum mons.   Nubi.

Ayualtes mons   Pylei montes

Ichthyophagi .   Arangas mõs.

ÆTHIOPIA INTERIOR.

Cinnami   Azania
fera Re-
gio.

Agisymba Regio.   Mafte

Athace.   P

Zipha mõs.

Dauchis mõs.

Lunę montes.

Mefcha mõs.   Anthropopha

Terra Ptolemeo   incognita.

Barditi mätes.

10   15   20   25   30   35   40   45   50   55   60   65   70

NORTHERN AFRICA

The nations of northern Africa with Muslim majorities form a line along the coasts of the Mediterranean Sea and the Atlantic Ocean. From east to west, they are Egypt, Libya, Tunisia, Algeria, Morocco, and the disputed Western Sahara, which is known to nationalist freedom fighters as the Saharawi Arab Democratic Republic.

Early Muslim geographers and chroniclers used the term *Maghrib* to describe the region of northern Africa (modern Algeria, Libya, Morocco, and Tunisia) that was conquered by the spread (*futuhat*) of Islam in the 7th and 8th centuries. They did not count Egypt as part of the Maghrib but grouped it with the Arabian Peninsula, Iraq, and Syria—the region often known as the "fertile crescent." Egypt and Syria were both conquered in 641 CE by one of the early followers of the Prophet Muhammad, Amr ibn al-As, during the Caliphate of Umar ibn Khattab (634-644); Egypt then became a province of the caliphate of Medina.

Maghrib is an Arabic term meaning, literally, "the west." Today the word has two popular meanings: it may refer specifically to the country of Morocco or to the time of the sunset prayer, the fourth of the five prayers (*salat*) that Muslims are required to perform daily. From the 7th century, the Maghrib was united as a single political entity until the end of the 8th century. Subsequently divided, it was later reunited several times under various rulers, notably those of the Almohad dynasty (1147–1229). Because the Maghrib is partially isolated from the rest of Africa by

the Atlas Mountains and the Sahara Desert, Algeria, Libya, Morocco, and Tunisia are closely linked economically, linguistically, politically, and topographically, as well as by religion. The cities of the Maghrib developed their own, distinctive behavioral mores (*adab*) and religious beliefs, which still differ in many ways from those in the rest of the Muslim world.

In the 7th and 8th centuries, the Maghrib became the center for Maliki jurists—Maliki is a madhhab, one of the four schools of Sunni Islamic law.

In the 7th and 8th centuries, the Maghrib became the center for Malikı jurists—Maliki is a *madhhab*, one of the four schools of Sunni Islamic law. Malikı practice is a fundamental conception of the legal codes that were formulated by Malik bin Anas (711–795) and still influence the constitution of the countries in the Maghrib today. Because the Marinid dynasty (Islamized Berbers who ruled Morocco from 1269 through 1465) was

This hand-colored copper engraving, produced in 1584, shows northern Africa as cartographers of the era imagined it.

eager to propagate the Maliki school of law, its sultans engaged in a long campaign to build many madrassas (religious colleges). In the middle of the 13th century, the start of the Reconquista—the "Reconquest," the name given to the Christian struggle to take back the Iberian Peninsula (modern Portugal and Spain) from the Muslim occupiers—created a flow of Islamic refugees across the narrow Strait of Gibraltar into northern Africa. The ensuing population boom caused great strains in the increasingly crowded cities. As the Arab traveler and author Leo Africanus (around 1485–1554) noted in *Descrittione dell'Africa* (1550; *A Geographical History of Africa*, 1600) on a visit to Morocco: "It was essential to find a roof under which we could shelter, which was not easy as the Andalusian [southern Spanish] immigrants, arriving in wave after wave in Fez, had taken over all the houses available."

Throughout history, the lives of people in the Maghrib have been dominated by sea transportation and trade. In 1989 Algeria, Libya, Morocco, and Tunisia— together with Mauritania—established the Arab Maghrib Union to promote cooperation and economic integration. Originally envisioned by the Libyan leader Muammar-al-Qaddafi as an Arab superstate, the union was expected eventually to function as a northern African common market.

EGYPT

The commercial and political center of modern Egypt was founded in 641 as a garrison for the conquering Muslim army led by Amr ibn al-As. Originally named al-Fustat, it grew into the city now known as Cairo and replaced Alexandria as the national capital.

Among the early rulers of Islamic Egypt were the Tulunids (868–905), a dynastic name derived from that of Ahmad Ibn Tulun, who was appointed governor of Egypt by the Abbasid Caliphate in Baghdad. In 969 the Fatimid armies from the region of northern Africa that is now Tunisia overran al-Fustat. The Fatimids, who ruled Egypt from 969 through 1171, belonged to the Ismaili branch of Shia Islam. They were named for Fatimah, a daughter of the Prophet Muhammad.

The Fatimids established the city of Cairo (al-Qahira). They gave the city its name, according to tradition, because on the day of its foundation the planet Mars (al-Qahir) was in the ascendant. Cairo prospered under the Fatimids. In 970 they founded Al-Azhar ("The Flourishing"), which is the second oldest functioning university in the world.

The Fatimids were succeeded by the Ayyubids (r. 1171–1252), whose most famous ruler was their founder, Salah ad-Din Yusuf ibn Ayyub (1138–1193), better known in the English-speaking world as Saladin, a great military leader and warrior who ruled Egypt and Syria.

The Mamluks succeeded the Ayyubids and ruled Egypt from 1252 through 1517. Before their rise to power, the Mamluks had been slaves, brought to Egypt and trained as soldiers from childhood. Ethnically they were mainly Kipchak Turks from the southern steppes of Russia and Circassians from the Christian areas of the northern Caucasus. Despite being slaves and non-Arabs, their status as professional soldiers and guards to the sultan gave them considerable political influence.

The Mamluks largely continued the policies of the Ayyubids, with power exercised by sultans, governors, and emirs (military commanders) who built many mosques, hospitals, and madrassas in Cairo, Aleppo, Damascus, and Jerusalem.

The Mamluks gained great prestige from their role as defenders of the lands of Islam (Dar al-Islam). The greatest Mamluk sultan is generally agreed to have been Baybars I (r. 1260–1277), who defeated an army of Christian Crusaders in 1250 at Al-Mansurah on the banks of the Nile River and ransomed its leader, King Louis IX of France. Baybars then defeated Hulegu's Mongols at the Battle of Ayn Jalut (Goliath's Well) in Palestine in 1260.

This undated, unsigned drawing depicts Saladin, the great Muslim leader who, in 1174, was proclaimed sultan of Egypt and Syria.

CAIRO

The view over the Cairo skyline combines traditional minarets with more modernist high-rise buildings.

The modern city of Cairo covers an area of more than 175 square miles (453 sq. km), although it is difficult to separate the city from some of its immediate suburbs. Bracketed by the desert to the east, south, and west and bounded to the north by the fertile delta of the Nile River, Cairo sits astride the river, although it spreads farther on the east bank than on the west. Cairo also includes several river islands, which play an important role in tourism and the social life of the city. As Egypt's principal commercial, administrative, and tourist center, Cairo contains many cultural institutions, business establishments, government offices, universities, and hotels, which together create a dense pattern of constant activity: the pyramids on the Giza Plateau, the Egyptian and Islamic museums, the Cairo zoo, the citadel, and hundreds of medieval monuments in the old city (Khan al-Khalili) are all very popular with tourists.

The outstanding buildings of the early Muslim period include the mosques of Amr ibn al-As (founded in 641–642) and Ahmad ibn Tulun (completed in 878) and the partially excavated mounds covering the site of the original garrison of al-Fustat.

The Mamluk Sultanate survived until 1517, when Egypt was conquered by the Ottoman Empire under the Turkish sultan Selim I (ruled 1512–1520). Egypt then continued under Ottoman rule until 1914. The later sultans found it difficult to govern the province from the Ottoman capital, Istanbul, but ruled vicariously through the semiautonomous Mamluks until Egypt was conquered in 1798 by the French under Napoleon Bonaparte (r. 1799–1815).

Muhammad Ali (an Albanian commander from Kavalla in Macedonia) expelled the French in 1801. He and his descendants then ruled Egypt until 1882, when the country became a de facto protectorate of Britain. From 1917 through 1936, the last two historically significant members of the Muhammad Ali dynasty— King Fu'ad and King Farouk—struggled to throw off British rule. In June of 1953, the monarchy was abolished and Egypt became an independent republic.

Under President Gamal Abdel Nasser (ruled 1956–1970), Egypt developed from an almost exclusively agrarian economy into a nation with a firm industrial base. Nasser's presidency was not entirely successful: he was defeated by Israel in the Six-Day War of 1967 and failed in his ultimate ambition to unite the whole Arab world under his leadership. Nasser ran Egypt as a police state. Nevertheless, he was a hero to many, and his posthumous reputation remains largely undiminished. Nasser's greatest lasting monument is the Aswan High Dam. Completed in 1970, this vast structure enabled the Egyptians for the first time to control the annual Nile River flood and to irrigate millions of acres of previously arid land. The construction of the dam led to an unprecedented international effort to save ancient treasures from the rising waters, including the famed temples of Abu Simbel, which were dismantled and moved to a nearby site.

On the death of Nasser, Anwar el-Sadat became the president of Egypt. With the assistance of U.S. president Jimmy Carter (in office 1977–1981), Sadat reached a peace agreement with Israel—the Camp David Accords—for which he and Israeli prime minister Menachem Begin were awarded the 1978 Nobel Peace Prize. Meanwhile, however, Sadat's economic policies failed and there was mounting domestic opposition to his conciliatory approach to Israel. Sadat was assassinated by Muslim extremists from a group called the Jihad Organization—a splinter group of the Muslim Brotherhood—in 1981.

During the presidency of Sadat's successor, Hosni Mubarak, Egypt's relations with Israel cooled, especially after the latter's invasion of Lebanon in 1982. Internal dissent is discouraged by the Egyptian security forces, and as a result there has been a notable rise in the number of guerrilla movements and acts of terrorism. Politically, the most significant opposition to Mubarak's rule is provided by the Muslim Brotherhood, which, though technically illegal, in 2009 held 88 seats in the People's Assembly.

LIBYA

Arab Muslims conquered most of the region now known as Libya in the seventh century. The invasion was led by Uqba ibn Nafi (622–683), a nephew of Amr ibn al-As. In 644, Uqbah ibn Nafi established a garrison in Libya and completed his conquest of the country by 655. Libya then became a part of the Umayyad Caliphate, which had its base in Damascus (the capital

of modern Syria). After the collapse of
the Umayyad Caliphate in 750, control
of the region passed to the Abbasid dynasty
(r. 750–1258). Libya enjoyed considerable
autonomy under a series of Abbasid-
sponsored lieutenant emirs, starting with
the Aghlabids (r. 800–909), who undertook
an ambitious program of public building
works and assembled a navy that was feared
throughout the Mediterranean. In the 16th
century, two of the provinces of Libya—
Cyrenaica in the east and Tripolitania in
the northwest—nominally became parts of
the Ottoman Empire. Libya enjoyed semi-
independence from the Ottoman sultans
under the Karamanlis (r. 1711–1835).
This dynasty was composed of descendants
of Ahmed Karamanli (1686–1745), a
Janissary (sultan's guard) who murdered
the Ottoman governor and usurped his
position. The Ottomans took power again
in 1835 and retained it until 1911, when
the region was invaded by Italy. It was
under the Italian occupation that Cyrenaica
and Tripolitania were formally united
with the southwestern province of Fezzan
to form the outline of the modern state.
In 1934, Italy began calling its colony
Libya, a name that had been used by the
ancient Greeks for all of northern Africa
except Egypt.

Libyan resistance to the Italians
eventually cost the lives of between 20
percent and 50 percent of the population.
Among the leaders of the rebels were
Omar Mukhtar (1862–1931) and Sidi
Muhammad Idris al-Mahdi al-Sanusi
(1890–1983). Although the Italians were
expelled at the end of World War II
(1939–1945), it was not until 1951 that
Libya achieved independence and became a
monarchy. Its first king was al-Sanusi, who
took the regnal name of Idris I.

Idris was a conservative ruler who
ignored his subjects' middle-class aspirations
and tried to resist the rising tide of pan-
Arab nationalism. In 1969, he was deposed
in a coup led by Muammar al-Qaddafi, a
28-year-old army officer. The new regime,
headed by the Revolutionary Command
Council (RCC), abolished the monarchy
and proclaimed the Libyan Arab Republic.
Qaddafi emerged as leader of the RCC
and eventually as de facto head of state.
He is referred to in all government
statements and in the official Libyan
press as the "Brother, Leader, and Guide
of the Revolution."

Libya's political system is based on
Qaddafi's *The Green Book* (1975), which
combines socialist and Islamic theories
and rejects parliamentary democracy and
political parties. Qaddafi exercises near total
control over major government decisions.
For the first seven years following the
revolution, Qaddafi and the RCC
completely overhauled Libya's political
system, society, and economy. In 1973
Qaddafi announced a "cultural revolution"
in schools, businesses, industries, and
public institutions that aimed to oversee
administration of those organizations in
the public interest. In 1977 Qaddafi
proclaimed the establishment of "people's
power," and changed the name of the
country to the Socialist People's Libyan
Arab Jamahiriya. (*Jamahiriya* was an Arabic
neologism meaning "republic ruled by
the masses.")

For many years, Libya sponsored
terrorist attacks on the West. In 1988 a
bomb exploded on board a Pan Am flight
from London, England, to New York,
killing all 243 passengers and crew and 11
people in the town of Lockerbie, Scotland,
on which the Boeing 747 aircraft crashed.

Suspecting Libya of involvement, the United Nations (UN) imposed sanctions in 1992. Libya remained isolated from the international community until 2003, when it finally admitted responsibility for the bombing. Since then, Qaddafi has successfully restored diplomatic and trading relations with many Western countries.

TUNISIA

The Arab conquest of 648–669 led to the development of the region of Tunisia formerly known as Ifriqiyya (the root of the English noun *Africa*). An Umayyad general, Uqbah ibn Nafi (622–683), founded the garrison of Kairouan, which later became the first major Muslim city

Nationalist leader Habib Bourguiba returns in triumph to Tunis from Paris after having achieved Tunisia's independence from France in 1956.

An Algerian soldier guards a street in Algiers during the political crisis that stemmed from the 1991 general election.

anywhere in northern Africa, predating even Cairo.

Tunisia flourished under Arab rule in the eighth century. Extensive irrigation installations were built to supply towns with water and to promote agriculture, especially olive production. From the 12th century to the 14th century, Tunisia—together with neighboring Morocco—received an influx of Muslim and Jewish immigrants, who fled from Andalusia (part of modern Spain) to escape the Reconquista. The Arab historian al-Umari (1301–1349) confirms the major shifts in demography resulting from the Reconquista. He notes that, "since Spain emptied itself of its [Muslim and Jewish] inhabitants, they have come to shelter under the wings of Tunis."

Several Arab and Berber dynasties governed Tunisia from the 9th century to the 16th century. The Aglabids (r. 800–909) were loyal to the Baghdad-based Abbasid caliph, Harun al-Rashid (r. 786–809), and presided over a renaissance in art, music, science, and religion. The Fatimids (r. 909–969) constructed a palatial city at al-Madiyyah but abandoned it in 969 to establish a new city, al-Qahira (Cairo), in Egypt. The Zirids and the Hammadids governed Tunisia from 972 to 1159 with one local headquarters at Kairouan and another at Qala'at bani Hammad in Algeria. They were succeeded by the Almohads (r. 1147–1229) and the Hafsids (r.1229–1574). The Turks, led by Uluj Ali, invaded Tunisia in 1570 and completed their conquest four years later. Tunisia then remained part of the Ottoman Empire until the 19th century. French troops occupied the country in 1881 and the bey (governor) signed a treaty acknowledging Tunisia as a French protectorate.

Although the French had acquired Tunisia through diplomatic maneuvers rather than through military action, as had been the case in Algeria, their colonialism proved no more welcome in Tunis than it was in Algiers. Widespread protests forced France in 1956 to announce its withdrawal from Tunisia, which became an independent republic the following year. Its first president, Habib Bourguiba (1903–2000), ruled for the next 31 years, during which he established a strict one-party state. Although Bourguiba's regime had a progressive veneer—it granted women greater freedom than they enjoyed in many Muslim states—it masked an underlying authoritarianism. The government clamped down harshly on Islamic fundamentalists.

Bourguiba was removed from power in a bloodless coup in 1987 and replaced by an army officer, Zine el Abidine Ben Ali (b.1936). In 1994, Ben Ali enacted electoral reforms that allowed the formation of a parliamentary opposition. However, the effectiveness of any legal political party other than the president's own Democratic Constitutional Rally remains dubious—Ben Ali won reelection in 1994, 1999, and 2004, each time with more than 90 percent of the vote. The radical Islamist Al-Nahdah (Renaissance) party is banned.

ALGERIA

Islam was introduced into Algeria by Arab military expeditions between 642 and 669. Prior to these invasions, most of the indigenous population followed either Christianity, which had been brought to the region during the late Roman period, or any of several local faiths espoused by the indigenous Berber people. Christians and Berbers then intermarried with Muslims to produce a heterogeneous society, which was subsequently ruled by Berbers who embraced Islam and became successively part of two great Muslim dynasties: the Almoravids (r. 1073–1146) and the Almohads (r. 1147–1229). There then followed more than 200 years of conflict and political instability, during which the use of Arabic spread to the countryside and sedentary Berber farmers were gradually Arabized.

In 1536 Algeria became part of the Ottoman Empire. The French invaded Algeria in 1830; before their conquest of the country was completed in the mid-1870s, the native population fell by one-third. Algerian independence movements led to the uprisings of 1954–1955, which developed into full-scale war with France. In 1962 French president Charles de Gaulle began peace negotiations, and Algeria became independent in the same year. In 1963 former rebel leader Ahmed Ben Bella was elected president, and Algeria adopted socialism. Ben Bella's party, the National Liberation Front (FLN), then dominated mainstream politics, but opposition gradually increased and culminated in a victory for the Islamic Salvation Front (FIS) in the first

Free Ports of Northern Africa

Located near the Strait of Gibraltar inside the entrance to the Mediterranean Sea, Ceuta is surrounded by Morocco but belongs to Spain. Around 150 miles (240 km) to the east of Ceuta lies the other Spanish exclave in northern Africa, Melilla. Both cities are free ports or free-trade zones in which goods may be landed, handled, manufactured, and reshipped without the usual customs formalities and fees. They are also the locations of strategically important Spanish military and naval bases.

Spain seized Melilla from the Berbers in 1497 and has retained it ever since, although not without local opposition: Moroccan forces almost captured it in 1921. Ceuta became a Spanish possession in 1580 after more than a century of Portuguese rule.

Morocco still claims Ceuta and Melilla and asks why Spain should retain these exclaves when the Madrid government objects to the occupation of Gibraltar by Britain. However, the Spanish argue that the situations are incomparable because, while Ceuta and Melilla are fully integrated into Spain as autonomous cities, Gibraltar is a British Overseas Territory, not a part of the United Kingdom of Great Britain and Northern Ireland.

The population of both cities—at the start of the 21st century, each had approximately 67,000 inhabitants—is around two-thirds Catholic and one-third Muslim. Both Ceuta and Melilla are heavily protected by armed guards and double fences with barbed wire and searchlights to discourage illegal immigration into Spain and, from there, into the wider European Community (EC).

round of the 1991 elections. Fear of this radical party prompted the Algerian army to intervene and postpone the second round of the elections. The ensuing military attempts to disband the FIS provoked opposition attacks on government targets. The government then partially relented, allowing the second round of the elections to go ahead but banning the FIS from participating. This provoked an insurgency, which degenerated into civil war. At least 100,000 Algerians were killed in the fighting, which continued until 1998. In the following year, Abdelaziz Bouteflika became president of Algeria in a rigged election. The military wing of the FIS, the Islamic Salvation Army, was disbanded in January of 2000.

In 2004, Bouteflika was reelected for a second term by a landslide majority. Nevertheless, widespread discontent remained and found expression through

extremist organizations such as the Salafist Group for Preaching and Combat (GSPC), which merged with Al-Qaeda in 2006 to form Al-Qaeda in the Lands of the Islamic Maghrib. This group has committed numerous acts of terrorism, including kidnappings, bombings, and suicide attacks on Algerian government targets and Western interests.

Morocco

The western campaign of Uqbah ibn Nafi reached the region of northern Africa now known as Morocco in 682. The original inhabitants—mainly nomadic Berbers, some of whom had espoused Christianity or Judaism during a brief earlier period of Roman rule—quickly converted to Islam. In 711 the Muslims used Morocco as their base for further territorial expansion, this time into southern Europe. Tariq-ibn-Ziyad, a

Muslim Berber general, led a force of 7,000 soldiers in response to a call for help from one faction in a civil war between the Visigoths in Andalusia. This expedition led to the establishment of an Islamic state in the Iberian Peninsula that endured until the 15th century.

Islam became firmly rooted in Morocco in 769 when Idris I—a descendant of Muhammad through the Prophet's daughter Fatimah and his son-in-law Ali—became the first ruler of the Idrisid dynasty that remained in power until 985. In the meantime, the city of Fez was founded in 808, and northern Morocco was unified as far as Tlemcen in Algeria.

The next major dynasty to govern Morocco was that of the Almoravids (r. 1073–1146), formerly nomadic Berbers who founded Marrakesh, which became the capital city. The Almohads (r. 1147–1229) captured Marrakesh in 1147 and, in 1195, the emir Yaqub al-Mansur (r. 1184–1199) defeated the Spanish and Portuguese kings at the Battle of Alacros, which led to the annexation of al-Andalus (Andalusia, Spain).

On ascending the throne, Ahmad al-Mansur (r. 1578–1603) reasserted Morocco's independence by skillfully turning the four European powers with covetous eyes on his realm against each other. Once the threats from England, France, Portugal, and Spain had been neutralized, Morocco entered a golden age of prosperity and artistic achievement.

Workers soak leather in the dye tubs of the tannery in the Leather Souq in Fez, which has existed on the same site since the 11th century. Sheep and goat hides are tanned and dyed to make the leather goods for which Morocco has traditionally been famous.

This photograph shows some of the typical desert landscape of Western Sahara.

In 1860 European colonialism returned to Morocco when the northern part of the country was occupied by Spanish forces. In 1912 the French imposed a protectorate under General Louis-Hubert-Gonzalve Lyautey (1854–1934). The colonial governors remained in control until 1956, when Morocco gained independence as a constitutional monarchy. The first king of the new era, Hassan II (r. 1956–1999), introduced political reforms that led to the establishment of a bicameral legislature: a lower house (the Chamber of Representatives) and an upper house (the Chamber of Counselors).

Hassan II was succeeded by his son, Mohammed VI (b. 1963), who has won plaudits from some commentators for improving the human rights of his subjects and worked to maintain moderately free news media. On the international stage, Mohammed VI has continued his father's work as a mediator between the Muslim world and the West. This role became increasingly important as tension between the two power blocs mounted after the Islamist terrorist attacks on New York and Washington, D.C., of September 11, 2001, and the subsequent U.S.-led invasions of Afghanistan and Iraq.

WESTERN SAHARA

Bounded on the west by the Atlantic Ocean, Western Sahara is bordered on its other three sides mainly by Morocco and Mauritania and also by Algeria, with which it has a 26-mile (42-km) frontier in its northeastern corner.

Much of the history of Western Sahara has been influenced by the actions of the nomadic Berbers, primarily the Sanhaja and Lamtuna peoples, and by the introduction of Islam and the Arabic language in the eighth century. The confederation of the Sanhaja and the Lamtuna led to the formation of the Almohad Dynasty (r. 1147–1229), which supplanted the Almoravids (r. 1073–1146). In the 16th century, Western Sahara was drawn into the Moroccan sphere of influence after Ahmad al-Mansur used the country as a through route for his expeditions in search of gold in the lands around the Niger River belonging to the Songhai people. This campaign culminated in 1593 with the Moroccan forces' capture of Timbuktu (a city in modern Mali). Partly as a result of this conquest, al-Mansur became known by the byname al-Dhahabi (the golden).

With its sparse population—even in the 21st century, it had only around 400,000 inhabitants in a territory of 102,700 square miles (266,000 sq. km), the size of Colorado—and few natural resources, Western Sahara was of little interest to the European colonial powers other than as a buffer between Morocco and Mauritania. At the Berlin West Africa Conference in 1884–1885—the main purpose of which was to establish the legitimacy of Portugal's claims to the Congo River basin—Western Sahara was awarded to Spain. For the next 90 years, the country was officially known as Spanish Sahara.

This move alienated the citizens of the nation itself and those of neighboring Morocco and Mauritania. Resentments festered during the 20th century and erupted in 1975 when Morocco organized the Green March, a mass demonstration of 350,000 unarmed citizens. Powerless to resist this popular movement, Spain withdrew and, in 1976, signed the Madrid Accords that divided the region between Morocco, which gained two-thirds of the territory, and Mauritania, which took control of the remainder.

These divisions were no more acceptable to Western Saharans than the previous arrangement and inspired the growth of the Polisario Front—the name is an abbreviation of "Popular Front for the Liberation of Saguia el-Hamra and Río de Oro" (the Spanish names for, respectively, the northern and southern extremes of Western Sahara). Founded in 1973 by the indigenous, nomadic people in opposition to the Spanish occupiers, the Polisario Front is a political and military organization that seeks independence for the whole country. In 1979 the Polisario Front was instrumental in forcing the withdrawal of Mauritanian forces, but it failed to advance its own cause—Morocco immediately annexed the one-third of Western Sahara that it had not previously owned. Forced to withdraw to Algeria, the Polisario Front—thought to number at the time around 15,000 people—used the neighboring country as its base for guerrilla raids on Moroccan bases in Western Sahara. This campaign continued throughout the 1980s. Morocco responded by constructing along its vulnerable borders a berm (earthen barrier), extending for 1,240 miles (about 2,000 km), which was completed in 1987.

Since then, the Polisario Front has continued its struggle to establish the Saharawi Arab Democratic Republic (SADR) in Western Sahara, despite having been weakened by internal rivalries and by a reduction in the covert military support it previously received from the government of Algeria. The intention is that SADR should be a secular state—its government in exile, which is headed by Mohamed Abdelaziz (b. 1947), has consistently condemned and distanced itself from Islamic fundamentalist terrorism.

See Also
The Eastern Mediterranean and the Arabian Peninsula 220-235 ❖ Sub-Saharan Africa 260-273 ❖ Western Europe 334-347 ❖

SUB-SAHARAN AFRICA

In spite of their numerous differences, the nations of Africa that lie to the south of the Sahara Desert have two main common features. One is savanna-dominated topography. The other is populations that are significantly—and, in some cases, almost exclusively—Muslim.

The Sahara is the largest desert in the world; it extends 3,000 miles (4,800 km) from west to east and between 800 miles (1,300 km) and 1,200 miles (2,000 km) from north to south. It is bounded to the west by the Atlantic Ocean, to the north by the Atlas Mountains and the Mediterranean Sea, to the east by the Red Sea, and to the south by solid dunes of impacted sand that extend across the greater part of central Africa. The semiarid savanna region directly to the south of the desert is known as Sub-Saharan Africa, the Sahel (border), or Bilad al-Sudan (land of black people). It extends through parts of 13 modern countries: Mauritania, Senegal, Mali, Ivory Coast, Ghana, Burkina Faso, Niger, Nigeria, Chad, Sudan, Ethiopia, Eritrea, and Somalia. Muslims form at least half the population in nine of these nations and significant minorities in the other four.

The earliest Muslim explorations of Sub-Saharan Africa probably took place in the ninth century. A lucrative trade then developed on the cross-desert caravan routes, with Arabs exporting salt and importing gold. Two hundred years later, Abu U'bayd al-Bakri (1014–1094), an Arab geographer from Córdoba (a city

in modern Spain), wrote a detailed description of Ghana. Although he may have exaggerated the influence of Islam on the ancient kingdom, much of his account has since been corroborated by archaeological evidence.

❖

The semiarid savanna region directly to the south of the desert is known as Sub-Saharan Africa, the Sahel (border), or Bilad al-Sudan (land of black people).

In Mali, Islam was well established by the reign of Mansa (emperor) Musa (r. around 1307–1337). The Muslim Berber travel writer Ibn Battuta (1304–1369) visited Timbuktu, a major city in Mali, in 1352 and described his experiences in his celebrated travel book *Rihla*. Of the black African citizens, he wrote: "These people are Muslim, punctilious in observing the hours of prayer, studying the books of law, and memorizing the Koran."

In addition to Ghana and Mali, the other region of Sub-Saharan Africa in

These fields in Mali are typical of the rural landscape of Sub-Saharan Africa.

THE FULANI

A Fulani herder watches cattle crossing the river in Diafarabe, Mali.

The Fulani are a predominantly Muslim people whose distribution throughout Sub-Saharan Africa transcends national boundaries. Thought to number more than 20 million in total, the Fulani are found in significant numbers in almost every country of the region and are most numerous in Senegal, Mali, Niger, and Nigeria. They are linked by their common language, Fula. They generally practice endogamy (marriage within their own group). Most male Fulani are polygynous (having more than one wife at a time). A typical household comprises the husband, his wives, and all their unmarried children.

Most modern Fulani maintain their traditional nomadic, pastoral existence, and these herders have the highest status within their society. However, since the 19th century, many Fulani have moved into urban life or become sedentary farmers. Such developments have been occasioned by economic necessity, notably by the periodic depletion of their herds through drought and food shortages. The consequent loss of social standing in their original communities led to their cultural absorption into their new surroundings. Nowhere was this effect more evident than in northern Nigeria, where the Fulani were fully assimilated by the Hausa people, adopting their language and culture and, indeed, after a series of wars (1804–1810), becoming their ruling elite.

While nomadic Fulani are often Muslims in name only, many urban and sedentary Fulani practice Islam in some of its strictest and most austere forms.

which Islam flourished was the Songhai Empire, which, at the height of its power in the 15th and 16th centuries, extended across much of western Africa. The Songhai rulers accommodated their Muslim subjects, who were mainly city-dwellers, and facilitated their trading activities, which were highly profitable to the state.

MAURITANIA

The earliest inhabitants of Mauritania in the common era were nomadic Berbers. After their conversion to Islam, from the 11th century they began to spread a particularly austere form of the religion to neighboring peoples along the caravan route that linked their settlements with Morocco. By the 15th century, Berbers were outnumbered by Arabs in Mauritania, and intermarriage between the two races had created a new people, known as the Moors. Mauritania first came under European influence in 1442, when the Portuguese established a port on the country's coast for the transportation of gold and slaves. The French later built a base farther south and eventually took control of the whole country. Mauritania achieved independence from France in 1960 and made Nouakchott its capital city. In 1976 Mauritania annexed the southern third of Spanish Sahara (now Western Sahara) but withdrew after three years of raids by guerrillas of the Polisario Front, which seeks independence for the territory. The civilian government of Mauritania was ousted in 1978 by a military coup. Two years later, the army introduced Sharia law. In 2005 the military dictator for more than 20 years, Maaouya Ould Sid Ahmed Taya, was deposed, and a military council was installed to oversee a transition to democratic rule. In 2007 independent

candidate Sidi Ould Cheikh Abdallahi became the first president of Mauritania to come to power in a fair and free election. His term ended prematurely a year later when the military deposed him and again took over the government.

Islam is Mauritania's state religion, and 99 percent of the nation's 3.3 million population are Muslim. Although there is only one major religion in Mauritania, there are many distinct ethnic groups. There is significant ethnic tension between the different communities.

SENEGAL

The region that comprises the modern republic of Senegal was part of the ancient Ghana kingdom. In the 11th century, Berbers from northern Africa converted the indigenous Fuzani and Tukulor peoples to Islam in the early phase of the Almoravid movement that swept northward through Morocco and into Spain. European colonization began in 1444, when the Portuguese staked a claim to Senegal; they were later displaced by the Dutch, who gave way in 1677 to the French. Meanwhile, Islam declined but revived in the late 18th century, when Tukulor Muslims established a confederacy based in the northern district of Fouta, from where they led a jihad (struggle) against colonial rule.

Senegal gained independence from France in 1960, first as part of the Mali Federation and then, a few months later, in its own right. In 1982 it attempted another union, this time with neighboring Gambia, but the resulting federation of Senegambia was dissolved in 1989. By the start of the 21st century, Senegal had become one of the most stable democracies in Africa in spite of an insurgency in the southeast of the country by the separatist

The mosque at Ouakam Beach in Dakar, Senegal, stands on a spectacular site overlooking the ocean. Dakar is one of the most important ports in West Africa.

Movement of Democratic Forces in the Casamance (MFDC). (Casamance is the region of Senegal that lies to the south of Gambia along the Casamance River.) This conflict remains unresolved after more than 25 years of sporadic fighting.

Muslims comprise some 94 percent of the total population (12.8 million) of Senegal. They are divided into three main Sufi brotherhoods (sects): the Qadiri, the Tijani, and the Mourides.

MALI

Islam was introduced into the region of Sub-Saharan Africa that comprises the modern republic of Mali by conquest in the 10th century. By the 13th century, most of the inhabitants were Muslims. Contacts with other parts of the Islamic world were strengthened by the trans-Saharan trade in gold, gum arabic (a clear, water-soluble adhesive), ivory, and slaves. In the 19th century, much of the territory was colonized by the French, who extended their sphere of influence south from Senegal. African Muslims who were opposed to European occupation formed jihads, which led in turn to the development of numerous local Islamic theocracies. Although France never completely eliminated these microstates, it took control of Mali in 1899 and made the region a part of French Sudan.

Mali gained independence from France in 1960, at the same time as Senegal. The two emergent nations were a federation for a few months but soon split into separate states. Mali was then ruled by dictatorship until 1991, when a military coup installed a republican democracy, which has since become one of the strongest governments of its type in all of Africa. Mali is a large country—around twice the size of Texas—but, because most of its land area is desert, it is sparsely populated and economically poor. Ninety percent of its 12.7 million citizens are Muslims.

IVORY COAST

Both Islam and European colonialism came to the region now known as Ivory Coast (Côte D'Ivoire) later than to neighboring countries because of its location far from the established caravan routes between northern Africa and Sub-Saharan Africa and its dearth of natural harbors on the Atlantic Ocean. The religion first became institutionalized in the kingdom of Bouna, which was created in the late 17th century by Bounkani, an immigrant from Dagomba (now Ghana). Bouna and the adjacent kingdom of Kong became important centers of Islamic learning.

It was not until the 19th century that the French—who had previously only a few small trading posts on this part of the Atlantic coast—made inroads into the upland savanna of the Ivoirian interior in an effort to set up coffee farms. France claimed Ivory Coast as a colony in 1893. The occupation was never popular with the indigenous population and inspired fierce resistance, particularly during World War I (1914–1918), when the French conscripted thousands of Ivoirians to serve in the armed forces in Europe. The colony was not brought fully under French control until the end of the first global conflict.

During World War II (1939–1945), Ivory Coast was ruled by representatives of the French Vichy government, which collaborated with the Germans and imposed racial laws along the lines adopted by the Nazis in Europe. Meanwhile, the Ivoirian coast was blockaded by the British navy, and the Ivoirians suffered significant privations as a result. In the postwar Ivory Coast, the independence movement gathered pace rapidly and, in spite of French efforts to crush it, soon became irresistible. In 1960 its leader, Felix Houphouët-Boigny, having previously served as a cabinet minister in two French governments, became the first elected president of the independent Ivory Coast. He ruled until his death in 1993. Thereafter, tensions mounted between Ivory Coast's numerous religious and ethnic groupings: the nation is 39 percent Muslim, 33 percent Christian, and 12 percent indigenous faiths. The remaining 16 percent are not members of any religious group. The main native peoples are Akans, Krous, Mandes, and Voltaiques. In 1999 the armed forces seized power and the nation descended into civil war. Although a peace deal was brokered

The Grand Mosque in Djenne, Mali, is the largest mud-brick building in the world.

with the help of the United Nations (UN) in 2003, the underlying causes of the conflict—including land ownership, the basis for nationality, and the qualifications for holding political office—remained unresolved, and fighting flared again in 2004. This time, the situation was further complicated by the involvement of France, which launched bombing raids after its peacekeeping troops were attacked by rebels. In 2007 a powersharing agreement brought in a transitional government, and there has since been an uneasy peace in Ivory Coast.

GHANA

Ghana is one of the Sub-Saharan African nations in which there is only a minority of Muslims—around 16 percent of a population of 24 million that is predominantly Christian. The modern republic lies around 500 miles (800 km) southeast of the ancient kingdom of Ghana for which it is named. The influence of Islam began in the eighth century, when the region became the southern terminus of trading routes to and from the Mediterranean ports of Libya, Morocco, and Tunisia. The inhabitants remained mainly Muslim until the 19th century, when Christianity was introduced by missionaries. Most of the missionaries came from Britain, which ruled Ghana until it achieved independence in 1957.

BURKINA FASO

One-half of the 15 million population of Burkina Faso—known until 1984 as Upper Volta—is Muslim. A French colony until 1960, the independent nation suffered a series of military coups during the 1970s and 1980s. The most recent army takeover took place in 1987. It was led by Blaise Compaore, who installed an electoral process and has won every presidential election held since then.

NIGER

Niger first came under the influence of Islam in the 10th century when Arabs and Berbers travelled south across the Sahara Desert in search of copper, the region's richest mineral resource. The religion subsequently influenced the three main ethnic groups—the Tuareg in the north, the Hausa in the center, and the Songhai in the west—but it did not predominate until the 20th century, when it became a focus for opposition to France, which invaded Niger in 1899 and completed its colonial conquest in 1917.

After World War II, the influence of France declined, and Niger declared independence in 1960. The nation's first president, Hamani Diori, set up a single-party dictatorship, which was ended by a military coup in 1974. In 1993 Niger held its first multiparty presidential election, which was won by Mahamane Ousmane of the Social Democratic Convention Party. Ousmane was toppled in a military coup three years later. The army held new elections that resulted in victory for its commander in chief, Colonel Ibrahim Baré Maïnassara. Maïnassara was assassinated in 1999, and another military faction then installed a transitional government that tried to establish democratic rule. Since the start of the 21st century, Niger's head of state has been an elected president, Mamadou Tandja of the National Movement for a Developing Society (MNSD). The MNSD faces numerous political problems, not the least of which are based on religious

practice. Although more than 90 percent of Niger's 12.6 million inhabitants adhere to the Sunni branch of Islam, there are major disputes over the desirability of introducing Sharia law.

NIGERIA

The modern republic of Nigeria has a population of 149 million and an immense ethnic diversity—it is home to more than 200 ethnic groups, the largest of which are the Hausa (29 percent of the population), the Yoruba (21 percent), and the Igbo (18 percent). The area was first visited by Arab and Berber traders in the 9th century and conquered by Muslim warriors in the 11th century. Islam then became well established, particularly in the major centers of the Hausa states and in the Borno region in the northeast of the country.

In the 19th century, a group of Muslim intellectuals—most of them Fulani (see box)—began a popular movement against the dilution of Islam by indigenous religious practices. In 1804, under the leadership of the mystic philosopher Usman dan Fodio (1754–1817), they withdrew to the northwest of the country and called on all true Muslims to rise against their rulers and install Sharia law. The ensuing armed jihad was joined by Muslims throughout northern Nigeria. Together they established a caliphate, each region of which had autonomy but pledged allegiance to Usman dan Fodio, who became the emir (governor) and made his seat of government in the purpose-built town of Sokoto.

Usman retired in 1811 to concentrate on theological matters, principally the ways in which the state could maintain strict adherence to the Maliki code of laws. The Sokoto caliphate was then divided into two

Umaru Musa Yar'Adua casts his vote in the 2007 Nigerian presidential election, which was won by his People's Democratic Party (PDP).

major emirates. One of the emirates, in the western part of the Hausa territory, was ruled by Usman's brother, the *wazir* (minister and deputy) Abdullahi. The other emirate was governed by Usman's son, the *wazir* Muhammad Bello.

Muhammad Bello continued the jihad. His military strength was based on cavalry but mounted soldiers could not penetrate the south of Nigeria because their horses succumbed to illness in the tropical rain forests. Nevertheless, at its zenith, the Sokoto caliphate extended from present-day Burkina Faso to Cameroon. All the Hausa states, parts of Borno, and several other districts became part of a single, cohesive theocracy.

In the part of Borno that remained outside the caliphate, there emerged a countermovement of Muslims who opposed jihad. Led by the scholar and statesman Shehu (Sheikh) Muhammad al-Amin al-Kanemi (1776–1837), they ousted the Seyfawa dynasty, which had ruled since the 11th century.

The Islamic revival in Nigeria—notably in the Sokoto caliphate and in Borno, but also in other parts of the country—was halted by the British, who gradually undermined the emirs and overthrew those who refused to cooperate with them— some in battle, others through political machinations. Sokoto itself fell in 1903.

Britain determined the modern boundaries of Nigeria and ruled the colony until 1960. On independence, Nigeria became a republic, but the government's efforts to control such a large and heterogeneous population inspired a (principally Igbo) secessionist movement in the east of the country, which broke away to form the independent nation of Biafra.

The rebellion was crushed in the ensuing Biafran War (1967–1970), during and after which Nigeria was governed by the military. In 1999 a peaceful transition to civilian government was completed under a new constitution. The following two presidential elections—in 2003 and 2007—were widely thought to have been corrupt, and significant tensions remain close to the surface, particularly between Christians and Muslims after some of the northern and central states chose to adopt Sharia law. Nevertheless, the administrations of President Olusegun Obasanjo (r. 1999–2007) and his successor, Umaru Musa Yar'Adua, have been the longest period of uninterrupted civilian government in the young nation's history.

CHAD

The earliest inhabitants of Chad were probably the dark-skinned troglodytes (cave-dwellers) described by the Greek historian Herodotus (484–420 BCE). In the common era, the region was peopled by the Berbers, who crossed the Sahara Desert from Tripoli in the eighth century in search of fresh grazing pastures. The first Berbers in Chad were pagans, but their descendants introduced the Muslim faith to the region.

Islam was strengthened in the 17th and 18th centuries under the influence of the rulers of neighboring Sudan, who expanded into Chad and sold many of the native animists into slavery. In the 19th century, the Muslim powers were torn apart by internecine rivalries. Into the resulting power vacuum came the French, who overthrew Rabih az-Zubayr—a Sudanese adventurer who ruled the country from 1883 through 1893. France took full control of Chad in 1900 and, 10 years later, incorporated it into French Equatorial Africa.

Chad achieved independence from France in 1960. The development of the new republic was inhibited by simmering tensions between the mainly Christian black population of the richer southwest of Chad and the nonblack Muslims in the underdeveloped, feudal north of the country. In 1963 the government declared a state of emergency in response to an alleged Muslim plot to overthrow it. From 1967 Chad became a one-party state. Around the same time, two guerrilla movements emerged. The Front for the National Liberation of Chad (Frolinat) operated primarily in the north from headquarters in southern Libya, while the Chad National Front (FNT) operated in the east-central region. Both groups aimed at the overthrow of the government, the reduction of French influence in Chad, and closer links with the Arab states of northern Africa.

Chad then endured nearly 30 years of civil war. During this period, the principal motivations of the fighting ceased to be Christian-Muslim rivalry and became more of a factional struggle in the north of the country. On several occasions, neighboring Libya was drawn into the conflict. Peace of a kind was achieved in 1990, and flawed presidential elections were held in 1996, 2001, and 2006. In 1998, another rebellion broke out in northern Chad. Although peace deals were periodically brokered, none of the agreements held, and sporadic fighting continued throughout the first decade of the 21st century.

The 10.3 million population of Chad is predominantly Muslim (53 percent). The largest minority is Christian (34 percent). However, in 2009, the country is dominated by

Khartoum, capital of Sudan, stands on the banks of the Blue Nile close to its confluence with the White Nile.

animists, who represent only 7 percent of the total population.

SUDAN

Sudan is the largest country in Africa—it is just over one-quarter the size of the United States. Of Sudan's population of 41 million, 70 percent are Sunni Muslims, most of whom live in the north of the country. The southern regions are occupied mainly by people who follow indigenous faiths (25 percent of the national total) and Christians (5 percent).

The name of the modern republic is derived from the old Arabic term for the region—Bilad al-Sudan (land of black people). Around the year 540, the people of Sudan—most of whom were then Christians—entered a series of treaties that bound them to Egypt. It was from Egypt that Islam entered Sudan, and the growth of the religion culminated in 1093 with the accession of a Muslim prince to the throne of Dunqulah, a city-state in Sudan on the banks of the Nile River.

In 1821 Sudan was formally united with Egypt, but the bond was broken in 1885 by a rebellion led by Muhammad Ahmad, who styled himself Mahdi (divinely guided one). The Mahdi sought to establish a government guided by the strictest precepts of Islam and to rid Sudan of foreign influences—not only Egyptian but also British (Egypt had been a de facto protectorate of Britain since 1882). The Mahdists took the capital, Khartoum, and expelled the occupiers, but their regime was overthrown after an Anglo-Egyptian army defeated them at the Battle of Omdurman on the outskirts of Khartoum in 1898. From then until 1956, Sudan was a part of the British Empire.

Independence brought to the surface many longstanding but previously submerged tensions between northern and southern Sudan. The inhabitants of the north of the country are mainly Arabic-speaking Muslims; those in the south are predominantly black Africans who are either Christians or who follow one of the many local religions. Even before the formal handover of power from the British to the Sudanese, the nation was already embroiled in a civil war that lasted until 1972. Before, during, and after this conflict, the government of Sudan consistently favored the Islamic north of the country over the non-Muslim south. The maintenance of such policies sparked in 1983 another civil conflict, which did not end until 2005. The second Sudan civil war had catastrophic effects on the whole population—although reliable figures are unobtainable, it is thought that 2 million people died, either in battle or in the war-induced famine, and that 4 million people became refugees. The peace treaty finally acknowledged the north-south divide by granting the southern rebels autonomy for six years, at the end of which a referendum on independence is planned.

ETHIOPIA

Ethiopia is one of the few nations of Africa to have experienced almost no European colonialism other than a brief occupation by Italy (1936–1941).

Christianity was the first of the three great monotheisms to be introduced into Ethiopia. The nation's orthodox church was established in the fourth century and has remained a powerful influence on the life of the nation with few disruptions ever since. Today it is the faith of 61 percent of the total population of 85 million. Islam

was brought to the region in the seventh century by refugees from Mecca. Today the religion is practiced by around 33 percent of Ethiopians. There are Muslims throughout the country, but they predominate in the Eastern Lowlands. They have generally received inferior treatment to Christians although, after the overthrow of the last emperor, Haile Selassie, in 1974, the Marxist Derg regime gave both Muslims and Christians equal but diminished status. (It was during the Derg period that most of the adherents of the third great monotheism, Jews—known in Ethiopia as Falashas—left the country, mainly for Israel.) The period of Derg rule was a disaster for Ethiopia, which was almost torn apart by a succession of coups, countercoups, popular uprisings, extensive droughts, and huge refugee problems. In 1991 the Ethiopian People's Revolutionary Democratic Front (EPRDF) ousted the communists, drafted a constitution, and, in 1995, supervised the country's first multiparty elections. The EPRDF has since been returned to power repeatedly, although there have been allegations of corruption and intimidation at each of the subsequent elections. Meanwhile, the status of Muslims has remained much as it was during Selassie's reign. Their lack of material and social advancement has aroused fears that they may become radicalized in the same way as many of the world's other Islamic societies.

ERITREA

Landlocked Ethiopia had long coveted Eritrea for its ports, and in 1952 the two countries were federated in a deal brokered by Britain, which had expelled the Italians from the region during World War II, and the United States. Ten years later, Ethiopia annexed its neighbor and provoked a war of independence that ended in 1991 when Eritrean rebels defeated government forces at the end of the Derg period. After their separation, the two countries failed to agree on their borders. This dispute led to another war (1998–2000), which was ended by the intervention of the UN. A Temporary Security Zone (TSZ)—15 miles (24 km) wide—was then set up along the frontier. It was abandoned in 2007, but the de facto line that subsequently appeared is still disputed by Ethiopia.

At the end of the first decade of the 21st century, the population of Eritrea was around 5.6 million. Although exact figures are unavailable, around one-half of the country's inhabitants today embrace Christianity, which has been established there since the fourth century. Around 200 years later, Islam was brought to Eritrea by traders and refugees from the Arabian Peninsula on the other side of the Red Sea. As Muslim power and influence grew in the coastal region, many of the Christians withdrew into the Ethiopian Highlands. Today Islam remains the majority religion in the lowlands of the Horn of Africa, embracing perhaps as much as 80 percent of the local population. Most of Eritrea's Muslims are Sunnis. In an effort to reduce the rivalry between Christians and Muslims that has long affected all strata of Eritrean society, religious political parties are banned, and seats on the State Council of the National Assembly are divided equally between the two religions.

Muslim women wear full burqas as they make their way along a road in a village in Eritrea.

SOMALIA

Islam is the official religion of Somalia and the overwhelming majority of its 9.8 million people are Sunni Muslim. Within Somali society, the strongest allegiances have traditionally been to clans, which remain powerful today.

In the 19th century and the first half of the 20th century, the nation was ruled by European powers. The British Somalia protectorate gained independence on June 26, 1960, and, on July 1, the adjacent Italian colony followed it into the era of political self-determination. The two territories then united as a democratic republic, but their relationship was never easy. In 1969 President Cabdirashiid Cali Sharma'arke was assassinated. Mohamed Siad Barre then led an otherwise largely bloodless coup that introduced an authoritarian leftist government. Siad's regime was described as "scientific socialism," and it was held to be fully compatible with the Muslim faith. When Ethiopia entered a period of turmoil after the overthrow of the emperor Haile Selassie in 1974, Somalia conquered Ogaden which, though Ethiopian, had a large Somali population. When Ethiopia recaptured the province four years later, hundreds of thousands of Ogaden Somalis fled to Somalia. The military defeat and the influx of refugees severely weakened scientific socialism.

Siad's regime was backed by the Soviet Union and, when both collapsed in 1991, Somalia was consumed by factional, regional fighting and the country descended rapidly into anarchy. The UN intervened in 1993 to alleviate the suffering caused to the civilian population in the ensuing famine, but the humanitarian mission itself came under attack and was forced to withdraw two years later. After years of negotiations, peace was restored in 2004, and a transitional government was elected under the leadership of interim president Abdullahi Yusuf Ahmed. However, fighting resumed and, in June of 2006, troops of the Council of Islamic Courts (CIC)—a Muslim guerrilla force—took control of the capital, Mogadishu. The United States and other Western nations suspected that the CIC was linked to international terrorism, but these allegations were fiercely denied by the CIC's leader, Sheikh Hassan Dahir Aweys. Somalia government forces defeated the CIC in December of 2006 and, although that particular rebel group then collapsed, other movements sprang up out of its ashes. The most powerful new opponent of the transitional government was al-Shabaab (Youth) militia, some of whose leaders had trained or fought in Afghanistan and were believed to have been associated there with the terrorist organization Al-Qaeda.

The worst effects of the civil war were felt in the south of Somalia and caused a refugee crisis in neighboring Kenya as thousands of Somalis sought safety across the border. Meanwhile, the relatively stable north of the country declared itself independent as the Republic of Somaliland. Somaliland's progress toward constitutional democracy—it soon set up a tricameral parliament, all levels of which were freely elected—earned the self-styled nation increasing status in the international community. However, other African countries have stopped short of granting full diplomatic recognition to Somaliland—normalization of this new nation will be unachievable for as long as its borders are disputed and insecure and adjacent Somalia remains at war.

See Also

The Eastern Mediterranean and the Arabian Peninsula 220-235 ✦ Northern Africa 246-249 ✦

Chapter 14

SOUTH ASIA

Islam gained its first foothold in South Asia shortly after the religion was founded. Today it is the majority faith in three countries of the region—Afghanistan, Bangladesh, and Pakistan. There are also significant and politically influential Muslim minorities in India, Myanmar, and Sri Lanka.

The Arabs imported Islam to South Asia in the seventh century. Buddhism, Jainism, and Hinduism were long entrenched in the region when Arab seafarers sailed from the Arabian Peninsula and established trading posts in southern and southwestern India amid a largely receptive native population. The first mosque in India was built in 629, during the lifetime of the Prophet Muhammad (570–632). At the start of the relationship between the monotheistic Arabs and the polytheistic inhabitants of the Indian subcontinent, there was little conflict between them; local people converted to Islam willingly, not under duress.

In the eighth century, an Arab force led by Muhammad bin Qasim imposed its will on the Hindu and Buddhist populations of Sind (a region of modern Pakistan). However, the most significant effect of Islam in South Asia was created by the more nomadic and aggressive Arabs who forcefully spread their faith into Persia (modern Iran) and from there into Central Asia. Having adopted the new faith, the Turkic peoples of Central Asia spread out in all directions—into South Asia, Christian Byzantium (modern Istanbul, Turkey), Afghanistan, and India.

Islam was implanted in Afghanistan in the ninth century when the town of Ghazni was established by Persian Muslims who subsequently secured the city of Kabul and founded a dynasty. During this conquest, Hindu and Buddhist Afghans came under the influence of Islam so that, by the time of Mahmud of Ghazni—a warrior of Turkic origin who rose to power in 999—much of the region was already populated by Muslims. Mahmud's army then occupied the lands beyond the Amu Darya River in the north—much of the region that is now

❖

At the start of the relationship between the monotheistic Arabs and the polytheistic inhabitants of the Indian subcontinent, there was little conflict between them. . . .

Iran—as well as the valleys and plains extending east from Peshawar to the Indus River. Mahmud of Ghazni created the first significant Muslim empire in South Asia by forcibly expelling the Hindu population from the Indus Valley, a campaign that was notorious for its violence and slaughter.

The Hindu Kush is a great mountain range that divides Central Asia from South Asia.

Islam therefore came to South Asia by sea and land, through peaceful as well as aggressive action, and in the latter instance it came to conquer and to rule. In neither case, however, did it eliminate every vestige of the preexistent cultures. Even at the height of Muslim power—during the Sultanate of Delhi (1206–1526) and later, during the period of the Mughal Empire (1526–1857)—Buddhism, Hinduism, and Jainism survived, sometimes through accommodation with Islam but, failing that, in defiance of the conquerors' faith.

AFGHANISTAN

Afghanistan is a landlocked, mountainous country that borders China, Pakistan, Iran, and several Central Asian countries. Over the centuries many invading armies and migrating peoples have met in Afghanistan, giving the country a highly diverse ethnic and cultural identity. Afghanistan is home to communities of Pashtuns and Baluchs in the south; Turkmen, Hazaras, Uzbeks, and Tajiks in the north. The most commonly spoken languages are Dari and Pashto, but there are many others spoken in northern areas. It is common for Afghans to understand more than one language.

Although Afghanistan has remained a largely independent state since its founding, it has always struggled to form a national identity that could unite its dispersed and isolated tribal population. Tribalism is strong and perpetuated by the difficulties of communication and transportation across remote, mountainous terrain. As a result, there are numerous microcommunities whose members identify with local chiefs rather than with national leaders. The Pashtuns are the largest cohesive group, but they are also divided by regional and linguistic differences. Their settlements

range across the border with Pakistan (the Durand Line), which was created by the British in 1893.

The state of Afghanistan first emerged out of the unrest that followed the death of Persian leader Nader Shah—whose empire included large areas of Afghanistan and Central Asia—in 1747. Pashtun military commander Ahmad Shah Durrani was chosen to be the country's first emir by a council of tribal leaders in Kandahar.

In the 19th century Afghanistan found itself caught between the frontiers of the rival empires of Tsarist Russia and Britain. Neither Britain nor Russia wanted to risk triggering a global war by occupying the country, but both wanted Afghanistan as an ally. This made Afghanistan the battleground for a cold war—known euphemistically as the "great game"—between Britain and Russia. The two powers used diplomacy, covert operations, and occasional military attacks to influence Afghan politics. The British army invaded Afghanistan in 1839, 1878, and 1919, while the Russian army was involved in several clashes on the country's northern border in the 1880s. In 1893 the borders of present-day Afghanistan were defined by a treaty between the two European powers in which the Afghans had little involvement.

In 1919 the unpopular new emir of Afghanistan, Amanullah Khan (r. 1919–1929), launched an attack on British India across the Durand line. Britain could not afford another war so soon after World War I had ended and relinquished control over Afghanistan as part of a peace treaty.

The now fully independent Afghan government introduced a number of social reforms. Elementary education was made compulsory for both girls and boys, and the state followed the example of newly secular

Turkey and discouraged the wearing of the *hijab*. At the same time, however, the Pashtun elite excluded other ethnic groups from power and ruthlessly silenced political dissent.

After World War II, Afghanistan was once again caught in the middle of a cold war, this time between the Soviet Union and the United States. Both sides sought Afghanistan as a diplomatic ally and so supported many public projects to win favor with the emir, Mohammed Zahir Shah (r. 1933–1973). The largest of these projects, a dam built across the Helmand River, was partly funded by the United States. The project was intended to provide irrigation and hydroelectric power for southern Afghanistan. Engineering firms from the United States built new towns and

irrigation canals throughout the region, and Mohammad Zahir Shah planned to relocate many Pashtun tribesmen to the area. The project was a technical failure, however, and by the late 1960s the irrigation systems had failed to create even half the amount of viable farmland promised at the beginning. Construction of the hydroelectic plant had also ground to a halt. The failure of the project was a financial disaster for the Afghan government and brought it considerable criticism from opposition groups. In 1973, after the country's problems were exacerbated by two years of drought, Mohammad Zahir Shah was overthrown by the prime minister, Daoud Khan (1909–1978).

The Afghan capital, Kabul, lies in a deep valley in the eastern foothills of the Hindu Kush. The city has probably existed on the site for more than 3,000 years.

The Amu Darya River forms part of the northern border of Afghanistan. It was formerly known in the West as the Oxus River.

Daoud Khan's attempts to revitalize Afghanistan were unsuccessful and he was killed in the communist revolution of 1978. Although it was publicly welcomed by the Soviet Union, the revolution was an indigenous one—many prominent members of the communist People's Democratic Party of Afghanistan (PDPA) were students of Kabul's Western-funded universities. The PDPA's attempts to reform and secularize the country were met with hostility. Rebel groups formed in rural areas, and the brutal response of the PDPA only increased the rebels' public support. In 1979, motivated by Afghanistan's apparent slide into civil war, the Soviet Union invaded. One of the Soviets' first actions was to kill the leader of the PDPA, Hafizullah Amin (1929–1979). The Soviets blamed Amin for turning the people against communism. The Afghans resisted the invaders and rejected their new puppet government. Casualties on both sides were severe. The Afghan forces, known

as mujahideen, were aided by the United States and Pakistan, who provided them with the weapons and training they needed to drive Soviet forces out of the country.

The Soviet withdrawal in 1989 did not, however, bring peace to Afghanistan. The mujahideen splintered along tribal lines and the country fell into years of further civil war. Into this chaos came the Taliban—originally a student movement drawn from religious schools in Afghanistan and Pakistan. Its supporters were inspired by the teachings of the most austere Islamic traditions. The Taliban arrived in the country in 1994 and within two years had defeated almost all the warring factions. Exhausted by more than two decades of conflict, Afghans in significant numbers embraced the Taliban. In 1996, the Taliban seized Kabul and soon afterward took most of the country. In response to the growth of the Taliban, Afghanistan's minority ethnic groups—Hazaras, Tajiks, Turkmen, and Uzbeks—formed the Northern Alliance, a group that fought the Taliban and governed a small region in the northeast of the country.

Under the Taliban, Afghanistan became an Islamic state. Religious courts enforced a set of laws that mixed traditional Sharia with Pashtun tribal codes. Adultery, homosexuality, apostasy, and many other crimes were punishable by death. The religious police enforced laws on everything from beard length to the sale of music. Despite these repressive policies, the Taliban continued to be supported by many Afghans because they brought a measure of stability to the country. For example, the Taliban promised to crack down on the corrupt local officials and warlords who had grown wealthy by extorting money from the people.

The rule of the Taliban was ended in 2001 when a U.S.-led military coalition invaded the country and drove them from power. Although the period of open warfare was relatively short-lived, the heavy air attacks that characterized the early phases of the conflict caused lasting damage to Afghanistan's already inadequate infrastructure.

Since the invasion of Afghanistan, the country has been officially governed by president Hamid Karzai and a democratically elected parliament, with support from coalition forces. In practice, however, Hamid Karzai's government has struggled to assert its influence beyond Kabul, and in rural areas power is typically vested in tribal leaders or local warlords. In some parts of southern Afghanistan, local Taliban commanders have exploited this power vacuum to assert control over many villages and towns. Beginning in 2009, however, coalition forces have redoubled their efforts to expel the Taliban from southern Afghanistan. Thousands of additional U.S. troops have been sent to the country, and funding for the Afghan national army has been significantly increased.

Questions remain, however, over the conduct of the Afghan government, which many argue must be reformed before the people can be expected to place their trust in its institutions. Investigations have found evidence of widespread corruption and discrimination in the police and civil service, as well as little respect among regional leaders for the laws of the new government. Additionally, Afghanistan remains the single biggest grower of opium poppies in the world.

The August 2009 presidential election, which was won by Hamid Karzai, was marred by allegations of widespread voter intimidation, electoral fraud, and fears over security. It is estimated that voter turnout was very low—between 30 and 50 percent—and almost nonexistent in some Taliban-dominated areas.

PAKISTAN

Pakistan came into being in August 1947 as a result of the Partition of India. From 1947 to 1971 Pakistan was formed of two states—known as West Pakistan and East Bengal (later East Pakistan)—located on opposite sides of the Indian subcontinent. After a brief civil war in 1971, East Pakistan declared independence and renamed itself Bangladesh.

Although Pakistan was planned to have a Muslim majority and be sympathetic to Muslim culture, it is not clear whether its founders intended it to be primarily secular or Islamic in character. The attitude of Muhammad Ali Jinnah (1876–1948), leader of the Muslim League and Pakistan's first governor general, is a frequently contested issue. His public statements on the intended nature of Pakistan's government were ambiguous—he argued both for and against secularism at different points in his career. Tensions between secularists and Islamists have been at the heart of many internal conflicts in Pakistan's history.

Over the course of Pakistan's history, civilian governments have alternated with periods of military rule. The first period of civilian democratic rule was characterized by the ethnic conflict and unrest that followed the partition of India. In 1958, Field Marshal Ayub Khan (1907–1974) seized control of the country and began to push Pakistani society in a more secular direction. He placed restrictions on polygamy and reformed Islamic laws relating to alimony payments and divorce. After the 1965 war with India over the disputed region of Kashmir ended in a stalemate, opposition to Ayub Khan's regime grew. In 1969 he handed power to General Yahya Khan, who was replaced by Zulfikar Ali Bhutto (1928–1979) in the 1971 election.

The 1970s saw a resurgence of Islamic influence in Pakistani politics. In the 1977 general election Zulfikar Ali Bhutto was challenged by the Pakistan National Alliance, a political coalition that promised to implement Sharia. Bhutto officially won the election but was deposed by General Muhammad Zia ul-Haq (1924–1988) amid widespread accusations of vote rigging.

Under Zia-ul-Haq, Pakistan became an Islamic state. The existing legal system was replaced with one based on Sharia. Under this new system crimes could be punished by flogging, amputations, or execution, and acts such as blasphemy, apostasy, and adultery were made illegal. During the

The main road through the Khyber Pass between Afghanistan and Pakistan is relatively easy to police. However, in the surrounding hills, the border line is practically unenforceable, and Pashtuns pass between the two countries more or less as they please.

THE PARTITION OF INDIA

On August 14th, 1947, the country commonly known as British India was formally dissolved. At midnight, the powers of the British administration were transferred to the governments of two new nations—Pakistan and India—ending over 150 years of colonial rule. For groups like the Muslim League and the Indian National Congress (INC), this was the culmination of decades of campaigning, but for many activists it was a far from ideal conclusion to their work.

Early supporters of Indian independence envisioned a single, unified country encompassing all of British India. Over time, however, disputes emerged between Muslim activists and the mostly Hindu members of the largest independence group, the Indian National Congress. Muslim leaders were angered by the limited role that the INC appeared to be willing to grant Muslims and concerned by the lack of concrete assurances that the rights of Muslims would be respected in an independent India. In 1906, a group of Muslim leaders formed the Muslim League to protect the interests of the Muslim community. Negotiations between the INC and the Muslim League often ended in frustration, however, and by 1930 its leader, Muhammad Iqbal, had given his support to the idea of a separate Muslim state. Some Muslims were enthusiastic supporters of this proposal, while others thought it was simply a useful bargaining tool in negotiations over the role of Muslims in India after independence.

In 1947 the British government passed the Indian Independence Act, which stipulated that India would be divided into two nations—one Muslim and one Hindu—no later than June 1948. The Muslim state was formed of two territories—East and West Pakistan (present-day Bangladesh and Pakistan, respectively)—separated by the Hindu state of India.

The British plan for partition was a compromise drawn up in just over a month by a British administration under pressure from the government in London. It split the existing states of Bengal and Punjab in half and left some religious groups, such as the Sikhs, divided between the two countries. Due to the speed at which the process took place, there was little time for people to prepare. In the aftermath of partition, millions were forced to migrate from one country to another, often with nothing more than what they could carry. Sikhs, Jains, and Hindus journeyed across the Pakistani border to India, while many millions of Muslims left India for Pakistan. In both India and Pakistan, mobs attacked minority communities, and it is estimated that millions died in interethnic fighting.

The partition plan left the princely states (semiautonomous regions within British India) to decide which country they wished to join. One of these states, Kashmir, chose not to join Pakistan despite having a mostly Muslim population. This caused a major dispute between India and Pakistan, which continues to this day.

1980s Pakistan became a major supporter of the mujahideen fighting the Soviet invasion in Afghanistan. Pakistan provided logistical support and acted as a transshipment point for military aid provided by the United States government. It also allowed groups of mujahideen to operate from the Federally Administered Tribal Areas (FATA) near the Afghan border, a move that would have serious consequences for the country in later years.

Today, Pakistan is organized as a federal republic. The country is divided into four provinces—Baluchistan, Sindh, Punjab, and the North-West Frontier Province (NWFP). Each of the provinces has its own elected government with authority over local matters. Pakistan's capital city, Islamabad, is located in a small territory similar to the District of Columbia in the United States. Another region, known as the Federally Administered Tribal Areas (FATA) is associated with the North-West Frontier Province but primarily ruled by a governor appointed by the president. There are also two areas of Pakistani controlled Kashmir—Azad Kashmir and the Northern Areas—which are under the control of the federal government.

The North-West Frontier Province is the smallest of Pakistan's provinces, located in the mountainous landscape to the north of the capital city, Islamabad. The politics and culture of the region are strongly influenced by Pashtun tribal traditions. The North-West Frontier Province's 21 million Pashtuns comprise around two-thirds of the area's population. In the provincial capital, Peshawar, as well as in the border regions, the Pashtun population is augmented by millions of Pashtun Afghan refugees. The province, along with the neigboring FATA, has long been a stronghold for Islamist groups fighting in Afghanistan. Since the ousting of the Taliban from power in Afghanistan in 2001, these groups have become increasingly active in Pakistan. In recent years the Taliban have been expanding from their established bases in the FATA and taking control of districts in the NWFP. According to some reports from early 2009 Islamist groups were openly in control of towns as little as 100 miles (160 km) from the capital city, Islamabad. With military assistance from the United States, the Pakistani government has since had some success in driving back the

Taliban, but many areas remain under partial Taliban control.

A survey conducted in December 2009 by the polling company Gallup found that only 5 percent of the Pakistani population thought that the Taliban had a positive influence. In the NWFP, where people have extensive direct experience of the Taliban, only 1 percent of those asked thought they had a positive influence.

Baluchistan comprises 45 percent of Pakistan's total land area, but it is the poorest, least developed, and the most sparsely inhabited of the four major provinces. The Baluch people are the dominant ethnic group in the region although there is also a significant Pashtun population. The Baluch community is divided between Pakistan, Iran, and Afghanistan, and the Baluch nationalist movement predates the formation of Pakistan. Baluch nationalists have frequently come into violent conflict with the Pakistani government, but so far all armed nationalist movements have been suppressed by the Pakistani military.

Formed into a province by the British in 1935, Sind was one of the principal regions in the creation of Pakistan in 1947. Its main city is Karachi, Pakistan's biggest port, commercial center, and—until the construction of Islamabad in the 1960s— the national capital. Karachi was also the destination for many of the millions of Muslims who fled India at partition, and even today it is known as a city dominated by the refugee (*muhajir*) community.

An early Arab settlement, Sind was the area from which Islam spread to other parts of South Asia and has been referred to as *Bab-al-Islam*, the "Gate of Islam." The province's population of over 40 million is composed of many ethnic groups, and native Sindhis, feeling insecure, have promoted "Sind for the Sindhis" movements that, from time to time, have perpetrated acts of violence against non-Sindhis. There is intense competition between Sindhis and the descendants of refugees who entered the province after the formation of Pakistan. Originally confined to the squalor of refugee colonies in Karachi, the *muhajir* are currently more than 15 percent of the province's population and play an important role in Sind's commercial life. Native Sindhis, who represent more than 65 percent of the total population, generally live in rural areas.

Punjab is the most populous province in Pakistan and also the most prosperous.

During the partition of India in 1947, the province was created from the Muslim-majority western half of the Punjab region. Its capital, Lahore, was a major administrative and cultural center during the period of British rule, and before that, one of the capitals of the Mughal empire. The province's cities are home to the country's most prestigious educational and cultural institutions, as well as many of Pakistan's important industrial and commercial centers. Islamabad, the capital city of Pakistan, is located a short distance to the north of the Punjabi city of Rawalpindi.

KASHMIR

Adjoining Punjab is Kashmir, a mountainous region in the Himalayas,

Peaks of the Himalayas rise behind a pasture high in the hills of Kashmir, a predominantly Muslim region of South Asia. Although currently under Indian rule, Kashmir is also claimed by Pakistan.

This mosque stands in the middle of the Meghna River in Narayanganj, Bangladesh.

which has been the flash point for several conflicts between Pakistan and India. Prior to the partition of India, Kashmir was a princely state (a semiautonomous region within British India) with a largely Muslim population but a Hindu ruling family. During the partition of India, the the ruler of Kashmir, Hari Singh, appeared to favor independence rather than union with either Pakistan or India, a suggestion which angered both parties. Pakistani forces occupied the western half of the region soon after independence, leading Singh to cede his territory to India in exchange for

military support. The war between India and Pakistan reached a stalemate in 1948. At this point both sides appealed to the United Nations for a resolution to the conflict. The UN decided that the future allegiance of the region should be put to the people of Kashmir, but neither side would allow an election to be held until the other withdrew its forces from the area. As a result of this conflict, Kashmir remains a disputed region, divided between Indian and Pakistani areas of control. Subsequent wars between India and Pakistan, in 1965 and 1971, and a major border incident in 1999 also failed to end the controversy. In addition to the conflict between India and Pakistan, large sections of northeastern Kashmir were annexed by Chinese forces in 1962 after a brief war with India.

Although India still claims the entirety of Kashmir, the 1948 ceasefire line—known as the "line of control"—is the de facto international border between the two countries. Kashmir is divided into five distinct regions. Azad Kashmir and the Northern Areas are controlled by Pakistan, and the population of these regions is almost entirely Muslim. India, on the other hand, controls the states of Ladakh, Jammu, and the Kashmir valley. These three states are more ethnically mixed than the Pakistani-controlled areas. While the Kashmir valley is around 95 percent Muslim, Jammu is around 66 percent Hindu, and Ladakh is fairly evenly split between Buddhists and Muslims. The Indian government is in favor of formalizing the current line of control as the international border. This plan is opposed by many Pakistanis as it would leave the mostly Muslim region of the Kashmir valley under Indian control. It is unclear what the outcome would be if India and Pakistan agreed to allow the vote suggested by the UN in 1948, but some analysts have suggested that the population is most likely to vote for independence rather than union with either state.

BANGLADESH

Bangladesh is one of the most densely populated countries in the Muslim world. Its population of around 129 million lives in an area of river valleys and floodplains approximately the same size as the U.S. state of Iowa. With the exception of a short border with Myanmar in the mountainous southeastern corner of the country, Bangladesh is entirely surrounded by India. It is the youngest nation in South Asia, having only seceded from Pakistan in 1971.

Bangladesh was an administrative region created by the British in the eastern part of Bengal. With the partition of India in 1947, it became East Bengal (later renamed East Pakistan), one of the five provinces of Pakistan, separated from the other four by 1,100 miles (1,800 km) of Indian territory.

This unusual arrangement was problematic from the outset. Bengalis found themselves over a thousand miles from their national government, unable to speak the newly declared official language (Urdu), and marginalized by an electoral process designed to limit their influence. The situation worsened when Ayub Khan seized control of Pakistan in 1958, and consolidated power in the hands of the Punjabi political elite.

These tensions reached a climax following the elections of 1970. The Awami League—a Bengali nationalist party—won almost every parliamentary seat in East Pakistan. Despite being the largest single party in parliament, they were not allowed a role in the national government. As public unrest escalated into full-scale civil war, Pakistani forces targeted supporters of the Bengali independence movement. Thousands of activists and intellectuals were killed, and millions more Bengalis were killed or forced to flee the country. With the support of the Indian army, Bangladeshi forces defeated the Pakistani Army in 1971.

Since 1971, elected governments have alternated with military administrations although the last period of military rule ended in 1990. According to the last census, completed in 2001, Bangladesh has a population of 129 million, 83 percent of which are Sunni Muslim. Most of the remaining 17 percent are Hindu, although there are small Shia Muslim and Christian minorities. Bangladesh was established as a secular country, but over the years it has undergone a process of gradual Islamization that has alienated its Hindu minority and caused many to migrate to India.

Bangladesh must now contend with religious and political activists who demand a more strict Islamic state. Some of these activists use violent means in pursuit of their ends. Moreover, by arguing that only the purest representation of Islamic practices can usher in a new era for the people of Bangladesh, extremist religious and political movements have proliferated, and they can increasingly count on the support of millions of Bangladeshis who have become disenchanted with conventional secular politics.

INDIA

India is the second-largest country in the world, with a population of more than 1 billion. It has an extremely diverse population, with 27 official languages, numerous ethnic groups, and several major religious groups, including Hindus, Muslims, Christians, Sikhs, Buddhists, Jains, and Parsis. Although Hindus are the majority, representing around 80 percent of the population, Muslims are the most significant minority group. Furthermore, while Muslims only account for 13 percent of the Indian population, there are more Muslims in India today (around 138 million) than there are in most Muslim-majority countries.

Although it is often associated with military conquests and forced conversions, Islam has a long history of open interaction with the indigenous religions of India. Sufi philosophy and practices have had a profound influence on the character of Islam in India, as well as on Indian culture as a whole. Sufi mystics played an important role in spreading the message of Islam and attracting converts from the local population, and almost all major schools of Sufi thought are represented in India.

While Muslims only account for 13 percent of the Indian population, there are more Muslims in India today (around 138 million) than there are in most Muslim-majority countries.

Mughal Emperor Akbar the Great (1642–1605) was strongly influenced by Sufism and wanted to find some common ground between the many faiths of his diverse kingdom. Akbar proposed a new ethical system that he called the Din-i-Ilahi (Divine Faith). It combined the core principles of Hinduism and Islam, as well as elements of Christianity, Zoroastrianism, and Jainism. Few adopted the new faith, but Akbar continued to promote religious tolerance in his kingdom until his death.

Islam is also thought to have had a major influence on the ideas of Nanak (1469–1539) the founder of Sikhism. Many historians believe that Nanak was raised as a Muslim and may have even performed the hajj in his youth. Against a background of religious conflict, Nanak preached that all religions were equal in the eyes of God. His writings combine Sufi practices and beliefs with elements of Hindu philosophy. Today there are around 20 million Sikhs living in northern India and Pakistan.

Indian Muslims are primarily Sunni, but there is a Shia minority that makes up around 10 percent of the Muslim population. The ethnic origin of India's Muslims is a complicated and controversial issue with strong political connotations. Some historians have suggested that Indian Muslims are descended from medieval Arab and Persian invaders; others that they are primarily descended from Hindus that were forced to convert by Muslim rulers; and some believe Indian Muslims are the descendants of Buddhists who converted to Sufi Islam. Most historians agree that Indians converted to Islam in significant numbers during periods of Muslim rule but disagree over the circumstances under which these conversions took place. Recent genetic studies have suggested that Indian Muslims—with the exception of a very small number of isolated communities—are primarily the descendants of indigenous converts, whose genetic ancestry is almost identical to their non-Muslim neighbors.

India is an officially secular country that does not grant privileged status to any ethnic or religious community. In practice, however, significant disparities exist between different ethnic groups. The Muslim population in particular has high poverty rates, low literacy rates, and is underrepresented in the government and the civil service. This is partly the result of the partition of India—the creation of a Muslim state in the form of Pakistan led many Indian politicians to consider Indian Muslims as outsiders—and partly a symptom of India's wider problems with poverty, poor education, and corruption. Today, only five percent of government employees are Muslim. In some crucial areas of government employment this figure drops even lower—Indian Muslims represent only four percent of police officers and three percent of armed forces personnel. Muslims occupy just over five percent of the Indian Parliament's 543 seats.

Indian governments have made token gestures toward greater inclusion of the Muslim community in politics, but the number of Muslims elected to parliament has changed little in the last 20 years. While India has had three Muslim presidents (a largely ceremonial post), there has yet to be a Muslim prime minister. Despite acknowledgment of the problem by many major political parties, the number of Muslims in the 545-seat Indian parliament actually declined from 36 to 29 following the 2009 national election.

In addition to this political marginalization, Muslims are frequently the victims of intercommunal violence. In the immediate aftermath of partition, independence activist Mohandas Gandhi (1869–1948) went on a hunger strike to protest the attacks on the Muslim population by Hindu mobs in Delhi, Rajputana, and Jammu. Since partition, there have been several waves of violence directed at the Muslim community, including the nationwide violence that followed the demolition of the Babri Mosque in 1992 and the violence that swept through the state of Gujarat in 2000 following a deadly attack on a train carrying Hindu pilgrims.

SRI LANKA

Islam was brought to Sri Lanka by Arab seafarers and merchants. Settling along the coastal regions, they married local women and established distinct colonies. When the Portuguese arrived at the start of the 16th century, they forcefully displaced the Muslim traders who had populated the southwestern coast, driving them into the central highlands and onto the eastern coast of the island. The forced intermingling of Muslims with the Sinhalese Buddhists and Hindus during this time led to the adoption of some non-Muslim practices among Sri Lankan Muslims.

The Portuguese labeled the Muslims "Moors," a term traditionally used by Europeans to describe the Muslim peoples of North Africa. This term is still commonly used to describe Sri Lankan Muslims, who are the third largest ethnic group in the country today.

Comprising approximately 1,650,000, around 7.2 percent of the total Sri Lankan population, the Muslim Moors settled in the area of the island inhabited mainly by the Tamils (a Hindu people from India). The two cultures merged over time, with the Muslims adopting Tamil as their spoken language. The Muslim Moors are Sunnis, with some following the Hanafi school of Islamic jurisprudence, while others follow the Shafi'i school. The latter is thought to have been introduced by Muslim Malays, who came to Sri Lanka during the periods of Dutch rule (1658–1796) and British rule (1796–1900) to work as soldiers, policemen, and laborers in the tea plantations. The Muslims adopted the language and customs of the Tamils, rather than the Sinhalese, and the latter were assimilated into Muslim traditions.

Although intertwined with the Tamils, the Muslims did not ignore the Sinhalese rulers, with whom they entered into agreements that benefited both parties. The growth of Islam in Sri Lanka can be attributed to the relative peace prevailing between the several traditions throughout the 19th century. Moreover, unlike other areas exposed to Islamic invasion and occupation, there was little Muslim proselytizing, and it was only during the Portuguese period that the Muslims found themselves under significant threat.

They enjoyed greater freedom during the subsequent periods of Dutch and British rule, and consequently Muslim numbers increased in the 18th and 19th centuries. However, British colonial rule created problems that would adversely affect the Muslim Moors in the latter part of the 20th century. Britain's utilization of the Tamils to run their colonial administration undermined Sinhalese power and upset the delicate balance between the different communities. The significance of this change, however, was not realized until Sri Lanka's independence following World War II (1939–1945). The previously favored Tamil Hindus were confronted with a new political order dominated by the majority Buddhist Sinhalese and, with the latter seeking to restore their diminished influence, the Tamils rebelled. Moreover, a militant element, known as the Tamil Tigers, decided that the Tamil population of Sri Lanka should be free and independent of Sinhalese rule. The Tigers' campaign to establish an independent Tamil state on the island began in earnest in the 1970s. The ensuing war between the Sinhalese and the Tamils trapped the Muslim Moors in the middle of a struggle that they could not control.

This photograph of the main mosque in Rangoon, Burma (present-day Yangon, Myanmar) was taken in the last quarter of the 19th century.

In laying claim to the north and the northwest of the island, the Tamils drove out the Sinhalese. Asserting that the Tamil-speaking Moors were ethnic Tamils, the secessionists assumed that the Muslims would join their cause. However, when the Moors indicated their preference for the national government, the Tamil Tigers directed their assaults against Muslims remaining in the north of the country. Muslims nevertheless continue to reside in the Jaffna Peninsula, where they play key roles in the textile and gem trades, but those engaging in farming or commercial fishing are exposed to the daily battles between the Tamils and the Sinhalese. The forced removal of Muslims from the Tamil-controlled region became the stated policy of the secessionists.

A Tamil Tiger ultimatum in the 1990s to the remaining Moors to leave the northern areas or to face annihilation forced 100,000 Muslims to seek safe havens in the central and southern areas of the island that were controlled by the Sri Lankan army. In the meantime, the lives of the more affluent Muslims still residing in the north of the country came under renewed pressure, with many being kidnapped and held for ransom. Muslim fishermen, accused of working with the Sri Lankan maritime authority, have also been targeted, and their industry has been virtually wiped out. Today, Sri Lanka's

Muslim population—one-third of which is trapped in the northern and eastern areas of the country—is excluded from negotiations between the main combatants and largely ignored by them. The Muslims have held separate talks with the Liberation Tigers of Tamil Eelam (LTTE) but these have proved largely fruitless.

Following the defeat of the LTTE by Sri Lankan government forces in 2009, many Muslim refugees living in the south are considering returning to their ancestral homes in the north. Many analysts see this as unlikely to take place on any significant scale; Muslims that do return north would face difficulties taking back their property and the constant threat of a resurgence of violence.

MYANMAR

Myanmar—which was known as Burma between 1885 and 1989—is bordered by Bangladesh, China, India, Laos, and Thailand. Approximately 65 percent of its 48 million people are BaMa Buddhists. The military junta, which seized power in 1962, justifies its harsh rule in the name of preserving the unity of a country comprising eight principal ethnic groups and more than one hundred declared "races." The human complexity of Myanmar is more apparent in the hundreds of languages or dialects that are spoken in the hills, valleys, jungles, and mountain gorges that define the geography of the region. Although Theravada Buddhism is the dominant belief system, Myanmar has significant communities of Christians, Hindus, and Muslims. However, while the Hindus are associated with Buddhism, and the Christians have developed workable relations with the Myanmar government, the Muslims have been subjected to severe repression.

Officially, the Muslim population of Myanmar is placed at 3 percent, but the true figure may be as high as 10 percent. Myanmar Muslims are divided into four groups, the largest being the Rohingyas or Rakhines, perhaps several millions in number, who live in Arakan, a coastal strip on the border with Bangladesh, and in the Chittagong Hill Tract region. A 1982 citizen law denied Rohingya Muslims citizenship in Myanmar if they could not trace their family's residency in the country to the first quarter of the 19th century—something almost impossible to do in a country with very limited official records. The Rohingyas therefore are now essentially stateless and have little if any protection under the law. One of Myanmar's other Islamic groups is the BaMa Muslims, who are generally the progeny of Burmese converts to Islam; many of them are ethnically Chinese Hui. Another of the country's Muslim groups is composed of immigrants from surrounding countries who entered Myanmar during the British colonial period (1885–1948). A fourth group is the product of mixed marriages between Indian Muslims and indigenous Burmese. Together, there may be between 4 million and 6 million Muslims in Myanmar.

Although generally antipathetic to Islam, the rulers of Myanmar are most focused on neutralizing the Rohingya Muslims because it is they who appear to keep the door open to Muslim immigration into the country. The people have responded by forming the Rohingya National Alliance, a militant group that comprises the Arakan Rohingya Islamic Front and the Rohingya Solidarity Association. The Alliance has clashed with the military government, but it is no match for the Myanmar army and paramilitary

لِلاطفال الروهنجيين المهاجرين واللاجئين
(في ماليزيا)
MAKHAD AL ISLAMIAH TAHFIZUL QURAAN DARULAYTAM
(FOR DISPLACED ROHINGYA REFUGEE'S CHILDREN
IN MALAYSIA) NO 12C JLN 18, KG, CHERASBARU
KUALA LUMPUR

Exiled from their native Myanmar, these Rohingya Muslim children attend school in Kuala Lumpur, Malaysia.

forces. The flight of almost 400,000 Rohingyas to Bangladesh in the 1970s and again in the 1990s was not welcomed by the Bangladesh government, which repatriated most of the refugees in spite of their trepidation about returning to Myanmar. Nevertheless, an estimated 100,000 Rohingyas remain in Bangladesh under the care of UN humanitarian agencies. Many of these displaced people have become radicalized and militant, and the Bangladesh government has from time to time been compelled to act forcefully against them.

Muslims in Myanmar are widely denounced as terrorists and secessionists. In a fiercely anti-Islamic climate of opinion, the military government in the Myanmar capital, Yangon (formerly Rangoon), though generally unpopular, has gained widespread public support for its campaigns against Islam.

See Also
Iran 236-245 ❖
Southeast Asia 292-303 ❖ China 314-321 ❖

Chapter 15

SOUTHEAST ASIA

Southeast Asia is partly on the mainland between the Indian subcontinent and the southern edge of China and partly in a vast archipelago that extends to the north coast of Australia. This massive and diverse region is home to around one-fifth of the Muslim population of the world.

M any 20th-century Western commentators on Islam tended to overlook Southeast Asia or to regard it as merely a remote outpost of the religion. Today, however, the nations of southeastern Asia are hard to ignore. More than 200 million Muslims live in the region, a combined population only marginally lower than that of the traditional heartland of Islam in North Africa and the Middle East. Most live in the Muslim-majority nations of Indonesia, where 181 million of the 207 million inhabitants are Muslim, and Malaysia, where 12 million of the 23 million inhabitants are Muslim, but there are also significant Muslim minorities in Thailand (2.4 million), the Philippines (3.8 million), and Myanmar (1.9 million). The largest of the southeast Asian nations, Indonesia, is the most populous Muslim-majority nation in the world, ahead of Pakistan (160 million) and Bangladesh (129 million).

Although Muslim communities in the region remain essentially orthodox in terms of belief and doctrine, the cultural, linguistic, and geographical distance between southeastern Asia and the birthplace of Islam has inevitably resulted in differences in customs and attitudes.

Muslims attend prayers marking the end of the fasting month of Ramadan at Sunda Kelapa (the old port of Jakarta) in Indonesia. Indonesia is the world's most populous Muslim-majority nation.

HISTORICAL BACKGROUND

The introduction and establishment of Islam in Southeast Asia are poorly documented, although it is generally agreed that the faith was first brought into the region by maritime traders from the Arabian Peninsula. A few archaeological remains, such as inscriptions on tombstones, suggest a Muslim presence in

A few archaeological remains, such as inscriptions on tombstones, suggest a Muslim presence in the Southeast Asian archipelago as early as the 10th century.

the Southeast Asian archipelago as early as the 10th century. By the late 13th century, several Muslim states were thriving along the coasts of Sumatra, the Malay Peninsula, and Java. Small harbor kingdoms and sultanates emerged as the focal points of Islamic activity in the subsequent centuries. From these mercantile centers, Islamization spread inland. It is significant that the dissemination of the faith cannot be attributed to any one place or tradition.

Rather, the fragmentary nature of Muslim settlements created a complex process through which Islam was slowly and gradually adopted by a majority of the population, often in idiosyncratic and locally discrete ways. By the 16th century, Islam had supplanted Hinduism and Buddhism as the predominant religions in many parts of Southeast Asia.

In Southeast Asia, Islam has generally been tolerant, with a pronounced openness toward pre-Islamic traditions and indigenous customs. This has resulted in a high degree of local variation in Islamic practices and beliefs throughout the region. Introduced peacefully by trade, rather than violently by force of arms, Islam later consolidated itself through political support from local rulers. The new faith accommodated preexisting religions, principally Hinduism, Buddhism, and animistic beliefs (spirit worship). Instead of being eliminated or replaced, the pre-Islamic local customs and norms were preserved under Islam, although they were frequently reinterpreted or modified so as not to contradict the central tenets of Islam—that there was one God only, and that Muhammad was his Prophet.

Puppet Theater

An illuminating example of the ways in which pre-Islamic customs were reframed within Islamic traditions is provided by the development of *wayang*. *Wayang* is the classical form of Javanese drama in which the action is presented by puppets that are manipulated by rods and whose shadows are projected onto a translucent screen. This performance tradition was brought into Southeast Asia around the 10th century by Hindus from India. *Wayang* in Java subsequently remained faithful to its

religious roots; most productions were based on great Hindu epics, such as the Ramayana and the Mahabharata, although indigenous Malay legends were also adapted. Although there is no consensus about the subsequent history of the form, it gradually began to display Islamic influences. Some Muslims hold that the Javanese *wayang* tradition was invented by Muslim saints, who used it to spread the message of the Prophet Muhammad and to win converts to the faith. Although the *wayang* tradition predates the arrival of Islam in Southeast Asia, this insistence on Islamic roots highlights the distinctively Muslim features that were adopted by the local *wayang* traditions. Stories taken from the Hindu epics continued but were modified and supplemented by new narratives that dramatized the lives of Muslim heroes. Meanwhile, Islamic suspicion of figurative art gave rise to greater abstraction in the shape and form of the puppets.

Mystical Influences

Almost from the start of the Muslim period, Islam in Southeast Asia was shaped by Sufism, Islam's mystical tradition. Sufi orders helped to spread the message of Islam from the coastal regions farther inland. Emphasizing the cultivation of inner attitudes rather than the strict regulation of outward behavior, Sufi mysticism proved attractive to many indigenous people because it was similar to aspects of pre-Islamic devotional practices in the region and was generally characterized by an open and tolerant attitude toward local customs. The result was a syncretic mix of beliefs and religious practices.

The veneration of saints, based on the belief in their mediating power, occupied a central place in this tradition. The graves of Muslim saints became outstandingly important in the spiritual life of the community. It was at the saints' graves that believers prayed and made offerings in order to secure the saints' *barakah* (blessing). People might visit saints' tombs at any time of the year, but pilgrimages were most common on the anniversaries of each saint's birth and death. In some cases, these local pilgrimages came to rival the hajj in importance—in some regions, a prescribed number of visits to a local holy site might be counted as the equivalent of the traditional journey to Mecca.

The blending of indigenous and Islamic traditions—a hallmark of Sufi mysticism—was a major factor in the successful spread of Islam throughout the archipelago. A consequence of this Islamization process, however, was that some of the local customs incorporated into Muslim practice conflicted with strict Islamic law (Sharia).

LOCAL CUSTOMS AND ISLAMIC LAW

Many Western views of Islam are based on the premise that the religious law (Sharia) is unalterable and inviolable—the immovable cornerstone of the faith. The seeming nonchalance with which Muslim legal prescriptions are sometimes treated in Southeast Asia—together with the faith's tendency to compromise with local customs—have given rise to the false notion that Southeast Asian Muslims are somehow less than fully orthodox or only trivially Muslim.

This photograph shows *wayang* shadow puppets in Bali, Indonesia.

Other scholars, however, argue that many of the locally inflected customs found in Southeast Asian Muslim communities are commonplace throughout the Muslim world and that many have explicit bases in the sacred sources of the Koran and the Sunna (the life of the Prophet). The dominant framework of meaning in which these practices are interpreted is the Islamic

Originating in Western Asia, the ideas of the Muslim modernist movement reached Southeast Asia through increased contact between the two regions.

mystical tradition, not Islamic law. Instead of describing this nonlegalistic strand of Muslim expression as un-Islamic, these scholars suggest that it is better understood as an alternative voice within a religion that, although widely regarded as an unyielding monolith, is, in fact, pluralistic.

ISLAMIC MODERNISM

People who have devalued mysticism as inauthentic Islam have perhaps been excessively influenced by the Muslim modernist movement, whose strongly critical attitudes to Sufi-inspired traditions gained wide currency in the 20th century. The modernists advocated strict observance of Islamic law and the direct application of Koranic injunctions to everyday life. The stated target of Islamic modernism was the purification of the faith and the removal from it of the syncretistic elements that the reformers held responsible for the perceived backwardness and poverty of the Muslim community. Among the

principal targets of this movement were the veneration of saints and pilgrimages to their gravesites.

Originating in western Asia, the ideas of the Muslim modernist movement reached Southeast Asia through increased contact between the two regions. The number of pilgrims to Mecca—and the number of scholars and students traveling to other parts of the Arabian Peninsula, western Asia, and northern Africa—increased significantly in the late 19th century and the early 20th century. There, Southeast Asian Muslims became familiar with the reformist ideas of Jamal ad-Din al-Afghani (1838–1897) and Muhammad Abduh (1849–1905). One of the first Southeast Asian Muslims to promote the ideas of Islamic modernism in Southeast Asia was Sheikh Tahir Jalal ad-Din (1869–1957), who had been a student of Muhammad Abduh in Cairo, Egypt. On his return to Singapore, he founded the journal *al-Imam*, which quickly became a mouthpiece for the reformist movement throughout Southeast Asia. In Indonesia, Islamic reformism ambitions found expression through the Muhammadiyah organization.

STRUGGLE FOR INDEPENDENCE

Indonesia was ruled by the Netherlands from the early 17th century until 1945. Malaysia was governed by Britain from the late 18th century until 1963. In both countries, growing opposition to colonial rule after World War II (1939–1945) galvanized nationalist sentiments and inspired struggles for independence. During the period of British control of Malaysia, the indigenous Muslims had been seriously disadvantaged economically and socially as the colonial rulers discriminated against them in favor of non-Muslim immigrants of Chinese and Indian descent. In an attempt to strengthen the socioeconomic position of the Malay Muslims, reformers stressed the significance of Islam as an essential element in the development of a national consciousness. This Malay-Islamic identity turned religion into a potent force that challenged the British regime. Similarly, in Indonesia, Muslim movements were involved in the anticolonial struggle to achieve national independence and a bigger role for Islam in state and society.

Having helped these former colonies to gain independence, Islam then moved closer to center stage in public life, although none of the emergent nations of Southeast Asia became an Islamic state. The numerical strength of the Muslim population, in addition to the role that Muslim organizations had played in the anti-colonial struggle, raised the hopes for a greater acknowledgement of Islam in the political and social structures of the newly independent nations. While the postwar development of Indonesia and Malaysia was influenced significantly by the nations' colonial history, the resurgence of Islam elsewhere in Southeast Asia took a range of different forms, and today the religion has widely different profiles in Thailand and the Philippines.

THAILAND

In Thailand, which had never been under colonial control, Buddhism, particularly in its Theravada variant, remains the dominant tradition. Thailand's 3 million Muslims (around 4.6 percent of the population), most of whom are ethnic Malays, are concentrated primarily in the south of the country near the border with Malaysia. This region, which has strong cultural and

THE MUHAMMADIYAH

Inspired by Muhammad Abduh and established in Indonesia in 1912, the Muhammadiyah (Arabic, followers of Muhammad) tried to bring the Muslim faith into harmony with modern rational thought. The movement aimed to abolish the superstitious customs that were relics of pre-Islamic times, as well as many manifestations of Muslim traditionalism. The methods adopted by the Muhammadiyah in pursuit of those aims were in many ways similar to those of Christian missionaries. The organization established schools along modern lines, in which religion was taught together with a range of Western subjects, including Dutch, the language of the colonial rulers of the country. By the 1920s, the Muhammadiyah was the dominant force in Indonesian Islam. At the start of the 21st century, the movement had around 29 million members and remains the world's largest Muslim modernist mass organization. It retains a strong focus on the modernization of religious education and issues of social welfare.

ethnic ties with Malaysia, became part of the Thai polity only in the 18th century. Muslims there are Malay-speaking and have retained cultural and religious differences from the rest of Thailand that have made them repeatedly the target of assimilationist campaigns by the central government.

In the 1930s, the Thai government introduced educational and economic programs to promote a cohesive and inclusive national identity. One of the initiatives was the resettlement of Malay Muslims from southern Thailand to central and northern parts of the country. Living alongside Muslims of Persian and South Asian descent, the relocated Muslims were generally assimilated into the societal mainstream—they speak Thai and have adopted Thai conventions and norms. However, by those who remained in southern Thailand, the government policies were perceived as anti-Islamic and anti-Malay. The 1960s and 1970s saw the emergence of several separatist movements that demanded autonomy and the preservation of religious Malay culture.

The Thai government's response ranged from repressive military campaigns to attempts at appeasement, but at the start of the 21st century the conflict was still unresolved. Nevertheless, the status of Thai Muslims has improved since the 1990s. Increasing numbers of Muslims have been elected to the Thai National Assembly. As a result of their influence on the legislature, Muslims have gained religious and political rights and participated more fully than ever before in public life. New mosques have been built with public funds, and the government has acknowledged the rights of Muslims to wear Islamic dress in schools and at work in the civil service and to adopt Islamic names.

THE PHILIPPINES

The experience of Muslims in the Philippines has in many ways paralleled that of Malay Muslims in Thailand. Filipino Muslims, known as Moros, are concentrated in the southern Philippines and, like their coreligionists in Thailand, have largely opposed the central government in their quest for cultural and political self-determination. Historically, the Moros were self-governing and therefore free to develop their own culture and identity. Neither the Spanish—who united and controlled the Philippines from the 16th century onward and converted the population to Christianity—nor, later, the Americans fully conquered the Moros in the south. When the Philippines achieved independence in 1946, the southern territories were included in the new nation without the consent of the Moros, who did not regard themselves as Filipinos.

After independence, the Moros were increasingly marginalized. The situation was aggravated by the government's encouragement of Christians from the north to settle in the south. This led to severe land conflicts between the groups. The grievances gave rise to the establishment in the early 1970s of the Moro National Liberation Front, which sought to form an independent nation or, at least, an autonomous region. The breakdown of peaceful negotiations led to armed conflict, which ended in 1989 with the creation of the Autonomous Region of Muslim Mindanao. Although the violence did not cease, Muslims were later granted numerous concessions that enhanced their political and economic powers and allowed the implementation of some aspects of Islamic law. Greater control over their own affairs in the southern regions, however, has done little to increase the involvement of the Moros in the national government of the Philippines.

Meanwhile, in contrast to Thailand and the Philippines, Indonesia and Malaysia have, since independence, institutionalized Islam through the establishment of religious courts, state-sponsored Islamic education, and Islamic political parties. Significant differences, however, exist between Indonesia and Malaysia in the role, status, and articulation of Islam in public life.

INDONESIA TODAY

Indonesia's state ideology is based on five principles, known as Pancasila, the first of which is the belief in one God. Although the constitution is secular—there is no official state religion—the Pancasila requires all citizens to profess one of the state-recognized religions, which include Islam. This has made possible the promotion of Islam through state institutions, such as political parties, ministries, schools, and courts. Nevertheless, the exact interpretation of the Pancasila with regard to the proper status of Islam as the religion of the majority has remained the subject of debate.

The increasingly authoritarian government of Indonesian President Suharto (ruled 1967–1998) sought to depoliticize Islam and restrict it to spiritual, social, and cultural matters. This policy provoked an increase in Muslim civic activism that coincided with and reinforced the unprecedented Islamic resurgence in the country in the 1970s and 1980s. Muslim civic organizations and political parties joined the opposition against authoritarianism and corruption under Suharto, who was forced to resign.

After the fall of the dictator, Indonesia embarked on an ambitious democratization program. However, the nation's political future remains uncertain. Since 1998, there has been an increase in interethnic and interreligious violence, and political decentralization has allowed a number of provinces to introduce Islamic law. Nonetheless, Muslim support for a civil-pluralist Islam that is detached from the institutions of government is well organized. The Muhammadiyah and other large Muslim organizations have repeatedly asserted their commitment to democratic reform. Equally encouraging, the results of recent national elections have indicated that support for Muslim parties advocating the establishment of an Islamic state is marginal and that the majority of Indonesians continue to support the multireligious compromise enshrined in the Pancasila.

MALAYSIA TODAY

Malaysia is a multiethnic and multireligious society in which Malay Muslims form the majority. Islam is the official state religion, and around 60 percent of the population adheres to it. Most of the remainder are Buddhists, Hindus, Christians, and

Moro musicians perform at a traditional wedding in the Philippines.

observers of traditional Chinese religions. Although the Malaysian constitution guarantees these minorities freedom of worship, the regulation of religious affairs through government ministries and the courts of law has effectively restricted non-Islamic practices in Malaysia.

In spite of the connection between being Malay and being Muslim, the Islamic community in Malaysia displays varying attitudes toward the role of religion in the nation's political affairs. The divergent viewpoints are reflected in two of the most prominent political parties that appeal to the Malay-Muslim constituency. The United Malays National Organization (UMNO) is the country's largest political party. It is part of a coalition that has ruled Malaysia since independence. Although UMNO supports Muslim dominance in the state, it is more moderate than its

The United Malays National Organization (UMNO) is the country's largest political party. It is part of a coalition that has ruled Malaysia since independence.

counterpart, the Pan-Malaysian Islamic Party (PAS). In a significant indication of the political climate, the PAS has been in opposition since the late 1970s, and its importance as a national party has diminished. Regionally, however, the PAS has retained significant influence, particularly in the northeastern Malay Peninsula, where it demands the full implementation of Islamic law and seeks the establishment of an Islamic state.

In the 1980s, in a bid to discredit claims that UMNO and other governing parties were un-Islamic, the ruling coalition initiated its own Islamization campaign that upgraded religious education in schools and colleges. The International Islamic University of Malaysia was founded in 1983 in the capital city, Kuala Lumpur, and was charged with developing a comprehensive model of higher education based on the principles of the Koran. The jurisdiction of Sharia courts in the legal system was broadened, and Malaysia developed an interest-free banking system to conform with the Koranic proscription of usury.

Islam and the State

Greater openness as a result of democratic reform in many Southeast Asian countries has provided Muslims with improved opportunities for participation in political discourse. This process has been accompanied and reinforced by a great increase in public expressions of Muslim faith—attendances at mosques, the wearing of Islamic dress, participation in the hajj, and the observance of Ramadan. The extraordinary resurgence of Islam has ignited an intense debate throughout Southeast Asia over the proper relationship between Islam and the state. Three distinctive positions can be discerned.

Some observers are generally troubled by the resurgence of Islam in the public sphere. They question whether the faith, as widely interpreted, is compatible with democratic qualities such as human rights, equality, and political participation. The recent electoral success of Muslim parties— the political programs of which include the implementation of Islamic law—has amplified these anxieties. Proponents of secularism seek to limit the role of Islam to

the private sphere and to detach the religion from politics.

Meanwhile, traditionalists are united by their opposition to secularism, but they are often unable to agree over the extent to which Islamic law should be adopted by the state and over interpretations of the holy texts themselves. There are also divisions between them about the means by which they should attain their objectives. Most of those who desire an Islamic state aim to achieve it through consensus politics; only a minority—albeit a high-profile one—advocate violent seizure of the state.

The latter group includes two insurgent separatist movements in the Philippines—the Moro Islamic Liberation Front in Mindanao and the Abu Sayyaf Group, which calls for an independent Muslim nation in the south of the country. Another is the Jemaah Islamiyah group in Indonesia, which was held responsible for the Bali nightclub bombings in October 2002.

Although terrorist atrocities have alienated majority public opinion, there remain many political parties in Southeast Asia that call for the implementation of Islamic law. In Indonesia, the fall of the Suharto regime prompted almost immediately the establishment of more than 40 Islamic parties. However, most of these groups did not seek to make Islam the basis of the state but rather accepted

Supporters of the Prosperous Justice Party (PKS) wave and shout slogans at a rally in Yogyakarta, Indonesia, during the 2004 election.

the Pancasila as their political platform. The current strength of political Islam in Indonesia remains a matter of debate. Some observers believe that even the success of the Prosperous Justice Party (Partai Keadilan Sejahtera; PKS), which won 7 percent of the vote in the 2004 elections, may have been the result of a protest vote against an incompetent and corrupt political establishment rather than a deeply felt traditionalist impulse.

CIVIL ISLAM

Dissatisfaction with the ideology of an Islamic state on the one hand and the secularists' demands for the strict separation of Islam from state structures on the other has led to the emergence of a group who propose a third way to ensure the continuing involvement of Islam in the region's democratic and pluralist societies.

This group of Muslims has included some high-profile figures, such as Abdurrahman Wahid (b. 1940) in Indonesia and Anwar Ibrahim (b. 1947) in Malaysia. Both men have furthered the processes of democratic-pluralist reform and spoken out against intolerance and interreligious violence. Although they have both held high political offices in their public careers, they did not advocate Islamization from the top down through government regulation but from the bottom up—a grassroots process. Rather than enforcing religion through state bureaucracies, they assert that the proper place for Islam is in the sphere of civil society, which can be seen as occupying the public realm between the private sphere and the state. These "civil Muslims"—a term coined by the anthropologist Robert Hefner—hold that Islamic ideals should inform the work of social activist groups, civic associations, nongovernmental organizations (NGOs), and independent research organizations in order to counterbalance state power.

The emphasis on Muslim extra-state organizations has been more pronounced in Indonesia than in Malaysia. This is largely due to the historically different roles that Islam has played in the constitution and public institutions of the two countries. The constitutionally based political dominance of Muslims in Malaysia has meant that many of the country's Islamic movements have emphasized the importance of state intervention and government regulations as the means to implement Islamic ideals. In spite of these precepts, however, there has meanwhile been a rise in Muslim NGO activity throughout Southeast Asian societies. Many of these NGOs concentrate

ABDURRAHMAN WAHID

Abdurrahman Wahid was the fourth president of the Republic of Indonesia (1999–2001) and a prominent leader of the traditionalist Muslim mass organization Nahdlatul Ulama (NU), which, under his leadership, has made relief and development work its leading priorities. Wahid is among the most influential Muslim intellectuals of contemporary Southeast Asia with a high profile as a writer, a columnist, and a speaker. His intellectual agenda fuses the demand for the public role of Islam as a source of ethical and moral ideals with an outspoken opposition to the idea of an Islamic state. His role in advancing tolerance and understanding throughout Indonesia and Southeast Asia has won him many honors. In 1993 he received the Raman Magsaysay award, which is sometimes described as "the Asian Nobel Prize"; in 2003 he was presented with the Friends of the United Nations Global Tolerance Award. In the contemporary Indonesian discourse over Islam and society, Abdurrahman Wahid remains a prominent voice for pluralism and democratic reform.

on social welfare, while others aim at raising public awareness of human rights, democratic development, and interreligious harmony by drawing on Islamic values and ideals. In Indonesia, Muslim associational life independent of the state also includes the world's two largest Muslim mass organizations, Muhammadiyah and Nahdlatul Ulama. Both organizations have consistently emphasized their profiles as social welfare organizations with a staunch commitment to a pluralist Indonesia and consistently opposed any attempts to establish a theocracy that has Islam enshrined in its constitution.

POSSIBLE WAYS FORWARD

It is difficult to predict which view of Islam and the state will prevail. What is evident, however, is that there exists a great variety of positions within Southeast Asia concerning the political dimension of Islam. The role and status of Islam in any of these societies have less to do with static or unchangeable religious truths than with the social, cultural, and historical circumstances that influence Muslim voices in the public sphere. In spite of the unpredictable future outcome of this debate, it seems certain that the influence of Islam on politics and culture in Southeast Asia will persist.

Hundreds of Muslim men attend Friday prayers at a mosque in Jakarta on the Indonesian island of Java.

See Also

South Asia 274-291 ❖
China 314-321 ❖
Australasia and the Pacific 378-385 ❖

Chapter 16

CENTRAL ASIA

The Muslims of Central Asia are concentrated in Azerbaijan, Kazakhstan, Kyrgyzstan, Tajikistan, Turkmenistan, and Uzbekistan. In addition, 10 percent of the population of Russia are Muslim (around 14 million people). All these countries were formerly parts of the communist Soviet Union, whose policies had a strong and enduring effect on the practice of Islam throughout the region.

Most of the Muslim peoples of Central Asia are Sunnis. One exception is the Azeris (the Turkic people of Azerbaijan), who, like their southern neighbors, the Iranians, are Shiite Muslims. Another exception is the Pamiri people of the Gorno-Badakhshan autonomous region of Tajikistan, who are mainly Shias of the Ismaili sect. Ethnically, the Muslims of Central Asia are a diverse mix; they can be grouped under the major categories of Caucasian, Turkic, and Persian peoples. Abkhazians, Chechens, and Avars are among the main Caucasian groups. Tatars, Azeris, Karakalpaks, as well as the majority populations of Kazakhstan, Kyrgyzstan, Turkmenistan, and Uzbekistan, are Turkic. The Tajiks, the Iranians, and the Pamiris are all Persian peoples.

Traditionally, the peoples of northern Central Asia were nomadic, while the peoples of the south of the region were sedentary. On the northern steppes—which comprise Turkmenistan, Kazakhstan, northern Kyrgyzstan, Mongolia, and the adjacent regions of southern Russia—the inhabitants herded animals and migrated according to the climate and the pasture conditions. During the Soviet period (1917–1991), the nomads were compelled to settle, but the legacy of their historic culture is still apparent in their social structures, economy, and religious practices. The fertile valleys in the south—most of which are parts of present-day Uzbekistan and Tajikistan—benefit from the drainage systems of the Amu Darya River and the

> Ethnically, the Muslims of Central Asia are a diverse mix; they can be grouped under the major categories of Caucasian, Turkic, and Persian peoples.

Syr Darya River, which have enabled local residents to become sedentary and engage in agriculture. Sedentary life facilitated the development of two great cities, Samarkand and Bukhara (both in modern Uzbekistan), which prospered as stopovers on the Silk Road, along which a growing range of commercial goods was transported between China, India, and Europe. Central Asian scientists and philosophers were thus exposed to both eastern (Chinese

This mosque with four minarets is in Bukhara, Uzbekistan. Uzbekistan, which became independent from the Soviet Union in 1991, has around 27 million inhabitants, 88 percent of whom are Muslim.

and Indian) and western (Arab, Greek, and Roman) sources. They also made their own contributions to science. For example, Ulugh Beg (1394–1449) was a Timurid shah (king) of Samarkand and an astronomer who discovered errors in the computations of the 2nd-century Greek astronomer Ptolemy, whose work had previously been highly influential throughout the world.

Central Asia has been invaded many times—by Greeks, Persians, Turkic peoples, Arabs, Mongols, and Russians—and the culture of the region reflects a wide range of influences. Islam was introduced to the region by the Arab conquests, which began in the 8th century. The sedentary peoples of the southern valleys were Islamicized early on, and madrassas in the cities of this region became important centers of orthodox Muslim learning, as well as of Sufism. For example, one of the most authoritative collections of Hadiths (sayings of Muhammad) belonged to Imam Bukhari (810–870), a native of Bukhara. Abu Mansur al-Maturidi (853–944), a theologian from Maturid, a town near Samarkand, founded the Hanafi school of jurisprudence, which is now followed by the majority of Sunni Muslims in Turkey and Central Asia, as well as in present-day Afghanistan and Pakistan. Meanwhile, the Islamicization of the nomadic peoples of the northern steppes was a much more gradual process that continued into the 19th century.

The Arabs failed to establish long-term control over Central Asia, but the inhabitants of the region—especially the nomads—learned Islam mainly from Sufis and traders. Sufis were generally tolerant of local pre-Islamic religious rites, and so Islam in Central Asia retained traces of previous

shamanistic practices, especially among the former nomads. For example, Central Asians continued to venerate and make pilgrimages to the tombs (*zyarat*) of saints, where they tied pieces of cloth to the branches of surrounding trees and made wishes. There are no saints in orthodox Islam; in this context, sainthood is a shamanistic rather than a Muslim concept.

MODERATE TRADITIONS

There is little radical Islam in Central Asia, where the predominant form of the religion is very much enmeshed with the local cultures. Fundamentalism is almost nonexistent, especially in those parts of the region that were formerly parts of the Soviet Union.

In the 18th and 19th centuries, many revivalist and modernist approaches to Islam were developed in the Muslim world, especially in Egypt and India, which were both, at the time, British colonies. These movements called for a return to the core texts of Islam—the Koran and the Hadith—in search of answers to modern problems. One of the principal aims of these movements was to free Islam from beliefs and practices that were not integral parts of Islam but that had come to be considered Islamic. The ideas that motivated these movements were introduced to Central Asia through the Russian and the Soviet administrations.

RUSSIFICATION

The expansion of the Russian Empire into the Muslim lands began in 1552. First, the Tatars, who inhabited the basin of the Volga River, were taken under Russian control. Gradually, all of Central Asia and Siberia were conquered. The Russians soon realized that they could not establish control over the Muslims by suppressing Islam so they adopted an accommodationist approach, seeking to modify Islam so that it became more compatible with Russian culture and government. The Russians used the Tatars as their agents, sending them as teachers to instruct the Muslims. This process, which became known as Jadid reform or "the New Method," did much to spread modernism and modern Islam among the Muslims of Central Asia.

The Russian Empire fell after the Bolshevik revolution of 1917, and the communist Soviet era began. The Soviets maintained broadly the same policy toward the Muslims living within their borders but implemented it more directly and with greater vigor. Instead of using Tatars to introduce modern education and modernist views of Islam, the Soviet state set out to educate the Muslims in their own languages in public schools and to control people's spiritual lives by institutionalizing Islam. The result, which many scholars call "official Islam," had numerous facets. Four regional muftis (legal authorities) were established. Mosques had to be registered. Imams (prayer leaders) became employees of the state. They all propagated modernist Islam and led initiatives to abolish or reduce the wearing of the traditional head veil. They also purged un-Islamic, often superstitious, practices, such as the worship of saints.

Although, in general, Central Asian Muslims responded positively to Soviet educational and modernization policies, they resisted anything that they regarded as an attempt to institutionalize Islam. Opposition to "official Islam" was particularly strong in rural areas, where people still learned about the traditional faith from the local elders, whose teachings were often different from those of the state-sponsored Islam promoted by the Soviets. Unofficial mosques emerged in a dissident movement that became known as "parallel Islam." The state disapproved but was powerless to stamp it out. Indeed, this duality continues in the post-Soviet republics that have Muslim majorities. In these countries, the government promotes a secular, modern version of Islam and tries to control religious affairs through national muftis and official mosques with state-appointed imams. However, the people continue to practice the traditional form of Islam that has been passed down from generation to generation. Most of them worship at neighborhood mosques on every day of the week except Friday, when they attend the larger, state-sponsored mosques for communal prayer.

POST-SOVIET DEVELOPMENTS

After the dissolution of the Soviet Union in 1991, the newly independent governments of Central Asia faced a dilemma: Should they maintain the Soviet traditions of institutionalizing and continually modernizing Islam, or should they encourage the assertion of Muslim identity? For a while, the latter option seemed the more attractive because it was popular with the electorate. However, attitudes changed throughout the region in the 1990s, when civil wars broke out in Chechnya (a republic of Russia) and in Tajikistan. Although these conflicts were, in essence, caused by ethnic or tribal rivalries, they acquired religious overtones and became increasingly associated with radical Islamist movements. This development alarmed the governments of Central Asia and made them more cautious about using Islam as a means of political mobilization.

In Uzbekistan, the threat of Muslim radicalism and terrorist groups provided a pretext for the government to tighten its authoritarian grip. For example, the Uzbek government sought to justify the Andijan massacre of May 2005—in which hundreds of protesters were shot dead by security forces—on the grounds that the demonstration was organized by Islamist terrorist radicals. This claim has been hotly disputed by many commentators, who say that the shootings were carried out to suppress political opposition of all kinds.

Although government statements linking political opposition to radical Islam are not always credible, the fact remains that there was a resurgence of Islamist groups in Central Asia after the fall of the Soviet Union. The three most notable organizations of this kind were the Islamic Renaissance Party of Tajikistan (IRP), the Hizb-ut-Tahrir (HT), and the Islamic Movement of Uzbekistan (IMU). The IRP was part of the United Tajik Opposition, one of the warring parties in the Tajik civil war (1992–1997). The only legal Islamist political party in Central Asia, the IRP participates in elections and now holds seats in the Tajik parliament. Hizb-ut-Tahrir (Party of Liberation) aims to reestablish the caliphate, an Islamic state that rules over the entire Muslim world. This international radical group has active branches in Central Asia, but it does not engage in terrorist activities. It is organized in small groups known as *halqa* (circles), which are cellular—members of one circle do not know for certain about members of other circles. The IMU is the most active and violent organization of the three. It has engaged in terrorist crimes, such as kidnappings and, allegedly, the Tashkent

bombings of 1999 in which 16 people were killed and more than 100 people were injured. IMU militants and leaders operate from bases in Afghanistan, where they are involved in drug trafficking and have also cooperated with the Taliban and Al-Qaeda. U.S. operations in Afghanistan since the 2001 invasion have reportedly rendered the IMU ineffective.

Given that fundamentalist interpretations of Islam are alien to Central Asia, as previously discussed, it may initially seem contradictory that radical organizations, such as the HT and the IMU, should have gained support among traditionally moderate Muslims. However, numerous Central Asians have been attracted to these organizations because

Unofficial mosques emerged in a dissident movement that became known as "parallel Islam." The state disapproved but was powerless to stamp it out.

they represent a channel for political opposition to authoritarian regimes and provide economic benefits in environments that have been blighted by poverty, unemployment, and ineffective or nonexistent development policies.

The conflict in Afghanistan has directly threatened the stability, not only of the contiguous nations of Tajikistan, Turkmenistan, and Uzbekistan—in addition to Pakistan—but also of all of Muslim Central Asia. The displacement of refugees and the fear that the war might spread into other parts of the region have also contributed to the rise of Islamist militancy, as well as indirectly causing an increase in authoritarianism, drug use, and the incidence of HIV/AIDS.

REGIONAL ECONOMY

The nations of Central Asia have enormous economic potential based principally on the Caspian Sea basin, which contains the Baku oil field and the Shah Deniz gas field (Azerbaijan), as well as the Tengiz oil field (Kazakhstan). These are some of the world's largest known oil reserves. There are also significant, though smaller, oil and gas reserves in Turkmenistan and Uzbekistan.

However, the exploitation of these natural resources is inhibited by ownership disputes. The Caspian Sea is bordered by five nations—Azerbaijan, Iran, Kazakhstan, Russia, and Turkmenistan—which all vie for control of the fields themselves and the pipelines through which the oil is exported. One of the problems concerns

This photograph of rebels with rocket launchers was taken in 1995 during one of the wars in which Chechnya tried unsuccessfully to secede from Russia.

the unresolved question of whether the landlocked water should be classified as a sea or a lake—the distinction is of crucial significance in international law. Another difficulty is that no new treaties have been made to supersede those that date from the time when only two countries flanked the shores—Iran and the Soviet Union. The emergence of four new countries after the collapse of communism in 1991 has not been satisfactorily dealt with. The question today is whether the water boundaries should be based on the former treaty between the Soviet Union and Iran, or equal division (one-fifth for each nation), or a division proportional to the length of each country's shoreline. No agreements have yet been reached.

Decisions about the routes of pipelines have involved international powers, primarily the United States, and major oil companies, such as Chevron and British Petroleum (BP). Oil and gas reserves will not benefit Azerbaijan, Kazakhstan, and Turkmenistan unless these nations can bring their resources to the surface and transport them to world markets. Caspian oil was seen by Western governments as a means of diminishing their dependence on oil from the countries surrounding the Persian Gulf. Thus, Western nations and oil companies developed initiatives to cooperate with the governments of Central Asia on drilling and transportation. These moves benefited the countries of the region, because they enabled them to reduce their dependence on pipelines through Russia.

This policy resulted in the construction of the Baku-Tbilisi-Ceyhan crude oil pipeline, which extends for 1,099 miles (1,768 km) between the capital of Azerbaijan on the Caspian Sea and the Turkish coast of the Mediterranean Sea. Its

WOMEN IN CENTRAL ASIA

Although Muslim women in Central Asia do not suffer from the stereotypical restrictions and discrimination endured by their counterparts in other parts of the Islamic world, it would be misleading to conclude that they enjoy freedom and equal status with men. Burqa-type clothing is uncommon, and head veils are worn only in the most conservative areas. However, Muslim women are expected to dress conservatively in traditional clothes. They are also expected to adhere to certain traditions regarding their appearance, such as not thinning their eyebrows or cutting their hair before marriage and wearing the ornate new-bride's cap for a year after marriage. Although women and men are generally not segregated in society, dating is rare, and marriage is often arranged or, at least, depends upon parental consent. A woman who is not married by the age of 24 is seen as an anomaly, and newlyweds are expected to have their first baby in the first year of marriage.

As a result of the policies during the Soviet era, contemporary Central Asian women participate in many aspects of life, attending college and going out to work. However, the primary expectation of the woman is that she should be a good wife, daughter-in-law, and mother. Because of the male-dominated nature of workplaces and the family obligations of women, females tend to gain employment only in low-level, poorly paid jobs. Equality and freedom, which are guaranteed for women in most Western countries, are unfamiliar in Central Asia, where traditional society expects women to be subordinate and homebound.

course, which runs through Georgia, avoids both Iran and Russia. Commenced in 2001, the pipeline went into operation in May of 2005. Further pipelines are planned to carry oil from Kazakhstan, Turkmenistan, and Uzbekistan to Western ports while bypassing Russia and trouble spots in western Asia.

ISLAM AND EVERYDAY LIFE

The depth of religious observance in the countries of Central Asia is influenced by a variety of factors, principally the length of time that Islam has been established and the level of contact with, first, the Soviet Union and, more recently, with Russia. Muslims in the southern parts of the region—where life has traditionally been sedentary and madrassa education is well established—tend to be more conservative than those in the north, who converted to Islam much later. Rural Muslims are more conservative and pious than those in urban areas, where Soviet and Russian cultural policies held and continue to hold the greatest sway. The most extreme cases of Russification can be observed among the Tatars and the Kazakhs, most of whom

This photograph shows some of the 1,500 floating oil derricks erected by Azerbaijan to extract oil from the bed of the Caspian Sea.

have never learned their respective ethnic languages and have been educated exclusively in Russian.

Many of the strictest adherents to the traditional obligations of Islam—such as praying five times daily and fasting throughout the month of Ramadan—inhabit the Ferghana Valley on the borders of Uzbekistan, Kyrgyzstan, and Tajikistan. The valley was also the native district of Juma Namangani (1969–2001), the leader of the IMU, and the major recruiting district for his organization. This was both a cause and an effect of repression by the authoritarian Uzbek government, which bans all public displays of religious affiliation, such as long beards in men and burqa-type attire in women. Human Rights Watch, the U.S.-based monitoring agency, reports that, since the 1999 bombings, many ordinary Uzbek Muslims have been detained without trial on suspicion of being terrorists. Uzbekistan has thus reverted to the Soviet way of strictly controlling Islam by tightening its grip on mosques and *mahalla*s. A *mahalla* is a neighborhood composed of households on a few small blocks in a village or in an urban area. Each *mahalla* has its own community governing body, which is composed of *aqsaqal*s (literally, "white beards"). *Aqsaqal*s used to be the eldest, most experienced men in the *mahalla* but, after the Soviet transformation of the social institution of the *mahalla*, anyone who is respected by the community can become an *aqsaqal*, regardless of age or sex. Since Soviet times, *mahalla* committees have been local offices of the state apparatus.

It remains difficult to distinguish religion from secular traditions in Central Asia, where Islamic practices have been deeply integrated with social structures and norms. Family life, the neighborhood, and the ceremonies surrounding them always have Islamic components. None of the societies in question is governed by Sharia law. Marriage, divorce, child custody, inheritance, and property rights are all governed by secular legislation, as is the penal code. However, while Islamic rules are not legally binding in family and social relationships, they are still social norms.

The nuclear family is a relatively new development in Central Asian societies and is more common in towns and cities than in the countryside, where yurts (portable tents) are still much in evidence in *aul*s (small villages) that may be relocated according to preference or the changing seasons. Urban Muslims traditionally live with their paternal families in courtyards

Family life, the neighborhood, and the ceremonies surrounding them always have Islamic components. None of the societies in question is governed by Sharia law.

surrounded by several separate residential units, each of which includes a guest room, a kitchen, a bathroom, and the family quarters of each married couple and their children. Daughters go and live with their husbands' larger family when they marry.

Surviving oral traditions, such as the Kyrgyz legend of the epic hero Manas, and the works of authors such as Chinghiz Aitmatov (1928–2008) are valuable in understanding the nomadic lifestyle and its transformation during the Soviet period.

Cultural elements and social norms are reproduced most significantly within the

larger family. Children learn about Islam and its principles, and first perform their prayers, within the family context. Knowledge of Arabic or Arabic script is not common in Central Asia, so children in general do not learn to read and interpret the Koran in its original language in the family. If they ever learn Arabic or the Arabic script, they do so mainly from the imam of the neighborhood mosque. While the traditional and practical aspects of Islam are learned through the family, formal and theological aspects are learned from the imams of the *mahalla*.

*Mahalla*s tend to be ethnically homogeneous; however, a *mahalla* is not always inhabited by members of the same extended family or tribe. Especially in rural areas and in the old sections of the cities, the inhabitants of a *mahalla* invariably know about their neighbors and have close-knit social relationships with them.

Rites of passage, such as weddings, births, circumcisions, and funerals, are neighborhood affairs and are celebrated with elaborate ceremonies. It is not uncommon for families to organize weddings that greatly exceed their means because these events help to consolidate their status within the community. The imam of the *mahalla* mosque is always present at these ceremonies, where he recites passages from the Koran.

In 21st-century Central Asia, the traditional and the modern are not always easily reconciled. One area of conflict is clothing, which is often indicative of ethnic and religious identity. For example, all men are expected to wear skullcaps and hats (*doppe* in Uzbek, *kalpak* in Kazakh and Kyrgyz), especially during ceremonies. However, many young men increasingly prefer Western-style attire.

Kazakh Muslims pray at an outdoor funeral. Many Kazakh Muslims now live in China, where they fled during the Soviet era to avoid persecution by the dictator Joseph Stalin.

See Also
Iran 236-245 ❖
South Asia 274-291 ❖
China 314-321 ❖
Turkey and Eastern
Europe 322-333 ❖

Chapter 17

CHINA

Muslims comprise between 1.5 percent and 3.8 percent of China's population of 1.3 billion. Between one-fifth and one-half of Chinese Muslims live in the northwestern provinces; the remainder are distributed throughout the country. Their freedom, prosperity, and social status vary greatly from time to time and from place to place.

There have been Muslims in China since the earliest days of Islam. The faith was spread eastward from its Arabian heartland by Arab and Persian merchants whose predecessors had been trading by sea and along the Silk Road for centuries before the birth of the Prophet Muhammad. By the beginning of the 21st century, there were an estimated 20 million Muslims in China; some commentators put the figure closer to 50 million, which would make Chinese Muslims more numerous than their coreligionists in all the nations of the Arab world, excluding Egypt.

Although more than 90 percent of the population of China are Han Chinese, there are 55 recognized ethnic minority groups, 10 of which are predominantly Muslim.

Although more than 90 percent of the population of China are Han Chinese, there are 55 recognized ethnic minority groups, 10 of which are predominantly Muslim: the Hui, the Uighur, the Kazakh, the Dongxiang, the Kirghiz, the Salar, the Tajik, the Uzbek, the Bonan, and the Tatar. All but one of these groups are concentrated in the northwestern provinces of Xinjiang, Gansu, Ningxia, and Tibet. The exception is the Hui, of whom there are around 10 million dispersed throughout China. Descendants of Arab, Persian, and Central Asian Muslims who settled in China in the 13th century, the Hui have long adapted to their local environments. They speak Mandarin Chinese and they are culturally—although not, of course, religiously—almost indistinguishable from the Han. There are also Hui who have settled among some of China's other ethnic groups and, over the centuries, they have adopted the language and customs of their hosts. For example, the Hui in Tibet speak Tibetan, wear traditional Tibetan clothing, and are Tibetan in every way apart from the fact that they are Muslims, not Buddhists.

The Uighur are the second largest Muslim group in China; numbering close to 9 million, they are concentrated in the northwestern province of Xinjiang. When the communist People's Republic of China was established in 1949, approximately 90 percent of the population of Xinjiang was Uighur. Of Central Asian, Turkic origin,

Chinese Muslims make their way to the Niujie Mosque in Beijing to celebrate Eid al-Fitr, the festival that marks the end of the fasting month of Ramadan.

315

the Uighurs have their own language, culture, and religious traditions.

Because the Muslim population of China is so diverse and widely distributed, it is difficult to make generalizations about the practice of Islam in the world's most populous nation. However, it may be noted that most Chinese Muslims are Sunnis, that they follow the Hanafi legal tradition, and that they tend to be more observant in rural areas than in cities.

The Mongol Yuan Dynasty

The earliest Muslims in China settled in the port cities of Canton and Guangzhou. They were few in number and, like all foreign residents, they were required to live in designated districts, and their contact with the natives was restricted to business transactions. It was not until the Yuan dynasty (1279–1368), when the Mongols gained control of the Chinese Empire, that large numbers of Muslims settled in China. As Genghis Khan swept across Central Asia to the eastern edge of Europe, the Mongols took as hostages anyone they thought might be useful to them. Among those chosen were thousands of Muslim architects, artisans, astronomers, craftsmen, engineers, and physicians, who were all transported to China. Later, as the Mongol Empire in China grew, more and more Muslims from Central Asia and western Asia were appointed to prominent roles in the Yuan administration. Through intermarriage with the indigenous population and maintenance of their own cultural traditions, they began a line of Chinese Muslims that extends to the present day.

The Ming Dynasty

The Ming dynasty, which succeeded the Yuan dynasty, saw the return of China

to Chinese rule. The resentment and humiliation felt by the Chinese after almost a century of foreign domination prompted the introduction of numerous policies to reinstill traditional customs and cultural practices. Although the foreigners who had settled in China were allowed to remain, they were all required to dress in traditional Chinese clothes, adopt Chinese names, and learn Chinese.

In spite of these policies of forcible acculturation, many Chinese Muslims clung firmly to their historic traditions and, indeed, intensified their adherence to them. It was during the Ming dynasty that Islamic scholars in China began writing their religious texts in Chinese, rather than, as previously, in Arabic or Persian. Consequently, the most important Islamic terms and concepts had to be rendered into Chinese characters. Islam officially became known as *qing zhen jiao* (the pure and true religion); Allah was referred to as *zhen zhu* (the true lord); and mosques were known as *qing zhen si* (temples of the pure and true).

Meanwhile, the Chinese emperors continued to install their Muslim subjects in powerful positions. In 1405, the Emperor Yongle (r.1402–1424) initiated a program of maritime exploration that was commanded by Zheng He, a Muslim eunuch from southwestern China. Zheng He led seven major expeditions with fleets of hundreds of ships that sailed across the South China Sea, through the Straits of Malacca, and into the Indian Ocean and the Red Sea, stopping at ports in present-day Bangladesh, India, Indonesia, Iran, Kenya, Malaysia, Oman, Saudi Arabia, Somalia, Sri Lanka, Thailand, and Yemen. Unlike the European expedition to America led by Christopher Columbus in

1492—which numbered only three ships, the largest measuring 90 feet by 30 feet (about 30 m x 10 m), with a total crew of 90 men—Zheng He's fleets included dozens of ships, the largest 400 feet (122 m) long and 150 feet (45 m) wide, and crews totaling more than 27,000 men. These ships carried hundreds of tons of Chinese trading goods, including silk, porcelain, lacquerware, and other traditional craftworks that were exchanged for precious items and goods from the countries they visited.

Despite the undoubted success of these expeditions, China abandoned maritime explorations at around the same time as the European countries began theirs. The nation then entered a period of introspection and isolationism. The Ming dynasty ended in 1644 and was succeeded by the Qing dynasty, which ruled until the start of the 20th century.

UNREST AND REBELLION

The next major period of Chinese history saw the return of non-Chinese rulers. The Qing (or Manchu) were a powerful tribal people based in northeastern China. After gaining control of the Chinese Empire, they quickly set about consolidating their power. By this time, there were several areas of China with Muslim populations of more than one million. Some of these regions became the scenes of rebellions that left thousands of Muslims dead. In the northwest of the country, tensions within Islamic communities increased when

This portrait of Chinese Muslim naval commander and explorer Zheng He is displayed at a temple shrine in Penang, Malaysia.

Chinese Muslims who had been on pilgrimages to Mecca returned home and tried to introduce what they now saw as the correct religious practices. Many Chinese Muslims who had not experienced the outside world insisted on maintaining their now well-established traditions. As the conflict escalated, the Qing authorities played one side off against the other in an effort to divide and rule their potentially troublesome Muslim subjects. Government forces frequently switched allegiance from one group to the other and, when the unrest erupted into violence, they carried out harsh military campaigns that resulted in the deaths of thousands of Muslims.

In southwestern China, a very different set of circumstances led to a similarly devastating attack on the Muslim community. Between 1856 and 1872, a small, independent, Muslim kingdom flourished in southwestern China. It was ruled by a Chinese Muslim scholar, Du Wenxiu, who took the title Sultan Sulaiman and named his realm Ping Nan Guo (Kingdom of the Pacified South). Sulaiman's followers included other Chinese Muslims, as well as members of numerous indigenous groups and Han Chinese who had settled in the region centuries earlier. This multiethnic coalition was formed in response to Chinese government policies that discriminated against the local population in favor of the Han Chinese who had recently fled to the region from overpopulation in central China. Many of the tribal peoples succumbed to harassment by the Han Chinese settlers, abandoning their land and moving away, but the Chinese Muslims, who had settled in the region in the 13th century, stood their ground, refusing to be

pushed aside by the new immigrants and demanding their rights as Chinese citizens. In response, the local Han Chinese officials ordered the massacre of all the Muslims living in Kunming, the capital of Yunnan province. Tens of thousands of Muslims were murdered, including women and children. Having earlier sent delegations to Beijing seeking justice from the emperor and receiving no response, the Muslims of Yunnan then decided to take matters into their own hands, break with the Chinese state, and establish a safe haven for themselves. With the assistance of a wide range of ethnic groups, they set up an independent kingdom in the northwest of the province. Although many of the newly appointed officials were Muslims, many of the others were indigenous peoples of the region and local Han Chinese. The kingdom sought to treat everyone fairly, sharing resources and insisting that all children of both sexes be educated. This was the first time in Chinese history that education for girls had been mandated. The Kingdom of the Pacified South survived until 1872, when Chinese imperial forces were brought in to crush it. Up to 90 percent of the Muslims were massacred or fled the region. Today, more than 100 years later, the Chinese Muslim population of this region is still less than half of what it was before the massacres.

THE RISE OF THE COMMUNISTS

The fall of the Qing dynasty in 1911 resulted in a period of intense rivalry between the communists, led by Mao Zedong (1893–1976), and the nationalists, led by Chiang Kai-shek (1887–1975). In an effort to gain support, the communists promised the Chinese Muslims freedom of worship and a degree of autonomy. The communists eventually succeeded in driving out the nationalists, and in 1949 the People's Republic of China was established. Initially, the communists kept their promises to the Muslim population; provinces with Muslim majorities were designated as autonomous regions. Although it later became clear that these concessions were mainly cosmetic rather than substantial, the fact remains that, during the early years of communist China, the Muslims enjoyed freedom of religion and the government established official Islamic organizations and schools to train imams.

However, religion in China came under sustained attack during the Cultural Revolution (1966–1976). In an effort to rebuild his support base, Mao Zedong instigated a campaign against "the four olds" (old customs, old culture, old habits, and old ideas), which he believed were hindering China's efforts to become a strong socialist country. During this period all forms of religious expression were discouraged, and believers were denounced as superstitious or counter-revolutionary.

Islam was particularly strongly suppressed because it was associated with various ethnic groups that had distinct cultural identities and customs that differed from the majority of the population. There were widespread reports of copies of the Koran being burned in the streets and of Muslims being arrested, beaten, or publicly humiliated. Many mosques were closed down or appropriated as government buildings, and many more were left to fall into disrepair. The government encouraged or coerced large numbers of non-Muslims

Chinese Muslim Uighurs return to work sharpening knives after Ramadan. There are about 9 million Uighurs in China, mostly in Xinjiang province.

to relocate to Muslim areas in the hope that this would reduce Muslim influence on local politics and culture.

REVIVAL AND REBUILDING

The Cultural Revolution ended in 1976, but it was several years before the Chinese government began returning the mosques to their communities. Muslims then set about repairing and, when necessary, reconstructing their places of worship. When this process was completed, occasional Islamic studies classes were introduced for the children of Chinese Muslim families who had never previously had the chance to learn about their faith. Over the next 20 years, educational courses were expanded through the introduction of daily classes for preschool children and retirees, summer classes for schoolchildren, and afternoon and evening courses for working adults. In addition, small private

Islamic colleges were established around the country. Many of the graduates of these colleges went on to set up new schools in remote areas.

As the number of Chinese Muslim students seeking advanced religious training has increased, more and more of them have continued their studies overseas. In 1990, the first groups of students left China to study in Syria and Pakistan. More recently, students have traveled in increasing numbers to complete their education in Egypt, Iran, Malaysia, and Saudi Arabia.

XINJIANG

Covering a large area of northwestern China, the Xinjiang Uighur Autonomous Region is the traditional homeland of the country's second largest Muslim minority group, the Uighurs. The Uighurs are a Turkic people whose culture is closely related to that of the peoples of Central

A detachment of Uighur soldiers in the Chinese army parade in Gulja, Xinjiang province.

Asia, and whose language is part of the family of languages spoken in Central Asia and Turkey. From the early 1930s to the formation of the People's Republic of China in 1949, the state of Xinjiang was an independent country, known as the East Turkestan Republic. According to official Chinese accounts, the East Turkestan Republic voluntarily joined the People's Republic of China in 1949. Uighur nationalists and many Western historians, on the other hand, characterize this takeover as an invasion.

In 1949, when the People's Republic of China was established, approximately 80 percent of the population of Xinjiang were Uighur; there were also other large Muslim groups of Kazakhs, Tajiks, and Uzbeks. At that time, Han Chinese made up less than 7 percent of the total population of the region. As a result of the relocation policies of the cultural revolution, the Han Chinese community comprises 45 percent of the population of present-day Xinjiang.

In the 1990s, as the Uighur people saw their homeland coming increasingly under the control of outsiders, they became disenchanted with the Chinese state. Protests were common and there were reports of inter-ethnic violence in the state capital, Urumqi. The government dealt harshly with these protests and arrested all of those believed to be associated with the Uighur independence movement, including peaceful activists, journalists, and religious leaders.

Since 2001 the Chinese authorities have increasingly claimed that ongoing arrests are necessary to prevent terrorist attacks. Government reports assert that there are several Islamic extremist organizations operating in Xinjiang, trained and armed by neighboring Afghanistan. No evidence has been produced to support this claim,

however, and many outside observers believe that the accusation of extremism is being used to discredit and suppress the Muslim community. This includes such measures as replacing the Uighur language—previously the language of instruction in Xinjiang's schools and colleges—with Chinese from the third grade on.

In 2009 inter-ethnic tensions in Urumqi spilled over into widespread violence. The extent and nature of the violence is still disputed, but most observers estimate that around 200 people were killed. It is not clear which group instigated the violence, but it was officially blamed on Uighur militants. In November 2009, after a brief and secret trial, nine Uighur men were convicted of leading the riots and executed.

CONCLUSION

Today, Chinese Muslims are focusing on community development. In addition to preschools, projects now include hospitals, nursing homes, scholarships for Muslim students, and charitable activities to assist the poor. In the past, Chinese Muslim communities sought financial assistance from abroad, but they have a growing sense that they no longer need outside help. This increasing self-reliance can also be seen in the growing number of students who choose to pursue advanced degrees in Islamic studies in China rather than abroad. Although the Uighur Muslims are persecuted and most Chinese Muslims are poor, the broader Islamic community in China seems increasingly to derive strength from the fact that it is a minority group. As the global economic recession of the early 21st century tightened its grip on an already impoverished country, Muslim solidarity seemed to increase through a sense of common purpose.

See Also
South Asia 274-291 ❖
Southeast Asia
292-303 ❖ Central
Asia 304-313 ❖

OTOPARK FİYAT TARİFESİ

TURKEY AND EASTERN EUROPE

Contrary to popular perceptions in the West, Islam is not a monolith. The diversity of the Muslim world is nowhere more apparent than in Turkey and in eastern Europe, especially within the patchwork of the adjoining Balkan states of Albania, Bosnia and Herzegovina, Bulgaria, Kosovo, and Macedonia.

Turkey and the adjoining Balkan Peninsula have long been—and remain—a major intersection, not only between Europe and Asia but also between Christendom and the Muslim world. The regions and states in the southeastern corner

With the exceptions of Albania, Bulgaria, and Turkey, all the countries discussed in this chapter were components of Yugoslavia, a federated communist republic that was established in 1946 and disintegrated in 1991.

This *teqe* (a form of mosque used by Bektashi Muslims) in Konya is one of thousands of Islamic religious centers that thrive in modern Turkey, despite the fact that the state is strictly secular.

of Europe have been strongly influenced by their larger eastern neighbor for almost 1,000 years. Some of Turkey's effects on the Balkans have been benign—much of the region is cosmopolitan and culturally diverse as a result of regular contact between Christianity and Islam, particularly during the period of the Ottoman Empire, between the 14th century and the 20th century.

However, the wide range of competing commercial, ethnic, national, political, and religious interests have often confronted each other here and sparked numerous conflicts, the worst of which—notably World War I (1914–1918)—have had global repercussions. With the exceptions of Albania, Bulgaria, and Turkey, all the countries discussed in this chapter were components of Yugoslavia, a federated communist republic that was established in 1946 and disintegrated in 1991. The ensuing civil war there lasted for nearly four years and ended with the emergence of seven new, independent nations.

TURKEY

More than 90 percent of Turks are Muslims, but Turkey has been a secular state since 1928, five years after its foundation, when Islam was removed as the official religion and Sharia courts were abolished during the rule of the first president, Kemal Atatürk (1923–1938). The separation of religion and government in Turkey has since caused problems at various times. For example, Atatürk banned the wearing

Turks take to the streets of the capital, Ankara, in 2008 to protest the government's interference in the practice of religion. The painting depicts Ali Ibn Abu Talib, son-in-law of Prophet Muhammad; the photograph shows Kemal Atatürk, the founder of modern Turkey.

in public of traditional Turkish Muslim headgear—fezzes and turbans for men and head scarves for women. Although these restrictions were resented by strict Muslims, they were generally tolerated, especially after the one-party state gave way in 1950 to a multiparty democracy, under which religious teaching—previously banned in schools—was again permitted. Indeed, the ban on Islamic headgear caused less controversy than the constitutional amendment, passed in 2008, that restored the freedom of women to cover their heads on university campuses. This move outraged advocates of secularism, which

had by this time become established as the conventional view in Turkey.

Turkish secularism is maintained by the armed forces, which have intervened in politics and taken over the rule of the country on three occasions—1960–1961, 1971–1973, and 1980–1983. In each case, the declaration of martial law was at least partly justified by fears that the ongoing tensions between secularists and traditionalists might escalate into civil war. After each episode of military government, democracy was restored under a revised constitution.

Since the 1980s, support for pro-Islamic political parties in Turkey has increased dramatically, resulting in the expansion of the role of Islamist parties in Turkish politics in the last decade of the 20th century and the first decade of the 21st century. There has also been a marked increase in the number of private courses and establishments for religious teaching; many new mosques and madrassas (Muslim schools) have also been built. Modern Turkey may be characterized as a nation with an elite that is secularist and a general public that has maintained its traditional commitment to Islam. There is tension between the two but little open hostility. The 2002 general election was won by Adalet ve Kalkinma Partisi (AKP), the Justice and Development Party, a political organization with Islamist roots.

ALBANIA

After 500 years of rule by the Muslim Turks of the Ottoman Empire, Albania—which is bordered by the Adriatic Sea, Greece, Kosovo, Macedonia, and Montenegro but effectively cut off from

all four countries by mountain ranges—was around 70 percent Muslim until the communist takeover in 1944. The leaders of the revolutionary regime were hostile to religion and, in 1967, outlawed all forms of worship when they made the country officially atheist. They closed all the mosques and *zawiyah* (Sufi monastic foundations), as well as all the Christian churches; they confiscated all religious property; and they persecuted people who tried to maintain any faith. During the next 50 years, Albania—which not only shunned the capitalist West but also gradually alienated other communist states, which its rulers then denounced as revisionist—became one of the most isolated countries in the world.

After the death of the totalitarian dictator Enver Hoxha (r. 1944–1985), the government of Albania softened its atheistic line and allowed the reopening of places of public worship. Religious tolerance gained ground after 1992, when a general election brought to power a democratic coalition.

RELIGIOUS COMPOSITION AND NATIONAL IDENTITY IN ALBANIA

Albania today is a nation of people who share first and foremost an Albanian ethnic identity. Although the country is home to several significant religious communities—the four main ones are Sunni Muslims, Bektashis (a Sufi sect that takes its beliefs from both the Shiite and Sunni branches of Islam), Orthodox Christians, and Roman Catholics—the modern government is reluctant to gather statistics about the exact number of adherents to each faith, partly because it is fearful that such information could be divisive and partly because it wishes to encourage the perception that all of its citizens are in the first place Albanians, regardless of their religious persuasions.

A significant number of Albanians are neither Christians nor Muslims. The years during which the country was governed by an atheistic communist regime have left a profound influence on personal beliefs.

At the beginning of the 21st century, Anastasios, the archbishop of Tirana and patriarch of the Autocephalous (self-governing) Albanian Orthodox church, conceded that his country was "no longer a typically Muslim nation" and spoke of its diversification: Albanian Islam is different from Islam in the Arab world; there are two schools of Christianity; and there are a significant number of people who have little commitment to any religion.

Taken in 1945, this is one of the few extant photographs of Enver Hoxha, the communist leader of Albania (1944–1985).

Today the percentage of Albanians who describe themselves as adherents of Islam has returned to its precommunist level—the remainder are Albanian Orthodox (20 percent) and Roman Catholic (10 percent). However, part of the legacy of the intervening years is that most Muslims are religionists in name only—everyday life in Albania remains almost as secular as it was during the worst repressions of Hoxha. Although there are factions among Albanian Muslims—most are Sunnis, but there is a significant Sufi minority—there is little friction between

ISLAM AND LOCAL CULTURE: THE BEKTASHI

Founded in the 13th century and originally from Iran, the Bektashi are Muslim orders of Sufi mystics who spread during the 16th century into Anatolia (part of modern Turkey) and then into the Ottoman Balkans, particularly Albania. The Bektashi are traditionalists, but they are more relaxed than other Muslim sects in the observance of religious laws. They allow women and Christians to take part in their rituals, which include dancing and the drinking of wine. Such practices are forbidden by mainstream Islam.

When Turkey became a secular state in the 1920s, the Bektashi migrated to Albania. When Albania banned religion in 1967, they moved to other regions of the Balkans with Albanian Muslim majorities, notably Bosnia and Kosovo, as well as to the United States. A few also returned to Turkey, which had by then become a multiparty democracy with a more tolerant attitude to religion. Today the Bektashi are reestablished in Albania, with their world headquarters in the capital, Tirana.

One of the most significant consequences of the adaptability and the mobility of the Bektashi has been their assimilation of many of the traditional customs of the regions in which they have settled, a phenomenon that has been described as "localized otherness." Bektashi rituals vary enormously from time to time and from place to place, but that does not concern the leaders of the sect, who attach greater importance to the sincerity of believers' thoughts and the goodness of their actions than to their methods of demonstrating their faith. Central to the Bektashi worldview is the notion that charity begins at home: according to one of their sayings, "If you are not good at home, how can you be good anywhere else?" Their lodges (known as *teqe*) provide free accommodation to the needy, and they finance, when possible, good works in the local community.

The Bektashi use of national symbols is also noteworthy. The flag of Albania—a black, two-headed eagle on a red background—is draped or flown next to the Bektashi flag in every *teqe* and at all celebrations and functions. Bektashi believe that there is "no faith without country" and are committed to nationalism and serving their host nations. In practice, Bektashi is far removed from pan-Islamism. Although it spans several countries, its structure is cellular, with each component part taking care of its own affairs. This characteristic is typical of Islam in Turkey and in the Balkans as a whole.

the two groups, which are united by the common purpose of reestablishing Albanian national identity after half a century of isolation.

BOSNIA AND HERZEGOVINA

Founded in 1995 as the result of an agreement made in Dayton, Ohio, between the various factions in the civil war that followed the disintegration of Yugoslavia, the modern state of Bosnia and Herzegovina is composed of three main ethnic groups: Croats (around 20 percent of the population), who are mainly Roman Catholic; Serbs (around 33 percent), who are Orthodox Christians; and the largest group, Bosniacs (between 40 and 48 percent), most of whom are Muslims. The nation is bordered by the Adriatic Sea, Croatia, Montenegro, and Serbia.

Islam became established in Bosnia after the country was assimilated into the Ottoman Empire in the 16th century. Although it used to be thought that this Islamization came about through forced conversions or mass emigrations from

Alija Izetbegovic, Muslim president of Bosnia and Herzegovina (1990–2000), holds a press conference in Sarajevo in June 1998.

Turkey, most historians now agree that it was a natural process that occurred as more and more people moved from rural districts to the two main cities—Mostar and the modern capital, Sarajevo—which were prosperous and already Muslim-run. In the modern era, Bosnia and Herzegovina's declaration of independence from Yugoslavia in 1990 was led by a Muslim, Alija Izetbegovic (1925–2003). The election of Izetbegovic as president was provocative in the short term—it was one of the flashpoints that caused the ensuing three-and-a-half-year civil war between all three ethnic and religious groups. However, after the resolution of the conflict, the symbolism of a Muslim head of state helped to inspire a closer association of Bosnian Muslims with the Islamic faith as a means of cementing their unity. For Bosniacs, the memory of the war—during which all three sides had tried to clear various areas of all inhabitants other than their own group, a process known as "ethnic cleansing"—led to a further strengthening of their collective identity as Bosnian Muslims.

Today in Bosnia and Herzegovina, Islam is both a token of religious identity and a distinguishing feature of national identity. Modern Bosniacs not only attend mosques regularly but often also undertake pilgrimages to mountaintop retreats in the interior of the country. Nevertheless, it is noteworthy that their religious practices have incorporated a variety of local cultural traditions and now differ in many ways from those of mainstream Islam.

BULGARIA

Muslims in Bulgaria have always been comparatively few—they currently make up around 10 percent of a total population of 7.25 million, the overwhelming majority of whom are Orthodox Christians.

Islam emerged in Bulgaria while the country was part of the Ottoman Empire (1396–1798). The religion developed slowly and naturally—the colonial rulers made no attempt to populate Bulgaria forcibly with Turks or to convert all Bulgarians to Islam. Most of the Turks who did immigrate to Bulgaria were agricultural laborers who settled in the southern and eastern parts of the country and in some of the valleys of neighboring Macedonia and Thrace (a border region that occupies parts of modern Bulgaria, Greece, and Turkey). There they remained with little disturbance until Bulgaria became communist at the end of World War II (1939–1945). The new atheist state then encouraged the emigration of all religionists of non-

Bulgarian heritage. Most Bulgarian Muslims were of Turkish descent, and 155,000 people of this background were expelled from Bulgaria between 1949 and 1951.

In 1971, Todor Zhivkov (1911–1998), who had been the first secretary of the Bulgarian Communist Party from 1954, became the president of Bulgaria. On his appointment as the titular head of state, he introduced a program that was intended to increase the low birth rate of the ethnic Bulgarian population by encouraging larger families. When this policy failed to have any discernible effect, Zhivkov launched in 1984 a major campaign to "Bulgarize,"

Most Bulgarian Muslims were of Turkish descent, and 155,000 people of this background were expelled from Bulgaria between 1949 and 1951.

or assimilate, the country's 800,000 ethnic Turks. Turkish-language publications and radio broadcasts were banned, and all Turks were required to adopt Bulgarian names.

The ethnic Turks opposed these moves and clashed with Bulgarian security forces, often violently. In 1989, the government of neighboring Turkey announced its willingness to take in Turkish refugees from Bulgaria; shortly afterward, more than 300,000 ethnic Turks fled or were expelled from Bulgaria.

Another 300,000 Bulgarian Muslims emigrated in 1989, mainly to Turkey, to escape the upheavals that accompanied the fall of communism. Almost half of them returned after the passage into law of the 1990 Bulgarian constitution that guaranteed freedom of religious observance for all the main faiths. By the end of the first decade of the 21st century, Islam, while still a minority religion, was thriving unhindered in Bulgaria.

Kosovo

Kosovo is bordered by four countries, including Serbia, of which it was a part until it declared independence in 2008. The United States and the European Union (EU) recognize Kosovo, but several other important countries, including Serbia and Russia, do not.

From the 15th century, Kosovo—like all of Serbia—was part of the Ottoman Empire. Its inhabitants were a roughly equal mixture of Serbs and ethnic Albanians, but in the centuries that followed, many of the former—most of whom were Orthodox Christians—left the province and resettled in other parts of Serbia. Those who remained converted to Islam, which gradually became the majority religion. In the 20th century, the inhabitants made periodic attempts to break away from Serbia and join Albania.

In the 1920s and the 1930s, Serbia attempted to redress the ethnic imbalance by encouraging the resettlement of Serbs in Kosovo. However, such moves were resisted by the Muslim majority, who were briefly united with Albania by the occupying

Turkish women attend Friday prayers in an outdoor part of a mosque in Istanbul. The separation of the sexes in Islam is one of the main barriers to Turkey's application for admission to the European Union (EU).

Italians during World War II. Toward the end of the conflict, Italy was driven out of the region and the status quo was restored. Yugoslavia's new communist government crushed a revolt in Kosovo by ethnic Albanians and repossessed the province. Josip Broz Tito, the president of Yugoslavia (1953–1980), then granted Kosovo the status of an autonomous region (later an autonomous province) within the Yugoslav republic of Serbia. Tito's army left observant Muslims largely undisturbed, but it clamped down heavily on any political activities that could be construed as Albanian nationalism.

Meanwhile, the number of Serbs in Kosovo continued to diminish. In 2009, 88 percent of the population of just over 2 million are Albanian, making it the fourth country in Europe with a Muslim majority, after Albania, Bosnia and Herzegovina, and Turkey. Most Kosovans are Sunni Muslims, although there are also several variant Sufi groups. An association of dervishes, founded in Kosovo in 1974, currently claims a membership of 50,000.

MACEDONIA

Macedonia is a landlocked country of the southern Balkans that is bordered to the north by Kosovo and Serbia, to the east by Bulgaria, to the south by Greece, and to the west by Albania. Its inhabitants are culturally and ethnically diverse, and relations between the various groups have often been complicated by the correspondence between their ethnicity and their religions.

Around 66 percent of Macedonians are Slavs, who are closely related to Bulgarians and practice Orthodox Christianity. Most of the remainder are Albanians, Turks, or Roma (Gypsies). Many members of all three of these groups follow Islam—at the start of the 21st century, 25 percent of the Macedonian population claimed to be Muslim. They identify with both the Sunni and the Sufi traditions. Local folkloric traditions, such as belief in the evil eye and the hand of Fatima, are also widespread and are sometimes incorporated into the established religions.

As in other areas of eastern Europe, Islam became established under the Ottoman Empire, of which Macedonia was a part from 1453, when Constantinople (modern Istanbul) fell to the Turks, until 1913. Thereafter, Macedonia was incorporated into Yugoslavia, which was a kingdom between the two World Wars and then a communist republic until it split into its component parts in 1991. Five hundred years of Ottoman rule had a profound and lasting influence on all aspects of life in Macedonia, not only on

Five hundred years of Ottoman rule had a profound and lasting influence on all aspects of life in Macedonia, not only on religion but also on cuisine, customs, language, and lawmaking.

religion but also on cuisine, customs, language, and lawmaking. For much of the period, Macedonians were subjected to *devsirme* (blood tax), under which they were conscripted into the Turkish army or civil service and forced to adopt Islam, regardless of their own religions. They were also relocated according to the requirements of the colonial administration, with the result that Muslims were interspersed with Orthodox Christians throughout the area. While this policy helped to prevent the emergence of ethnic enclaves such as those that developed damagingly in Kosovo, the proximity of different groups also caused significant tensions.

In post-Ottoman Macedonia, birth rates fell among the Orthodox Christian population, as Christians, in response to the growing industrialization of the country, moved to jobs in the cities and, living mainly in apartments, tended to have fewer children. Meanwhile, the Muslims generally remained at work in agriculture and increased their numbers at between two-and-a-half and three times the rate of the Slavic majority. The social problems caused by this imbalance reached a crisis after the collapse of Yugoslavia brought economic hardship and political uncertainty to the whole country.

POLITICAL ISLAM

Although most of the crises that have affected the Balkans since the 1990s have involved Muslims, Islam was not the cause of any of the resulting conflicts. The common notion that the region is a frontier between two antagonistic cultures takes insufficient account of the fact that the Muslim populations of the countries under consideration here are anything but a cohesive unity.

After the fall of communism, the new nations that emerged from the wreckage of Yugoslavia legislated in an effort to prevent political parties from organizing on ethnic or religious grounds. The attempt was less than completely successful. Parties that were plainly faith-based evaded the issue by giving themselves uncontroversial names. These included the Democratic League of Kosovo, which, in fact, represented the nation's Albanian Muslims;

the Movement for Rights and Freedom (DPS), which represented the Turks of Bulgaria; and the Party for Democratic Action (SDA), which was run and supported by the Muslims in Bosnia and Herzegovina.

Nevertheless, by participating in the democratic process, these parties, and a host of others like them, had to prepare broad manifestos to attract support. The growth of Islamic parties in the Balkans is thus not attributable to a monolithic Muslim vote. In a democracy, there can be no power without a broad appeal to the electorate, and the voters in all the former Yugoslav states under discussion here are deeply heterogeneous.

In spite of that, there are still numerous Muslim minority parties in the region, which tailor their political agendas to small groups. Many of them campaign on a single issue; one leading example of the type is the Movement for Rights and Freedoms, a liberal party in Bulgaria that campaigns for the reintroduction of the traditional Turkish names outlawed by Bulgarization.

The entrance of Muslims as identifiable actors on the Balkan political stage has led to the renewed politicization of their ethnicity. In most of the nations under consideration here, this is a matter more of labeling and identification than of religious substance. The main exception to that general rule is in Bosnia and Herzegovina, where the SDA claims affinity with the Arab world, identifying itself with "martyrs of the faith" and supporting the principles of jihad, which, in this context, means "holy war." However, it is likely that such views are the product of the Bosniacs' long history of struggle to gain cultural independence from the Croats and Serbs

rather than of any effective form of pan-Islamism. The same motivation accounts for the desire of some Pomaks (Bulgarian Muslims) to be described as "Turks" and the growing preference of the Roma in Macedonia to call themselves "Egyptians" (a noun that is etymologically associated with "Gypsies").

Further evidence to support the theory that, throughout the Balkans, "Islam" is more of a social and political identifier than a religion (politically, at least) may be adduced from the fact that numerous Muslim institutions lag way behind other institutions in post-communist reconstruction. Many of the region's mosques remain in a state of relative neglect, and religious scholars in Bosnia and Herzegovina, Bulgaria, and Macedonia regularly complain about the imams' lack of knowledge of the Koran and the Hadiths (sayings of Muhammad). The apparent lack of enthusiasm for the restoration of traditional Islam, particularly when viewed alongside the revival of Muslim involvement in politics, suggests that the religion has become more of a convenient political banner than a way of life.

A Serb soldier takes cover behind a tank in 1999 during the war to prevent the secession of Kosovo from Serbia.

See Also
Northern Africa 246-249 ❖ Central Asia 304-313 ❖ Western Europe 334-347 ❖

Chapter 19

WESTERN EUROPE

The Muslim encounter with the West—in particular with Western Europe—dates from the beginning of Islam's expansion. However, the widespread introduction of Islam into western Europe occurred with the arrival of immigrants from regions that had been colonized in the 19th century by European powers.

The earliest documented Muslim settlement of western Europe occurred in 652, when a small Arab force established a toehold in Sicily. The first significant Arab inroads into this part of the continent came in 711, when the Umayyad dynasty conquered the greater part of the Iberian Peninsula (modern Portugal and Spain), which they named al-Andalus. There they became firmly established and, by the 10th century, almost the entire population of all but the northern extremities of the region along the Bay of Biscay had embraced Islam. However, non-Islamic (mainly Christian) forces hit back from the far north and gradually drove the Arabs south, with the result that, by the middle of the 13th century, the Muslim territory in Iberia had been reduced to the province of Granada, with its impregnable fortress, the Alhambra.

Meanwhile, other Arab groups advanced northward from Spain into France until they were repelled by the Franks under Charles Martel at the Battle of Tours in 732. The Muslim enclave in Sicily grew too, albeit more slowly and modestly. An emirate was established there in the 10th century, but it did not survive the Norman conquest of the 11th century.

In spite of the antipathy between Arabs and Christians in Europe, the whole continent was profoundly influenced by Arab thought and customs. Even after the Arab forces had finally been expelled from Granada in 1492 and the Reconquista (reconquest) of Spain was completed, Moriscos (Arab converts to Christianity) remained in Spain until the early 17th century.

❖

In spite of the antipathy between Arabs and Christians in Europe, the whole continent was profoundly influenced by Arab thought and customs.

Arab and western European cultures then developed along diverging lines until the 19th century, when European nations began to colonize regions with Muslim majorities—notably, northern Africa, eastern Africa, Malaysia, and parts of India—and the process of cross-fertilization began again. European settlers began to learn firsthand about Muslim life, and Muslims increasingly went to live and work

The minaret of the East London Mosque is viewed over Whitechapel High Street in the East End of London, England. This building is an important center of worship for the British capital's Muslims of Bangladeshi heritage.

STATISTICS

Today, the largest Muslim minority in Europe as a percentage of the total national population, as well as in absolute numbers, is in France, where the number of Muslims is estimated at 4.5 million out of a total of 64 million inhabitants. Other large Muslim minorities are found in Germany (3.3 million out of a total of 82 million), the United Kingdom (nearly 3 million in a population of 60 million), and the Netherlands (850,000 in a population of 17 million). In these countries, Muslims make up between 4 and 7 percent of the total population. The lowest Muslim population in western Europe is in Iceland, where Muslims currently comprise only 800 members of a total population of 300,000 (2.7 percent). In northern Europe the percentage varies between less than 1 percent in Finland and almost 3 percent in Denmark, Norway, and Sweden. In southern Europe, Italy, Portugal, and Spain have become favored destinations for Muslim immigrants, and the number of Muslim inhabitants (now less than 1 percent of the population) is increasing rapidly.

A Muslim child waves a French flag at a protest in Paris opposing a proposed ban on head scarves in schools.

in the countries whose forces had occupied theirs—for instance, significant numbers of Algerians went to live and work in France, and numerous Pakistanis and Bangladeshis settled in parts of Britain.

MODERN DEMOGRAPHY

At the start of the 21st century, there were thought to be more than 13 million Muslims living in western Europe, making up about 3 percent of the total population. However, no reliable statistics are available because most European countries do not include religious affiliations in their population censuses. A further problem

with estimating the number of European Muslims is that, in some countries, the younger generation of Muslims disappears from the statistics altogether because their parents were born in Europe. Another difficulty lies in determining with any accuracy the number of conversions—from Islam to Christianity or, increasingly, vice versa—in each country.

There is an enormous diversity of Muslim minorities in western Europe. The most numerous ethnic group has its roots in the Maghrib, an area of northern Africa that includes Algeria, Libya, Mauritania, Morocco, and Tunisia. The immigrants are mainly Arabic-speakers and Berbers from Algeria, Morocco, and Tunisia. The Berbers are a non-Arab people who lived in northern Africa before the rise of Islam but came under its influence and are now mainly Muslims.

The second-largest ethnic group is the Turks, who, like the Maghrib Muslims, come mostly from rural areas. The third-largest group is made up of immigrants from Bangladesh, India, and Pakistan. Also scattered throughout western Europe are significant numbers of Muslim refugees who have fled political upheaval in their home countries. They mainly come from Afghanistan, Iran, and Iraq in western Asia,

Somalia in Africa, and Bosnia and Herzegovina in eastern Europe, as well as from several other countries.

PHASES OF IMMIGRATION

In France, the statistical dominance of North African Muslims is entirely a product of France's former colonial empire. The first significant group of Muslims to settle in France in the 20th century was composed of North African and Senegalese mercenaries who had been recruited to fight in the French colonial wars, including a group that formed the vanguard of the Allied troops that liberated Paris from Nazi occupation. There is also a significant

This 1930s photograph shows North African cavalrymen taking part in an Armistice Day parade in Algiers. Such Muslim cavalrymen served in the armed forces of the colonial rulers of Algeria, Morocco, and Tunisia.

number of Harkis in France. Harkis are Algerian soldiers who fought with the French colonial government to suppress the Algerian revolution. They settled in France after 1962 to avoid reprisals in Algeria after that country gained its independence.

In the Netherlands, the first Muslim immigrants came from the former Dutch colonies, Indonesia and Surinam. In Britain, the early Muslim immigrants came from British colonies in South Asia and Africa. Small numbers of Muslims had always lived and studied in Europe; decolonization brought much larger numbers of new arrivals.

Although Germany was also a colonial power—among its African possessions at one time were Tanzania and Togo—after the nation's defeat in World War II

The boycott signaled the end of a period of reconstruction and prosperity and led to an economic depression and widespread unemployment.

(1939–1945) it welcomed few immigrants until the 1960s, when it received a growing stream of guest workers who came to relieve the shortage of manual labor during the postwar economic reconstruction. Most of the immigrants to Germany during this period were from Turkey, but there were also Moroccans and Yugoslavs—almost all of them were Muslims.

The western European host countries fully expected that these foreign laborers would be in their countries only temporarily and that they would return to their homelands as soon as their short-term

contracts had expired. The laborers, too, believed that their stay in western Europe would be temporary. Therefore, during this period, most of the immigrants had little contact with Europeans and made little effort to learn the languages of their host countries. Interaction was further restricted by the guest workers' long working hours and their separation from ordinary local life in compounds with, generally, cramped and undesirable living conditions. Another obstacle to integration was that many companies recruited workers from the same region or village, with the result that they seldom needed or had the opportunity to meet anyone outside a small circle of people they already knew.

After 1974, the second phase of Muslim settlement of western Europe began. It was triggered by the oil embargo, which was declared by several oil-producing nations during the 1973 Yom Kippur War between Israel and its Arab neighbors. The boycott signaled the end of a period of reconstruction and prosperity and led to an economic depression and widespread unemployment in Europe. As a consequence, European economies underwent a dramatic restructuring that reduced the demand for unskilled labor. Within Europe, service industries grew, while manufacturing jobs were exported to Asia. Many low-skilled immigrants lost their access to the European labor market. Several European nations, including France, Germany, and the Netherlands, were eager to shrink the ranks of the unemployed and offered financial incentives for the repatriation of labor immigrants to their countries of origin. Although many of the laborers did indeed return home, especially those who had been living in Spain and Italy, most of the Moroccans and the Turks decided to stay

because they were better off in Europe, even without a job, because of welfare payments. The efforts of western European governments to reduce the number of foreigners in their countries therefore had exactly the opposite effect to that intended. In many nations, immigration actually increased substantially as Muslims took advantage of European laws that allowed for family reunification with permanent right of abode.

The number of Muslim inhabitants in Europe continued to increase through the growth of families: many young Muslims preferred to marry someone from a shared cultural and religious background who was not too "Westernized." The issue of "importing" a spouse has inspired strong political and public debate. One important topic in this debate is the lack of integration into and knowledge of European culture and the national language of the country of destination by the new partner. Second, and more sensitive, is the issue of arranged marriages with partners from abroad.

The third phase of the immigration and settlement of Muslim minorities in western Europe was the result of global political instability and of wars, especially during the 1990s. A large number of people from different countries in Africa, eastern Europe,

Kurdish Muslim refugees from Iraq pass through Amman Airport in Jordan on their way to starting a new life in Sweden.

and western Asia have sought refuge in western Europe and have augmented the number and the diversity of Muslim minorities there.

INSTITUTIONALIZATION OF ISLAM

Among the Muslim immigrants living in western Europe in the 21st century, Islam is an important mobilizing force. During the first phase of Muslim immigration and settlement, the governments and political parties of the host nations paid little attention to the aspirations of Muslims and, as a result, many immigrant workers were isolated in Western societies. They maintained their focus on the countries that they had left behind, and usually their sole ambition was to earn enough money as guest workers to lead a comfortable life on their inevitable return home.

However, that attitude changed during the later period of family reunification, when Muslims saw that their future and their children's future lay in western Europe. As a consequence, they began to express their need to institutionalize their faith more strongly. Europeans and their governments recognized the need for change in order to integrate Islam and the Muslim minorities into their societies.

The establishment of mosques was an important step in the institutionalization of Islam in western Europe. In the 1960s, there were merely a few dozen mosques in western Europe. They were constructed either by and for diplomats or by missionaries who sought to convert Christians to Islam. From the 1970s, the number of religious centers, prayer houses, and mosques increased considerably. From

This store in Lille is one of many Muslim-run businesses that have prospered in France since the end of the colonial period.

the 1980s, a number of organizations emerged in western Europe representing Muslim interests at the national level. Also, because of family reunification, Muslims began to interact more extensively with their host societies. Most significantly for the future, their children attended local schools, where they learned the local language better than their parents.

Meanwhile, the immigrants maintained their cultural roots, and western Europe witnessed the introduction of Islamic schools and broadcast media. Muslims in western Europe gained the right to slaughter their meat according to halal (Islam-approved) rituals; they built their own cemeteries and formed their own political parties; and Muslim spiritual advisors began to complement Christian ministers in hospitals, prisons, the armed forces, and other organizations.

By institutionalizing their faith in these ways, Muslim immigrants to western Europe were able to integrate with the host community while at the same time preserving religious and cultural traditions. This approach created solidarity and a sense of common purpose for followers of Islam in non-Muslim countries. The result was Muslim communities throughout western Europe that have synthesized ancient religious practices with modern customs.

EUROPEAN EFFECTS ON ISLAM

Muslims do not shape the development of their religious communities in isolation; they are influenced by the society in which they live. As a result, the way in which Islam has been institutionalized in western Europe is different from in more traditional Muslim societies and has also varied significantly from country to country.

Most western European countries are, in principle, secular nation-states, but some countries—including Denmark, Greece, and the United Kingdom—have an established (national) church. In France, on the other hand, church and state are in theory kept strictly separate, although, in practice, the dividing line is sometimes blurred. In spite of these differences, all western European nations have established social formations that are, in religious and ideological respects, permeated with Christian or humanist elements. These elements are reflected in nearly all aspects of life, from legislation to national holidays. With the presence of large numbers of Muslims, questions arise as to whether, and to what degree, Islam can be incorporated into these historically determined systems.

Western European countries also differ in their specific histories and the historical development of citizenship. The proportion of Muslims who are citizens varies between European countries, largely because each nation has its own naturalization rules. For example, in Germany, only a small percentage of immigrants are naturalized citizens, because citizenship was historically related to descent—a person could not be a German unless his or her parents were also German. In France, citizenship was historically connected to place of birth—a person born in a French overseas colony did not necessarily qualify as French in the same way as, in the early 20th century, a New Zealander, for example, was automatically eligible for British citizenship because New Zealand was a part of the British Empire and later a member of the British Commonwealth. Both Germany and France have now changed their rules to allow more immigrants to become fully entitled citizens.

European countries also differ in the ways and the degree to which they allow individual citizens and groups to organize themselves on religious or ethnic grounds. France has an assimilationist policy, under which immigrants are expected to comply with the common rules like everyone else; exclusive groups based on faith or ethnicity are regarded as undesirable. The Netherlands, on the other hand, has religious diversity firmly established in its history and enshrined in its laws, accommodating ethnic and religious diversity in what is known as a pluralistic approach.

In addition to differences between western European nations, there are differences within each country that influence the establishment of Islamic institutions. For example, the founding of a religious institution, such as a mosque, may be of no concern at the national level but may cause problems locally for practical reasons.

MAINTAINING LINKS

Many Muslims in western Europe maintain strong relations with their home countries. The first generation, in particular, kept its focus on the countries of origin; in the second half of the 20th century, it was common to see Muslim guest workers in France and Germany packing their automobiles with family members and goods and setting off to Morocco or Turkey for their summer vacation.

In some cases, the governments of the countries of origin try to maintain their influence on emigrants. The Diyanet, a department of the Turkish Foreign Ministry, has about 1,200 imams stationed throughout Europe for this purpose. Although these imams are well educated, they often do not speak the languages of

the countries in which they are stationed. Another common criticism is that they often know too little about the specific concerns and situation of European Muslims to be adequate spiritual leaders for European Muslims.

Another issue is that of dual nationality. Although some western Europeans prefer immigrants to renounce their foreign nationality and commit themselves to their adopted country, it is not always desirable or possible for them to do so. Turks cannot give up their nationality without losing inheritance rights in their native land. Moroccans are not allowed to give up their

In some cases, the governments of the countries of origin try to maintain their influence on emigrants.

nationality at all and, in some cases, have been forced to submit to Moroccan law even while living abroad.

ACCULTURATION CONCERNS

The concept of integration has become more popular in western Europe. Most countries have placed an increasing emphasis on their expectations of Muslims and concentrate policy on increasing active Muslim participation in society. A 2006 survey in Berlin, Germany, and Paris, France, found little difference between Muslim and non-Muslim respondents when questioned about what Muslims need to do to integrate into the larger society. An overwhelming majority of Muslim respondents to the survey stated that learning the language, finding a job, getting a better education, and celebrating the national holidays were among their main concerns and desires.

However, the term *integration* implies a process of give and take on both sides and, partly as a result, western European governments currently find themselves in a dilemma. On the one hand, they are coming to realize that they must find ways to fund and support the development of an independent Islam in Europe. Foreign funding and foreign imams preaching to European Muslims are now regarded as undesirable. In the Netherlands, all imams are required to take an acculturation program, which teaches them the Dutch language and aspects of the law. On the other hand, issues of national security and anti-terrorism influence policy throughout Europe, while the anti-Islamic rhetoric of right-wing politicians hinders the process of acculturation.

These conflicting priorities have led to some contradictory signals from European governments toward Muslim minority populations. For example, while France is moving toward a wider application of the ban on the head scarves traditionally worn by Muslim women, the government at the same time announces that it is creating a foundation to fund "French Islam." Britain, which has gone furthest of all European countries with anti-terrorist laws, which affect many Muslims, also promises to allow Shariah law to be used in courts for some disputes.

ANTI-ISLAMIC SENTIMENTS

Anti-Islamic sentiments in western Europe long predate the events of September 11, 2001, when Muslim terrorists destroyed the twin towers of the World Trade Center in New York and caused serious damage to the Pentagon in Washington, D.C., outrages now widely known as "9/11." These sentiments are founded on centuries-old prejudices and have been reinforced by anxiety about the rapid recent changes that have seen greater numbers of Muslims than ever before settle in western Europe. In the aftermath of 9/11 and other terrorist acts committed in Madrid, Spain, and London,

THE *HIJAB* IN FRANCE

The *hijab*—the Islamic head scarf traditionally worn by many Muslim women and teenage girls—has been the topic of emotional debate all over western Europe, where it is perceived by many non-Muslims as a symbol of repression that women have been forced to adopt by patriarchal societies.

In France, the wearing of the *hijab* has been a particularly sensitive issue since 1989. The debate was essentially concerned with Muslim girls wearing the *hijab* in public schools and was sparked when three girls were expelled from school when they refused to uncover their heads. The move to ban the *hijab* was generally welcomed in France, where the law states that there can be no religious interference in government affairs, nor government interference in religious affairs. Religion is entirely a private matter, and religious symbols are therefore excluded from the public sphere. In 2004, a new law was passed that prohibited the wearing of visible religious symbols in French public schools. The banned items included Muslim *hijab*s, Jewish yarmulkes, and large Christian crosses. Students are permitted only discreet symbols of their faith, such as small crucifixes, Stars of David, or Fatima's hands.

England, some Europeans have feared that Islam aims to undermine all of Western society.

Before these attacks, many Europeans believed that, in the modern age, the importance of religion in everyday life was declining and they expected that, over time, Muslim immigrants would assimilate in European societies, that their children would grow up with European attitudes, and that they would lose their religious distinctiveness. However, these expectations have now been confounded. Instead, not only in Islam but also in other religious groups (for example, evangelical Christians and Hindu Nationalists), religious identification has in fact increased since the beginning of the 21st century, partly in response to globalization, which is sometimes interpreted as a code for U.S. expansionism.

The growing tension between the Muslim world and the West was highlighted by the American political scientist Samuel Huntington in his 1993 book *The Clash of Civilizations and the Remaking of World Order*, which identified Islam as one of the major religious, cultural, and ideological systems that were inherently incompatible—and likely to clash—with Western values. Huntington's thesis has found many followers since 9/11, but it has often been simplified to accommodate emotional arguments.

Widespread damage was caused in several poor urban districts of France in November 2005 when Muslims rioted to protest their unequal treatment by the authorities.

THE RUSHDIE AFFAIR

A major clash between freedom of speech and sensitivity toward religion followed the publication in 1988 of *The Satanic Verses* by Salman Rushdie (b. 1947), a British novelist of Indian heritage. Soon after the book first appeared, hundreds of young Muslims in Bradford, a city in northern England where around 20 percent of the population are Muslim, burned the book in the streets and requested the government to ban it. The author spent most of the decade in hiding after he was condemned to death by a fatwa (decree) issued by the Ayatollah Ruhollah Khomeini, the leader of Iran.

Many Muslims were offended by what they regarded as the author's lack of respect toward the Prophet Muhammad, especially because of Rushdie's own Muslim background. Furthermore, the anger was combined with the social and economic problems of numerous Muslims in Britain, fueling the protests there. Many of the demonstrators, especially of the younger generation, used the occasion to voice their resentment at their marginalization in Western society. At the same time, some Western politicians and intellectuals seized on the affair to condemn Islam as inherently incompatible with Western values.

Huntington himself recognized that for every such action by extremists there would be opposite reactions, as moderates on both sides sought to reduce violence by increasing mutual understanding.

ETHNICITY, POVERTY, AND ISLAM

Muslim immigrants to western Europe are typically city dwellers. They are drawn to the urban environment in search of work. In many cases, Muslim immigrants who first arrived in western European cities moved to areas where housing was cheap and work was nearby. Over the following years, many European nationals moved out of these areas and were replaced by more immigrant families.

Currently, many Muslim communities thrive in ethnic enclaves where they make up a majority of the population. In all western European countries, Muslim communities comprise among the poorest ethnic groups. Research has shown that many European Muslims face social discrimination in housing, education, and employment. The second generation, who were either born in Europe or immigrated to Europe at a very young age, has experienced many of the same disadvantages. The unemployment rate among Muslims is higher than among European nationals, a disparity that even affects members of the younger generation who have the same qualifications as their European peers. Although, in theory, national law gives equal rights to all citizens, many young Muslims do not feel that they are granted the same opportunities as Europeans. Urban problems in poor city districts all over Europe have been a topic of political debate and public unrest over the years. These suburbs have high rates of unemployment and crime. Young men and boys with roots in countries that are perceived as strongly orthodox, such as Pakistan and Somalia, are particularly perceived as troublemakers.

In the media and in political and public debate, the problems these youths face are perceived as ethnic and their Muslim background is often mentioned in the debates. However, young people of the current generation are, in fact, more often disconnected from their families, from the values connected to their culture of origin, from the mosque, and from the European educational system. Muslim parents and social workers have been quoted as saying that such people are delinquents not because they are Muslim but because they are not Muslim enough. Meanwhile, the youths themselves often feel that Western societies have exploited their parents, who helped to build their adopted nations, and are unwilling to submit to the same treatment themselves.

NEW ISLAMIC IDENTITIES

There is great diversity in modern Muslim communities in western Europe, as their members discover new ways of following their faith through processes known as secularization and individualization. Such processes enable individuals to choose those aspects of the faith that they prefer to practice publicly and those that they regard as private matters for their own conscience. As a result, many modern Muslims in western Europe cannot be recognized as adherents of the faith by their clothing, as is traditional. Instead, they "wear" their Islam entirely on the inside.

Sometimes known as "New Muslims," these people also tend to separate their ethnicity from their religion. The wide geographical range of Muslims and the increased access to global information, particularly through the Internet, have enabled young Muslims to identify themselves with the international *ummah* (community of believers) on an international rather than a national or a regional basis.

While adapting to many aspects of life in western Europe, large numbers of young Muslims resist those aspects of Western life that they view as corrupting. They are drawn to a fundamentalist interpretation of Islam, notably Salafism and, to a lesser extent, Wahhabism (which is linked to the current rulers of Saudi Arabia). The concept of fundamentalism is a confusing one. The term not only embraces those Muslims who are both theologically and politically conservative but can also be applied to other religious groups. Although the labels commonly attached to Islamic fundamentalists—"Islamists" and "Islamic radicals"—are often used indiscriminately, there are major differences between terrorists (a tiny minority) and a much larger group who are religiously conservative and seek only to follow the instructions of the Koran in their worship.

There is also a growing Muslim elite emerging in western Europe. An increasing number of Muslims are educated at universities and become high earners. In most European countries, Muslims are now represented in national or local politics. Many Muslim politicians are not from the second generation but are new immigrants who came to western Europe as political refugees, students, or both. They are mostly concerned with issues of the integration of Muslims into wider society. At the same time, many of them represent the interests of Muslims and strive for the equal treatment of Islam as a fully accepted European religion.

CHALLENGES AND OPPORTUNITIES

The presence of growing Muslim minorities in western Europe has presented a wide range of challenges and concerns, which are addressed by both immigrants

A member of the Al-Muhajiroun Islamic organization protests next to a poster of Osama bin Laden outside Downing Street in London in 2004.

and by the European nations. Although the Muslim presence has been established since the end of World War II (1939–1945), there is still much work to be done to incorporate the Muslim minority fully into European societies. In recent years, much attention has been given to the radicalization and marginalization of Muslim youth in western Europe. Meanwhile, however, a Muslim elite has emerged, largely unnoticed but increasingly powerful and influential. Often highly educated, its members have become part of the middle and upper classes and taken increasingly active roles in local and national politics.

Although there is undoubtedly some evidence to support the notion of a clash between Western and Islamic civilizations in contemporary Europe, especially since 9/11, most of it is derived from the actions of terrorists, whose crimes attract the maximum publicity and therefore tend to drown out the views of the majorities on both sides of the cultural divide. For example, surveys conducted in several western European cities repeatedly show that an overwhelming majority of their Muslim residents embrace democracy, but findings of that kind do not make headline news. However, many Muslims also believe that they are not being given equal opportunities to benefit from some of the most attractive aspects of European life, such as religious tolerance, equality under the law, and personal dignity. While a generation of youth with roots in Islamic countries struggles to find its way in western European society, politicians and individuals are striving to come to terms with the new reality that Muslims are now Europeans, too.

See Also

The Eastern Mediterranean and the Arabian Peninsula 220-235 ❖ Northern Africa 246-249 ❖ Turkey and Eastern Europe 322-333 ❖ United States and Canada 348-361 ❖

UNITED STATES AND CANADA

The earliest Muslim immigrants to North America were African slaves. Many of them were converted to Christianity but reverted to Islam in the 20th century. Subsequent immigrants have remained faithful to Islam, which is now thought to have more than 9 million followers in the United States and Canada.

M uslim immigration to North America began in the early 16th century, when the first slaves were forcibly imported from western Africa, in some parts of which Islam had already been established for almost 500 years. During the 17th century and the 18th century, the Muslim faith spread through Senegal, Gambia, Futa (part of modern Mauritania and Senegal), and Futa Djallon (a mountainous region of modern Guinea). Meanwhile, slave traders continued to seize the inhabitants of these regions, and more and more of those shipped westward across the Atlantic Ocean were Muslims. There were also unknown numbers of animists and believers in local deities.

Between the early 16th century and the late 19th century, it is estimated that around 11 million Africans were forcibly transported to the Americas as slave laborers. Most were sent to the colonial plantations of South America and the Caribbean—around 4.8 million are thought to have been transported to Brazil alone—but a significant proportion were sent to mainland North America. In 1808 the United States banned the importation of slaves. Estimates of the number of Africans living there by that

time vary because no one kept reliable immigration records. Emory University's Trans-Atlantic Slave Database puts the figure at around 390,000, while in *Africa Remembered: Narratives by West Africans from the Era of the Slave Trade* (1967), Philip D. Curtin of Johns Hopkins University estimates that, between 1711 and 1810, slave traders brought 1.6 million slaves to North America from western Africa.

■ ❖ ■

In 1808 the United States banned the importation of slaves. Estimates of the number of Africans living there by that time vary because no one kept reliable immigration records.

Regardless of the true figures at the start of the 19th century, the 1860 census shows that, by then, the slave population of the United States was around 4 million. The exact provenance of these immigrants was unknown for many years; the great majority of enslaved African Muslims remained anonymous or were known only

The Islamic Center in Toledo, Ohio, is one of 3,000 mosques in the United States.

by foreign-looking names on plantation owners' property lists. However, in *African Muslims in Antebellum America: A Sourcebook* (1984), Allan D. Austin of Springfield College, Massachusetts, persuasively demonstrated that significant numbers of slaves in this period belonged to three, mainly Muslim, African peoples: the Fulani, who are widely but sparsely distributed between Lake Chad and the Atlantic coast in modern Cameroon, Guinea, Mali, Niger, Nigeria, and Senegal; the Hausa of southern Niger and northwestern Nigeria; and the Malinke, who inhabit parts of the Ivory Coast (Côte d'Ivoire), Gambia, Guinea, Guinea-Bissau, Mali, and Senegal.

During the Reconstruction period (1865–1877) that followed the Civil War (1861–1865), a significant—but, again, unknown—number of American slaves returned to Africa. For the remaining part of the 19th century and the first quarter of the 20th century, the African American Muslims who stayed behind had almost no political influence in the United States, and non-Muslim Americans had little awareness of Islam within their national borders. The most famous American Muslim of this period was Alexander Russell Webb (1846–1916), a white journalist, newspaper owner, and sometime U.S. consular representative in the Philippines. Webb converted to Islam in 1887 and, six years later, started a missionary organization, the American Muslim Propagation Movement, which was based in New York.

20TH-CENTURY TRENDS

A new phase of Muslim immigration to North America began around 1900, when the United States attracted displaced people from western Asia. The trickle of incomers became a tide after the disintegration of the Ottoman Empire at the end of World War I (1914–1918). Most of the refugees came from the region known at the time as Greater Syria—present-day Jordan, Lebanon, Palestine, and Syria—but other nationals were also represented in the diaspora. In 1915, Albanians established the first associations of immigrant Muslims in the United States. They built a mosque in Biddeford, Maine, and, by 1919, completed another in Connecticut. In 1926, a group of Polish-speaking Tatars built a mosque in Brooklyn, New York.

The flow of Muslims into the United States was reduced, first by the 1921 Emergency Quota Act, and then by the Immigration Act of 1924, which superseded the earlier legislation. These federal laws restricted the number of immigrants who could be admitted from any country to 2 percent of the number of people from that country who had already been U.S. residents at the time of the census of 1890. The legislation succeeded in its main aim, which was to limit immigration from southern and eastern Europe and from Asia. Thereafter, only a few openings were set aside for immigrants from the Muslim world. During this period, the few Muslim immigrants to the United States were mainly Turks, Kurds, Albanians, and Arabs.

THE NATION OF ISLAM

Of the Muslims who had entered the United States before the immigration laws were passed, a small group established a community in Ross, North Dakota. In 1934, Lebanese immigrants built a simple, white-framed mosque with a green dome at Cedar Rapids, Iowa. Meanwhile, in 1930, the first African American mosque in the United States was completed in

THE AHMADIYAH AND THE QADIANI

In the 1920s, Muslim missionaries in the United States initiated efforts to spread Islam among the African American community, especially among players and followers of jazz music. In the forefront of this evangelical movement were the Ahmadiyah.

Ahmadiyah is a term that may be applied generally to various Sufi groups (Muslim mystics). However, in this context, it refers specifically to a sect that was founded in India in 1889 by Mirza Ghulam Ahmad (1839–1908). Ahmad and his followers believed that he was the living incarnation of leading mystical figures in three major religions—Christianity, Hinduism, and Islam. He claimed to be the Christian Messiah and the Hindu god Krishna, as well as both a *buruz* (reappearance) of the Prophet Muhammad and the *mahdi* (divinely guided one), a messianic being who, some Muslims believe, will bring justice, universal equality, and true religious faith for a period of between 7 and 9 years before the end of the world.

The Ahmadiyah were eager to convert unbelievers to their religion and, to that end, they engaged in a peaceful worldwide jihad (struggle). They continued their mission after the death of Gulam Ahmad but, after his elected *khalifah* (successor), Mawlawi Nur-ad-Din, died in 1914, they split into two groups. One group downgraded Gulam Ahmad to the status of reformer (*mujaddid*), but the other group, the Qadiani, continued to regard Ahmad as a prophet (*nabi*) and redoubled their efforts to spread the word.

When India was partitioned in 1947, the Qadiani moved their headquarters to Rabwah, Pakistan, and then established bases in western Africa, Europe, and India, as well as in the United States. Today they are a well-financed, highly organized global missionary organization that preaches a variant form of Islam in which Gulam Ahmad is afforded comparable status as a prophet with Muhammad. Although Qadiani nonconformism sometimes attracts opposition from orthodox imams, most Muslims are generally well disposed toward a movement that promotes their religion and shows it in a favorable light.

In the 20th century, the Qadiani branch of the Ahmadiyah attracted large numbers of African Americans, not only to its own version of Islam but also to mainstream Islam. They gained many of their converts through an energetic publication program, which created a new mass-market readership for the Koran, the Hadith (sayings of Muhammad), and other important works of Islam that had previously been difficult to obtain in English translations in anything other than expensive, scholarly editions.

The success of these publications was both a cause and an effect of the African Americans' increasing consciousness of their real or presumed Muslim roots. Throughout the United States and in many other countries, Islam was increasingly regarded as a viable alternative to white supremacism and Western imperialism. Among the most prominent people who are believed to have been influenced by Ahmadiyah evangelism was Marcus Garvey (1887–1940). Garvey founded the Universal Negro Improvement and Conservation Association and African Communities League, usually known as the Universal Negro Improvement Association (UNIA), in his native Jamaica in 1914. From 1916, he set up branches of the organization in Harlem, New York, and other black ghettos in northern U.S. cities, which, for a time, had a considerable African American following. Although there is no evidence that Garvey was himself a convert to the Ahmadiyah, it is generally agreed that his work was to some extent inspired by, and his popularity partly attributable to, the evangelical activities of the Qadiani.

Pittsburgh, Pennsylvania. The second African American mosque, in Cleveland, Ohio, opened two years later. The construction of these two buildings reflected the African Americans' growing consciousness of their ethnic and religious heritage, a new self-awareness that developed symbiotically with the emerging Nation of Islam. This organization grew out of the Moorish Science Temple of America, which had been founded in 1913 in Newark, New Jersey, by Noble Drew Ali, the adopted Islamic name of Timothy Drew (1886–1929). In 1930, Wali Fard Muhammad (born Wallace D. Fard) claimed that he was the reincarnation of Drew and founded the Nation of Islam in Detroit, Michigan. Fard's associate, Elijah Muhammad (born Elijah Poole) then established another branch of the movement in Chicago, Illinois. In 1934, Elijah Muhammad intervened to stop

infighting and took control of the whole organization. Fard was sidelined into retirement, but his memory was venerated by Elijah Muhammad, who depicted his predecessor as a combination of Allah, the God of Islam, and Jesus, the Son of God in the Christian faith. This image was designed to appeal to religious-minded African Americans who, by this time, could be divided into two broad categories— those who had maintained or wanted to return to Islam and those who were converts or the descendants of converts to Christianity. The Nation of Islam preached traditional Muslim values—such as the importance of a strong family life—and upheld traditional Muslim prohibitions— such as those on drinking alcohol, eating pork, using tobacco, and taking illicit drugs. The organization captured the hearts and minds of many African Americans at the temples and the parochial schools that it

THE NATION OF ISLAM

Elijah Muhammad, the leader of the Nation of Islam, preached that "the white race" had been created by Yakub, a mythical black scientist who lived in Mecca, and that it was a force for evil. (In Elijah Muhammad's view, "the white race" comprised Europeans and Jews.) Although Allah, the God of Islam, had permitted whites to dominate for 6,000 years, their allotted time in charge of the world had ended in 1914. From that time onward, black people would assert themselves and take over the reins of power. In pursuit of that objective, Elijah Muhammad advocated economic self-sufficiency. He advised and encouraged African Americans to start their own businesses as the first step toward the creation of a separate black nation, which was to comprise the U.S. states of Alabama, Georgia, and Mississippi.

In an effort to reawaken African Americans to their heritage, the Nation of Islam encouraged them to drop their "slave names" and adopt Muslim names instead. The most famous early convert was the world heavyweight boxing champion Cassius Clay, who, in 1964, changed his name to Muhammad Ali. Other African Americans renounced their surnames and, while searching for an appropriate Muslim alternative, used the letter "X." One of the first people to make this change was Malcolm Little, who was known as Malcolm X until he finally settled on el-Hajj Malik el-Shabazz. Later, Louis Walcott became Louis X until Elijah Muhammad bestowed on him the Muslim name Abdul Haleem Farrakhan. Walcott later became famous under a combination of his original "slave name" and his new Islamic name—Louis Farrakhan.

set up in major population centers across the United States.

At the end of this initial period of growth, the Nation of Islam was suppressed after the United States entered World War II (1939–1945) in 1941 because the organization called on its members to refuse military service. Restrictions were lifted after the conflict and the Nation of Islam then renewed its appeal to the postwar generation, particularly after Malcolm X (born Malcolm Little; 1925–1965) was appointed head of the New York Temple. A highly controversial leader, Malcolm X attracted many new converts to the Nation of Islam but alienated others who regarded some of his pronouncements as unacceptably extreme. He also made enemies within his own organization, and it was likely a group of

them who assassinated him in 1965.

In the early 1970s, the Nation of Islam remained divided by doctrinal and political disputes. This situation persisted for as long as Elijah Muhammad remained in charge but, after his death in 1975—by which time, there were no fewer than 75 Nation of Islam centers across the United States— the organization was taken over by one of his sons, Wallace, who took the name Warith Deen Mohammed. Based on his extensive study of the Koran, he brought in radical, doctrinal changes, renouncing the organization's former racial and nationalist attitudes and its memorialization of Fard as an incarnation of God. Wallace also changed the name of the organization, first to the World Community of al-Islam in the West and, in 1978, to the American Muslim Mission. These changes paved the

Louis Farrakhan (at the microphones, wearing a bow tie) addresses a Nation of Islam meeting in Chicago, Illinois, in 1985.

way for the reintegration of the Nation of Islam into the broader African American Muslim community; the organization was disbanded in 1985.

LOUIS FARRAKHAN

African American Muslims who did not wish to follow the Nation of Islam along the path toward orthodoxy formed new organizations. One of the fragmentary groups—which, like two of the others, retained the original Nation of Islam name, was founded in 1978 by Louis Farrakhan (born 1933). Farrakhan—who had succeeded Malcolm X as leader of the New York Temple—began with only a few thousand supporters but, thanks to his skills as an orator and his energetic self-promotion, soon found himself at the head of a regenerated international movement, which made its headquarters at Elijah Muhammad's former mosque in Chicago and also had branches in Britain and Ghana.

Like Malcolm X, Farrakhan was a controversial figure, particularly during the 1984 U.S. presidential election when, after having announced his support for African American candidate Jesse Jackson, he alienated a wide range of public opinion by making references to Jewish American slaveholders in the antebellum period that were widely denounced as anti-Semitic. However, Farrakhan later withdrew those remarks and aligned himself more with consensus liberal opinion. Having entered mainstream politics, he shared church pulpits with Christian ministers and actively supported education programs and anti-drug initiatives. At the start of the 21st century, Farrakhan's Nation of Islam had an active membership of between 10,000 and 50,000 people.

MODERN DEMOGRAPHICS

The number of immigrants to the United States from western Asia increased greatly after World War II when the U.S. Immigration and Nationality Act of 1965 ended national quotas. By the 1980s, immigrants from the Arab world were second in number only to immigrants from South Asia and eastern Asia. According to the 1990 census, 82 percent of Arabs in the United States were U.S. citizens, but only 63 percent of those people were born in the country. Most Arab Americans are of Lebanese or Syrian heritage; many of these people were displaced in the wake of the establishment of the state of Israel in 1948 and in the aftermath of the Arab-Israeli Six-Day War in 1967. However, by 2010, they had been joined in the United States by growing numbers of Iraqis and Palestinians who fled the Persian Gulf War (1990–1991) and the Iraq War (2003–2010).

North American Muslims have several different doctrinal traditions. As in other parts of the Muslim world, the Sunnis are in the majority, while Shiite Muslims

LATE-20TH CENTURY U.S. IMMIGRATION

This table shows the U.S. census figures for the number of immigrants from predominantly Muslim countries during two consecutive 10-year periods:

Country	1980–1989	1990–1999
Egypt	31,400	27,900
Iraq	19,600	26,800
Jordan	32,600	25,000
Lebanon	41,600	29,900
Pakistan	61,300	70,500
Syria	20,000	16,600

account for the second-largest following. All four major schools of Islamic jurisprudence—Maliki, Hanafi, Shafi'i, and Hanbali—are found among the Sunni Muslims, while the Shiite community adheres to the Jafari school of Muslim law. In a 2006 survey conducted by the Council on American-Islamic Relations (CAIR), of 1,000 Muslim registered voters, about 36 percent said that they were Sunni, 12 percent identified themselves as Shiite, and 40 percent called themselves "just a Muslim." A 2007 poll in *Newsweek* magazine found that 50 percent of native-born American Muslims identified themselves as Sunnis, while 53 percent of foreign-born American Muslims so described themselves. The same survey showed that 7 percent of native-born American Muslims described themselves as Shiites, as against 21 percent of foreign-born American Muslims.

A study commissioned in 2001 by CAIR estimated that the total number of Muslims living in the United States was between 6 million and 7 million. African Americans comprised 42 percent of that total; 24.4 percent were of Indian or Pakistani origin; 12.4 percent were Arabs; 5.2 percent were African; 3.6 percent were Iranian; 3.2 percent were Albanians; 2.4 percent were Turks; 2 percent were from Southeast Asia; and 1.6 percent were white Americans. The remaining 3.2 percent were from various other countries.

The total number of American Muslims increased significantly during the first decade of the 21st century. In 2008, another survey conducted on behalf of *Newsweek* estimated the total number of Muslims in the United States at between 7 million and 8 million. The U.S. states with the highest concentrations of Muslims were California

THE ISLAMIC CENTER, WASHINGTON, D.C.

The Islamic Center in Washington, D.C.—the foundation stone of which was laid in 1949 and which was opened in 1957 by President Dwight D. Eisenhower—was not the first mosque to be established in North America, but it was the first to be built in a major U.S. city. The Islamic Center employs a unique aesthetic vocabulary; the architect, Abdur Rahman Rossi, chose motifs, both internally and externally, from Egypt. Several pious inscriptions embellish the interior walls and ceilings and they have been arranged in a configuration of linear symmetrical patterns. The Beautiful Names of Allah (*Asma Allah al-Husna*) and several familiar verses from the Koran are inscribed in large framed borders of script with smaller framed panels of ornamental script.

Muslims leaving the Islamic Center in Washington, D.C. The imposing minaret of the structure is 160 feet (49 m) tall.

(1 million), New York (800,000), Illinois (420,000), Indiana (180,000), Michigan (170,000), Virginia (150,000), Texas (140,000), and Ohio (130,000).

PLACES OF WORSHIP

As the number of practicing Muslims in the United States has increased, so, too, has the number of mosques. The completion of the Islamic Center in Washington, D.C., in the 1950s marked the beginning of a flurry of building work, as mosques appeared in every major North American city with a significant Muslim population. Among the largest and most important mosques today are those in Atlanta (Georgia), Boston (Massachusetts), Houston (Texas), and New York City in the United States and Toronto and Montreal in Canada. There are more than 3,000 mosques in North America that were established in the second half of the 20th century.

Although neither of the two main Islamic religious texts provides clear rules as to how a mosque should be laid out or what it should look like, the Koran does stress the overall role of the edifice as a place for the remembrance of Allah. The Hadith (sayings of Muhammad) contains a list of profane actions that are forbidden in a mosque. For example, the proscription of human or animal imagery (iconography) attempts to ensure that the essence of sacred art always remains reflective, contemplative, and theocentric. The acceptance of revealed truths requires a keen intellect (*al-aql*), purity of heart (*qalb*), and piety of soul (*ruh*). Most important, the mosque is a fellowship hall in which men and women gather to pray on a daily basis, to read the Koran, and to engage in a wide range of pious activities; its design should therefore always facilitate those activities.

Within these broad guidelines, the design and appearance of the urban mosques of North America differ enormously, reflecting the wide-ranging global roots of the Muslim population. Many immigrant communities invoke one particular cultural style and imagery, largely because of their country of origin and nostalgia. However, the ground plan of a mosque's fellowship hall for men and women is a fundamental criterion, as is the requirement that the prayer hall should be oriented so that worshippers face toward Mecca while they pray. The correct direction is indicated by a niche (*mihrab*) in the wall that faces the holy city.

Out of a wide variety of styles, three visual patterns emerge. One is the use of designs derived from plant life; such patterns are often known in the West as arabesques. Another common denominator is the use of Arabic calligraphy, which, regardless of the vernacular in any part of the world, remains the most revered art form in Islam because it conveys the word of Allah in its purest form, without the risk of anything being lost in translation. The third common characteristic is tessellation (the repetitive ordering of a geometric pattern). Although these three features do not often occur together, an exception to that general rule may be seen in rural Abiquiu, New Mexico, where in 1980 Egyptian architect Hassan Fathy designed Dar al-Islam (abode of tranquillity), a Muslim village community. By using locally available adobe (bricks made of sun-dried earth and straw), Fathy made his structures appear to have developed gradually rather than from a single project of works. As he himself described it: "Tradition is a key element of culture. When the craftsman was responsible for much of the work of building, traditional art came out of the subconscious of the community. The village built by accretion is more harmonious than the one built on the drawing board; it is held together by an accumulated culture, rather than by one individual's idea of harmony."

Yet, in spite of the widely varying architecture, the functions and purposes of Muslim religious buildings are remarkably homogeneous throughout the continent of North America. Every mosque serves as an Islamic center—it is the heart of the Muslim community, where the faithful gather to participate in communal worship, to be educated, to marry, and to engage in social activities. The mosque is also a place of contemplation and repose, a spiritual sanctuary—indeed, in the view of many Muslims, this is its primary function. Mosques also play an important role in the broader Muslim community and its relations with the outside world. The imams and their ancillaries work productively to address social concerns, such as education, health care, and poverty relief, and to provide training for a wide range of jobs.

ORGANIZATIONS

By 2010, the largest Islamic organization in the United States was the American Society of Muslims (ASM), whose founding leader was Warith Deen Mohammed. Most of the ASM's membership of between 2 million and 3 million was African American. Almost as large as the ASM was the Islamic Society of North America (ISNA), an association of mainly immigrant Muslims. The third most important organization was the Islamic Circle of North America (ICNA), which is open to all Muslims, regardless

of their ethnicity. Together with its affiliated youth organization, the Young Muslims, the ISNA is thought to be almost as large as the ASM and the ICNA.

There are, in addition, several other administrative bodies that cater to some of the Muslim community's more specialized needs. These include the Islamic Supreme Council of America (ISCA), which aims

NUMBER OF U.S. MOSQUES, STATE BY STATE

In addition to the figures shown, in 2001 there were 11 mosques in the District of Columbia, making a nationwide total of 1,209.

State	Mosques	State	Mosques
Alabama	23	Montana	2
Alaska	3	Nebraska	4
Arizona	23	Nevada	3
Arkansas	8	New Hampshire	1
California	227	New Jersey	86
Colorado	17	New Mexico	6
Connecticut	21	New York	140
Delaware	3	North Carolina	34
Florida	57	North Dakota	3
Georgia	41	Ohio	66
Hawaii	2	Oklahoma	14
Idaho	3	Oregon	12
Illinois	57	Pennsylvania	67
Indiana	23	Rhode Island	5
Iowa	14	South Carolina	15
Kansas	6	South Dakota	1
Kentucky	8	Tennessee	15
Louisiana	24	Texas	67
Maine	1	Utah	3
Maryland	30	Vermont	2
Massachusetts	23	Virginia	37
Michigan	23	Washington	24
Minnesota	9	West Virginia	4
Mississippi	10	Wisconsin	19
Missouri	21	Wyoming	2

to interpret traditional Muslim law and accommodate it within the context of modern Western society.

In the political sphere, there are several groups that lobby for Muslim interests and against negative depictions of Islam. The most influential of these groups is the CAIR, which works with the U.S. president and the executive branch of the government on domestic safety and foreign policy in the aftermath of the terrorist attacks on New York and Washington, D.C., of September 11, 2001. Also important is the Muslim Public Affairs Council (MPAC), which, in its mission statement, describes itself as working "to offer the public a portrayal that goes beyond stereotypes in order to elucidate that Muslims worship God, abhor global terrorism, stand against oppression, and are part of a vibrant American pluralism."

Of the large number of Muslim charities in the United States, the most important are the Inner-City Muslim Action Network (IMAN) and Islamic Relief USA, which is the American branch of Islamic Relief Worldwide. Much of the work of both organizations is in social development projects. They also provide emergency relief, both in the United States and abroad, and distribute food during Ramadan, the Muslim month of fasting.

Among other noteworthy organizations is the Muslim Women's League, which aims to raise the awareness of Muslims and non-Muslims of female issues within Islam and in relation to American society as a whole.

CANADA

There have been Muslims in Canada for almost as long as the nation has existed. In 1867, Canada became a self-governing dominion while retaining links to Britain; four years later, the first Canadian census recorded 13 Muslims; their provenance is unknown. Around 1882, there began a small influx of Arabs from the Ottoman Empire. In 1931, the census recorded 10,070 Canadians of Arab origin, 645 of whom were Muslims. Canada's first mosque was opened in Edmonton, Alberta, in 1938.

Significant Muslim immigration to Canada began after 1967, when a new Immigration Act was passed into law by the government of prime minister Lester B. Pearson (in office 1963–1968). The revised legislation removed previous restrictions on non-white immigration and Canada's traditional preference for people of European origin. Canada then became one of the favorite refuges sought by people displaced by the civil war in Lebanon (1975–1990) and the revolution in Iran (1979). These incomers were later joined by Muslims fleeing the civil war that broke out in Somalia in 1991 and by Bosnian Muslims during the conflicts that followed the disintegration of Yugoslavia in the same year. Muslim immigration was further encouraged by the passage into law in 1982 of the Canadian Charter of Rights and Freedoms, which guarantees freedom of religious expression and, among other measures, permits the wearing of the *hijab* in schools and at places of work.

Iranians, Lebanese, Somalis, and Bosnians now comprise the majority of Canada's Muslim population, which, at the start of 2010, was estimated to exceed 1 million, just under 3 percent of the national total of 33.5 million. Most of the remainder have come from almost every Muslim country in the world—notably, Algeria, Bangladesh, Pakistan, Syria, and

Turkey—in search of personal safety and improved educational and employment opportunities. There is also a small number of converts.

Most Canadian Muslims settled in the province of Ontario, where they are concentrated in and around the city of Toronto. The next largest Muslim community is in Vancouver and surrounding British Columbia. There are also strong Muslim presences in almost every other city in Canada.

CANADIAN ORGANIZATIONS

As befits a community comprised of around 60 ethno-cultural groups, Canadian Muslims have numerous organizations that represent their own interests and interact with other sectors of society. Many of these organizations are protean and mutable, realigning and reforming themselves to reflect the preoccupations of their members. One of the most firmly established organizations is the Canadian Islamic Congress (CIC), the nation's largest independent, non-profit Muslim body. The CIC claims to be "the independent voice of Canada's Muslims—Sunni and Shia, men and women, youth and seniors." It is moderate and mainstream and has the support of most of Canada's mosques.

The Muslim Association of Canada (MAC) is a national, grassroots organization with branches in 11 Canadian cities. Its main aim is to build Islam in Canada from within, by encouraging faith-based education that is fully attuned to the requirements of the Western job market.

The government of Canadian prime minister Lester B. Pearson enacted legislation in 1967 that gave Muslims greater freedom than before to immigrate to Canada.

The Canadian Council on American-Islamic Relations (CAIR-CAN) is the main Muslim advocacy and civil liberties organization. Based in Ottawa, CAIR-CAN is independent of its U.S. equivalent, CAIR, although the two bodies join forces in matters that concern them both.

The Muslim Canadian Congress (MCC) was founded in 2002 to provide a voice for people who were unrepresented by existing organizations. Liberal, antiauthoritarian, and largely secular, the MCC advocates the complete separation of religion and the state and offers support

Pakistani Canadian actor Sitara Hewitt arrives at the 2007 Gemini Awards ceremony. Hewitt portrays a devout Muslim physician in Canadian Broadcasting Corporation's television series *Little Mosque on the Prairie.*

not only to practicing Muslims but also to anyone who identifies himself or herself as a Muslim.

An offshoot of the MCC, the Canadian Muslim Union also advocates the complete separation of religion and the state but aims for even greater inclusiveness than its parent organization, encouraging both Muslims and non-Muslims who have ties to the Islamic community to involve themselves in its activities and its online discussion groups.

Some organizations cover both Canada and the United States. Prominent among these is the Islamic Society of North

The importance of Muslims in modern Canadian life is both reflected in and enhanced by the prominence of Islam and Islamic issues in the broadcast media.

America (ISNA), which raises funds and directs humanitarian work throughout the world. Its most notable interventions have come in Darfur, a region of Sudan suffering from war and civil conflict, and the areas of South Asia that were devastated by the Indian Ocean tsunami in December of 2004.

The city of Toronto is the venue for an important Muslim festival, called Reviving the Islamic Spirit, which has been held annually every midwinter since 2003. The attendance at the inaugural event—3,500 people—has increased in every subsequent year. Each year's festival explores a different theme, such as the life of the Prophet Muhammad and Canadian Muslim identity.

CANADIAN MUSLIM DEMOGRAPHICS

Muslims are the youngest social grouping in Canada, with a median age of 28.1 years. The median age of the nation is 40.4 years. Less than 10 percent of Canadian Muslims were born in Canada, but 68 percent of them have Canadian citizenship.

Some 37 percent of Canadian Muslims are of South Asian descent; most of this group are of Indian or Pakistani heritage. The next largest groups are those of Arab descent (21 percent) and those from the Caribbean (14 percent). In a 2007 opinion poll, more than 80 percent of Canadian Muslims said that they were generally content with life in their country—apart from the winter weather.

CANADIAN FILM AND TELEVISION

The importance of Muslims in modern Canadian life is both reflected in and enhanced by the prominence of Islam and Islamic issues in the broadcast media. Among the most prominent emerging Canadian filmmakers are Saide Kardar and Zarqa Nawaz.

Born in Iran, Kardar immigrated to Canada as a child. He is the director of *Homegrown Muslims* (2007), a documentary about the practice of Islam by young people in Toronto.

Nawaz—a British-born Canadian writer and director of Pakistani heritage—first came to prominence as the producer of *Me and the Mosque* (2005), a documentary financed by the National Film Board of Canada about the role of women in Islam in world history and modern Canada, with special reference to her own experience. Nawaz then devised *Little Mosque on the Prairie*, an award-winning sitcom produced by the Canadian Broadcasting Corporation (CBC) and screened worldwide after its pilot episode was critically acclaimed on first airing in 2007.

See Also
Western Europe 334-347 ❖ Mexico, Central America, and the Caribbean 362-369 ❖ South America 370-377 ❖

Chapter 21

MEXICO, CENTRAL AMERICA, AND THE CARIBBEAN

The Muslims of Mexico, Central America, and the islands of the Caribbean are few in number, but they are increasingly aware of their heritage and identity. In addition, since the late 20th century, Islam has attracted converts throughout the region.

There is a broad consensus that the first Muslim presence in the Caribbean, Central America, and Mexico was established in Cuba, Haiti, and Panama by slaves who were brought from Africa by Spaniards in the 16th century. However, the slave trade does not fully account for the introduction of Islam into every part of the region. For example, in Trinidad and Tobago, it was the indigenous Amerindians who were enslaved by the Spanish. It is therefore unlikely that Muslims arrived there before the locals were freed from slavery by the British, who, from 1839, encouraged indentured workers to migrate from Asia in order to fulfill the islands' labor needs. (An indenture is a contract that binds one person to work for another for a stated period.)

The next influx of Muslims began in the late 19th century, when immigrants from western Asia came to Central America and some of the Caribbean islands to escape the injustices to which they were subjected under the Ottoman Empire. This westerly movement of peoples intensified when the Ottoman Empire disintegrated at the end of World War I (1914–1918).

The most recent period of growth was caused by the conversion of small but significant numbers of indigenous peoples to Islam. This trend emerged in the 1990s and was sustained throughout the first decade of the 21st century.

❖

The most recent period of growth was caused by the conversion of small but significant numbers of indigenous peoples to Islam.

The number of Muslims currently residing in the Caribbean, Central America, and Mexico is difficult to determine with any degree of accuracy because Islam is seldom identified as a distinct religion in national censuses. Where official statistics do exist, they are often out of date and incomplete and regularly indicate population levels lower than those reported by the Muslim communities themselves. There may be several reasons for such anomalies. One possible cause of inconsistency is that

This mosque in Port of Spain, Trinidad, is the focal point of worship for the island's estimated 71,000 Muslims.

The Tzotsil
Mayans from
Chiapas, Mexico, are
among the native
Amerindian peoples
who have been
increasingly attracted
to Islam.

community religious leaders may overstate the size of their membership in order to attract further investment and sponsorship. Another possibility is that assimilation into a new culture modifies the newcomers' social and religious practices. As a consequence, the level of attendance at mosques may not give an accurate reflection of the number of Muslims, especially because there is now a growing trend among them to worship at home. There are also significant—but usually uncounted—numbers of Muslims who take temporary residence in the countries of the region while attempting to overcome problems with legal documentation and immigration to the United States.

Taken as a whole, the population of the Caribbean, Central America, and Mexico is thought to be around 1 percent Muslim. Proportionally, the country with the largest Muslim population is Trinidad and Tobago, with just under 6 percent. The smallest

According to official records, of the 8,240 immigrants from western Asia who came to Mexico between 1878 and 1951, only 343 were Muslims.

Muslim groups are in Cuba, the Dominican Republic, and Haiti (less than 0.1 percent of the populations).

MEXICO

Mexico is the largest—and, with 111 million inhabitants, the most populous—country in the region. Most Mexicans are Catholics—76.5 percent of the population. It is uncertain where Mexico's first Muslims came from or when they began to arrive. They may have been refugees from Spain at the end of the Reconquista (the repossession by Christian forces of the Iberian Peninsula, which had been occupied by Muslims since the 13th century). They may have been slaves who were brought over by ship from Africa in the 16th century. Another possibility is that they were Moriscos, who were evacuated from Spain in the early 17th century. (*Morisco* is a derogatory term applied to former Muslims

in Spain who had nominally adopted Catholicism but who were suspected of having secretly retained their Islamic faith and, as such, were persecuted by the Spanish Inquisition.)

There was certainly an influx of Muslim immigrants in the late 19th century, when people fled western Asia in order to avoid Turkish impositions under Ottoman rule, such as military conscription. Here again, the exact figures are disputed. According to official records, of the 8,240 immigrants from western Asia who came to Mexico between 1878 and 1951, only 343 were Muslims. However, some historians have stressed that these immigrants may have been strongly motivated to conceal their religious beliefs on arrival in a predominantly Catholic country.

Estimations of the number of Muslims in Mexico at the start of the 21st century varied between 2,000 and 300,000. Accurate figures are unobtainable because the census does not require respondents to make any statements about their religious affiliations. Regardless of its numerical strength, the most remarkable feature of Mexico's Islamic community is the high percentage of its members who are recent converts from Catholicism or pre-Columbian religions. These new followers of Islam are thought to account for as much as half of the total number of Mexican Muslims. This development is thought to be, in part, a belated reaction against the forcible imposition of Christianity on the residents of Mexico during the period of Spanish colonial rule before independence in 1821. It is also believed that the economic inequality of modern Mexico has made the social justice advocated by Islam attractive as a more equitable way of ordering society.

The main Muslim organization is the Centro Cultural Islámico de México (CCIM), which was founded in 1994 by Omar (born Mark) Weston, a British-born immigrant convert. Although the CCIM failed in its attempt to construct a mosque in Mexico City, after the withdrawal of funding by the Saudi Arabian embassy, and had to close its two prayer halls in the capital, it has maintained Dawamigo, a *dawa* (missionary office) near the main university, the Universidad Nacional Autónoma de México (UNAM), in the capital's Coyoacán district.

Dawamigo has done much to raise the awareness of Islam among the general public, offering Arabic language classes and the sale of Arab foodstuffs, clothing, and other goods. CCIM also operates a retreat called Dar as Salaam outside the capital, near Cuernavaca in the state of Morelos. Dar as Salaam has a library, a swimming pool, residential accommodation, and beautiful views over Lake Tequesquitengo. It was designed to be a leisure and educational center for the Muslim community, and numerous conferences are held there, together with various festivities of the Muslim calendar, such as Eid al-Fitr. CCIM has assisted the development of communities in other parts of Mexico, including Guadalajara, Monterrey, and San Cristobal de las Casas, and the organization attracts converts to Islam from all over Mexico through the Internet and by means of outreach work, which is carried out by its representatives in person. There are other, smaller, Muslim communities in Aguas Calientes, Morelia, Puebla, Veracruz, and Zacatecas.

The other main center of the conversion of indigenous Mexicans to Islam is in the southern state of Chiapas. There, a Sufi group, an affiliate of the Spanish Comunidad Islámica en España, also known as the Muribatun Movement, attempted to attract members of the Zapatista Army of National Liberation (Ejército Zapatista de Liberación Nacional, EZLN). The EZLN is an armed revolutionary group that declared war on the national government on New Year's Eve, 1993, to protest the signing of the North American Free Trade Agreement (NAFTA), which, they claimed, would harm local farmers. The leader of the EZLN's Muslim converts is Sheikh Abd al-Qadir as-Sufi al-Murabit, a Scot whose birth name was Ian Dallas. His writings are critical of capitalism, Western hegemony, and positivist science. However, in spite of rumored links with terrorist groups, it appears that this small organization is isolated and more concerned with maintaining its madrassa (Koranic school) than with the overthrow of Western society.

BELIZE

Belize—population 308,000—is a small country bounded by Mexico, Guatemala, and the Caribbean Sea. It is predominantly Catholic but has one officially recognized Muslim organization, the Islamic Mission of Belize, which was founded in the 1960s and received state approval as a religious body in 1978. The Islamic Mission is active in the Muslim community and functions on a pan-Islamic basis, focusing on the *ummah* (religious community) as a whole and ignoring factional divides, such as the long-standing schism between Shiites and Sunnis.

In cooperation with the government, the Islamic Mission runs an elementary school that provides basic education for young children and caters to their spiritual needs. While this is an Islamic school, children do not need to be Muslims to attend. The Mission plans to develop part of a 350-acre (142-hectare) site leased from the government in the Jannahville area of Belize City into an Islamic quarter in which Muslims can combine homes, occupations, and education in a self-sufficient community. The success of this project will be key to the future development of Islam in Belize.

COSTA RICA

Costa Rica has two small Islamic communities. The larger community is in the capital, San José; most of the remaining Muslims reside in the city of Alajuela. The Centro Cultural Musulmán de Costa Rica, which is situated in San José, has strong links with other Latin American Muslim organizations, especially those in Costa Rica's two neighbors, Nicaragua and Panama. Another Muslim community, the Centro Islámico de Costa Rica, meets in the capital's Omar mosque. There is also a *dawa* and a *tabligh* (calling and conveying) missionary group called al-Markaz, which has been active in propagating the Islamic message. The Muslims of Costa Rica are mainly a mixture of immigrants from Egypt, Lebanon, Libya, and Palestine, together with some converts from Colombia and Costa Rica itself.

EL SALVADOR

El Salvador has two main Muslim groups, a Shiite community and the Centro Islámico Árabe Salvadoreño, both of which are composed mainly of immigrants. El Salvador has received immigrants from Lebanon, Palestine, and Turkey, most of whom were Christian, although a small number of Lebanese and Turkish Muslims founded the

Mezquita de la Luz mosque in the capital, San Salvador. The Centro Islámico Árabe Salvadoreño promotes Islam in the print media and on television. The group is dedicated to correcting misinterpretations of Islam and its history, in addition to increasing awareness of the religion. An outreach center, the Villa Palestina, provides medical care, education, vocational training, and facilities for worship for 163 local Muslim families suffering from economic hardship. The Shiite community has done much to publicize Islam in El Salvador since 2004, when it began producing literature about the religion and founded an Islamic library, which is named Fatima az-Zarah, after the daughter of the Prophet Muhammad. Arab immigrants in El Salvador have generally integrated successfully into the wider Catholic community, with several individuals making valuable contributions to public life, although there is something of a renaissance of Arabic cultural traditions among the second and third generations of immigrants, who are exploring their cultural heritage.

GUATEMALA

The vast majority of Guatemala's Muslim community is composed of Arab immigrants from Palestine. They are active in missionary work and offer classes in Islam to teach people about the faith. Their mosque is the Mezquita Al Dawa Islámica de Guatemala. Estimates place the Muslim population in the low thousands but, once again, there is a lack of accurate data.

HONDURAS

Honduras is thought to have one of the region's larger Muslim populations, although accurate figures are unobtainable because the national census contains no questions about religious affiliation. The proportion of Arab immigrants is higher in Honduras than in any other country of Central America or the Caribbean. The two main Muslim communities, the Centro Islámico de Honduras and the Comunidad Islámica de Honduras, are located in Cortés and San Pedro Sula, respectively.

NICARAGUA

Nicaragua has a significant minority of Muslim immigrants and converts to Islam but, again, no accurate figures are available to determine exact numbers.

A mosque was established in 1999 in the Ciudad Jardin area of the capital, Managua, and this has provided a spacious place of worship for the country's Muslim community. The chief Muslim organization in Nicaragua is the Asociación Cultural Nicaragüense-Islámica.

The Shiite community has set up a new organization called the Centro Cultural Islámico Nicaragüense, which actively communicates what it means to be a Muslim to the wider population, including the indigenous Amerindian peoples.

PANAMA

In 1552 Spanish colonists brought African slaves to Panama to work in their copper mines. The captives were Malinke, a West African people who are still recorded as an ethnicity in Panama today. According to Panamanian folk history, the Malinke were Muslims who narrowly escaped death when their ship sank as it neared Central America. Almost 500 of them swam for the shore, reaching Panama. There they appointed one of their number, a man named Bayano, to lead them against the Spanish slave masters. It is said that, even at this time, several mosques were established.

Bayano was captured by the Spanish conquistador Pedro de Ursúa, who sent him into exile where he later died, after which it is said that all remnants of Islam were eradicated from Panamanian society. Today, this story is used to support the contention that the ancestors of some modern Panamanians might have been Muslims centuries ago.

Panama has four principal places of worship, founded by different segments of the Muslim community. Most immigrants arrived during the 20th century and came to Panama from Lebanon and South Asia, especially India and Pakistan. During the 1970s, Panamanian Muslims were influenced by the Nation of Islam, an African American movement and organization, founded in 1930 in the United States, whose teachings combined traditional Islam with black nationalist ideas. In the 21st century, Panama's Muslim groups, such as the Centro Cultural Islámico de Colón, have made themselves open to all citizens, regardless of their religion, to increase general awareness of Islam.

THE CARIBBEAN

It is generally agreed that most of the Muslims who currently inhabit the Caribbean are descendants of immigrants from India and Indonesia who came to work as indentured laborers after Britain—which ruled many of the islands of the region—abolished slavery in the 19th century. African slaves were first brought to the Caribbean island of Hispaniola (now divided between the Dominican Republic and Haiti) by the Spanish in 1501. Later, the French took Muslim slaves from West Africa to their dominions in the region—Guadeloupe, Haiti, and

Martinique. By the start of the 21st century, Martinique had become the adopted home of a sizable immigrant population from Palestine.

Few Caribbean islands have mosques, so Muslims pray in private homes or in public halls. However, in Trinidad and Tobago, the strong Muslim presence—5.8 percent of the 1.2 million population—is large enough to support a religious organization called the Anjuman Sunnat-ul-Jamaat Association (ASJA), which employs a small full-time staff. The organization operates libraries, several schools, and a bank that offers interest-free credit facilities. Sunni Islamic activities throughout the Caribbean are coordinated through the Caribbean Islamic Secretariat, which was founded in 1988 and conducts missionary work, promotes economic development, produces Islamic literature, and coordinates Muslim education.

In Cuba, Muslim diplomats attend the Arab House. This purpose-built 1940s building in the capital, Havana, is partly a place of communal worship and partly a museum of Arab culture. Non-diplomats pray in private homes as the construction of religious buildings is not permitted by the communist regime. However, the Muslim World League (MWL) has entered negotiations with the Cuban government for the establishment of an official place of Muslim worship on the island.

In Jamaica, there are several Muslim organizations, including the Islamic Education and Dawa Center and the Islamic Council of Jamaica in Kingston. Other islands have religious communities but often no formal place of worship. For example, in Antigua and Barbuda, the immigrant population from Lebanon and Syria has its own International Islamic Society and a Muslim Student Association

at the local American University, but neither island has a mosque.

The Islamic community in Barbados is another that traces its connection with Islam back to the slave trade, although later immigration has added diversity to the Muslim population. Nationally, Islam is represented by the Barbados Muslim Association, and there are several places of worship, including the Madina, Makki, and Jumma *masjid* (prayer halls). Other Caribbean states have fewer facilities, meaning that the education of Muslim children can be an issue. In the Bahamas, for example, Muslim parents have made representations to the government for respect of their constitutional rights, because their children are subjected to an exclusively Christian education in the local schools.

The influence of Islamic culture is evident in the Moorish style of these buildings in Havana, Cuba.

See Also
United States and Canada 348-361 ❖
South America 370-377 ❖

Chapter 22

SOUTH AMERICA

The 13 modern nations of South America all have Muslim populations that, though small in percentage terms, are of considerable historical significance and growing political importance in the 21st century.

The exact date of the first arrival of Islam on the continent of South America is unknown. It is possible—but unlikely—that some Moors (Portuguese and Spanish Muslims) accompanied the earliest explorers and invaders on their voyages across the Atlantic Ocean from the Iberian Peninsula in the 16th century. What is almost certain—but largely undocumented—is that many, if not most, of the slaves brought to South America from West Africa between the 16th century and the 19th century were Muslims. However, nearly all of the forced laborers who survived were converted to

❖

The first modern wave of immigrants came from Egypt, Lebanon, Palestine, and Syria as Muslim Arabs fled the disintegrating Ottoman Empire.

Christianity. The most recent period of Muslim immigration to South America began in the mid-19th century, when political conditions in Asia created a diaspora of economic migrants and refugees, and has continued into the 21st century. The first modern wave of immigrants came from Egypt, Lebanon, Palestine, and Syria as Muslim Arabs fled the disintegrating Ottoman Empire. They were later joined by many migrants from India, Indonesia, and Pakistan.

ARGENTINA

With around 500,000 practicing Muslims in a total population of 41 million, Argentina has South America's largest active Islamic minority. Although the early history of European settlement of the country is poorly documented, it seems unlikely that Muslims came to Argentina with the first wave of Portuguese and Spanish explorers in the 16th century or with the 19th-century influx of Spanish and Italian settlers who eventually formed the majority of the immigrant population. Most of the Muslims in modern Argentina are Arab immigrants or the descendants of Arab immigrants from Lebanon and Syria. They began to arrive during and after the dissolution of the Ottoman Empire at the end of World War I (1914–1918). In addition to the practicing Muslim population, there are an estimated 3.5 million Argentines of Arab heritage. Among them is the family of Carlos Menem (b. 1930), who converted to

Carlos Menem, president of Argentina (1995–1999), was the son of Muslim immigrants from Syria. Although he converted to Christianity in the 1960s, his wife and son remained faithful to Islam.

Christianity (which, for the greater part of the 20th century, was the state religion) in order to achieve his political ambitions. Menem later became the president of the republic (r. 1989–1999). The requirement for the head of state to be a Roman Catholic was abolished in 1994, and that legislation coincided with a new phase of Muslim immigration, mainly from South Asia.

Argentina has numerous mosques, the largest of which—the King Fahd Islamic Cultural Center in a prosperous residential district of Buenos Aires—was completed in 1989. There are other mosques in the national capital and in several regional centers. They are most concentrated along the Triple Frontier, the three-way border between Argentina, Brazil, and Paraguay.

BOLIVIA

The officially documented number of Muslims in Bolivia is very small—only around 1,000 people out of a population of 9.8 million—but they exert a large and visible influence on the life of the nation. Their high profile has caused some commentators to speculate that the actual number of believers in Islam is much higher. The importance of the Muslim faith is reflected in the proliferation of Islamic organizations throughout the country. Among the most prominent of these organizations are the Centros Islámicos Bolivianos (CIB; Bolivian Islamic Centers), which were created in 1986 by Imam Ahmed Amer Abu Sharar, a Palestinian immigrant. The CIB currently has branches in the cities of Santa Cruz, Sucre, and Cochabainba. The CIB also has Bolivia's only mosque, which was completed in 1994 in Santa Cruz. In Sucre,

there is a Muslim group called the Mulumana Casilla, and in Santa Cruz there is an outreach community known as the La Paz Islamic Center, which aims to spread Islam into La Paz. The British-based charity Muslim Aid works in Bolivia to support groups of indigenous people who have converted to Islam, providing them with, among other things, laptop computers to enable them to communicate with fellow Muslims worldwide.

BRAZIL

During the European colonial period, which began in the 16th century, Brazil had more Muslims than any other country in South America. Most of them—perhaps as many as 3 million—were slaves who had been forcibly transshipped from West Africa by the Portuguese. Muslims played a major role in the Bahia Uprising of 1835, in which around 300 African slaves rose against their masters. The revolt was put down within 3 hours by the colonial armed forces. Between 50 and 100 of the rebels were killed in the fighting; most of the others were later executed or banished. In response to this insurrection, the Portuguese rulers launched a campaign to convert African slaves to Christianity. Nevertheless, it is thought that, by the start of the 20th century, there were still around 100,000 Muslims in Brazil.

The next wave of Muslim immigration to Brazil came after World War I and comprised Arab refugees from Lebanon and Syria. At the start of the 21st century, estimates of the number of Muslims in Brazil varied widely. The lowest total—27,239—was determined by the 2000 census. Most of these people lived in and around São Paulo. However, independent research by the Pontifical Catholic University in Rio de Janeiro has put the

number of Muslims in Brazil at almost 2 million—1 percent of the total population of 199 million. There are four main groups: African Brazilians of Muslim heritage who have assimilated into mainstream society; descendants of the early-20th-century Arab immigrants; a more recent influx of Muslims who immigrated from South Asia in the late 20th century; and an unconfirmed number of converts who were influenced by the life and work of Malcolm X (1925–1965), the African American leader who himself converted to Islam and articulated concepts of race pride and black nationalism. The figure of 2 million includes both active practitioners and nominal followers of Islam.

CHILE

The Muslim population of modern Chile is small—just over 3,000 out of a population of 16.6 million—but Islam has been present in the country since the arrival of the earliest European explorers. In *Chronicles of the History of Chile*, Aurelio Díaz Meza (1879–1933) noted that at least one Morisco (a convert from Islam to Catholicism) accompanied the Spaniard Diego de Almagro (1475–1538) on his expedition to the region. Later, the immigration statistics of 1854 record the arrival of a handful of Arab immigrants, and the 1895 census records 58 Muslims living in the north of Chile. There were 1,498 Muslims in Chile in 1907. Most of these immigrants were reported to have come from Lebanon, Palestine, and Syria after the collapse of the Ottoman Empire. Members of this community founded Chile's Sociedad Unión Musulmana (Society of Muslim Union) in 1926. Among the nation's other Islamic organizations is the Sociedad Musulmana de Chile (Muslim Society of Chile). Under the military dictatorship of general Augusto Pinochet (r. 1973–1990), the activities of these Muslim associations,

This photograph shows the Mosque of Foz do Iguazu on the Brazilian side of the Triple Frontier—the three-way border between Argentina, Brazil, and Paraguay.

373

along with all other nongovernmental organizations, were severely restricted. The fall of the military dictatorship in 1990 brought many social and economic reforms that enabled the Muslim community to take a more prominent role in Chilean society. The first mosque in Chile, the Mezquita as-Salam in the capital, Santiago, was commissioned in 1989 and was opened in 1995 by the king of Malaysia. Another place of worship, the Bilal mosque in Iquique, was completed in 1999. Among other focal points of Islamic faith and religious instruction is the Centro Cultural Mohammed VI—named for the king of Morocco—in Coquimbo. In addition to

After the September 11 attacks there was a backlash against Chilean Muslims by a small minority who saw Islam as synonymous with terrorism.

the immigrant Muslim community, a small, but significant proportion of the Chilean Muslim population are converts to Islam from Christianity. Conversion has been attributed to a number of factors including the increased visibility and community participation of Muslims; anti-secular sentiment in South America; and a sense of identification among some Chileans with their Moorish or West African ancestry. After the September 11 attacks there was a backlash against Chilean Muslims by a small minority who saw Islam as synonymous with terrorism. Most modern Chilean Muslims are Sunnis. There is also a Shiite minority and a small number of Sufis; most of the latter group are converts of non-Arab heritage.

COLOMBIA

At the start of the 21st century, the estimated number of Muslims in Colombia was around 10,000—less than 0.02 percent of the population of 45.6 million. Although Muslims form only a very small minority, the national capital, Bogotá, has at least five Islamic centers, and there are other Muslim community organizations in the provincial cities of Guajira, Maicao, Medellín, Nariño, San Andrés, and Santa Marta. Maicao is the location of Colombia's principal Islamic place of worship, the Mosque of Omar Ibn Al-Khattab, the second-largest mosque in South America. The city also has several Islamic elementary and secondary schools—facilities that do not exist anywhere else in Colombia. From 2007, Colombia was the location for a Spanish-language remake of *O Clone* (The Clone), the popular Brazilian TV soap opera, first screened in 2002, about a Muslim girl torn between her Islamic heritage and modern society.

Most of Colombia's Muslims are the descendants of immigrants from Lebanon who came to the country in the 1920s at around the same time as a larger group of Arabs who espoused Maronite Christianity.

ECUADOR

Most of Ecuador's first Muslims were traders from Egypt, Lebanon, Palestine, and Syria who fled to South America to escape World War I (1914–1918) and World War II (1939–1945). The main areas in which they settled were Quito and Guayaquil, although they eventually dispersed to inhabit Esmeraldas, Los Ríos, and Manab as well. Many Muslims assimilated readily into Ecuadorian culture, sometimes adopting Christianity, at other times intermarrying with native Ecuadorian people. More recent waves of immigration—from Pakistan and

The child of a Colombian mother and a Lebanese immigrant father, Faryd Mondragón became in 1993 the first Muslim to represent the Colombian national soccer team, for which he was the goalkeeper.

West Africa in the last quarter of the 20th century—have increased the Muslim proportion of Ecuador's 14.5 million population, although its exact numerical strength is unknown.

Founded in 1994, the Sunni Centro Islámico del Ecuador became the first Ecuadorian Muslim organization to be recognized by the state. This organization is active in the dissemination of Islamic literature in the Spanish language and provides a place of worship for two of each of the daily prayers and the Friday sermons. However, there is as yet no Islamic school in Ecuador. Most Ecuadorian Muslim women wear the *hijab* and long dresses.

FRENCH GUIANA

There are no statistics to confirm the number of Muslims in French Guiana, although it is thought to be a very small percentage of the total population of only 221,000. It is reported that the Muslim immigrant community hails chiefly from Afghanistan and Lebanon. There are Islamic schools and community halls for worship in both Kourou and Cayenne.

GUYANA

According to official statistics, around 7 percent of the 772,000 population of Guyana is Muslim. This figure is relatively reliable because it has been determined by the Organization of Islamic Countries (OIC), of which Guyana has been a member since 1998.

Guyana's first Muslims were probably African slaves, but it appears that their religious practices were either abandoned or suppressed. Islam has been in Guyana continuously only since South Asian immigration—principally from India—began under colonialism in 1838. The OIC reports that there are at least 125 *masjid* (prayer halls) across the country.

A Muslim woman crosses the bridge over the Paraná River between Paraguay and Brazil.

In addition to the OIC, there are several other formal Muslim organizations, including the Guyana Islamic Trust, the Guyana Muslim Mission, the Guyana United Sad'r Islamic Anjuman, the Hujjatal Ulamaa, the Muslim Youth, the Rose Hall Town Islamic Center, the Tablighi Jamaat, and a Salafi group.

Since the 1970s, the government of Guyana has officially recognized several non-Christian religious days as national public holidays. The major Muslim festivals that are now recognized by the entire country include Eid al-Fitr (the end of Ramadan, the sacred month of fasting), Eid al-Adha (the feast of sacrifice), and Mawlid (the birthday of the Prophet Muhammad). The specific dates of these holidays vary from year to year according to the Islamic lunar calendar.

PARAGUAY

Paraguay has a very small Islamic minority. Although there are no confirmed figures, it is estimated that there are only around 500 Muslims in a total population of 7 million. Most Paraguayan Muslims are the descendants of immigrants from Lebanon, Palestine, and Syria who came to South America as refugees from political upheavals in their native countries. The major Islamic organization in Paraguay is the Centro Benéfico Cultural Islámico, which operates in and around the capital, Asuncíon.

PERU

Most of the Muslims in Peru—around 1,000 people in a total population of 29.5 million—immigrated from Iran and Palestine during the 20th century. It has been suggested by historians that some Peruvian Muslims may be the descendants of Moorish evacuees who left Spain (particularly Granada) in the late 15th century at the end of the Reconquista (the repossession by Christian forces of the Iberian Peninsula, which had been occupied by Muslims since the 13th century). The modern Muslim community in Peru has no official mosque—prayers are held in local community centers—but it does have an Islamic school. Its principal organization is the Asociación Islámica del Peru (Islamic Association of Peru), which is based in the capital, Lima. Occasionally, as in other countries of South America, Arab architectural influences may be found in Peru, notably in some of the pilasters used in balconies and columns.

SURINAME

The first Europeans to visit Suriname were Spaniards, who sailed there in the 16th century. The land was then settled by the English in the 17th century and became a Dutch colony in 1667. Slaves were brought from Africa to work the land—many of these people may well have been Muslims, but they were nearly all converted to Christianity. After the abolition of slavery in 1863, there was a new influx of workers, this time mainly from India and Java. It is from this wave of immigrants that most of the Muslims in modern Suriname are descended. Since gaining independence from the Netherlands in 1975, Suriname has received a small wave of Muslim refugees from Afghanistan.

According to the 2004 census, 19.6 percent of the population of Suriname are Muslim—94,000 of the national total of 481,000 people. This, in percentage terms, is the highest concentration of any country in South America. However, census figures are not wholly reliable because some

people may conceal their religious commitments, while other people may have inadvertently been omitted from the surveys. Some commentators have suggested that the total number of Muslims in Suriname may be as high as 135,000— 28 percent of the population. Whatever the true overall figure, the census showed that the concentration of Muslims varies greatly from region to region of Suriname— between 0.2 percent and 40.4 percent.

URUGUAY

The Muslims of Uruguay—between 300 and 400 people in a total population of 3.5 million—have no mosque. Their two main places of worship are the Islamic Center in Canelones and the Egyptian Islamic Center in the grounds of the Egyptian Embassy in the capital, Montevideo. The latter was Uruguay's first formal place of Muslim worship, bringing immigrants and converts together for Friday prayers.

VENEZUELA

Estimates of the Muslim population of Venezuela vary widely between 100,000 and 750,000 out of a national total of 27 million. However, as in other nations of South America, there are no definitive statistics. The Muslims are most concentrated in the capital, Caracas, and on Margarita Island, in the Caribbean Sea off the northeast mainland. Most Venezuelan Muslims are Arabs of Lebanese, Palestinian, and Syrian extraction. There are also Muslims of Iranian and Turkish heritage, together with some indigenous converts. The Mosque of Sheikh Ibrahim Al-Ibrahim in Caracas is the largest Islamic religious building in South America. There are other mosques in several provincial cities, including Maracaibo and Yaracuy.

See Also

United States and Canada 348-361 ❖ Mexico, Central America, and the Caribbean 362-369 ❖ Australasia and the Pacific 378-385 ❖

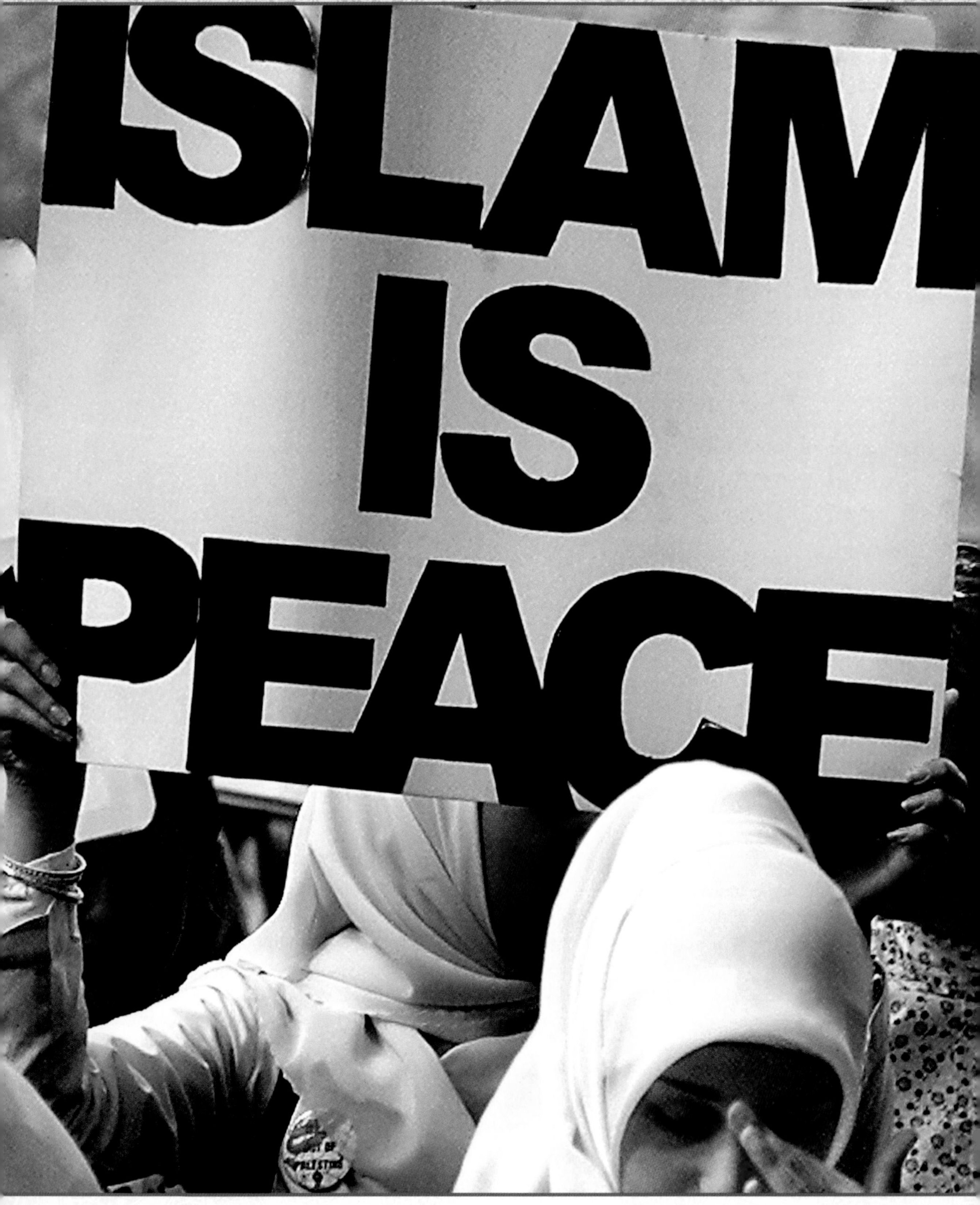
ISLAM
IS
PEACE

Chapter 23

AUSTRALASIA AND THE PACIFIC

Over the years, migrants from Asia, Europe, and Africa have worked or settled in Australasia—Australia, New Zealand, Fiji, Papua New Guinea, and the neighboring Pacific Ocean islands—for economic or political reasons. Muslim settlement in Australasia has been facilitated by geographical proximity to Asia, and Muslims have commuted to or settled primarily for economic reasons.

The first settlers in Australia and New Zealand were predominantly Caucasians of Christian faith. Fiji was a British colony until 1970, and Papua New Guinea was also under European control for several centuries. Historically, economic factors may have motivated people to move to Australasia. However, in the contemporary period, some refugees and asylum seekers have fled persecution in their respective countries to settle, particularly in Australia and New Zealand.

AUSTRALIA

Muslim contact with Australia can be traced before European settlement; in the 17th century Macassarese people from Indonesia made trade links with the indigenous Australians. British-European settlement on the Australian continent occurred when British and Irish convicts were transported there between 1787 and 1868. Although a few Muslim convicts from the British colonies arrived in Australia, official Muslim settlement began with the arrival of Afghans in the 1860s,

when they were introduced as camel drivers for exploration purposes. By 1901 Afghan camel drivers numbered between 2,000 and 4,000.

Other early Muslim ethnic groups were the Malays, Javanese, Indians, and Albanians. Malay people from the Indonesian Archipelago were mostly Muslims. In the

Official Muslim settlement in Australia began with the arrival of Afghans in the 1860s.

1870s Malays worked as pearl divers in Western Australian waters, particularly in Broome. They were single men and came to Australia as indentured laborers under contract, usually for between three and seven years. They often worked in exchange for accommodation, food, and other essentials, or for passage to a new country, rather than for any monetary reward. The Malay indentured pearl divers

Young Muslims march in a peace rally in Sydney, Australia, in 2001 to protest against Australia's material support for the war in Afghanistan.

were retained for long periods as they provided cheap labor and acclimatized more easily to the conditions and requirements of the industry than did Europeans. Muslims from the Indonesian island of Java arrived in Queensland as indentured laborers in the early 1880s to work in the sugar industry. After serving a contractual term, the Javanese laborers were free to farm or take up their own trades. Indian Muslims, who mostly arrived in the 1890s, worked with the Afghan laborers. Some were also employed as street vendors, cloth merchants, or shopkeepers.

The Afghans and some Indians lived in towns, that were segregated from the white

This stone marks the grave of Afghan camel driver Zeriph Khan. He was buried in Bourke Cemetery, New South Wales, in 1903.

community. They were allowed to build mosques, and their imams were also permitted to enter Australia for short periods of time. The Afghan camel drivers are regarded as the founders of Islam in Australia; they constructed the first mosque at Marree, South Australia, in 1882. Although this mosque no longer exists, some major mosques built by the early Afghan settlers (together with some Indian settlers) still stand: Adelaide, South Australia (built 1890); Broken Hill, New South Wales (built 1891); Perth, Western Australia (built 1905); and Brisbane, Queensland (built 1907).

In the 1890s Australia experienced an economic depression and a shortage of employment opportunities. Non-Europeans were alleged to have worked at lower rates than white laborers, thus seemingly taking their jobs. Apart from economic fears, there were also racial concerns that the continent would be contaminated by "nonwhite" people. In 1901 the Immigration Restriction Act initiated the "White Australia" period, which reduced the number of Asian laborers, also known as aliens. Under this act, aliens who attempted to enter Australia had to submit to a medical examination and a dictation test of 50 words in any language chosen by the immigration officer. This test was crudely discriminatory because the language chosen was unlikely to be understood by the applicant; however, it remained policy until 1958. The "White Australia" policy resulted in a rapid decline of non-European migrants (including Muslims) and the deportation of many existing aliens.

Albanians arrived in Australia in the 1920s and worked mainly as agricultural laborers and land clearers. Being white, they were allowed to bring their families

with them. However, because Italy occupied Albania during World War II, the Albanian settlers became viewed as "enemy aliens" and were alleged to be a fascist threat; some Albanians were interned.

The Muslim population was very small during the "White Australia" period. In 1947 Muslims numbered 2,704. Between 1964 and 1966 a shift of immigration policy occurred with an emphasis on integration; finally, in 1973, a multicultural policy was introduced that aimed to impart equal opportunities to all Australians

Australia's Muslims are heterogeneous in language, color, and ethnic culture; the only element they share is their religion.

irrespective of their race, color, ethnic origin, or religion. Turkish and Lebanese Muslims arrived in relatively large numbers in 1969 and 1970, respectively, and the 1980s saw a larger rise in the Muslim population overall. The immigration intake since the 1970s has mostly been for economic reasons and Australia's need for labor, while some people have also been accepted for humanitarian reasons. In 2006 Australia's Muslim population was 340,392, or 1.7 percent of the national population.

Australia's Muslims are ethnically diverse, coming from nations including Afghanistan, Albania, Bangladesh, Bosnia, Eritrea, Ethiopia, Fiji, India, Indonesia, Iran, Iraq, Lebanon, Malaysia, Pakistan, Palestine, Sri Lanka, Somalia, Sudan, South Africa, and Turkey. Australian converts to Islam are known as reverts. Australia's Muslims are heterogeneous in language, color, and

School children at Risallah College Primary School in Sydney take part in a lesson exploring the acceptance of different faiths in Australian culture.

ethnic culture; the only element they share is their religion. Although religion and culture are different aspects of ethnicity, it is argued that all Muslims share an Islamic culture, which can often be identified through names, dress code, and eating and drinking habits. Such identity makes them a distinct cultural group separate from the predominantly Anglo-Celtic and European Christian Australian population.

Australia's Muslim community includes more than 100 groups, representing the interests of Muslims at a local or regional level. Islamic councils representing the broader Muslim community exist in all Australian states and territories and come together in a national body, the Australian Federation of Islamic Councils. There are 10 Islamic primary schools in Australia, 11 combined primary and secondary schools, and approximately 100 mosques, mainly in New South Wales and Victoria.

Muslims in Australia vary from

professionals to tradespeople; however, some Muslims are disadvantaged in the labor market. In 1996, 2001, and 2006 the unemployment rate of Australian Muslims was three times higher than the national average. Some Muslims who look conspicuous because of their Islamic attire have been vilified by some members of the wider community. This has intensified since the terrorist attacks on the United States on September 11, 2001, largely because asylum seekers have been perceived as terrorists. Some Islamic schools and colleges have been vandalized, and the Kuraby Mosque in Brisbane was burned down in an arson attack on September 22, 2001.

Although the terrorist acts of militant Muslims since 9/11, including the Australian Embassy bombing in Jakarta in 2003, may have influenced some mainstream Australians, the aftermath of the 9/11 attacks has had a positive effect in other respects. It has encouraged some

Australian Muslims to devise initiatives to explain themselves and their religion better to other Australians, informing the wider community that extremists form only a tiny minority of the 1.4 billion Muslims worldwide. Interest in Islam and Muslims among mainstream Australians has increased, and many seminars, conferences, and community events have been held to foster better understanding. The result of such initiatives is hoped to be greater tolerance and understanding between cultural groups and a more integrated multicultural Australian society.

NEW ZEALAND

A Muslim presence in New Zealand could be seen as early as 1874. The 1874 census reports that a few Muslims worked with the Chinese in the goldfields in the south of the country. Some Indian men of Gujarati Muslim background arrived in the early decades of the 20th century and opened small shops, mainly in the towns south of Auckland. Under the "White New Zealand" policy, which ran between 1900 and 1974, nonwhite immigrant men were not allowed to bring their wives and families with them; however, when their sons turned 18 years old they could be brought over to work.

The first Indian Muslim to come to New Zealand was Ismail Bhikoo. In the 1930s Bhikoo's five sons arrived in New Zealand. In 1950 Suleiman Bhikoo, along with 15 other Muslims, formed the New Zealand Muslim Association in Auckland. Initially its membership consisted of the few Gujarati families living in the area, who gathered in private homes to observe the *salat* (Muslim prayer), attend Koran classes, and participate in religious celebrations. As their numbers grew, the need for a larger, fixed place of worship and education became necessary. Thus an ordinary house was bought and converted to an Islamic center in Auckland in 1957.

New Zealand maintained its restrictive immigration policy during the 1960s but gradually came to realize that the country's future lay in Asia. In the 1970s New Zealand relaxed its immigration policy toward Asia and expanded its markets there after Great Britain, upon which New Zealand had relied for agricultural exports, entered the European Economic Community. In 1972 the government reviewed its immigration policy and in 1974 announced the abandonment of "White New Zealand" and introduced a new policy that would secure "a unified and nondiscriminatory approach to New Zealand's needs." New Zealand has since endorsed ethnic diversity by ratifying a number of international conventions and domestic legislation based on eliminating discrimination and assuring fundamental rights for all citizens, including minorities.

In the 1950s and 1960s, some Islamic immigrants arrived from Turkey and the Balkans, but New Zealand's Muslim population remained very low, having numbered just 205 in 1951. The 1960s and 1970s saw the arrival of some Fijian Indians, and in 1971, the Muslim population in New Zealand was 779, increasing to 36,072 by 2006. New Zealand's Muslims now reflect most of the huge geographic expanse from Morocco in the west to Indonesia and the Philippines in the east, and from central Asia and the Balkans in the north to sub-Saharan Africa in the south. There has also been a small number of converts to Islam among New Zealand's Maori population.

PAPUA NEW GUINEA AND THE PACIFIC ISLANDS

Muslims in Papua New Guinea form a tiny minority. In July 2007 the total population was 5,795,887. A large majority of Papua New Guineans are Christians (96 per cent in 2000), although many combine their Christian faith with traditional indigenous beliefs and practices. There were about 2,000 Muslims in Papua New Guinea (0.03 per cent) in 2003. In 1988, Muslims set up the first Islamic center, and by 2007 there were six more. The first mosque was built in Port Moresby. Although the number of Muslims in Papua New Guinea is negligible, there have been incidents of discrimination and Islamophobia against them. According to the United States Department of State's annual report on religious freedom, Muslims were subjected to sporadic minor attacks, such as small fires at or in the only mosque in the country.

There is a small Muslim concentration in other Pacific islands such as the Solomon Islands, New Caledonia, Vanuatu, and East Timor. Islam is more established in East Timor where Muslim adherents form 5 per cent of the total East Timorese population. East Timor's former Primer Minister, Mari Alkatiri, was a Muslim.

A coup in Fiji in 1987 led to an influx of Fijian Indians, including many Muslims, and the continuing political uncertainties in Fiji led to more Fijian migrants entering New Zealand. New Zealand is noted for its generous refugee policy. The 1990s saw the arrival of many Somalian refugees; later Somalian migrants arrived to join their families. Other groups of Muslim refugees came from Iraq, Bosnia, Kosovo, and Kurdistan. In 2001, New Zealand accepted 208 refugees from Afghanistan.

Several regionally based Muslim organizations are affiliated with the national organization, the Federation of Islamic Associations of New Zealand (FIANZ). FIANZ has an appointed board of ulema (Islamic scholars) consisting of seven imams, who hold university degrees in Sharia (Islamic law) and who lead the congregations of New Zealand's seven mosques. There are two Islamic schools in New Zealand. The Al-Madinah School is coeducational, and the Zayed College is a girls' school. FIANZ is also involved with the certification of meat as halal. There is a huge halal meat export market to the Middle East, and in 2004, halal meat exports to the Islamic world were in excess of NZ $200 million.

New Zealand's Muslims follow both Sunni and Shia branches of Islam, which causes some division within the Muslim community. In New Zealand there is disagreement between those Muslims who celebrate the Prophet Muhammad's birthday and those who do not. The Muslims of Sufi tradition (mostly South Asian Muslims) celebrate the Prophet's birthday. There is also a division between those who insist on a more liberal interpretation of Islam and those, often labeled fundamentalist, Salafi, or Wahhabi, who insist on a strict interpretation.

Many Muslims suffered personal assaults following the terrorist attacks on the United States on September 11, 2001. After the London bombings in July 2005, graffiti was sprayed on an Auckland mosque; in Dunedin dung was thrown on Muslim women, and eggs were thrown at the mosque. Some Muslims felt that the media failed to recognize diversity among Muslims. Under New Zealand's security laws, some citizens who appear visibly different because of their beards or Islamic attire have been stopped and searched. In March 2003, the Algerian-born refugee Ahmed Zaoui was alleged to be a security threat to New Zealand and was refused refugee status. Zaoui was

imprisoned despite the Refugee Status Appeal Authority finding that he was a legitimate refugee. Finally, in September 2007, New Zealand Security Service objections were withdrawn, thus allowing Zaoui to remain in New Zealand. Overall, however, Muslims in New Zealand are content with their settlement and the freedom to practice their religion.

Fiji

Between 1879 and 1916, indentured Indian Muslims worked in the sugarcane fields in Fiji. After the indentured labor system was abolished in 1920, Indo-Fijians settled in the sugarcane belts. As the number of Muslim Indians increased through indenture and migration, they gradually established various Islamic organizations, including the Fiji Muslim League in 1926. Muslim schools were established in Fiji in the 1950s, and by 1995 there were 21

Sunni primary schools and eight Sunni high schools.

Fiji's Muslims sought to obtain equal opportunities in employment and education through political representation. In 1964 Fijian-born Siddiq Koya of the Federation Party became the Indo-Fijian leader and addressed the social disadvantage of Indo-Fijians. In 1970 Fiji gained independence from Great Britain, and Muslims asserted themselves more strongly. According to provisional results from the 2007 census, Fijian Muslims comprised 6.5 percent of the total population.

Fiji has witnessed three military coups since 1987. Because of this political instability and to seek better economic opportunities, some Fijian Muslims moved to Australia or New Zealand. However, the presence of mosques, schools, and Islamic associations remains a visible reminder of Fiji's Muslim community.

Fiji's Muslims make up around 6.5 percent of the total population. This mosque in Nadi on the Fijian island of Viti Levu is one of many dotted around the island group.

See Also
Southeast Asia 292-303 ❖ China 314-321 ❖ United States and Canada 348-361 ❖ South America 370-377 ❖

GLOSSARY

ayatollah a high-ranking Shiite Muslim cleric. Holders of the title are experts in various aspects of Islam, particularly law, ethics, and philosophy.

Ba'ath a secular political party advocating the formation of a single Arab socialist nation. It has been in power in Syria since 1963 and was the ruling party in Iraq from 1968 to 2003.

bida any innovation in the practice of Islam that is not derived from the traditional Sunna of the Muslim community.

caliph (from *khalifah*, Arabic: "successor") a religious and political leader of Islam; successor to Muhammad. The office and realm held by a caliph is called a caliphate.

emir a military commander, governor of a province, or a high military official.

Fatah (Palestine National Liberation Movement) Arab political and military organization, founded in the late 1950s. Until the 1990s, Fatah was a militant organization affiliated with the Palestine Liberation Organization (PLO). Since the 1993 peace accords between the PLO and Israel, it has acted as a political party within Palestine.

fatwa a legal opinion. In the West, the term has been widely taken to mean "death sentence." This incorrect translation arose after the fatwa of 1989 in which Ayatollah Ruhollah Khomeini (ruler of Iran, 1979–1989) publicly condemned the Indian British author Salman Rushdie (b. 1947) for his book *The Satanic Verses*.

fiqh Islamic jurisprudence. *Fiqh* expands and develops Sharia law on the basis of the continuing judgments and rulings of Muslim jurists. The term is used particularly with reference to judgments concerning the observance of rituals and morals, and with social legislation. A person trained in *fiqh* is known as a *faqih* (plural: *fuqaha*).

Grameen Bank a Bangladeshi bank founded in 1976 to provide small loans to poor individuals. It advances money to borrowers in the expectation that they will repay the debt because of their sense of honor and in response to peer pressure. In this, the Grameen Bank differs from Western-style banks, which require security for any loan.

Hamas (Arabic: "zeal") a militant Palestinian organization founded in 1987. Hamas opposed the 1993 peace accords between Israel and the Palestine Liberation Organization (PLO). Hamas has both political and military wings, and has had a majority in the Palestinian Legislative council since 2006.

Hezbollah (Party of God) a Shiite militant group in Lebanon with links to Iran. Since its founding in the 1970s, Hezbollah's terrorist activities have been a significant source of tension between Israel and Lebanon.

hijab a veil that covers the hair and usually the neck of Muslim women. The term is used generally for any form of modest Islamic dress, including the burqa (which covers the entire face and body) and the chador (an outer garment or open cloak thrown over the head and held closed in front). The *jilbab*—a long, loose-fitting coat that covers the entire body, except for hands, feet, face, and head—may be complemented by the *khimar* (a wraparound scarf) and the *niqab* (a veil). The notion, common in the West, that Islam requires believers to cover their bodies almost completely has no basis in the Koran, which requires only the wearing of the *khimar* (head scarf)

hudud the traditional punishments mentioned in Sharia law. In Sharia, punishments are of two classes—*hudud*, in which they are laid down by the Koran and Sunna; and *tazir*, in which case the court has more discretion in the form of punishment. *Hudud* punishments include death by stoning, flogging by 80 or 100 strokes, and amputation of limbs. The punishments apply to such crimes as adultery, theft, or slander against women.

iddah the cooling off period before the finalization of a divorce. A Muslim husband may end his marriage simply by saying "*Talaq*" (I divorce you) to his wife. No religious or judicial process is involved. The man may change his mind at any time during the *iddah*, the waiting period during which he must still maintain his wife. If, in the meantime, the wife discovers that she is pregnant, the *iddah* is extended until the birth of the child.

ijtihad the use of rational principles to deal with religious matters that are not explicitly covered in the Koran or the Hadith or by *ijma* (scholarly consensus). When Islam was first established, all jurists had the right to exercise *ijtihad*; such people were known as *mujtahids*. Shiite Muslims still recognize their leading jurists as *mujtahids*, but the majority Sunnis have maintained since the 13th century that scholars could no longer use *ijtihad* and had to be bound in all cases by established precedents.

Islamist an ideologue who seeks to create a society based in Muslim values. The term encompasses a wide spectrum of political views and is loosely applied. It first entered common English usage to describe Muslim fundamentalists during the Iranian Revolution in 1979. It gained wider currency after the terrorist attacks on the United States by members of al-Qaeda on September 11, 2001. However, the word is not synonymous with "terrorist"; an Islamist may work for change through legitimate political channels.

jihad usually translated as "to strive" or "to struggle," the term has often been misapplied by non-Muslims who have taken it to be synonymous with holy war.

madhhab an Islamic school of law or *fiqh* (religious jurisprudence). Sunni Muslims have four main *madhhabs*—the Hanafi, the Hanbali, the Maliki, and the Shafi'i. Based on the teachings of the theologian Imam Abu Hanifah (700–767), the Hanafi *madhhab* is used today in Central Asia, India, Pakistan, and Turkey. Hanbali is the most fundamentalist of the four main *madhhabs*. It is founded on the teachings of Ahmad ibn Hanbal (780–855), a literalist who rejected personal opinion, analogy (*qiyas*), and Mutazilah rationalism on the grounds that they were liable to cause sinful *bida* (innovations). The Hanbali *madhhab* is used in Saudi Arabia. The Maliki *madhhab* is based on the teachings of the imam Malik ibn Anas (715–795). It stresses the Hadiths (sayings of Muhammad) and analogical reasoning (*qiyas*) as the bases of judgment. Maliki law is practiced today in northern and western Africa, in Sudan, and in some of the Persian Gulf states. The Shafi'i *madhhab* was founded by Abu Abd Allah ash-Shafi'i (767–820), who favored the use of *qiyas* (analogical reasoning) when no valid precedents for the case under consideration could be found in the Koran or in the Hadiths. This school of law operates today in eastern Africa and Indonesia.

mujahid (Arabic: "one engaged in jihad") although the term has long been used for anyone who is struggling, either internally or externally, for the Muslim faith, the use of the plural—*mujahideen*, meaning "holy warriors"—was not widespread until the 18th century in India. The word gained much broader currency through its adoption by several guerrilla groups fighting the Soviet occupation of Afghanistan (1979–1989).

Muslim Brotherhood an Islamic organization founded in Egypt in 1928 by Hasan al-Banna (1906–1949) to promote the Koran and the Hadiths as the proper basis for a just and decent society. After 1938, it became radically politicized, rejecting secularism and Western values. Suppressed in Egypt after 1954, the Muslim Brotherhood operated under cover until the 1980s, when it reemerged as a mainstream political grouping.

Nation of Islam a 20th-century African American religious movement that combined black nationalism with some of the tenets of Islam. Founded in 1930 by Wallace D. Fard, the Nation of Islam preached traditional Muslim values and practices in addition to unorthodox beliefs such as African racial superiority and the divinity of Wallace D. Fard. Elijah Muhammad became leader in 1934. The movement achieved great prominence in the 1950s and 1960s through the work of Malcolm X. After the death of Elijah Muhammad in 1975, the Nation of Islam renounced its former racial and nationalist attitudes and gradually disbanded. However, the organization was later reestablished as a national movement by Louis Farrakhan.

Organization of the Islamic Conference (OIC) an international organization established in 1971 to promote the common interests of Muslims throughout the world. Member states include Afghanistan, Algeria, Bahrain, Bangladesh, Benin, Brunei, Burkina Faso, Cameroon, Chad, Comoros, Djibouti, Egypt, Gabon, Gambia, Guinea, Guinea-Bissau, Indonesia, Iran, Iraq, Jordan, Kuwait, Lebanon, Libya, Malaysia, Maldives, Mali, Mauritania, Morocco, Niger, Oman, Pakistan, Qatar, Saudi Arabia, Senegal, Sierra Leone, Somalia, Sudan, Syria, Tunisia, Turkey, Uganda, United Arab Emirates, and Yemen.

qiyas analogical reasoning in Islamic law, where it replaced *ijtihad* (rational principle), which was regarded as being arbitrary in many cases. *Qiyas* is based on the principles set out in the Koran and the Sunna and applied to matters not specifically discussed in either.

shah king of Iran or Persia. The title was also adopted elsewhere, most notably by the rulers of Afghanistan before the overthrow of the monarchy in 1973.

Sharia the religious law of Islam, originally codified in the eighth century. There is no one Islamic law—rather there are several different schools of Islamic law. The main division is between the Sunni and Shiite branches of Islam, which have further divisions within them.

sheikh an honorific title that predated Islam in the Arabian Peninsula and was later applied by Muslims, first to any male older than 50 years, and later to heads of state, religious leaders and theologians, college principals, and learned men.

Sunna (Arabic: "custom") the record of the Prophet's deeds. The Sunna is second in authority only to the Koran in shaping Muslim worldviews and behavior. As a result, the literature recording it, while not technically scripture, functions in much the same way as holy writ. The Sunna is articulated in the Hadiths (the

sayings or deeds of Muhammad). The authenticity of each Hadith is subjected to close scrutiny by Muslim scholars, who apply *tafsir* (exegesis) to distinguish true accounts of the Prophet from fabrications that were interpolated in order to advance a particular doctrine or point of view.

Taliban Islamic fundamentalist political grouping that emerged in 1994 in Afghanistan. In 1996, it took over most of the country, apart from the northeastern region, and reconstituted Afghanistan as an Islamic emirate with assistance from Pakistan and some of the oil-rich Arab states. The Taliban interpretation of Islamic law was oppressively strict: criminals had their hands or feet amputated; women were forbidden to work; girls were excluded from schools; the burqa was made compulsory; and all music, sports, and television were barred. In 2001, in response to that year's 9/11 attacks on New York City and Washington, D.C., the United States invaded Afghanistan in a bid to topple the regime.

Wahhabism an ultraconservative interpretation of Sunni Islam characterized by a very strict adherence to Islamic law as well as to the practices of the early Islamic *ummah* (religious community). Its restrictions include the mandatory covering of women in full-length black cloaks. The ruling royal family of Saudi Arabia is Wahhabi.

FURTHER READING AND RESEARCH

Reference

Armstrong, Karen. *Islam: A Short History*. New York: Mordern Library, 2002.

Calvert, John. *Islamism: A Documentary and Reference Guide*. Westport, CT: Greenwood Press, 2008.

Esposito, John L. *What Everyone Needs to Know about Islam*. New York: Oxford University Press, 2002.

Esposito, John L. (ed.). *The Oxford Encyclopedia of the Islamic World*. New York: Oxford University Press, 2009.

Grieve, Paul. *A Brief Guide to Islam: History, Faith, and Politics: The Complete Introduction*. New York: Carroll and Graf, 2006.

Lewis, Bernard, and Buntzie Churchill. *Islam: The Religion and the People*. Indianapolis, IN: Wharton Press, 2009.

Martin, Richard C. (ed.). *Encyclopedia of Islam and the Muslim World*. New York: Macmillan Reference USA, 2004.

Nagy, Luqman. *The Book of Islamic Dynasties: A Celebration of Islamic History and Culture*. London: Ta-Ha Publications, 2008.

Nasr, Seyyed Hossein. *Islam: Religion, History, and Civilization*. San Francisco: Harper, 2003.

Robinson, Francis (ed.). *The Cambridge Illustrated History of the Islamic World*. New York: Cambridge University Press, 1996.

Ruthven, Malise. *Islam in the World*. New York: Oxford University Press, 2006.

Shepard, William E. *Introducing Islam*. New York: Routledge, 2009.

Turner, C. *Islam: The Basics*. New York: Routledge, 2006.

Ünal, Ali. *An Introduction to Islamic Faith and Thought*. Somerset, NJ: Tughra Books, 2009.

Zepp, Ira. *A Muslim Primer: Beginner's Guide to Islam*. Fayetteville: University of Arkansas Press, 2000.

Beliefs and Practices

Bravmann, M. M. *The Spiritual Background of Early Islam: Studies in Ancient Arab Concepts*. Boston: Brill, 2008.

Caner, Emir Fethi. *More than a Prophet: An Insider's Response to Muslim Beliefs about Jesus and Christianity*. Grand Rapids, MI: Kregel Publications, 2003.

Caner, Ergun Mehmet. *Unveiling Islam: An Insider's Look at Muslim Life and Beliefs*. Grand Rapids, MI: Kregel Publications, 2002.

Dakake, Maria Massi. *The Charismatic Community: Shi'ite Identity in Early Islam*. Albany: State University of New York Press, 2007.

Dawood, N. J. (trans.). *The Koran*. New York: Penguin Books, 1990.

Drummond, Richard Henry. *Islam for the Western Mind: Understanding Muhammad and the Koran*. Charlottesville, VA: Hampton Roads Publishing, 2005.

Farah, Caesar E. *Islam: Beliefs and Observances.* Hauppauge, NY: Barron's, 2003.

Gordon, Matthew. *Understanding Islam: Origins, Beliefs, Practices, Holy Texts, Sacred Places.* London: Duncan Baird, 2002.

Gulevich, Tanya. *Understanding Islam and Muslim Traditions: An Introduction to the Religious Practices, Celebrations, Festivals, Observances, Beliefs, Folklore, Customs, and Calendar System of the World's Muslim Communities, including an Overview of Islamic History and Geography.* Detroit, MI: Omnigraphics, 2004.

Hazleton, Lesley. *After the Prophet: The Epic Story of the Shia-Sunni Split in Islam.* New York: Doubleday, 2009.

Kabbani, Muhammad Hisham. *Encyclopedia of Islamic Doctrine.* Mountainview, CA: As-Sunna Foundation of America, 1998.

Khan, Ruqayya Yasmine. *Self and Secrecy in Early Islam.* Columbia, SC: University of South Carolina Press, 2008.

Lane, Jan-Erik. *Religion and Politics: Islam and Muslim Civilization.* Burlington, VT: Ashgate, 2009.

Marranci, Gabriele. *The Anthropology of Islam.* New York: Berg, 2008.

Marshall, Paul A. *Islam at the Crossroads: Understanding Its Beliefs, History, and Conflicts.* Grand Rapids, MI: Baker Books, 2002.

McCullar, Michael D. *A Christian's Guide to Islam.* Macon, GA: Smyth and Helwys, 2008.

Paas, Steven. *Beliefs and Practices of Muslims: The Religion of Our Neighbours.* Zomba, Malawi: Good Messenger Publications, 2006.

Ramadan, Tariq. *The Messenger: The Meanings of the Life of Muhammad.* New York: Penguin Books, 2008.

Rippin, Andrew. *Muslims: Their Religious Beliefs and Practices.* New York: Routledge, 2005.

Safran, Janina M. *The Second Umayyad Caliphate: The Articulation of Caliphal Legitimacy in al-Andalus.* Cambridge, MA: Harvard University Press, 2000.

Schwartz, Stephen. *The Other Islam: Sufism and the Road to Global Harmony.* New York: Doubleday, 2008.

Sherwani, Muhammad Habibur Rahman Khan (translated by Syed Moinul Haq). *Hazrat Abu Bakr: The First Caliph of Islam.* Lahore, Pakistan: Muhammad Ashraf, 1963.

Swarup, Ram. *Understanding the Hadith: The Sacred Traditions of Islam.* Amherst, NY: Prometheus Books, 2002.

Walker, Paul E. *Fatimid History and Ismaili Doctrine.* Burlington, VT: Ashgate, 2008.

Culture

Adeney, Miriam. *Daughters of Islam: Building Bridges with Muslim Women.* Downers Grove, IL: InterVarsity Press, 2002.

Behrens-Abouseif, Doris, and Stephen Vernoit. *Islamic Art in the 19th Century: Tradition, Innovation, and Eclecticism.* Boston: Brill, 2006.

Blair, Sheila, and Jonathan Bloom. *Rivers of Paradise: Water in Islamic Art and Culture.* New Haven: Yale University Press, 2009.

Broug, Eric. *Islamic Geometric Patterns.* New York: Thames and Hudson, 2008.

Burckhardt, Titus. *Art of Islam: Language and Meaning*. Bloomington, IN: World Wisdom, 2009.

Clot, André (translated by John Howe). *Harun al-Rashid and the World of the Thousand and One Nights*. New York: New Amsterdam, 1989.

Curatola, Giovanni, and Gianroberto Scarcia (trans Marguerite Shore). *The Art and Architecture of Persia*. New York: Abbeville Press, 2007.

Fakhry, Majid. *Averroës, Aquinas, and the Rediscovery of Aristotle in Western Europe*. Washington, D.C.: Georgetown University Press, 1997.

Goodman, Lenn Evan. *Avicenna*. Ithaca, NY: Cornell University Press, 2006.

Grabar, Oleg. *Islamic Visual Culture, 1100–1800*. Burlington, VT: Ashgate, 2006.

Grabar, Oleg. *Masterpieces of Islamic Art: The Decorated Page from the 8th to the 17th Century*. New York: Prestel, 2009.

Gruendler, Beatrice, and Louise Marlow (eds). *Writers and Rulers: Perspectives on Their Relationship from Abbasid to Safavid Times*. Wiesbaden, Germany: Reichert, 2004.

Husain, Salma. *The Emperor's Table: The Art of Mughal Cuisine*. New Delhi, India: Lustre Press, 2008.

Jones, Owen. *Ornament and Design of the Alhambra*. Mineola, NY: Dover Publications, 2008.

Kellner-Heinkele, Barbara, Joachim Gierlichs, and Brigitte Heuer (eds.). *Islamic Art and Architecture in the European Periphery: Crimea, Caucasus, and the Volga-Ural Region*. Wiesbaden, Germany: Harrassowitz, 2008.

Khalili, Nasser D. *Visions of Splendour in Islamic Art and Culture*. London: Worth Press, 2008.

McCaughrean, Geraldine (ed.). *One Thousand and One Arabian Nights*. New York: Oxford University Press, 1999.

Michell, George. *The Majesty of Mughal Decoration: The Art and Architecture of Islamic India*. New York: Thames and Hudson, 2007.

O'Kane, Bernard. *The Treasures of Islamic Art in the Museums of Cairo*. New York: The American University in Cairo Press, 2006.

Rogers, J. M. *The Arts of Islam: Treasures from the Nasser D. Khalili Collection*. Sydney, Australia: Art Gallery of New South Wales Press, 2007.

Ruggles, D. Fairchild. *Islamic Gardens and Landscapes*. Philadelphia: University of Pennsylvania Press, 2008.

Welzbacher, Christian. *Euro Islam Architecture: New Mosques in the West*. Amsterdam, Netherlands: SUN, 2008.

Modern Society

Ageron, Charles Robert (translated and edited by Michael Brett). *Modern Algeria: A History from 1830 to the Present*. Trenton, NJ: Africa World Press, 1991.

Ahmed, Akbar S. *Journey into Islam: The Crisis of Globalization*. Washington, DC: Brookings Institution Press, 2007.

Aslan, Reza. *No God but God: The Origins, Evolution, and Future of Islam*. New York: Random House, 2006.

Ayoob, Mohammed. *The Many Faces of Political Islam: Religion and Politics in the Muslim World*. Ann Arbor: University of Michigan Press, 2008.

Bhutto, Benazir. *Reconciliation: Islam, Democracy, and the West*. New York: Harper, 2008.

Blauer, Ettagale. *Mauritania*. New York: Marshall Cavendish Benchmark, 2009.

Braswell, George W. *Islam and America: Answers to the 31 Most-Asked Questions*. Nashville, TN: Broadman and Holman, 2005.

Cesari, Jocelyne (ed.). *Encyclopedia of Islam in the United States*. Westport, CT: Greenwood Press, 2007.

Collins, Robert O. (ed.). *Civil Wars and Revolution in the Sudan: Essays on the Sudan, Southern Sudan, and Darfur, 1962–2004*. Hollywood, CA: Tsehai Publishers, 2005.

Coughlin, Con. *Khomeini's Ghost: The Iranian Revolution and the Rise of Militant Islam*. New York: Ecco, 2009.

Delgado, Kevin. *Morocco*. Detroit, MI: Lucent Books, 2006.

Dresch, Paul. *A History of Modern Yemen*. New York: Cambridge University Press, 2000.

Farmer, Brian R. *Understanding Radical Islam: Medieval Ideology in the Twenty-first Century*. New York: Peter Lang, 2007.

Gelletly, LeeAnne. *Somalia*. Broomall, PA: Mason Crest Publishers, 2008.

Gerges, Fawaz A. *America and Political Islam: Clash of Cultures or Clash of Interests?* New York: Cambridge University Press, 1999.

Gershoni, Israel, Hakan Erdem, and Ursula Woköck (eds.). *Histories of the Modern Middle East: New Directions*. Boulder, CO: Lynne Rienner Publishers, 2002.

Gillespie, Carol Ann. *Bahrain*. Philadelphia: Chelsea House Publishers, 2002.

Hunter, Shireen T. (ed.). *Reformist Voices of Islam: Mediating Islam and Modernity*. Armonk, NY: M. E. Sharpe, 2009.

Jensen, Erik. *Western Sahara: Anatomy of a Stalemate*. Boulder, CO: Lynne Rienner Publishers, 2005.

Jinju, Muhammadu Hambali. *Islam in Africa: Historico-Philosophical Perspectives and Current Problems*. Zaria, Nigeria: Bello University Press, 2001.

Kramer, Martin S. *Arab Awakening and Islamic Revival: The Politics of Ideas in the Middle East*. Piscataway, NJ: Transaction Publishers, 2008.

Mackintosh-Smith, Tim. *Yemen: The Unknown Arabia*. New York: Overlook Press, 2000.

Marcovitz, Hal. *Islam in Africa*. Philadelphia: Mason Crest Publishers, 2007.

Marr, Phebe. *The Modern History of Iraq*. Boulder, CO: Westview Press, 2004.

McAmis, Robert Day. *Malay Muslims: The History and Challenge of Resurgent Islam in Southeast Asia*. Grand Rapids, MI: W. B. Eerdmans, 2002.

Miller, Debra A. *Kuwait*. Farmington Hills, MI: Lucent Books, 2005.

Morrison, John, with additional text by Adam Woog. *Syria*. New York: Chelsea House, 2009.

Nydell, Margaret K. *Understanding Arabs: A Guide for Modern Times*. Yarmouth, ME: Intercultural Press, 2006.

O'Kane, David, and Tricia Redeker. *Biopolitics, Militarism, and Development: Eritrea in the Twenty-first Century*. New York: Berghahn Books, 2009.

Owtram, Francis. *A Modern History of Oman: Formation of the State since 1920.* New York: I. B. Tauris, 2004.

Polonskaya, Ludmila, and Alexei Malashenko (eds.). *Islam in Central Asia.* Reading, England: Ithaca Press, 1994.

Radu, Michael. *Islam in Europe.* Broomall, PA: Mason Crest Publishers, 2006.

Rashid, Ahmed. *Jihad: The Rise of Militant Islam in Central Asia.* New Haven: Yale University Press, 2002.

Salibi, Kamal S. *The Modern History of Jordan.* New York: I. B. Tauris, 1993.

Shelley, Toby. *Endgame in the Western Sahara: What Future for Africa's Last Colony?* New York: Zed Books, 2004.

Tanner, Stephen. *Afghanistan: A Military History from Alexander the Great to the Fall of the Taliban.* Karachi, Pakistan: Oxford University Press, 2003.

Tomohiko, Uyama (ed.). *Empire, Islam, and Politics in Central Eurasia.* Sapporo, Japan: Hokkaido University Press, 2007.

Turner, Richard Brent. *Islam in the African-American Experience.* Bloomington: Indiana University Press, 2003.

Vandewalle, Dirk (ed.). *Libya since 1969: Qadhafi's Revolution Revisited.* New York: Palgrave Macmillan, 2008.

Young, Mitchell (ed.). *Islam.* Farmington Hills, MI: Greenhaven Press, 2006.

Islamic World

Bowen, Wayne H. *The History of Saudi Arabia.* Westport, CT: Greenwood Press, 2008.

Caner, Ergun Mehmet. *Unveiling Islam: An Insider's Look at Muslim Life and Beliefs.* Grand Rapids, MI: Kregel Publications, 2002.

Chinyong Liow, Joseph, and Nadirsyah Hosen (eds.). *Islam in Southeast Asia.* New York: Routledge, 2009.

Corrigan, Jim. *Kazakhstan.* Philadelphia: Mason Crest, 2005.

Engineer, Asgharali. *Islam in Post-Modern World: Prospects and Problems.* Gurgaon, India: Hope India Publications, 2008.

Esposito, John L. *The Future of Islam.* New York: Oxford University Press, 2010.

Esposito, John L., and Dalia Mogahed. *Who Speaks for Islam? What a Billion Muslims Really Think.* New York: Gallup Press, 2007.

Gordon, Alijah. *The Propagation of Islam in the Indonesian-Malay Archipelago.* Kuala Lumpur, Malaysia: Malaysian Sociological Research Institute, 2001.

Habeeb, William Mark. *Turkmenistan.* Philadelphia: Mason Crest, 2005.

Harmon, Daniel E. *Kyrgyzstan.* Philadelphia: Mason Crest, 2005.

Israeli, Raphael. *Islam in China: Religion, Ethnicity, Culture, and Politics.* Lanham, MD: Lexington Books, 2002.

Losleben, Elizabeth. *The Bedouin of the Middle East.* Minneapolis, MN: Lerner Publications, 2003.

Nomachi, Kazuyoshi. *Mecca the Blessed, Medina the Radiant: The Holiest Cities of Islam.* New York: Aperture, 1997.

Rashid, Ahmed. *Jihad: The Rise of Militant Islam in Central Asia.* New York: Penguin Books, 2003.

Sagdeev, Roald, and Susan Eisenhower (eds.). *Islam and Central Asia: An Enduring Legacy or an Evolving Threat?* Washington, DC: Center for Political and Strategic Studies, 2000.

Tyler, Aaron. *Islam, the West, and Tolerance: Conceiving Coexistence.* New York: Palgrave Macmillan, 2008.

WEBSITES

Aga Khan Archnet
www.archnet.org
Website that provides profiles of all sites of architectural interest in the Muslim world, along with numerous diagrams, photographs, and academic papers.

Bedouin
www.geographia.com/egypt/sinai/bedouin.htm
Website that covers all aspects of the culture and history of the desert-dwelling people.

Berbers
i-cias.com/e.o/berbers.htm
Website that gives an accessible introduction to the history and significance of these peoples who lived in northern Africa before the arrival of Islam.

Comparative Islamic Studies
www.equinoxjournals.com/ojs/index.php/CIS/index
The website of an academic journal dedicated to the study of Islam.

Exploring Religions—Islam
uwacadweb.uwyo.edu/religionet/er/islam/index.htm
A website about different aspects of Islam from the University of Wyoming.

Islam
www.bbc.co.uk/religion/religions/islam
Website with a comprehensive outline of Muslim beliefs and an account of the religion's historical development.

Islamic-American Zakat Foundation
www.iazf.org
Information about an organization that provides food, shelter, clothing, and transportation to the needy.

Islamic Finder
www.islamicfinder.org/Hcal/index.php
Website showing the Muslim calendar; converts Gregorian dates into *hijri* dates and vice versa.

Islamic Philosophy Online
www.muslimphilosophy.com
A site covering the history of Muslim thought.

Mecca
i-cias.com/e.o/mecca.htm
Description of the city; includes a list of key dates in the history of the city.

Muslim Students Association National
www.msanational.org
A website dedicated to the needs of Muslim students in North America.

Online Hadith Collection
www.hadithcollection.com
Website providing translations of the full text of all the major collections of Hadith; also includes introductions that explain the origins of each collection and its author.

Online Koran Project
www.al-quran.info
Website that provides searchable translations of the Koran in many languages.

Oxford Islamic Studies Online
www.oxfordislamicstudies.com
Comprehensive resource of nearly four thousand entries plus primary documents.

Sunni and Shiite Muslims
hnn.us/articles/934.html
An essay explaining the origin of the central split in the Muslim world.

Tariq Ramadan
www.tariqramadan.com
Website of Swiss-Muslim intellectual Tariq Ramadan; includes lectures, debates, and essays by Ramadan and other Muslim intellectuals.

Academic Institutions Teaching Islamic Studies

Abbasi Program in Islamic Studies at Stanford University
www.stanford.edu/dept/islamic_studies/index.html
Find out about undergraduate and postgraduate courses on Islamic subjects.

Arabic and Islamic Studies, Georgetown University, Washington
arabic.georgetown.edu
Learn about Georgetown's Arabic and Islamic program for students.

Center for Middle Eastern Studies, Harvard University
cmes.hmdc.harvard.edu
Information about Harvard's courses aimed at increasing awareness and understanding of the cultures and politics of western Asia.

Center for Middle Eastern Studies, University of California at Berkeley
cmes.berkeley.edu/Programs/grants_alfalah.html
Find out about the center's program to promote better understanding of Islam in the United States.

Center for Middle Eastern Studies, University of Chicago
www.cmes.uchicago.edu/index.html
Learn about the courses available in the languages and civilizations of western Asia.

Department of Near Eastern Studies, Cornell University
www.arts.cornell.edu/nes/index.html
Learn about courses in western Asian archaeology, history, religion, and literature.

Department of Near Eastern Studies, Princeton University
www.princeton.edu/~nes
Visit this website to find out about Princeton's program of Islamic studies.

Institute of Islamic Studies, McGill University, Montreal
www.mcgill.ca/islamicstudies
Information about this Canadian university's program of courses on the Muslim world.

Islamic Legal Studies at Harvard Law School
www.law.harvard.edu/programs/ilsp
Find out about Harvard Law School's research program to advance understanding of Islamic law.

Islamic Studies Program, University of Michigan
www.ii.umich.edu/ii/aboutus/specialinit/isi
Information on the university's program, which has more than 50 faculty members.

Middle East Center, University of Pennsylvania
mec.sas.upenn.edu
Learn about the courses centering on raising awareness of the circumstances in present-day western Asia.

Middle East Studies, Brown University, Rhode Island
www.watsoninstitute.org/middleeast
Learn about the courses, including Arabic and Islamic history, offered at Brown University.

Middle East Studies Program, University of Wisconsin-Madison
mideast.wisc.edu/index.htm
Visit this website to find out information on courses covering western Asian culture and religion.

Middle Eastern Studies, University of Texas
www.utexas.edu/cola/depts/mes
Information on the college's western Asian program that has been running for five decades.

Religious Studies, Yale University
yale.edu/religiousstudies/fields/islamic.html
A website outlining Yale's program of Islamic studies.

INDEX

political repression
Afghanistan and 277, 278, 279
Albania and 325
Bulgaria and 329
China and 319–320, 321
Egypt and 251
Iran and 239, 241, 243
Thailand and 298
Uzbekistan and 308, 312
polygamy 15, 32–35, 39, 262
polygyny 32
population
Bahrain 232
Bangladesh 285, 286
Brazil 372–373
Central America and the Caribbean 365
Chad 269–270
China 315
free ports, Northern Africa and 256
India 286
Iraq 228, 229–230
Kuwait 234
Lebanon 225
Mali 265
Myanmar 290
Northern Africa 248
Saudi Arabia 230, 231
South America 377
Southeast Asia 293
Syria 228
Thailand 297
United States 354–356
Western Sahara 259
population growth, employment and 98
Portugal
Islam in 336
Kuwait and 232
Mauritania and 263
Oman and 234
Senegal and 263
Sri Lanka and 288
post-Soviet era, Central Asia and 307–309
poverty 142–143, 345
see also economic issues
prayer 66–67, 178–179, 356
pre-Islamic Arabia
gender roles and 69
Iraq and 228

Oman and 234
polygamy and 32
slavery and 183
women's rights and 175
prenuptial agreements 129
see also marriage contracts
Price, Daniel E. 175
privacy 26
private schools 102
progressive Muslims 152–153, 177–178, 194
Progressive Muslim Union 178
property rights 69
prophets, American Society of Muslims (Nation of Islam) and 136
proselytizing, freedom of religion and 182–183
Prosperous Justice Party (Indonesia) 301, 302
prostitution 50, 52–53
provinces, Pakistan and 281–282
public accommodations, religious practices and 191
public life, gender and 66
public opinion
Islamism and 152, 209
United States and 218–219
Punjabi language 96
Punjab province, Pakistan 283

Q

Qaddafi, Muammar al-
Arab Maghrib Union and 248
government of 147, 252
Islamic socialism and 151, 163
Islamism and 194–195
Qadiani sect 351
Qadiri Sufism 264
al-Qaeda 164–167
Algeria and 256
Islamism and 152, 197, 198
Jihad Organization and 208

Saudi Arabia and 231
Somalia and 272
terrorism and 208–209, 210–211, 216
Yemen and 235
Qajar dynasty 237
qanun (secular law) 116
Qaradawi, Yusuf al- 211
al-Qarawiyin Mosque 70
al-Qarawiyin School 93
Qasim, Muhammad bin 275
Qatar 98, 232, 234–235
Qing dynasty 317–318
qurbani (charity) 137
Qutb, Sayyid
democracy and 148, 197
Islamism and 194, 205, 207
theodemocracy and 160
Wahhabism and 201

R

Rabia al-Adawiyya 176
racial profiling 188, 190–191
racism, Nation of Islam and 352
radical Islam 196–197, 198
Rafsanjani, Ali Akbar Hashemi 243, 244
Rahman, Aisha Abdel 76
Rahman, Omar Abdel 166
Ramadan 82, 137
Ramallah Center for Human Rights Studies 187
rape 176
Ras al-Khaimah 232
Rashid, Harun al- 92, 254
Rashid, house of 204
Raziq, Ali Abd al- 156
Reagan, Ronald 241, 244
Reconquista, the 248, 254, 335
Reconstruction period, U.S. 350
Red Crescent 132, 138–139
reform movements
Iran and 120–121, 243–244
Southeast Asia and 296–297

refugees
Australasia and the Pacific 379
Brazil and 372
Canada and 358
Europe and 337, 339–340
Kurdish people and 339
New Zealand and 384–385
Pakistan and 282, 283
Palestinian refugees and 224, 225, 226, 227
Somalia and 272
regional variations
community life and 9
education and 94–95
employment and 98–99, 102–105
family life 24–26, 26–27
see also countries
relativism, human rights and 169–170
relief agencies 138–139, 140, 141
religious beliefs
Albania and 325, 326
Chad and 269–270
family life and 25–26
Malaysia and 299–300
marriage and 37
Myanmar and 290
Northern Africa and 247
Oman and 234
Sudan and 270
religious education 26–27, 106–107
religious identity
clothing and 83, 87
Eastern Europe and 332–333
family life and 27–31
gender roles and 79–80
immigration to Europe and 345–346
Muslims in the United States and 26–27
religious leadership
feminism and 177–178
gender roles and 66–67, 81–82
Islamic states and 156–157
political leadership and 158, 196